The Springer Series on Challenges in Machine Learning

Series editors

Hugo Jair Escalante, Astrofisica Optica y Electronica, INAOE, Puebla, Mexico
Isabelle Guyon, ChaLearn, Berkeley, CA, USA
Sergio Escalera, University of Barcelona, Barcelona, Spain

The books of this innovative series collect papers written by successful competitions in machine learning. They also include analyses of the challenges, tutorial material, dataset descriptions, and pointers to data and software. Together with the websites of the challenge competitions, they offer a complete teaching toolkit and a valuable resource for engineers and scientists.

More information about this series at http://www.springer.com/series/15602

Sergio Escalera • Markus Weimer
Editors

The NIPS '17 Competition: Building Intelligent Systems

 Springer

Editors
Sergio Escalera
Department Mathematics & Informatics
University of Barcelona
Barcelona, Spain

Markus Weimer
Microsoft (United States)
Redmond, Washington, USA

ISSN 2520-131X   ISSN 2520-1328   (electronic)
The Springer Series on Challenges in Machine Learning
ISBN 978-3-030-06867-7   ISBN 978-3-319-94042-7   (eBook)
https://doi.org/10.1007/978-3-319-94042-7

This Springer imprint is published by the registered company Springer Nature Switzerland AG
The registered company address is: Gewerbestrasse 11, 6330 Cham, Switzerland

Foreword

Years after the first KDD cup that pioneered the idea of associating competitions with data science conferences in 1993, the NIPS conference has launched its competition program. The NIPS workshops however have been hosting competitions since 2001 when the "learning from unlabelled data competition" was first launched, followed by the NIPS 2003 "feature selection challenge" and many more. Since 2013, there is a yearly workshop for competition organizers, the "Challenges in Machine Learning" workshop. This all contributed to grow a community of challenge organizers and increasing more rigorous standards of evaluation.

For its first edition, the NIPS competition program has brought to the community a very exciting set of events covering a wide range of machine learning topics. Among 23 pier reviewed proposals, 5 were accepted:

- The Conversational Intelligence Challenge
- Classifying Clinically Actionable Genetic Mutations
- Learning to Run
- Human-Computer Question Answering Competition (Quiz Bowl)
- Adversarial Attacks and Defences

Evaluation was based on the quality of data, problem interest and impact, promoting the design of new models, and a proper schedule and managing procedure. The online competitions lasted between 2 and 6 months. The Quiz Bowl competition was also run live between a team of human champions and the winning artificial system.

The workshop also included a presentation of the AI XPRIZE (https://ai.xprize. org), a 4-year contest run by IBM to encourage entrepreneurship in AI, featuring milestone results in mental health and addiction monitoring, drug design, satellite imaging of crops, virtual tutors, decontamination, and other exciting topics. A presentation was also made by the organizers of the DeepArt competition (https:// deepart.io/nips/), which featured art posters decorating the NIPS conference, made with Deep Learning technology.

This book gathers contributions of the organizers and top ranking participants. Having attended the competition workshop, I was particularly impressed. How much can be expected from a handful of researchers tackling a task for such a short time? A lot indeed.

Some competitions advanced more classical aspects of machine learning such as the competition on "Classifying Clinically Actionable Genetic Mutations" but others explored successfully completely new grounds. The "Adversarial Attacks and Defences" competition examined the problem of making learning systems robust against being confused by samples closely resembling training samples, but having an entirely different meaning. This problem is particularly important to avoid malicious attacks such as modifying traffic signs to cause road accidents by fooling the computer vision systems of autonomous vehicles.

In the Learning to Run competition, the organizers provided a rather elaborate human musculoskeletal model and a physics-based simulation environment. The goal was to teach the human avatar to run through an obstacle course as quickly as possible by controlling the muscles and joints (see a video of the winners https://www.youtube.com/watch?v=8xLghMb97T0).

Two competitions dealt with natural language processing tasks and approached as closely as to get to the state of the art in artificial intelligence. The "Conversational Intelligence Challenge" competition used the scenarios of chatbots, imitating the famous Turing test. The "Human-Computer Question Answering Competition" has a regular offline version, and then the winning system competed against human champions of the Quiz Bowl game, a game similar to Jeopardy, the quiz show one year ago by IBM's Deep Blue computer. Impressively, a neural-network based system won the game against the human champions, see the YouTube video https://www.youtube.com/watch?v=0kgnEUDMeug, with considerably less human effort and compute power than Deep Blue.

But of course, the results are only as good as the data, and progress can really be made only over a period of time with the organization of recurrent events providing each year new fresh data of ever better quality. Efforts made by governments to open up data to the public will hopefully nicely complement research and competition programs in every domain of machine learning. We wish long-lasting success and impact to the future NIPS competition programs.

UPSud/INRIA, Univ. Paris-Saclay, France   Prof. Isabelle Guyon
and ChaLearn, USA
NIPS 2017 General Co-Chair

Editor Notes This book consists of the reports from the competitions of the inaugural NIPS competitions track at NIPS 2017 in Long Beach, CA.

Competitions have become a staple in the research calendar. They allow us to gage what works and what does not, force us to develop novel approaches to problems outside the usual, and provide us with new data sets to develop machine learning approaches for. But with all the competitions happening already, and some even professionally organized by companies devoted to the task, one might ask: What can a NIPS workshop track add that is not covered? What is its niche?

When we considered the task of chairing this workshop track, we asked ourselves exactly that question. We identified a couple of *hopes* for this new track:

- Academic rigor: This being the NIPS community, its workshop track was to be as academically rigorous as the best out there.
- Spotlight novel problems: We envisioned the NIPS community to have enough draw for novel problems and data sets to be proposed as competitions.
- Generate new benchmark data sets: One of our goals was to attract new and interesting data sets to be released for the competitions.

In order to attract truly novel and hard competitions, and to make best use of the NIPS audience, we added a twist to our call for proposals: In addition to the known format for data science competitions, we introduced a new format: Live competitions to be held science-fare style at NIPS itself.

In retrospect, the gamble with both the new track at NIPS and the novel format paid off: In response to our call, we received 23 proposals. Selecting the top five of those to be run as part of the track was a difficult process, as many more were exciting. Our selection process was aided by reviewers with experience in running and winning competitions. It focused on the goals outlined above as well as practical matters of running successful competitions.

Four competitions were run in the "traditional" mode data science competition style:

- "Classifying Clinically Actionable Genetic Mutations"
- "Learning to Run"
- "Adversarial Attacks and Defences"
- "The Conversational Intelligence Challenge"

One was live competition:

- "Human-Computer Question Answering Competition"

The results of the first four were presented in the workshop at NIPS, and the latter one was run at NIPS. During that workshop, we witnessed the first win of a computer against five humans in quiz bowl. This achievement is remarkable, as Quiz Bowl is arguably harder than Jeopardy, and the winning solution was achieved on a minuscule budget compared to IBM's landmark achievement in that game. Even more remarkable was the reaction in the audience: Instead of celebrating the win for our community, we immediately switched gears to discussing how to make next year's competitions *harder* for the computer.

Hence, the NIPS community deserves the competitions track. But more so, the competitions deserve to be exposed to this community. We are looking forward to next year's incarnation. But before we do, we would like to thank the NIPS Foundation, the organizing committee of NIPS 2017, and the organizers of the five successful competitions and the XPRIZE and DeepArt linked competitions for their support and tireless work. Special thanks to Prof. Isabelle Guyon, who bring to us the idea and the real possibility to incorporate competitions at NIPS. Without it, we would not have established a new stable in the NIPS schedule.

Sergio Escalera and Markus Weimer
NIPS Competitions Chairs 2017

Contents

Chapter 1
Introduction to NIPS 2017 Competition Track

Sergio Escalera, Markus Weimer, Mikhail Burtsev, Valentin Malykh, Varvara Logacheva, Ryan Lowe, Iulian Vlad Serban, Yoshua Bengio, Alexander Rudnicky, Alan W. Black, Shrimai Prabhumoye, Łukasz Kidziński, Sharada Prasanna Mohanty, Carmichael F. Ong, Jennifer L. Hicks, Sergey Levine, Marcel Salathé, Scott Delp, Iker Huerga, Alexander Grigorenko, Leifur Thorbergsson, Anasuya Das, Kyla Nemitz, Jenna Sandker, Stephen King, Alexander S. Ecker, Leon A. Gatys, Matthias Bethge, Jordan Boyd-Graber, Shi Feng, Pedro Rodriguez, Mohit Iyyer, He He, Hal Daumé III, Sean McGregor, Amir Banifatemi, Alexey Kurakin, Ian Goodfellow, and Samy Bengio

Abstract Competitions have become a popular tool in the data science community to solve hard problems, assess the state of the art and spur new research directions. Companies like Kaggle[1] and open source platforms like Codalab[2] connect people with data and a data science problem to those with the skills and means to solve it. Hence, the question arises: What, if anything, could NIPS add to this rich ecosystem?

---

[1] https://www.kaggle.com/
[2] http://codalab.org/

S. Escalera (✉)
Department Mathematics & Informatics, University of Barcelona, Barcelona, Spain
e-mail: sergio@maia.ub.es

M. Weimer
Microsoft (United States), Redmond, WA, USA
e-mail: Markus.Weimer@Microsoft.com

M. Burtsev · V. Malykh · V. Logacheva
Moscow Institute of Physics and Technology, Moscow, Russia
e-mail: burtcev.ms@mipt.ru; valentin.malykh@phystech.edu; logacheva.vk@mipt.ru

R. Lowe
McGill University, Montreal, QC, Canada
e-mail: ryan.lowe@cs.mcgill.ca

© Springer International Publishing AG, part of Springer Nature 2018
S. Escalera, M. Weimer (eds.), *The NIPS '17 Competition: Building Intelligent Systems*, The Springer Series on Challenges in Machine Learning,
https://doi.org/10.1007/978-3-319-94042-7_1

1

In 2017, we embarked to find out. We attracted 23 potential competitions, of which we selected five to be NIPS 2017 competitions. Our final selection features competitions advancing the state of the art in other sciences such as "Classifying Clinically Actionable Genetic Mutations" and "Learning to Run". Others, like "The Conversational Intelligence Challenge" and "Adversarial Attacks and Defences" generated new data sets that we expect to impact the progress in their respective communities for years to come. And "Human-Computer Question Answering Competition" showed us just how far we as a field have come in ability and efficiency since the break-through performance of Watson in Jeopardy. Two additional competitions, DeepArt and AI XPRIZE Milestions, were also associated to the NIPS 2017 competition track, whose results are also presented within this chapter.

I. V. Serban · Y. Bengio
University of Montreal, Montreal, QC, Canada
e-mail: iulian.vlad.serban@umontreal.ca; yoshua.bengio@umontreal.ca

A. Rudnicky · A. W. Black · S. Prabhumoye
Carnegie Mellon University, Pittsburgh, PA, USA
e-mail: air@cs.cmu.edu; awb@cs.cmu.edu; sprabhum@andrew.cmu.edu

S. P. Mohanty
École Polytechnique Fédérale de Lausanne, Lausanne, Switzerland
e-mail: sharada.mohanty@epfl.ch

Ł. Kidziński · C. F. Ong · S. Delp
Stanford University, Stanford, CA, USA
e-mail: lukasz.kidzinski@stanford.edu; ongcf@stanford.edu; delp@stanford.edu

J. L. Hicks
Department of Bioengineering, Stanford University, Stanford, CA, USA
e-mail: jenhicks@stanford.edu

S. Levine
Department of Electrical Engineering and Computer Sciences, University of California, Berkeley, CA, USA
e-mail: svlevine@eecs.berkeley.edu

M. Salathé
School of Computer and Communication Sciences, EPFL, Lausanne, Switzerland
e-mail: marcel.salathe@epfl.ch

I. Huerga · K. Nemitz
Director of Engineering and Applied Machine Learning, Memorial Sloan Kettering Cancer Center, New York, NY, USA
e-mail: huergasi@mskcc.org; nemitzk@mskcc.org

A. Grigorenko
Lead Data Scientist, Memorial Sloan Kettering Cancer Center, New York, NY, USA
e-mail: grigoreak@mskcc.org

All these competitions emphasize advancing the state of the art of Neural Information Processing Systems as opposed to solving a singular instance of a data science problem. And this focus is the answer to the question what NIPS can add to the rich tapestry of competitions out there. And as you will find in this and other chapters in this book, the advances made are substantial.

L. Thorbergsson · A. Das
Sr Data Scientist, Memorial Sloan Kettering Cancer Center, New York, NY, USA
e-mail: thorberl@mskcc.org; dasa@mskcc.org

J. Sandker · S. King
Talent Community Manager, Memorial Sloan Kettering Cancer Center, New York, NY, USA
e-mail: muchaj@mskcc.org; kings1@mskcc.org

L. A. Gatys
University of Tuebingen, Tuebingen, Germany
e-mail: leon.gatys@bethgelab.org

J. Boyd-Graber
Computer Science, iSchool UMIACS, Language Science, University of Maryland, College Park, MD, USA
e-mail: jbg@umiacs.umd.edu

S. Feng · P. Rodriguez
Computer Science, University of Maryland, College Park, MD, USA
e-mail: shifeng@cs.umd.edu; pedro@snowgeek.org

S. McGregor
Technical Lead, IBM Watson AI XPRIZE, XPRIZE Foundation, Culver City, CA, USA

Member of Technical Staff, Syntiant Corporation, Irvine, CA, USA
e-mail: NIPSCompetitionBook@seanbmcgregor.com

A. Banifatemi
Artificial Intelligence Lead and IBM Watson AI XPRIZE Lead, XPRIZE Foundation, Culver City, CA, USA
e-mail: amir.banifatemi@xprize.org

I. Goodfellow · S. Bengio
Google Brain, Mountain View, CA, USA

A. S. Ecker · M. Bethge
University of Tübingen, Germany

M. Iyyer
UMass Amherst, Amherst, USA

H. He
Stanford University, California, USA

H. Daumé III
University of Maryland, Maryland, USA

A. Kurakin
Google, San Francisco, Bay Area, USA

1.1   The Conversational Intelligence Challenge

Recent advances in the area of natural language processing driven by deep neural networks have sparked a renewed interest for dialogue systems in the research community. In addition to the growing real-world applications, the capacity to converse is closely related to the overall goal of AI. The Conversational Intelligence Challenge had a goal to unify the community around the challenging task of building systems capable of intelligent conversations. Teams were expected to submit dialogue systems able to carry out intelligent and natural conversations about snippets of Wikipedia articles with humans. At the evaluation stage of the competition participants, as well as volunteers, were randomly matched with a bot or a human to chat and score answers of a peer. The competition had two major outcomes: (1) an assessment of state-of-the-art dialogue systems quality compared to human, and (2) an open-source dataset collected from evaluated dialogues.

1.1.1   Task

The goal of competing bots was to maximize an average score of dialogs rated by human evaluators. The evaluation was performed through a blind cross testing of bots and other human users in a series of chat sessions. Members of participating teams, as well as volunteers, were asked to log into an anonymous chat system and communicate with randomly chosen bot or another human user. No information about identity of the peer was provided. Both peers received the text of a snippet from a Wikipedia article. Discussion of the article proceeded till one of the peers ended dialog. Then human user was asked to score the quality of every response and the dialog as a whole.

1.1.2   Running the Competition

The Conversation Intelligence Challenge was split in four stages. Starting from the beginning of April of 2017 participants submitted applications consisting of a proposal describing details of scientific approach and statement of work as well as a system architecture and relevant technical information. After review of applications teams were invited to submit working solutions for the qualification round till the middle of July, 2017. During the last week of July these solutions were evaluated by participants of the summer school-hackathon DeepHack Turing[3] and volunteers.

This evaluation process generated the dataset of rated human-to-bot and human-to-human dialogs. Dataset of rated dialogs was open sourced and participating teams were able to tune their solutions on these data. Two weeks before the NIPS

---

[3]http://turing.tilda.ws/

conference final versions of bots were run in the test system and final evaluation round was started and lasted till the day before the Competition track session at NIPS.

Competing teams were required to provide their solutions in the form of executable source code supporting a common interface (API). These solutions were run in isolated virtual environments (containers) and were not be able to access any external services or the Internet to prevent cheating. The master bot created by organizers facilitated communication between human evaluators and the competitors' solutions. It was implemented for popular messenger services[4] and allows to connect a participant to a randomly selected solution or peer and log the evaluation process.

1.1.3 Outcomes

Major goals of the competition were establishing a new non-goal-driven but still topic-oriented task for dialogue, probing the current level of the conversational intelligence for this task and collecting dataset of evaluated dialogs.

Ten teams applied for the challenge and six of them were able to submit working solutions. Final score of the dialogue quality for the best bot was 2.746 compared to 3.8 for human.[5] We found that human-to-human dialogs were longer and humans used shorter utterances. Higher length of dialogs possibly indicates higher engagement of peers. It was also found that human performance in dialogue at both utterance and dialogue levels is generally rated high, but not exclusively high, which suggests that either human utterances or scores (or both) are not always reliable.

As a result of data collecting effort 4.750 dialogues were recorded in total. Among them there are 2.640 human-to-bot and 359 human-to-human *long* dialogues where each participant produced at least three utterances. The dataset is available in the competition repository[6] and as a task in ParlAI framework.[7]

Participation in this type of challenges requires significant engineering effort. To make the entrance in the field easier the source code of participated solutions was published in the repository of the competition.[8] A well-documented baseline solution for the future competition will also be available.

Better promotion of the competition in academy and industry is needed to get more participating teams and volunteers for evaluation. Another measure to increase

---

[4]http://m.me/convai.io or https://t.me/convaibot

[5]Possible scores were from one to five with former corresponding to the bad and the latter to the excellent dialogue quality.

[6]http://convai.io/data/

[7]http://parl.ai/

[8]https://github.com/DeepPavlov/convai/tree/master/2017/solutions

engagement of human evaluators might be to change the task from discussion of incidental text snippet to the discussion focused on the topics that are more interesting to the user.

The first Conversational Intelligence Challenge was a successful attempt to test the ground for a large scale dialogue system competition with evaluation by human volunteers. Results of the competition demonstrate that current state of conversational artificial intelligence allows to support dialogue with a human on a given topic but with quality significantly lower compared to human. Closing this gap will not only bring a major progress in solving fundamental problems of artificial intelligence research but also open possibilities for a wide range of industrial applications. We are looking forward to continue exploration of possible solutions to the problem of making machines talk like humans with the next Conversational Intelligence Challenges.

1.2   Classifying Clinically Actionable Genetic Mutations

The increase in genetic sequencing capabilities combined with the decrease in cost have been instrumental for the adoption of cancer genetic testing in the clinical practice. Genetic testing may detect changes that are clearly pathogenic, clearly neutral or variants of unclear clinical significance. Such variants present a considerable challenge to the diagnostic laboratory and the treating clinician in terms of interpretation and clear presentation of the implications of the results to the patient. There does not appear to be a consistent approach to interpreting and reporting the clinical significance of variants either among genes or among laboratories. The potential for confusion among clinicians and patients is considerable and misinterpretation may lead to inappropriate clinical consequences. Currently this clinical interpretation of genetic variants is being done manually.

This is a very time-consuming task where a clinical pathologist has to manually review and classify every single genetic variant based on evidence from the clinical literature. MSK pioneered the creation of OncoKB, a knowledge base where evidence for these genetic variants is being collected, and manually curated. It takes a molecular pathologist around 3 h to curate a single variant. To date more than 88 million genetic variants have been discovered in the Human Genome by the 1,000 Genomes project.[9] Therefore this task is completely unfeasible via the current manual processes.

The scope of this competition was to develop a classification model that can compete with a human curator in some of the tasks described. This would have a considerable high impact on the health care and cancer domains.

---

[9]http://www.nature.com/nature/journal/v526/n7571/full/nature15393.html

1.2.1   Task

This is a classification task with the main goal of using the evidence from the literature to classify the genetic variants in one of the *Oncogenicity* and *Mutation Effect* classes.

There are four **Oncogenicity** classes, *Likely Oncogenic, Oncogenic, Likely Neutral* and *Inconclusive*. There are nine **Mutation Effect** classes, *Likely Gain-Function, Loss-of-function, Likely Loss-of-function, Likely Neutral, Inconclusive, Neutral, Gain-of-function, Switch-of-function, Likely Switch-of-function*.

When the curator decides to investigate a genetic variant, she currently has to manually carry out two tasks. First, she has to manually search the medical literature to identify abstracts that can provide evidence for the interpretation of the genetic variant of study. Second, she needs to read and interpret all these abstracts to ultimately classify the genetic variant in one of the *Oncogenicity* and *Mutation Effect* classes. This second task is the most time consuming, and the goal of this competition. In a real-world scenario our curators would still make manual searches when a new genetic variant needs to be studied. But getting into this competition we could envision a situation where after identifying abstracts containing potential evidence from the literature, the human experts would pass them as input to a model that classifies them into their corresponding *Oncogenicity* and *Mutation Effect* classes.

1.2.2   Data

The data for this competition was made available in the public domain via the OncoKB Data Access[10] page. It could be accessed via REST APIs, or simply downloaded in two different versions - Actionable Variants[11] or All Variants.[12]

The Table 1.1 below shows a detailed description of a manually annotated genetic variant in the Actionable Variants data set. The first column *Gene* refers

Table 1.1 Detailed description of a genetic variant in the data set

A sample annotation					
Gene	Alteration	Oncogenicity	Mutation effect	PMIDs for mutation effect	Abstracts for mutation effect
ERBB2	L869R	Likely oncogenic	Likely gain-of-function	21531810, 26305917, 16397024	Hyman et al.

---

[10] http://oncokb.org/#/dataAccess

[11] http://oncokb.org/api/v1/utils/allActionableVariants.txt

[12] http://oncokb.org/api/v1/utils/allAnnotatedVariants.txt

to the gene that is being annotated. *Alteration* represent the aminoacid change for that specific mutation. *Oncogenicity* denotes whether or not this specific mutation has been identified as oncogenic, or cancer-causing, in the literature. *Mutation Effect* represent the effect of this mutation in downstream molecular pathways. *PMIDs for Mutation Effect* represents the Pubmed abstracts that the human curator had to read to be able to classify the *Oncogenicity* and *Mutation Effect* of the specific variant. Pubmed abstracts are publicly available via the National Library of Medicine's REST API. Finally *Abstracts for Mutation Effect* provides links to specific abstracts from the medical literature that might have been made available in selected conferences such as the American Society of Clinical Oncology (ASCO). These are also abstracts that the human curator will have to manually analyze in order to classify this genetic variation in one of the *Oncogenicity* and *Mutation Effect* classes.

1.2.3 Running the Competition

This competition was particularly challenging to run due to the size of the data set, with less than 10,000 observations. This particular problem is very common in the medical domain where obtaining manually labeled samples is extremely costly and very often machine learning practitioners need to come up with creative ways to counter for this limitation.

In our case, we decided to run this competition in two stages. During the first stage (June 26th, 2017 to September 25th, 2017) participants would have access to the OncoKB samples available in the public domain. And a short second stage (September 26th, 2017 - October 2nd, 2017) where we made available a holdout dataset with 1,000 samples. Finally, participants were evaluated only against the holdout dataset made available during stage two of the competition.

In terms of logistics, we used the Kaggle platform to run this competition. In our case this worked particularly well since we were able to leverage Kaggle's community to encourage users to participate in our competition. One factor to emphasize for future organizers of this type of competitions is that selecting the right platform to run your competition is one of the critical decisions to make.

1.2.4 Outcomes

Our main goal getting into this competition was twofold. First, we wanted to introduce the Machine Learning Community with real world challenges in health care that could potentially be solved via Machine Learning. Second, we wanted to leverage this community to find out a solution for a very particular problem that we at MSKCC have, classifying clinically actionable mutation.

We can now definitely say that we achieve these two goals. On the one hand we had more than 1,500 participants taking part and submitting at least one solution to our competition. This definitely proves that the competition was a success in terms of raising awareness within the community. On the other hand, the best scenario possible for MSKCC was that at least one of the participants would come up with an innovative solution to our particular problem that we could implement and deploy into our production clinical pipeline. Thanks to this competition we found not just one, but two. The solutions from the Cornell University and Uber Technologies teams are currently being evaluated by our clinicians for their integration within our clinical workflow. Therefore, we also clearly achieved our second goal of finding a solution that would have a clear clinical impact. These two solutions will be described in detail in two separate chapters in this volume.

1.3 Learning to Run

Synthesizing physiologically accurate movement is a major challenge at the intersection of orthopedics, biomechanics, and neuroscience. An accurate model of the interplay of bones, muscles, and nerves could potentially allow to predict variability in movement patterns under interventions (e.g. a surgery) or new conditions (e.g. an assistive device or prosthetics).

In this challenge, participants were tasked to build controllers for a neuromusculoskeletal system without any experimental data, i.e. solely through exploration of simulated physics. The role of a controller was to observe sensory information and actuate muscles in order to make the model move forward as quickly as possible, while avoiding obstacles. Over the course of 4 months 442 participants submitted 2154 controllers. The competition has proven not only that the task is approachable despite high dimensionality of the solution space, but also that the movement patterns generated through reinforcement learning resemble human gait patterns.

1.3.1 Task

Given a neuromusculoskeletal model, i.e. a set of bones connected by joints and muscles attached to the bones, participants were tasked to make the model move as far as possible within 10 seconds of simulation time. To control the models, they were sending signals actuating muscles causing the model to move according to predefined dynamics. Decisions were taken on a discretized time-grid of 1000 equidistributed time-points.

Actuation signals were defined as vectors $a_t = [0, 1]^{18}$ corresponding to excitation of 18 muscles (0 – no excitation, 1 – full excitation). The simulation of dynamics was performed in OpenSim (Delp et al. 2007) – a physics engine dedicated to musculoskeletal simulations.

For the purpose of this section, the simulation engine can be seen as a function M from the space of states and muscle actuations to the space of states. Let S_t be a state of the system at time t, then:

$$S_{t+1} = M(S_t, a_t).$$

Participants did not observe the entire state, but only a function $O(S_{t+1})$ which included positions and velocities of the center of mass, bodies, and joints. Simulations were terminated either when the time finished (i.e. after 1000 time-steps) or when the vertical position of the pelvis fell below 0.65 meter, what was interpreted as a fall.

The objective of the competition was to build a controller synthesizing the fastest movement, without falling and without extensive use of ligaments. We quantified this objective through a reward function. At each step of simulation, agent receives a reward $r(t)$ defined as

$$r(t) = d_x(t) - \lambda\sqrt{L(t)},$$

where $d_x(t)$ is the change of position of pelvis in this time-step, $L(t)$ is the sum of squared forces generated by ligaments at time t and $\lambda = 10^{-7}$ is a scaling factor. Let T be the termination time-step. The total score of the agent is the cumulative reward till T, i.e. $R = \sum_{t=1}^{T} r(t)$.

In order to enforce building robust controllers, we introduced two types of obstacles, randomly chosen for each simulation. First, we had variable strength of the psoas muscles simulating an injury. Second, we placed spherical obstacles along the path, enforcing adaptation of the steps. Information about both kind of obstacles was included in the observation vector.

1.3.2 Running the Competition

The competition was running in two stages: the open stage (4 months) and the play-off stage (2 weeks). In the open stage, participants were interacting with the grading server iteratively, at every time-step. Thanks to an elementary API, this allowed for very simple on-boarding of participants. In the play-off stage, participants were asked to prepare a docker container with their solution. This allowed for testing the solution in exactly the same environments and for reproducibility of the actual controllers, which was crucial for a post-hoc analysis of the results.

For running the challenge we needed a customized platform. First, our challenge did not rely on any data, so it did not fit classical data science settings, typical to platforms like Kaggle. Second, both stages of the challenge required customized solutions: the first one requires direct interaction with the grader, while the second one requires a docker-based infrastructure. These circumstances directed us towards open platforms and we decided to host the challenge on the crowdAI,[13] while leveraging OpenAI gym (Brockman et al. 2016) infrastructure for grading. Implementations of all components of our challenge, i.e. the simulation engine, the grading server, the docker-based grading system as well as the entire crowdAI platform are all open source.

1.3.3   Outcomes

The objective of the challenge was to answer two questions: (1) Are the modern reinforcement learning techniques capable of solving high-dimensional non-linear continuous control problems? (2) are the movement patterns emerging from reinforcement learning physiologically relevant? Due to the very large space of solutions and no theoretical guarantees on finding global solutions with reinforcement learning, we cannot expect to definitely answer these questions through a challenge. Instead, we rather perceive them as exploration of potential new directions of research in computational biomechanics.

Top solutions submitted to the challenge partly answer both questions. First, the winning solution was running at around 4.5 m/s, equivalent to fast human jogging. The running gait pattern is very complex and the fact that it emerge under very weak assumptions imposed on the controller is most remarkable. Second, we observed weak similarities in angular joint kinematics between the top solutions and experimental data on running. We discuss them in detail in the "Learning to run" chapter (Kidziński et al. 2018).

1.4   Human-Computer Question Answering Competition

Question answering is a core problem in natural language processing: given a question, provide the entity that it is asking about. When top humans compete in this task, they answer questions incrementally; i.e., players can interrupt the questions to show they know the subject better than their slower competitors. This formalism is called *quizbowl* and was the subject of the NIPS 2015 best demonstration.

In this year's iteration, competitors could submit their own system to compete in a quiz bowl competition between computers and humans. Entrants created systems that receive questions one word at a time and decide when to answer. This then provided a framework for the system to compete against a top human team of quizbowl players in a final game.

---

[13]http://crowdai.org/

1.4.1 Data

We created a server to accept answers to a set of questions and provided quiz bowl question data to train and validate systems. This data also comes with preprocessed text versions of the Wikipedia pages associated with each answer in the training set. We encourage the use of external data in addition to what we have provided.

1.4.1.1 Test Set

The test set had possible answers from any Wikipedia page. However, many of the answers will likely be in the train set (the same things get asked about again and again). Around 80% of test questions are about answers in the train set. The test questions were written by quiz bowl writers based on the standard high school distribution.

1.4.2 Competition

The competition had two phases: a machine competition to select a top computer team and a human-machine phase to pit the top computer entry against a strong team of trivia experts.

1.4.2.1 Machine Evaluation

We evaluated systems (and humans) in pairwise competition. The system that gives a correct answer first (i.e., after requesting the fewest number of words) gets 10 or 15 points (15 points are available for early, correct buzzes). A system that gives an incorrect answer first will lose 5 points. There is no penalty for guessing at the end of a question. The system with the higher overall score wins.

Participants interacted with a server architecture that replicates the process of playing a quiz bowl game. Systems get each word in the question incrementally and can decide to answer (or not) after every word. We break ties randomly when systems are evaluated against each other.

1.4.2.2 Human-Machine Evaluation

The top computer team faced off against six strong trivia players from the Los Angeles area and from the NIPS community. The questions came from the same pool of questions used in the computer competition. The system OUSIA decisively won the competition, 475–200 (Fig. 1.1).

Fig. 1.1 Our human-computer competition at NIPS 2017. The top computer submission faced off against a team of top trivia players from the LA area

1.4.3 Outcomes

In the competition overview chapter, we describe how this competition is not the final word for comparing question answering abilities of humans and machines. In many ways, this competition is tilted in favor of the machines, and we can improve the competitiveness of the competition through adversarial writing of questions, forcing machines to interpret speech, changing the difficulty of questions, and focusing on questions whose answers are less well-represented in Wikipedia.

1.5 Adversarial Attacks and Defenses

Most existing machine learning classifiers are highly vulnerable to adversarial examples. An adversarial example is a sample of input data which has been modified very slightly in a way that is intended to cause a machine learning classifier to misclassify it.

Adversarial examples pose security concerns because they could be used to perform an attack on machine learning systems, even if the adversary has no access to the underlying model.

The purpose of adversarial attacks and defenses competition was to increase awareness of the problem and stimulate more researchers to explore potential solutions. In this competition participants were invited to submit methods which craft adversarial examples (attacks) and classifiers which are robust to adversarial examples (defenses). Attack methods were ranked based on how many times they fool defenses and defense methods were ranked based on their accuracy on adversarial examples.

1.5.1 Task and Evaluation Metrics

Adversarial attacks and defenses competition had 3 tracks and participants were invited to submit a solution in one or several tracks:

- **Non-targeted adversarial attack.** In this track participants were invited to submit a method which performs non-targeted adversarial attack, i.e. given an input image generate adversarial image which potentially be misclassified by a defense.
- **Targeted adversarial attack.** In this track participants were invited to submit a method which performs targeted adversarial attack, i.e. given an input image and a target class generate adversarial image which potentially be classified as a given target class by a defense.
- **Defense against adversarial attacks.** In this track participants were invited to submit an image classifier which is robust to adversarial examples.

During evaluation all attack methods were run on the provided dataset to craft adversarial images, then these adversarial images were fed into all defenses and classification labels were computed.

An attack got 1 point each time it was able to fool a defense on a single image. If attack was unable to fool a defense or was unable to generate adversarial image then it got 0 points for that image. A defense got 1 point for each correctly classified image and 0 points for incorrect classification or failure to produce classification label. Points for each submission were added together and then normalized (using common normalization constant for all submissions), such that the final scores of all submissions were in the range [0, 1], where 1 means success on all images and 0 means failure on all images.

1.5.2 Dataset

Dataset of source images which were fed to attacks was composed of ImageNet-compatible images. We constructed this dataset by collecting images available online under CC-BY license, automatically cropping and classifying these images with help of the state-of-the art ImageNet classifier, then manually verifying labels and discarding images with invalid labels.

We prepared two datasets. DEV dataset contained 1000 images and was provided for development of the solutions as well as for evaluation of development round. FINAL dataset contained 5000, was kept secret and was used for final evaluations of all solutions.

1.5.3 Running the Competition

Competition was announced in May 2017, launched in the beginning of July 2017 and finished on October 1st, 2017. Competition was run in multiple rounds. There were three development rounds (on August 1, 2017, on September 1, 2017 and September 15, 2017) followed by the final round with submission deadline on October 1st, 2017.

Development rounds were optional and their main purpose was to help participants to try and test their solution. Final round was used to compute final scores of submissions and determine winners.

We partened with Kaggle,[14] which hosted competition web-site, forum, leaderboard and was used to upload submissions. During the evaluation of each round, we disabled submission uploads and took all already uploaded submissions from Kaggle and run them on our customly build infrastructure on Google Cloud[15] platform. Then results were published online and submission upload was re-enabled.

1.5.4 Outcomes

Main goals of the competition were to increase awareness of the adversarial examples and stimulate researchers to propose novel approaches to the problem.

Competition definitely increased awareness of the problem. Article «AI Fight Club Could Help Save Us from a Future of Super-Smart Cyberattacks»[16] was published in MIT Technology review about the competition. And in the end we got 91 non-targered attack submissions, 65 targeted attack submission and 107 defense submissions participating in the final round.

There were good results and interesting approaches among the submissions. Best non-targeted attack achieved 78% success rate against all defenses on all images. Best targeted attack achieved 40% success rate, which is quite impressive because targeted black box attacks are generally hard. Top defense submission got 95% accuracy on all adversarial images produces by all attacks. This indicates that it may eventually be possible to be robust to adversarial examples at least in the black box situation (i.e. when attacker is unaware of the exact defense).

---

[14]www.kaggle.com

[15]www.cloud.google.com

[16]https://www.technologyreview.com/s/608288

Tools, competition datasets and several baseline method were published online[17] as a part of development toolset. Additionally most of the participants released their submissions under open source licences[18] as was required by competition rules.

1.6 IBM Watson AI XPRIZE Milestones

The IBM Watson AI XPRIZE is a 4 year competition awarding a $5 million prize purse to teams improving the world with artificial intelligence (AI). Teams competing for the prize are permitted to propose the grand challenge they will solve with AI and judges select advancing teams in each year of the competition. Teams advance on the basis of technical and logistical achievement and the importance for humanity of the team's presumed solution.

The competition began in 2017 with 148 teams competing to solve problems in sustainability, robotics, artificial general intelligence, healthcare, education, and a variety of other grand challenge problem domains (see Table 1.2). The first judgment round winnowed the field to 59 teams. Of these 59 advancing teams, 10 teams were nominated for Milestone Awards and two teams won Milestone Awards.

Table 1.2 High level problem domain descriptions for teams competing for the IBM Watson AI XPRIZE. The rows are ordered from domains with the highest advancement rate (top) to the lowest advancement rate (bottom). Figure 1.2 gives additional details on advancement rates

Problem domain	Team count	Example problem area
Humanizing AI	7	Moral and ethical norming
Emergency Management	5	Planning disaster response logistics
Health	13	Drug efficacy prediction
Life Wellbeing	21	Augmenting the visually impaired
Environment	8	Automated recycling
Education/Human Learning	17	Intelligent tutoring system
Civil Society	11	Online filter bubbles
Health Diagnostics	12	Radiography image segmentation
Robotics	5	Robotic surgery
Knowledge Modeling	7	Automated research assistant
Civil Infrastructure	9	Earthquake resilience testing
Business	19	Optimizing social investment
Artificial General Intelligence	8	* (all of them)
Brain Modeling and Neural Networks	6	Cognition emulation

---

[17] https://github.com/tensorflow/cleverhans/tree/master/examples/nips17_adversarial_competition

[18] Links to code of non-targeted attacks: https://www.kaggle.com/c/6864/discussion/40420, targeted attacks: https://www.kaggle.com/c/6866/discussion/40421, defenses: https://www.kaggle.com/c/6867/discussion/40422

1.6.1   Running the Competition

Teams submitted competition plans to the XPRIZE Foundation in the first quarter of 2017. Following a survey of team problem areas, the XPRIZE Foundation recruited a panel of 34 judges with core competencies in either artificial intelligence research (e.g., natural language processing, robotics, etc.) or team problem areas (e.g., cancer diagnosis, civil society, etc.). Teams submitted four page First Annual Reports in September. Judges bid on these reports within the EasyChair conference management system and an assignment algorithm generated a proposed set of reviewers. XPRIZE staff then adjusted EasyChair report assignments to ensure that every team would be reviewed by at least one AI researcher.

Judge reviews separated teams into Milestone Nominees, advancing, and rejected groups on the basis of their *overall rating, importance for humanity, existing solution status, progress indicators,* and *technological capacity for solving the problem.* The 10 teams with the highest average overall rating were nominated for Milestone Awards.

The judges then each reviewed two additional teams from the Milestone nominee list and labeled one of the teams as having the better First Annual Report. After ranking the teams from the pairwise comparisons, the top two teams were awarded a total of $15,000 during the NIPS Competition Track.

1.6.2   Outcomes

The characteristics of advancing, rejected, and awarded teams highlight the problem domains with the greatest challenges and opportunities for improving the world with artificial intelligence. Our NIPS Competition Track chapter surveys the problem domains and technologies of the IBM Watson AI XPRIZE, details the prize judgement process executed to date, and treats the advancement decisions of judges as opportunity indicators for the "AI for Good" movement (see Fig. 1.2). The results show where AI researchers may fruitfully direct their efforts to address problems that are simultaneously important for humanity, technically challenging, and feasible to solve within 4 year timelines.

1.7   Neural Art Challenge

Since its introduction in 2015, Neural Style Transfer (Gatys et al. 2016) has had a big impact in a number of areas. It not only produces beautiful artistic pictures, which attracted world-wide media attention. But it also introduced novel perceptual loss functions to measure image similarity, which was particularly useful for fields such as image processing and image synthesis.

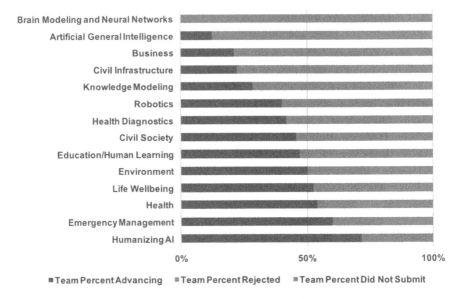

Fig. 1.2 Stacked percent bar charts for the 148 teams. The first series (blue) represents percentage of the teams within the problem domain advancing. Similarly, the orange and gray bars represent teams that were judged and rejected and did not submit a report, respectively

Neural style transfer requires two ingredients: a photograph that defines the content and a painting that defines the style. The algorithm then combines the two and renders the content of the photograph in the style (or texture) of the painting. The rendering is done via a so-called pre-image search. We iteratively update the content image by gradient descent until it minimizes the sum of two loss functions: a content loss and a style loss. Both losses are computed in the feature space obtained by passing the images into a deep convolutional neural network (VGG-19 (Simonyan and Zisserman 2015)) trained on large-scale image recognition (ImageNet (Russakovsky et al. 2015)). The content loss tries to match the activations of the content image and the rendering in a high-level convolutional layer (conv4_2). These high-level layers are relatively invariant to low-level features like color or small local perturbations, which allows for some flexibility in changing the style while maintaining the important shapes (content) of the image. The style loss tries to match spatial summary statistics (correlations of feature maps) between the style image and the rendering in a number of layers. Matching summary statistics enforces that the texture features from the style image are transferred onto the rendering, but does not constrain their spatial arrangement. The resulting image looks like the content of the photograph has been swapped into the painting.

The goal of the Neural Art Challenge was not to advance science in any way, but instead to demonstrate the breadth of artistic effects that can be achieved with this simple image synthesis procedure. Our main goal was to engage the NIPS community in a fun project to decorate the conference center with neural art.

1.7.1   Task and Evaluation Metric

Participants generated neural artworks using the free online service DeepArt.io.[19] The goal was to create aesthetically pleasing images. We determined the best artwork by a democratic vote.

1.7.2   Running the Competition

We divided the challenge into two stages: an online stage where everyone all over the world was free to cast a vote, and an on-site stage at NIPS where only conference participants could vote. The top 50 artworks from the first stage were qualified to the second stage, as well as 12 "editor's picks", which we added to increase diversity.

In the first stage, participants used DeepArt.io to generate neural artworks. They submitted a link to their best pieces to the competition website,[20] which we set up for this purpose. To ensure image quality sufficient for printing on 24" × 36" posters, we instructed participants to submit only images with a resolution of at least two megapixels.

Submission for the first stage opened on October 25, 2017 and closed on November 22, 2017. During this time, all submissions were shown on the submission website in random order (sorting by 'most recent' and 'most popular' was also possible). Anyone could vote for artworks by clicking on a 'vote' button next to each image.[21]

In the second stage, the top 50 submissions from stage 1 and the 12 editor's picks were exhibited as posters in the conference center on the Grand Ballroom Concourse (outside the hall used for the poster sessions). NIPS participants could vote for their favorite posters via an online form. Access to this form was restricted to users with a NIPS user account. The voting was open from Monday, December 4, 9am to Thursday, December 7, 2017, 9am PST.

The final winner and the two runners up were announced at the Competition Track Workshop on Friday, December 8, 2017.

1.7.3   Outcomes

The first stage received 456 submissions from 125 artists. The 12 top-ranked submissions are shown in Fig. 1.3.

---

[19]Disclosure: Alexander Ecker, Leon Gatys, Łukasz Kidziński and Matthias Bethge are founders and shareholders of DeepArt UG (haftungsbeschränkt), the company operating https://deepart.io.

[20]http://deepart.io/nips

[21]To detect cheating, we logged voters' IP addresses and other meta information. We identified a handful of cheaters and removed their images from the competition usually within a day.

(1.) By Raghavendra Adla   (2.) By Thu Nguyen Phuoc   (3.) By Mehrdad

(4.) By José   (5.) By Philips Kokoh Prasetyo   (6.) By Dario

(7.) By Giovanni   (8.) By SeungHyun   (9.) By Philips Kokoh Prasetyo

(10.) By Suraj Subramanian   (11.) By Alexis Jacq   (12.) By Rasmus Tirsgaard

Fig. 1.3 Top 12 submissions from the first (online) stage

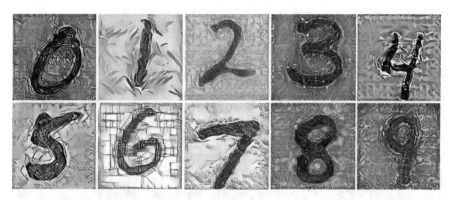

Fig. 1.4 Ten digits from the popular MNIST dataset made it into the top 50 during the online phase of the competition

After the first stage, we determined the 50 top-ranked submissions that were suitable for printing. Three submissions had to be removed: two because of low image quality and one because the artwork had identical content and style image (i. e. the original was reproduced rather than a neural artwork). A notable fun fact is that all ten digits of the popular MNIST dataset made it into the final round (Fig. 1.4). Finally, because space and budget allowed, we added another 12 images as "editors' picks" in order to increase diversity and include a couple of late submissions that did not have enough time to accumulate votes.

The poster exhibition was very well received at the conference. The final winner and the two runners up are shown in Fig. 1.5. The "spaghetti theme" featuring Albert Einstein in third place (16.5% of votes) has been a popular internet meme some time in 2016. In second place with 17.5% were the drawings of popular neural network architectures in the style of Leonardo da Vinci. The final winner with 18.6% of votes is – perhaps surprising – the image of a cat in an abstract, polygonal style. This artwork was also one of the most popular ones during the online phase.

1.8 Discussion

Results Overall, the competitions track of NIPS 2017 was a success. Some competitions advanced the state of the art in other sciences such as "Classifying Clinically Actionable Genetic Mutations" and "Learning to Run". Others, like "The Conversational Intelligence Challenge" and "Adversarial Attacks and Defences"

(1.) By SeungHyun

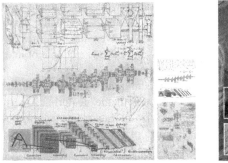

(2.) By Joseph Paul Cohen

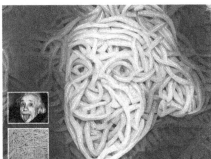

(3.) By Rasmus Tirsgaard

Fig. 1.5 Final winner (top) and two runners up (bottom). Insets show content and style images used to create the artwork

generated new data sets that we expect to impact the progress in their respective communities for quite some time. And "Human-Computer Question Answering Competition" showed us just how far we as a field have come in ability and efficiency since the break-through performance of Watson in Jeopardy.

The selection of competitions emphasizes advancing the state of the art of Neural Information Processing Systems as opposed to solving a singular instance of a data science problem. We believe that this particular angle provides a big enough niche for competitions at conferences as opposed to on data science platforms.

Advise for future organizers Running multiple competitions is an approach that paid off: It is more laborious than just a single competition. At the same time, it allows for accepting a wider range of competitions. This lessens the pressure on each individual competition to carry the burden of being *the one* competition. It also makes the track more attractive to more people overall.

One major challenge that inhibits the use of competitions is the lack of human participation, where desired. One approach that did work was to have a two-stage competition: First have the machines compete with one another, then ask humans to enter the competition.

We wish our successors in organizing NIPS Competitions track all the best.

Acknowledgements The NIPS 2017 Competition track was sponsored by NIPS and ChaLearn.

The Conversational Intelligence Challenge was partially sponsored by Facebook, Flint Capital, IVADO, Microsoft Maluuba, Element AI.

The Learning to Run Challenge was organized by the Mobilize Center at Stanford University, a National Institutes of Health Big Data to Knowledge (BD2K) Center of Excellence supported through Grant U54EB020405, and by the crowdAI.org platform. The challenge was partially sponsored by NVIDIA, Amazon Web Services and Toyota Research Institute.

The Neural Art Challenge was sponsored by a number of sponsors, who we would like to thank. DeepArt.io sponsored the high-resolution renderings. ChaLearn.org sponsored the printing of the posters. Prices were sponsored by NVIDIA.

The IBM Watson AI XPRIZE is sponsored by IBM Watson.

References

Greg Brockman, Vicki Cheung, Ludwig Pettersson, Jonas Schneider, John Schulman, Jie Tang, and Wojciech Zaremba. Openai gym. *arXiv preprint arXiv:1606.01540*, 2016.

Scott L Delp, Frank C Anderson, Allison S Arnold, Peter Loan, Ayman Habib, Chand T John, Eran Guendelman, and Darryl G Thelen. Opensim: open-source software to create and analyze dynamic simulations of movement. *IEEE transactions on biomedical engineering*, 54(11):1940–1950, 2007.

Leon A. Gatys, Alexander S. Ecker, and Matthias Bethge. Image style transfer using convolutional neural networks. In *Proceedings of the IEEE Conference on Computer Vision and Pattern Recognition*, pages 2414–2423, 2016.

Łukasz Kidziński, Ong Carmichael Sharada, Mohanty, Jennifer Hicks, Sean Francis, Sergey Levine, Marcel Salathé, and Scott Delp. Learning to run challenge. In Sergio Escalera and Markus Weimer, editors, *NIPS 2017 Competition Book*. Springer, Springer, 2018.

Olga Russakovsky, Jia Deng, Hao Su, Jonathan Krause, Sanjeev Satheesh, Sean Ma, Zhiheng Huang, Andrej Karpathy, Aditya Khosla, and Michael Bernstein. Imagenet large scale visual recognition challenge. *International Journal of Computer Vision*, 115(3):211–252, 2015.

Karen Simonyan and Andrew Zisserman. Very deep convolutional networks for large-scale image recognition. 2015.

Chapter 2
The First Conversational Intelligence Challenge

Mikhail Burtsev, Varvara Logacheva, Valentin Malykh, Iulian Vlad Serban, Ryan Lowe, Shrimai Prabhumoye, Alan W. Black, Alexander Rudnicky, and Yoshua Bengio

Abstract The first Conversational Intelligence Challenge was conducted over 2017 with finals at NIPS conference. The challenge IS aimed at evaluating the state of the art in non-goal-driven dialogue systems (chatbots) and collecting a large dataset of human-to-machine and human-to-human conversations manually labelled for quality. We established a task for formal human evaluation of chatbots that allows to test capabilities of chatbot in topic-oriented dialogue. Instead of traditional chit-chat, participating systems and humans were given a task to discuss a short text. Ten dialogue systems participated in the competition. The majority of them combined multiple conversational models such as question answering and chit-chat systems to make conversations more natural. The evaluation of chatbots was performed by human assessors. Almost 1,000 volunteers were attracted and over 4,000 dialogues were collected during the competition. Final score of the dialogue quality for the best bot was 2.7 compared to 3.8 for human. This demonstrates that current technology allows supporting dialogue on a given topic but with quality significantly lower than that of human. To close this gap we plan to continue the experiments by organising the next conversational intelligence competition. This

M. Burtsev (✉) · V. Logacheva · V. Malykh
Moscow Institute of Physics and Technology, Moscow, Russia
e-mail: info@convai.io; burtcev.ms@mipt.ru; logacheva.vk@mipt.ru;
valentin.malykh@phystech.edu

A. Rudnicky · A.W. Black · S. Prabhumoye
Carnegie Mellon University, Pittsburgh, PA, USA
e-mail: sprabhum@andrew.cmu.edu; awb@cs.cmu.edu; air@cs.cmu.edu

I.V. Serban · Y. Bengio
University of Montreal, Montreal, QC, Canada
e-mail: iulian.vlad.serban@umontreal.ca; yoshua.bengio@umontreal.ca

R. Lowe
McGill University, Montreal, QC, Canada
e-mail: ryan.lowe@cs.mcgill.ca

© Springer International Publishing AG, part of Springer Nature 2018
S. Escalera, M. Weimer (eds.), *The NIPS '17 Competition: Building Intelligent Systems*, The Springer Series on Challenges in Machine Learning,
https://doi.org/10.1007/978-3-319-94042-7_2

future work will benefit from the data we collected and dialogue systems that we made available after the competition presented in the paper.

2.1 Introduction

Dialogue systems are traditionally divided into several types according to their purposes. Question-answering systems (Sukhbaatar et al. 2015) can give information on a particular topic or a range of topics. Goal-oriented dialogue systems (Bordes and Weston 2016) can accomplish a task such as looking for flights or ordering a pizza. Finally, chatbots (Serban et al. 2017) are just capable of having a chat. Their goal is to make a conversation interesting and enjoyable for a user.

Creating a chatbot is probably the most challenging task in this field of research. A chat without a particular topic or any other restriction is too general task. In contrast to dialogue systems of other types, chatbot often has no context, i.e. it does not know anything about user's goals in a conversation. Therefore, it is hard to tell which capabilities a chatbot should have to be considered good and how one could comprehensively test all these capabilities. Giving user a task of just chatting and then reporting how good was the conversation is not a reliable setting, because users might have too different expectations. In this case scores from different users will not be comparable.

A well-performing chatbot is often more difficult to develop than a goal-oriented system. Pre-defined scenarios and sets of rules which are common in goal-oriented systems are insufficient to produce natural conversations in chit-chat settings. To address richness of human communication development of chatbots relies much more on Machine Learning (ML) algorithms, which makes it less deterministic. There currently exist no established best practices of developing good chatbots, but it is a subject of active ongoing research.

There is another aspect that sets chatbots apart from goal-oriented systems and makes their development so challenging. When interacting with a goal-oriented system user has one or several pre-defined goals which are known to the system. In contrast to that, when chatting to a bot user has an implicit goal hidden from the bot. Moreover, this goal can change throughout the conversation. We assume that correct prediction and appropriate treatment of the peer's conversational goals makes a dialogue natural. Therefore, a good chatbot should be able to identify these user's goals and construct a dialogue with respect to them.

To explore possible approaches to the challenge of open-ended communication in natural language, different chatbots should be tested on a variety of tasks that emerge in a free-flow dialogue. Competition of dialogue systems is one of the ways to organise a large-scale interaction between human and bots. A scenario for such competition should be challenging enough to highlight the main capabilities of a target system, but constrained in order to make evaluations comparable.

Finally, even a meaningful dialogue between a chatbot and a human is difficult to evaluate automatically. The reason for that is the absence of evaluation metrics.

While goal-oriented systems can be evaluated with the percentage of successful dialogues (when user's task was accomplished) and for Q&A systems we can compare a given answer to a correct one, for chatbots there is no formal measure of success or correctness. The goals of a chatbot are to generate answers which (i) are natural and (ii) suit the context. Naturalness is often measured with perplexity of a generated string with respect to some language model (Serban et al. 2015). This metric is often used to evaluate chatbots, but it cannot check the adequacy of answer. In order to measure this suitability, researchers often use metrics that compare a generated string to some oracle answer (e.g. BLEU (Papineni et al. 2002) and METEOR (Lavie and Agarwal 2007) originally used for evaluating Machine Translation models). This is not an optimal way of evaluating chatbots either, because a relevant answer can be different from an oracle (Liu et al. 2016). The latest works on the evaluation of dialogue systems suggest training evaluation metrics on a set of human-labelled dialogues (Lowe et al. 2016, 2017). However, obtaining such corpora takes much time and effort, so they do not exist in big number.

Following these conclusions, we designed Conversational Intelligence Challenge (ConvAI)—a competition of chatbots which addresses all the mentioned challenges of chatbot development and testing. First of all, we suggested a new scenario of human-to-bot conversations. In the beginning of a conversation both participants of a conversation receive a snippet of around 100 words on some particular topic. The task is to discuss this text. A human user can evaluate utterances emitted by a chatbot during the conversation. When the conversation is over, the user is asked to evaluate the overall dialogue. As a result, humans rate the submitted chatbots and a dataset of scored dialogues is accumulated. The proposed competition task has the following properties:

- Pre-dialogue text acts as a proxy for dialogue context. In a regular setting we need a long conversation history to check if a chatbot is good at memorising facts. The provided text alleviates this need. Inconsistency of chatbots within a dialogue is often reported as one of their major problems (Li et al. 2016), so finding a way to keep and reuse conversation history in chatbot's memory is one of the main sought-after goals for developers.
- At the same time, this text sets the focus of discussion and conversation becomes topic-oriented. Conversations with no topic are often reported to be boring for users (Yu et al. 2016) and do not allow to test the capabilities of chatbot. If a conversation has no particular topic, a chatbot can always produce overly general answers which suit the immediate context but do not form a meaningful conversation.
- By giving user a task of discussing an article we also made an effort to limit the range of possible user goals. Within this task user behaviour can be guided by a number of goals: she can ask for clarification of the information in the article or express her opinion about it. Our intuition is that the task becomes easier for dialogue systems and also more interesting for users. Although we do not track user goals and do not test systems' capability of predicting these goals, we assume that a successful conversation implies correct prediction of the goals.

- Last but not the least, data collection is more time-efficient than in previous experiments on chatbot evaluation. In contrast to them, in our setup dialogues and their quality scores are collected jointly.

The first ConvAI competition was organised in 2017. 10 research teams submitted their chatbots and 6 of them met technical requirements to participate in the main competition. During the competition almost 1,000 volunteers took part in scoring. As a a by-product of human evaluation of submitted chatbots we collected a corpus of human-to-machine dialogues manually labelled for quality at the level of dialogues and utterances. To have a reference, we also collected a significant number of human-to-human conversations. The task was the same, peers receive a text and then should discuss it and evaluate each other. This allowed to get larger number of successful dialogues and compare the properties of human-to-human and human-to-bot conversations.

The closest analogue of the competition is the Amazon Alexa Prize competition.[1] This competition aimed at building a socialbot that can converse coherently and engagingly with humans on popular topics. Another small-scale analogue is Loebner Prize.[2] There is also Build It Break It competition proposing a new type of shared task for AI problems that pits AI system "builders" against human "breakers" in an attempt to learn more about the generalisation capabilities of current NLP technology.[3] The key differences of our competition are:

- a large number of evaluators,
- deliverables:
  - an open-source dataset created as a result of the competition and potentially highly valuable for research community,
  - open-source chatbots developed by participants of the competition that can be used as user simulators or serve as a baseline for future competitions,
- judges produce graded evaluation of dialogues and individual answers (as opposed to only utterance-level evaluation used in previous work),
- every conversation has a specific topic—to discuss a randomly selected Wikipedia article.

The chapter is organised as follows. In Sect. 2.2 we describe the competition task and experimental setup. Section 2.3 contains short descriptions of dialogue systems that participated in the competition. In Sect. 2.4 we give the results of the competition, specifically how the chatbots were perceived by human volunteers. Then, in Sect. 2.5 we analyse the collected dataset. Finally, we discuss the results and outline directions for future work in Sect. 2.6.

---

[1] https://developer.amazon.com/alexaprize

[2] https://en.wikipedia.org/wiki/Loebner_Prize

[3] https://bibinlp.umiacs.umd.edu/

2.2   Competition Description

2.2.1   Task

The goal of the competition was to test the ability of a dialogue agent (chatbot) to discuss the content of a short excerpt from Wikipedia article with a user. The evaluation was performed through a blind cross-testing of bots and human users in a series of dialogues. We also included human-to-human dialogues in order to address possible poor quality of bots and to compare the statistics for human and machine peers. Occasional connection of two humans also serves for gamification of the data collection process. If a volunteer does not know if her peer is a human or a bot, she will probably be more engaged into the conversation and eager to chat in order to discover that.

Volunteers logged into an anonymous chat system and communicated either with a bot or with another human user according to the following scenario:

1. volunteer is connected with a random peer. The peer can be a chatbot or other human user. No information about identity of the peer is provided,
2. peers receive text extracted from a Wikipedia article,
3. volunteer discusses the content of the article with the peer as long as she wishes and evaluates peer's responses during the dialogue,
4. once the dialogue is finished, the volunteer evaluates the quality of the dialog as a whole.

The peers were encouraged to discuss the text shown prior to the conversation, but they were not strictly required to stay within this topic. Evaluation of individual responses was optional, whereas dialogue-level evaluation was compulsory. All conversations were in English.

2.2.2   Structure of the Competition

The competition started in May 2017 and lasted until the 9th of December 2017. It consisted of four stages:

- **Qualification round**. Registered participants submitted applications consisting of two parts: (1) proposal describing architecture of their system (2) code of system for testing. Systems which accomplished technical requirements were selected for the first round.
- **First round** of chatbot evaluation and data collection: July 2017. This round was conducted at the scientific hackathon DeepHack[4] where participants had a task

---

[4]http://turing.tilda.ws/

to chat with submitted systems and use the generated data to train models for prediction of dialogue score. Half of the data was collected at this stage.

- **Intermediate stage** between two rounds: August–November 2017. Data collection continued in the background and all the data was released into the public domain. ConvAI teams were able to learn from this data and improve their dialogue agents. In addition to that, some participants also reported collecting similar data on their own.
- **Second (final) round**: 20th of November—9th of December. Dialogues collected during this round were used to define the winner of the competition. The majority of dialogues were collected at NIPS-2017 conference. We asked the research community to volunteer for the competition by chatting with systems and scoring their answers.

Participants were allowed to submit new versions of their systems any number of times between the first and the second rounds.

2.2.3 Pre-dialogue Texts

The tested dialogue systems belonged to the same type, i.e. chatbots. This means that they did not have to identify any particular goal of a dialogue and accomplish it. However, in order to give a meaningful topic of conversation and encourage more informative responses from both humans and robots we supply peers with a context, which is a paragraph from the SQuAD dataset (Rajpurkar et al. 2016). These paragraphs originally come from Wikipedia articles. From now on the paragraphs that come before dialogues will be referred to as *contexts*, because they serve as contexts for the dialogues.

To the best of our knowledge, such technique has not been used in chat data collection experiments before. Our intuition was that by providing peers with a *context* we would achieve a number of goals:

- make conversations more interesting and diverse because the lack of diverse and informative responses has been identified as one of problems of collecting human-to-bot conversations (Yu et al. 2016),
- test dialogue systems in the setting where they should accomplish some task and have a chat, i.e. act as a goal-oriented system and a chatbot within the same conversation,
- test the systems' ability to store in memory a number of facts and refer to them appropriately. Short-term memory of what has been said during dialogue is one of crucial problems in the development of dialogue systems (Li et al. 2016). Making a system have a talk about a text is an easy way to test its memory without a long conversation,
- enable developers to test their systems easily and automatically before the competition, without having to resort to crowd-sourcing experiments.

2.2.4 Evaluation

During the conversation user can evaluate the quality of her peer's answers. Below every peer's utterance a user is shown two buttons: "thumbs up" (good/appropriate utterance) and "thumbs down" (bad/inappropriate utterance) to indicate whether the answer was appropriate or inappropriate, respectively. During the analysis of results we interpreted "bad" scores as 0 and "good" scores as 1. This evaluation is not compulsory, user can continue the conversation without giving scores to peer's utterances.

After the conversation is finished, user is asked to evaluate the whole dialogue along three dimensions:

- overall quality of dialogue (referred to as *quality*),
- breadth of dialogue—how thoroughly peers discussed the topic suggested in the opening text (*breadth*),
- engagement of peer into the conversation (*engagement*).

All three parameters are given scores from 1 (bad) to 5 (good). Initially, dialogue-level scores were compulsory: a user could not start a new conversation without scoring the previous one. However, after the first round we changed this setup. Now, user is still asked to type in scores for the three dialogue-level metrics and cannot start a new conversation straight away, but if the system does not get the response from the user for 10 min, the evaluation is discarded and dialogue stays without scores.

2.2.5 Volunteers

We did not impose any requirements on volunteers. All the information about the competition was in English, so we expected volunteers to have some knowledge of English, but we did not check their level of English. Since data collection was anonymous, we do not have any information on volunteers' background or age.

The majority of volunteers who participated in the first round of data collection were students of Computer Science from Russian universities, another part are data scientists also based in Russia. Most of them are native speakers of Russian with different level of proficiency in English. The total number of volunteers was a bit over 250 people, but half of them had only one conversation. The number of active contributors (users who conducted at least 10 dialogues) was 64 people, they conducted 85% of all dialogues. Every active contributor participated in 36 dialogues on average.

Volunteers who contributed to the evaluation at the final round were a bit different: since we advertised the competition at the NIPS-2017 conference, many of volunteers belong to research community. The statistics here are similar to those of the first round: half of the people conducted only one dialogue, and only around 10% conducted 10 dialogues or more. The average number of dialogues from active contributors was only 17 this time.

2.2.6 Framework

We created a framework for collecting conversations of humans and bots which operates on Telegram[5] and Facebook Messenger[6] messaging services.

The framework is written in Scala language and distributed as a Debian-style Linux package. It consists of three main parts:

- connector—a module to connect to external messaging systems like Telegram;
- server—a module to provide interface for participating systems;
- router—a module to connect external users with participating systems or other external users.

The competition system has two connectors - one for Facebook Messenger and another one for Telegram instant messaging platforms. They have almost the same functionality, except that Facebook Messenger does not allow to put arbitrary emojis as reactions to utterance. The external users connect to the system through these messengers. Figures 2.1, 2.2, and 2.3 show the Telegram user interface: Fig. 2.1 shows a pre-dialogue context, Fig. 2.2 contains a screenshot of a dialogue between a

Fig. 2.1 Pre-dialogue context

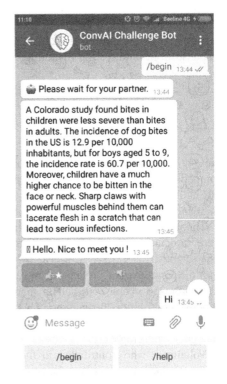

Fig. 2.2 Dialogue of two
peers and utterance-level
evaluation

volunteer and a peer (apparently a chatbot) and utterance-level scores ("thumbs up") given by the volunteer. Figure 2.3 shows the process of dialogue-level evaluation performed at the end of dialogue.

The *server* provides API which is a simplified version of Telegram server API. It supports only plain text messages and `put message` and `get message` commands. That was made intentionally to simplify switching from our server to Telegram messaging system for participants in case they want their system to be available directly.

The *router* connects a user with a randomly chosen competing bot. To collect data for human-to-human dialogues volunteer is connected to another volunteer with the probability of 0.1.

The data is stored to MongoDB.[7] Alongside the system we provide scripts to dump MongoDB database to JSON. The dumped record contains the dialogue *context*, the utterances from both sides, evaluated values for utterances and dialogue as a whole, identities for both sides. The scripts have an option of data anonymisation, since we need to publish collected data and protect personal data of the users. An anonymised dialogue does not contain participants' identities.

---

[7]https://mongodb.com

Fig. 2.3 Dialogue-level
evaluation

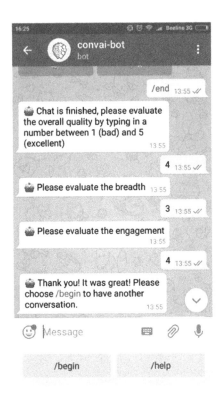

The source code of the framework is published.[8]

2.3 Participants

A total of 6 chatbots participated in the final round of the competitions. We provide
their brief descriptions. All solutions are available online.[9]

2.3.1 RLLChatbot

The Reasoning and Learning Lab Chat Bot team from McGill University presented
their system RLLChatbot to the NIPS 2017 Conversational Intelligence Challenge.

---

[8]https://github.com/deepmipt/convai-testing-system

[9]https://github.com/DeepPavlov/convai/tree/master/2017/solutions

The team divides their approach into two high-level steps: generation of candidate responses and controlling the conversation flow.

2.3.1.1   Generation of Candidate Responses Based on News Article and Dialogue History

The team used an ensemble of generative models, retrieval models, and rule-based models to generate those responses:

- HRED trained on Twitter&Reddit,
- Neural Question Generator trained on SQuAD,
- DrQA trained on SQuAD,
- a topic extractor model,
- a fact generator model,
- a set of predefined regexp rules to answer common queries,
- ALICE bot.

2.3.1.2   Controlling the Conversation Flow

At each turn, the generated candidate responses from each model are fed into a neural network that scores the responses based on their estimated human score (trained to predict "thumbs-up" vs "thumbs-down" label of candidate response). The system then returns to the user the candidate response that has the maximum score based on this evaluation. Here are some features used as input to the scoring network:

- Average word embeddings (dim 300) for candidate, previous turns, article.
- Embedding Similarity between candidate & previous turns and article.
- Message topic for candidate and previous user message: one-hot vector for greeting, personal question, affirmation, negative, request, politic.
- Bigrams, trigrams, entities and non-stop words overlap between candidate & previous turns and article.
- Confusion, intensifier, 'wh' and negation word percentage for candidate & previous user message.
- Length of article and of conversation history.
- Vader Sentiment of candidate and previous user message.

2.3.2   kAIb

This system was submitted by a team from the School of Electrical Engineering, Korea Advanced Institute of Science and Technology and AIBrain company.

The proposed dialogue system consists of three modules: dialog act classifier (DA), question-answering (QA), and chit-chat (CC). The DA classifies whether the message requires the question-answering or the chit-chat function. According to the classification results, the corresponding module generates a response.

To answer factual questions about the articles, the QA employs the Passage-Question Matching Network (PQMN) that is trained on SQuAD. The network matches questions and passages with attention mechanisms and finds the answer spanning section. Sometimes, users ask factual questions beyond the provided articles. In order to answer them, the team has collected another wiki article database, and the related passage is retrieved by passage retriever from this database. These additional passages are also fed into the PQMN to answer the question.

To answer the chit-chat type messages, the CC firstly generates diverse response candidates by employing both a rule-based model and sequence-to-sequence (Seq2seq) neural models. Then it selects the most appropriate response among the candidates. In detail, for the rule-based model, the system utilises the ALICE bot and additional rules. For the seq2seq models, the team trained diverse neural networks with different data and network architecture.

2.3.3 bot#1337

The dialogue system bot#1337 was submitted by the team from Moscow Institute of Physics and Technology. This system is capable of conversing with humans about a given text. The conversation is enabled by a set of skills, including chit-chat, topic detection, text summarisation, question answering and question generation. The system has been trained in a supervised setting to select an appropriate skill for generating a response.

System allows to focus on skill implementation and provides a simple and effective approach for dialogue management. Skills with a lot of dialogue data could be easily added to the conversational agent, other skills could be added by writing few key phrases for the dialogue manager. The bot is implemented with open source software and open data. Source code of bot#1337 is available on Github.[10]

In future work the bot#1337 team is planning to add frame-based skills, improve conversational agent by iteratively testing on users, develop a dialogue quality scorer trained on human evaluations, build a simulator and apply reinforcement learning to maximise dialogue quality scores.

---

[10]https://github.com/sld/convai-bot-1337

2.3.4   Poetwannabe

Poetwannabe system was developed by a team from the University of Wroclaw. Its full description can be found in Chorowski et al. (2018).

Poetwannabe is a dialogue system able to conduct a conversation with a user in natural language. The conversations can concern an excerpt of encyclopedic or news articles. The primary function of the dialogue system is to provide a context-aware question answering (QA) functionality. However, since the QA module works in the context of a conversation, the systems secondary function is to maintain a general conversation.

The system is composed of a number of sub-modules which independently prepare replies to user prompts and assess their confidence. The system runs the submodules in parallel, then selects the most confident one. To answer questions, the dialogue system relies heavily on factual data sourced mostly from Wikipedia and DBpedia, as well as real-world data of user interactions in public forums, and data concerning general literature. An information retrieval module retrieves facts from the databases, and scores their relevance to the conversation. The selected passages are used to generate answers using a question-answering module. The QA module is built on the SQuAD question answering task, which recently gained momentum in the deep learning community.

To handle general user prompts the system mainly retrieves responses from a large dialogue corpus harvested from the Internet. Using word2vec, the system embeds a large dataset of utterances with their contexts, and retrieves best matching utterance pairs from the associated database. The database covers a wide range of responses, from simple phrases and expressions to long statements. Poetwannabe also uses a version of Alicebot as a separate response generating module. Those less specific modules do not introduce new information to the user, but rather sustain the conversation and mimic the behavior of a human peer. Where applicable, modules are trained on large datasets using GPUs. However, to comply with the competition's requirements, the final system is compact and runs on commodity hardware.

2.3.5   PolyU

This system was developed by a team from The Hong Kong Polytechnic University. The system uses four strategies to enhance existing sequence-to-sequence conversational models:

1. *Fusion of retrieval-based and generation-based models.* This technique is targeted at enriching users input utterances to get a more comprehensive view of what the user "intends to say". The current input utterances are enriched with other similar input utterances, and with other similar input-response pairs in the training data. Such input utterance enrichment is formulated as a kind of query expansion using relevance feedback model.

2. *Knowledge-augmented generation-based model.* The team incorporates the extra knowledge base into conversational models, so that they can refer common sense to background knowledge as a real human. For example, when the user mentions the politician Hillary Clinton, it is better for the conversational models to know relevant information and news about her. In particular, the team adopted Freebase as a knowledge base.
3. *Generation-based model with structured attention.* Including structured attention increases the diversity of generated responses. Structured attention allows the decoder to focus on fine-grained and more accurate relevant information in the input utterances, which reduces the amount of information needed to attend. It also serves as an extra mechanism to keep track of what has been generated by the decoder so far.
4. *Continuous learning process with reinforcement learning.* A dialogue is considered as a reinforcement learning problem where rewards are either duration of the conversation process or positive dialogue states.

More information about this system can be found in Shen et al. (2017).

2.3.6   *DeepTalkHawk*

This is a system presented by a team from University of Massachusetts Lowell. It is a conversational agent with hierarchical structure, which supports the following functionality:

1. *Discover relevant concepts in the article* using a bidirectional LSTM with a CRF layer at the top.
2. *Generate meaningful questions* with respect to relevant concepts from the article and the chat messages. A discriminator is trained to guide the training of the question generator. The discriminator takes in a question sequence and outputs a confidence score on whether the input is a real question in the dataset or a machine-generated question. The generator is trained as a policy network, using REINFORCE algorithm, with the probability score assigned by the discriminator as its reward.
3. *Answer questions based on the article.* The article and question are read by separate Long-Short Term Memory recurrent networks to produce a representation per token. A Match-LSTM network analyses both representations to effectively read over the passage again, using information from the question to highlight candidate tokens for an answer. Finally, a Pointer Net uses the output of the Match-LSTM to produce the answer to the question using token words from the article.
4. *Generate non-answer comments* related to the article based on the relevant world knowledge. This module is trained on user responses collected from Reddit.
5. *Decide which of the above functionality should be invoked* at each turn, and maintain a representation for the dialogue state to improve discourse.

2.4 Results

Performance of all teams in the competition was evaluated both after the first and the second round. Only *long* dialogues that had at least 3 utterances from each participant were taken into account. The results of the first round were computed on dialogues collected by the end of the round. Final rating was obtained from the data collected during the second round. Since all participating chatbots were updated between the first and the second rounds, the scores given before November 20 did not reflect the quality of final systems.

Each dialogue was rated according to three parameters: *quality*, *breadth* and *engagement*. Since the *quality* metric encompasses the overall impression of the dialogue, the official criteria determining the competition winner was based on the average value of this metric. However, we also report other metrics for completeness.

2.4.1 First Round

During the human evaluation round we added some extra bots to increase the diversity and to reduce chances for users to interact with the same bot. Those extra bots were also evaluated but not included to the official ranking. In the tables below names of bots which participated in the competition are written **in bold**.

The evaluation of bots was computed using 1400 *long* dialogues. The distribution of those dialogues across different systems is not even because some chatbots were shut down after conducting less than 100 dialogues due to technical problems. Other differences in the number of dialogues are attributed to the fact that some chatbots had short dialogues more often because they were not able to capture user's attention for a long time.

Table 2.1 shows the average scores of individual dialogue-level metrics and the average of all scores given to dialogues of a bot ("Total" column). The scores are mostly poor. The average values for bots range from 1.3 to 2.3 and dialogue-level metrics are strongly correlated at the system level. We also included average human score given to human volunteers by their human peers. As expected, human dialogue quality is much higher than those of chatbots.

The utterance-level scores produce a slightly different ranking of bots (shown in Table 2.2). However, it shows strong correlation (Pearson r of 0.85) with dialogue-level ranking at the system level. Here we see a larger variation: the average utterance-level scores range from 0.5 to 0.06. This ranking is not guaranteed to be fair because each bot has on average 50–70% of rated items, and the unrated ones were discarded for this evaluation. On the other hand, this holds for all bots.

Table 2.1 Dialogue-level quality of bots. Bots are sorted from best to worst according to the averaged values of all metrics (**Total** column). Bots **in bold** are those which participate in the official competition

Bot name	Quality	Engagement	Breadth	**Total**	# dialogues
poetwannabe	2.366	2.310	2.207	2.294	201
DATA Siegt	2.320	2.400	1.953	2.224	150
bot#1337	2.295	2.219	2.094	2.203	270
RLLChatBot	2.228	2.244	2.024	2.165	231
Plastic world	2.181	2.319	1.993	2.164	140
poetess	2.172	2.207	2.069	2.149	26
kAIb	2.011	1.991	1.780	1.928	222
Q&A	2.000	1.833	1.833	1.889	5
DeepTalkHawk	1.427	1.433	1.401	1.420	155
PolyU	1.329	1.286	1.271	1.295	9
Human	3.800	3.755	3.548	3.701	620

Table 2.2 Average utterance-level quality of bots ("0" for bad answers and "1" for good answers). Bots are sorted from best to worst. Bots **in bold** are those which participate in the official competition

Bot name	Quality
DATA Siegt	0.512
poetwannabe	0.467
kAIb	0.453
bot#1337	0.433
RLLChatBot	0.430
poetess	0.380
Plastic world	0.372
Q&A	0.326
DeepTalkHawk	0.195
PolyU	0.061

2.4.2 Final Round

In the final round we used chatbots only from the six official participants of the competition for data collection. This time, they were evaluated based on 292 dialogues.[11] Table 2.3 shows the final results of the competition. Here we again used averaged *quality* scores as the primary metric, but we also provide *engagement* and *breadth* for completeness.

Due to the small number of dialogues used for the evaluation the results of this round were ambiguous: they did not allow us to define a single winner—the 1st prize was shared between teams **bot#1337** and **poetwannabe**. However, according to our refined results (the ones reported here), there were only two significantly different groups of systems: the top three (**bot#1337, poetwannabe, RLLChatBot**) and the bottom three (**kAIb, PolyU, DeepTalkHawk**). The differences of scores within

---

[11] Unfortunately, we were not able to collect any more dialogues during the round

Table 2.3 Results of the final round. The official metric is **Quality**

System ID	Quality	# dialogues	System ID	Engagement	System ID	Breadth
bot#1337	2.779	68	RLLChatBot	3.231	bot#1337	2.676
poetwannabe	2.623	53	bot#1337	2.809	RLLChatBot	2.462
RLLChatBot	2.462	13	poetwannabe	2.623	poetwannabe	2.415
kAIb	2.2	35	kAIb	2.057	kAIb	1.657
PolyU	1.75	28	PolyU	1.964	PolyU	1.286
DeepTalkHawk	1.262	42	DeepTalkHawk	1.286	DeepTalkHawk	1.262

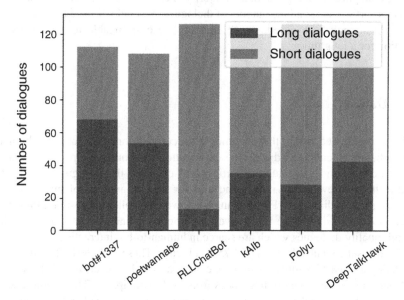

Fig. 2.4 The number of short and long dialogues for each system in the final round

these groups are not significant. This result is consistent throughout all metrics—although systems' positions in ranking differ, these shifts are not statistically significant.

This suggests that the competition should have three winners. However, there is an additional parameter that should also be considered—the number of dialogues used for evaluation. The framework described in Sect. 2.2.6 assigned bots to human volunteers randomly with equal probability. This means that the numbers of dialogues conducted by different bots are similar. On the other hand, the number of *long* dialogues used for evaluation depends on the bot's quality and differs significantly for participating systems. We provide the number of *long* dialogues for every chatbot in the left part of Table 2.3. It shows that although dialogues conducted by **RLLChatBot** are good, their number is four to five times less than that of other winning systems. The number of long and short dialogues for all chatbots is also shown in Fig. 2.4. It is clearly seen that the overall number of dialogues ranges from 110 to 125, whereas *long* dialogues constitute different percentages of this amount.

The analysis has shown that such low number of dialogues is due to the fact that **RLLChatBot** had many dialogues with no utterances or dialogues where the chatbot did not produce any answers: it was often not able to maintain the conversation due to its internal technical problems. Thus, the system failed to fully accomplish technical requirements of ConvAI. Hence, while its answers might have been adequate, we were not able to collect a sufficient number of them to achieve statistical significance.

We should note that the situation when a well-performing system has low number of *long* dialogues is not typical: in the majority of cases we see a correlation between system's performance and the number of dialogues that could be used for evaluation. As it has already been noted, worse chatbots are often unable to capture user's attention for a long time.

2.5   Dataset

As it was mentioned, one of the outcomes of the competition is the dataset of human-to-bot dialogues collected during the competition. Although the primary goal of the data collection was to rate the participating chatbots, the dialogues can also be used to train an evaluation metric and also for manual analysis of main features of human-to-bot dialogues. For the latter goal we also collected a small number of human-to-human dialogues: they serve for comparison and also provide examples of high-quality dialogues which are scarce in human-to-bot interaction.

The dataset contains the total of 4,750 dialogues. These include 4,224 human-to-bot dialogues and 526 human-to-human conversations. However, only half of these dialogues have three or more utterances from both participants. The dialogue-level evaluation showed that a half of dialogues were considered bad (were rated with "1"). The utterance-level evaluation shows a similar result, there, over a half of utterances were also labelled as bad.

We tested this data on a task of training an automatic metrics of dialogue quality. We organised a hackathon where multiple research teams developed their metrics. Besides that, the data was used by participants of ConvAI to update their chatbots between the first and the second rounds. They used the conversations collected in the first round. However, some of them reported not using neither dialogue-level nor utterance-level labels because of their low reliability.

The full description of the collected dataset is given in Logacheva et al. (2018).

2.6   Discussion and Future Work

We organised a competition of chatbots with a goal of establishing a new task for dialogue systems research. The task is to discuss a topic defined by a short textual description. This focuses user goals in dialogue around the provided text and allows to explore approaches to the challenging problem of meaningful topic-oriented dialogue. In order to speed up the process of dialogue labelling we suggested that it should be conducted during the generation of dialogue by volunteers who chat with bots. Finally, we crowdsourced a part of dialogues from the research community during NIPS-2017 conference.

Through the course of the competition we collected a dataset of human-to-bot and human-to-human conversations which are labelled for quality. This dataset proved to be useful. Many participants used it to improve their systems between the first and the second rounds of the competition.

The main decisions to be made in terms of the system evaluation scenario were (1) choice of texts used as topics of conversations, (2) evaluation process: who and when should evaluate the dialogues, which metrics should be used. Below we analyse the setup we chose and suggest possible improvements.

2.6.1 Data

One of the major sources of complaints from volunteers were the pre-dialogue contexts. Those were excerpts from Wikipedia articles taken from the SQuAD corpus. These texts were originally not supposed to be used as seed texts for dialogues. Many of them are full of factual information and are not of general interest. Therefore, most of people did not like them and some admitted not reading them at all. This observation corroborates our results which have shown that humans and chatbots quite rarely discuss the content of provided texts.

Nevertheless, the problem of topics for conversations is still crucial in conversations between humans and non-goal-oriented systems. We suggest that we still need to define topics in further data collection experiments. However, the topics should be defined in a different way. They should be shorter and more interesting for users. One of options would be using news titles or interesting facts as contexts, because they are short and often catchy so that users will be more excited to discuss them. Alternatively, we could formulate topics as individual words or phrases ("Music", "French cuisine") and offer participants one or several of them to discuss.

Another aim which we did not fully accomplish in our data collection experiments is explicit definition of user goals. We assumed that by providing dialogue context we would constrain user goals to a subset related to this context. It was expected that user would be eager to express her opinion, learn her peer's opinion or clarify some information from the text. However, this constraint did not hold for the majority of conversations, because users rarely talked on pre-defined topics. One possible way to fix this in the future is to generate a set of goals and give them to user in a particular order. In such a scenario we will be able to make dialogues from different systems more comparable and identify flaws of systems better.

Every dialogue in the dataset has scores from only one user. This results in unstable labels and our inability to estimate their uncertainty. Since we do not have multiple labels for one object, we cannot compute user agreement. This also makes scores noisy. Besides that, the majority of teams reported that during the intermediate stage of the competition they used only collected dialogues, and not their scores. However, this issue can be solved by performing additional scoring of recorded dialogues by several assessors in order to make the scores more reliable.

2.6.2 Evaluation

Our hypothesis is that a dialogue should be evaluated by the person who had a chat and immediately after it in order to give the fresh impression of the conversation. Such evaluation better reflects user satisfaction than evaluation performed by a user who reads a completed dialogue.

However, on-the-fly labelling might create a number of problems. In our case it primarily affected utterance-level evaluation. The instruction for evaluators did not explicitly say that scoring of utterances was optional. As a result, significant share of participants tried to label every utterance of their peers. This disrupted the natural dialogue flow. Therefore, we need to work on gamification of the process.

Another possible improvement of our evaluation setup is to get rid of three dialogue-level metrics. As we have already reported, they strongly correlate, which suggests that users do not see the difference between them. This corroborates previous experiments with multiple metrics for evaluation of dialogues (Lowe et al. 2017). Volunteers also reported having difficulties with multiple metrics and noticed that different people interpreted *breadth* and *engagement* metrics in different ways. We suggest to use only one dialogue-level metric (overall quality) in the future.

2.6.3 Organisational Aspects

Data collection experiments always require a way of motivating people who generate data. When the data generation process requires expert knowledge (e.g. translation from one language to another), the only option is to pay for accomplishing the task. However, in many cases labelling of the data can be conducted by almost anyone or by people with expertise which is quite common, for example, the ability to have a conversation in English. In such cases a common choice is *crowdsourcing*—generation of data by volunteers who work for free or for a small payment.

Our data collection setup belongs to the latter case, that is why we decided to crowdsource the dialogues. However, motivation of volunteers in crowdsourcing scenarios is still a problem. An option for increasing the volunteer engagement is gamification of data collection process. It can include competition of volunteers so that the ones who conducted more conversations have higher score. Besides that, we could motivate user by making conversations more interesting, for example, by including topics which user is more eager to discuss. Another option would be to give volunteers an explicit task such as "Find the system's opinion on X" and give a reward depending on the accomplishment of this task. Meanwhile, the quality of chatbots can also be defined by user success in the task, in a way that a good chatbot should be able to understand user intentions and answer her questions appropriately.

Scoring of dialogues is also challenging for users. Some of them find it difficult to use a 1-to-5 scale and understand how a dialogue with quality of "3" differs from the on with quality of "4". Therefore, the next edition of data collection experiments should include detailed instructions for the labelling task with examples of good and bad dialogues and all intermediate states.

2.6.4 Future Work

Results of the first Conversational Intelligence Challenge competition demonstrate viability of crowdsourcing approach to the evaluation of the dialog systems and dataset generation. Still, the quality of topic-oriented conversations produced by bots submitted to the competition is far from human level.

In the next year's competition participants will be able to use this dataset from the beginning. In addition to that, we will collect more conversations during the next competition. Although we are unlikely to collect much larger amount of data, new evaluation setup will make it more accurate and thus more useful.

Finally, this year's competition provided the set of open-source dialogue systems that can be used by next year's participants as a baseline. Alternatively, such models can be used as user simulators. Therefore, the next year's participants will be able to take an existing state-of-the-art solution and improve upon it. We expect that the next year's chatbots will be more successful and more interesting to talk to.

Acknowledgements Participation of MB, VL and VM was supported by National Technology Initiative and PAO Sberbank project ID 0000000007417F630002.

References

Bordes, A. and Weston, J. (2016). Learning end-to-end goal-oriented dialog. *CoRR*, abs/1605.07683.

Chorowski, J., Łańcucki, A., Malik, S., Pawlikowski, M., Rychlikowski, P., and Zykowski, P. (2018). A Talker Ensemble: University of Wrocaw entry to the NIPS 2017 Conversational Intelligence Challenge. *NIPS 2017 Competition track Springer Proceedings*.

Lavie, A. and Agarwal, A. (2007). Meteor: An automatic metric for mt evaluation with high levels of correlation with human judgments. In *Proceedings of the Second Workshop on Statistical Machine Translation*, StatMT '07, pages 228–231, Stroudsburg, PA, USA.

Li, J., Galley, M., Brockett, C., Gao, J., and Dolan, B. (2016). A persona-based neural conversation model. *CoRR*, abs/1603.06155.

Liu, C., Lowe, R., Serban, I. V., Noseworthy, M., Charlin, L., and Pineau, J. (2016). How NOT to evaluate your dialogue system: An empirical study of unsupervised evaluation metrics for dialogue response generation. *CoRR*, abs/1603.08023.

Logacheva, V., Burtsev, M., Malykh, V., Polulyakh, V., and Seliverstov, A. (2018). ConvAI Dataset of Topic-Oriented Human-to-Chatbot Dialogues. *NIPS 2017 Competition track Springer Proceedings*.

Lowe, R., Noseworthy, M., Serban, I. V., Angelard-Gontier, N., Bengio, Y., and Pineau, J. (2017). Towards an automatic turing test: Learning to evaluate dialogue responses. In *Proceedings of the 55th Annual Meeting of the Association for Computational Linguistics (Volume 1: Long Papers)*, pages 1116–1126, Vancouver, Canada.

Lowe, R., Serban, I. V., Noseworthy, M., Charlin, L., and Pineau, J. (2016). On the evaluation of dialogue systems with next utterance classification. *CoRR*, abs/1605.05414.

Papineni, K., Roukos, S., Ward, T., and Zhu, W.-J. (2002). Bleu: A method for automatic evaluation of machine translation. In *Proceedings of the 40th Annual Meeting on Association for Computational Linguistics*, ACL '02, pages 311–318, Stroudsburg, PA, USA.

Rajpurkar, P., Zhang, J., Lopyrev, K., and Liang, P. (2016). Squad: 100,000+ questions for machine comprehension of text. In *Proceedings of the 2016 Conference on Empirical Methods in Natural Language Processing*, pages 2383–2392, Austin, Texas.

Serban, I. V., Sankar, C., Germain, M., Zhang, S., Lin, Z., Subramanian, S., Kim, T., Pieper, M., Chandar, S., Ke, N. R., Mudumba, S., de Brébisson, A., Sotelo, J., Suhubdy, D., Michalski, V., Nguyen, A., Pineau, J., and Bengio, Y. (2017). A deep reinforcement learning chatbot. *CoRR*, abs/1709.02349.

Serban, I. V., Sordoni, A., Bengio, Y., Courville, A. C., and Pineau, J. (2015). Hierarchical neural network generative models for movie dialogues. *CoRR*, abs/1507.04808.

Shen, X., Su, H., Li, Y., Li, W., Niu, S., Zhao, Y., Aizawa, A., and Long, G. (2017). A conditional variational framework for dialog generation. In *Proceedings of the 55th Annual Meeting of the Association for Computational Linguistics (Volume 2: Short Papers)*, pages 504–509.

Sukhbaatar, S., Szlam, A., Weston, J., and Fergus, R. (2015). End-to-end memory networks. In *NIPS-2015: Proceedings of the 28th International Conference on Neural Information Processing Systems*, pages 2440–2448.

Yu, Z., Xu, Z., Black, A. W., and Rudnicky, A. I. (2016). Chatbot Evaluation and Database Expansion via Crowdsourcing. In *WOCHAT workshop at IVA-2016*, Los Angeles, California.

Chapter 3
ConvAI Dataset of Topic-Oriented Human-to-Chatbot Dialogues

Varvara Logacheva, Mikhail Burtsev, Valentin Malykh, Vadim Polulyakh, and Aleksandr Seliverstov

Abstract This paper contains the description and the analysis of the dataset collected during the Conversational Intelligence Challenge (ConvAI) which took place in 2017. During the evaluation round we collected over 4,000 dialogues from 10 chatbots and 1,000 volunteers. Here we provide the dataset statistics and outline some possible improvements for future data collection experiments.

3.1 Introduction

The development of dialogue systems is hampered by the inability to evaluate them automatically. This problem is particularly crucial for non-goal-oriented dialogue systems (chatbots (Serban et al. 2016)). In contrast to goal-oriented dialogue systems, chatbots do not have any formal criterion of successful conversation. Their quality is based on user experience, it cannot be easily formalised.

A recently suggested solution to this problem is to train a model to predict user rating of dialogue (Lowe et al. 2017). Such model should be trained on real user scores. However, the existing models cannot perform well enough to replace human scores. One of the main obstacles to good quality is insufficient training data. While there exist many datasets of human-to-human conversations (Serban et al. 2015), human-to-bot conversations with quality labellings are scarce.

The First Conversational Intelligence Challenge (ConvAI (Burtsev et al. 2018)) aimed at evaluating the performance of chatbot systems. Human volunteers conversed with chatbots and evaluated them. As a byproduct of this evaluation we acquired a dataset of human-to-bot conversations labelled for quality. This data can be used to train a metric for evaluating dialogue systems. Moreover, it can be used in

V. Logacheva (✉) · M. Burtsev · V. Malykh · V. Polulyakh · A. Seliverstov
Moscow Institute of Physics and Technology, Moscow, Russia
e-mail: info@convai.io; logacheva.vk@mipt.ru; burtcev.ms@mipt.ru;
valentin.malykh@phystech.edu; malykh.va@mipt.ru

© Springer International Publishing AG, part of Springer Nature 2018
S. Escalera, M. Weimer (eds.), *The NIPS '17 Competition: Building Intelligent Systems*, The Springer Series on Challenges in Machine Learning,
https://doi.org/10.1007/978-3-319-94042-7_3

the development of chatbots themselves: it contains the information on the quality of utterances and entire dialogues, that can guide a dialogue system in search of better answers.

We describe the statistics of collected data,[1] analyse its properties and outline some possible improvements for future data collection experiments.

3.2 Data Collection

The aim of the ConvAI competition was to establish a task for evaluating non-goal-oriented dialogue systems. Such systems do not have any particular goal in conversation. In order to fully test their capabilities and make the task more formal we specified a constraint on the topic of conversations: a chatbot and a human volunteer should discuss an excerpt from a Wikipedia article that we provide. These texts were taken from the SQuAD dataset (Rajpurkar et al. 2016). The peers are encouraged (but not strictly required) to discuss this text. We further refer to this text as dialogue *context*.

We created a framework for collecting conversations of humans and bots which operates on Telegram and Facebook messaging service. When a user starts a conversation, the framework randomly assigns her a bot or another user, so the user does not know if she is talking to a bot or a human.

During the conversation user can evaluate the quality of peer's answers. Below every peer's utterance a user is shown two buttons: "thumbs up" and "thumbs down" to indicate whether the answer was appropriate or inappropriate, respectively. This evaluation is not compulsory, user can continue the conversation without giving scores to peer's utterances.

After the conversation is finished, user is asked to evaluate the whole dialogue along three dimensions: overall *quality* of dialogue, *breadth* of dialogue (how thoroughly peers discussed the topic suggested in the opening text) and *engagement* of peer. All three parameter are given scores from 1 ("low") to 5 ("high").

The data collection was conducted in three stages:

- **first round**—July 2017. This round was conducted during the hackathon[2] at MIPT, Moscow. There, around a half of the data was collected.
- **intermediate period** between two rounds—August–November 2017. Data collection continued in the background, participants of the competition had a possibility to improve their systems using the data collected during the first round.

---

[1]The dataset is available at http://convai.io/2017/data/

[2]http://turing.tilda.ws/

- **final round**—November–December 2017. In the end of November participants submitted final versions of their systems, dialogues collected since then were used for the final evaluation of chatbots. The majority of dialogues from this round were collected during NIPS-2017 conference.[3]

Overall, 10 chatbots and 1,000 volunteers participated in data collection. Volunteers were students and members of research community.

The full description of the task and the framework can be found in Burtsev et al. (2018).

3.3 Statistics of Dialogues

The dataset contains the total of 4,750 dialogues. These include 4,224 human-to-bot dialogues and 526 human-to-human conversations. The average number of utterances per dialogue is 10.5 and the average utterance length is 7.1 words. The distribution of dialogue lengths is shown in Fig. 3.1. It can be seen that over 1,600 dialogues contain 0 to 5 utterances, and dialogues of over 30 utterances are extremely rare. The dataset includes a significant number of empty dialogues (dialogues with zero utterances) and one-sided dialogues (dialogues with zero utterances from one of users). If the "silent" side is volunteer, it means that she lost interest in a dialogue immediately after it began. The culprit was often the pre-dialogue *context* which was often long and contained many numbers, names and

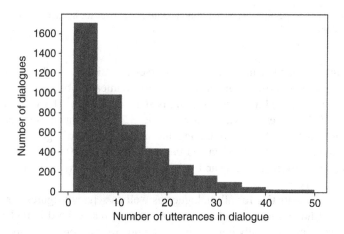

Fig. 3.1 Distribution of dialogue lengths in utterances

---

[3]https://nips.cc/Conferences/2017

Table 3.1 Dataset statistics: number of dialogues with different characteristics

	All dialogues	Human-to-bot	Human-to-human
Total number of dialogues	4,750	4,224	526
Empty dialogues	272 (5.7%)	251 (5.9%)	21 (4%)
One-sided dialogues[a]	1125 (23.7%)	1076 (25.5%)	49 (9.3%)
Long dialogues[b]	2,640 (55.6%)	2,281 (54%)	359 (68.2%)
Utterances per dialogue	10.49	10.36	11.55
Words per utterance	7.08	7.14	6.62
Unique words per dialogue	45.72	45.00	49.58

[a]*One-sided* dialogues are dialogues where one of users did not produce any utterances
[b]*Long* dialogues are dialogues consisting of at least three utterances from each participant

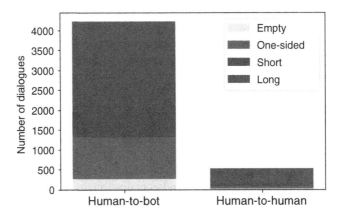

Fig. 3.2 Distribution of empty, one-sided, short and long dialogues for human-to-bot and human-to-human dialogues

other unengaging factual information. Conversely, a "silent" chatbot is usually a system which did not produce any answer due to technical problems.

The statistics of dialogues are summarised in Table 3.1. The distribution of dialogues of different length is also shown in Fig. 3.2. These statistics are computed for the whole dataset. When computing the number of words per utterance we excluded 20 dialogues which contained utterances of over 100 words—these were cases when users were copying and pasting dialogue *context* or typing in other senseless answers.

We give joint statistics for all dialogues as well as separate figures for human-to-human and human-to-bot dialogues, as these turn out to be different in some respects. Two humans usually have longer and more diverse conversations (in terms of the number of used words) than a human and a bot. These facts are apparently related: if a peer uses richer vocabulary, she is better at capturing her partner's attention for a longer time. On the other hand, utterances themselves are shorter in human-to-human dialogues. This probably suggests that humans try to be more explicit when talking to machine so that it understands them better. Moreover,

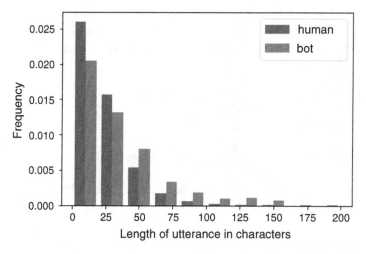

Fig. 3.3 Distribution of dialogue lengths in utterances

as Fig. 3.3 shows, humans tend to generate shorter utterances in general. While dialogue systems try to generate meaningful and grammatically correct sentences which are usually relatively long, humans can output extremely short answers, e.g. "?", "Oh", ":)".

The statistics are computed for the whole dataset collected from July to December 2017. However, its parts (dialogues collected during the first, second rounds as well as during the intermediate stage of the competition) expose the same regularities. This suggests that different types of users (i.e. students and members of international research community) behave more or less similarly and that the changes in systems performed between the first and the second round of competition did not affect their behaviour too much.

3.4 Dialogue-Level Evaluation

After the end of a dialogue a user was asked to rate it in terms of three parameters: peer's *engagement*, *breadth* and overall *quality* of dialogue. Similarly to previous experiments on dialogue data collection (Lowe et al. 2017), we found that these three dialogue-level metrics are strongly correlated: Pearson r scores between any two of those metrics is 0.86–0.87. Volunteers reported having difficulties with interpreting the additional metrics (*engagement* and *breadth*). They said that the interpretations could vary considerably from one person to another. Many of them could not identify the difference of additional metrics and the *quality* score, hence their high correlation.

The distribution of overall quality scores is plotted in Fig. 3.4. We computed scores for *long* and *short* dialogues separately and discovered that *long* dialogues

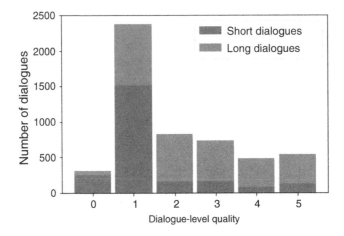

Fig. 3.4 Distribution of dialogue-level quality scores

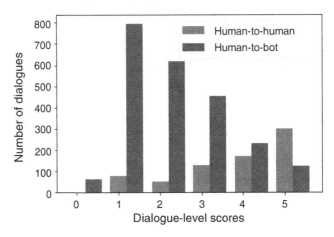

Fig. 3.5 Distribution of dialogue-level evaluation of human and bot peers

are unsurprisingly better than *short* ones: while 66% of *short* dialogues were rated with "1" and another 11% were not rated (unrated dialogues are given a score of "0"), for *long* dialogues these values are only 29% and 2%, respectively. As we can see, the majority of dialogues which were given scores from 2 to 5 are long.

As we expected, quality of human and bot dialogues differ significantly. Figure 3.5 shows the distribution of dialogue-level quality scores separately for bots and humans. Humans perform much better. They were given the score of "5" in the majority of cases, while bots' most common score is "1". We should note though, that performance of human participants of dialogues was occasionally rated low—volunteers gave score of "1" to dialogues with human peers in around 10% of cases. This can indicate that users produced utterances which were irrelevant to the previous dialogue. Alternatively, a user could just dislike answers from her peer, although they were grammatical and relevant. Finally, a user could just rate dialogues randomly.

The latter situation occurs in human-to-bot dialogues as well. We conducted manual analysis of some human-to-bot dialogues that were rated high and found out that some of these dialogues are of quite low quality and shouldn't be considered as examples of successful human-bot interaction. This observation requires more thorough analysis. We suggest that highly-rated dialogues should be re-rated, preferably by several users.

Note that dialogue-level evaluation was provided by all users, so human-to-human dialogues were evaluated twice. This gave us a possibility to compare the evaluation of the same dialogue by two participants. It turned out that in 38% of cases ratings from both users matched, and in another 29% the difference between them was 1. This indicates quite high agreement.

3.5 Utterance-Level Evaluation

As opposed to the quality of dialogues, quality of utterances was evaluated in terms of a binary scale: "good" vs "bad" utterances. "Good" scores were interpreted as 1, while "bad" were 0.

This task is apparently difficult to perform during the conversation: 45.6% of utterances were not rated. On the other hand, there can be a different interpretation of the absence of score: a user might not be sure whether a response was good or not. However, a ternary scale ("good"/"not sure"/"bad") is often also misleading (Yu et al. 2016), so we suggest that the binary scale should be used for this kind of evaluation.

In order to better understand why we got so few utterance-level scores, we performed analysis of scores. Our intuition is that if unrated items mean ambiguous quality, then percentage of such items should be close for all dialogues. On the other hand, if some users do not rate utterances because they find on-the-fly evaluation difficult, the distribution of ranked utterance within a dialogue will be user-dependent.

We discovered that the latter hypothesis is true: 30% of dialogues have no rated utterances, whereas in 35% all or most of utterances (at least 90%) have a score. The average percentage of rated utterances for dialogues with at least one rated utterance is 74.8%. This means that if a user rates utterances in a dialogue, she tries to rate all of them. One of the reasons of such behaviour could be the length of a dialogue. It could happen that as a conversation gets longer, user gets tired of giving ranks to items, so longer dialogues might have smaller percentage of rated utterances. However, we did not find any correlation between the length of dialogues and the percentage of rated utterances in them.

The distribution of utterance-level quality scores themselves is shown in Fig. 3.6 (unrated utterances were discarded). As with dialogue-level scores, here humans

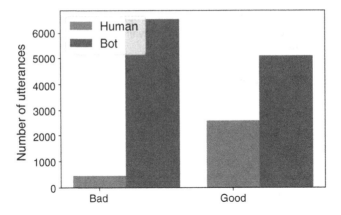

Fig. 3.6 Distribution of utterance-level quality scores for humans and bots

perform much better, but also occasionally produce some utterances which were rated as bad by a peer: 14% rated user responses were considered inappropriate. For bot utterances this number equals 56%.

3.6 Other Properties of Data

We were interested to see if utterance-level scores matched the dialogue-level ones: if the overall dialogue is good, are individual utterances also appropriate within the dialogue? In order to check that, we took an average of utterance-level and dialogue-level scores and computed their correlations (only for dialogues where at least one utterance was rated). It turns out that utterance-level and dialogue-level scores have a moderate correlation of 0.6. The plot in Fig. 3.7 shows their correspondence. This holds for all three dialogue-level metrics. This means that while the overall impression of a dialogue depends on scores of individual answers, it is not fully defined by them. A chatbot can be interesting to chat with despite occasional fails and, conversely, individual answers that fit into the context do not always make a good conversation.

We also tried to find correlation of dialogue-level quality with any dialogue properties, e.g. number of utterances or unique words in a dialogue. However, we found no such correlation.

Besides that, we decided to check how useful is the context that is provided in the beginning of every conversation. We suggested that all participants of a dialogue discuss the provided paragraph of text, hence adding an implicit goal to conversation. Therefore, we wanted to check if the contexts were used as conversation topics. We did that by checking if the most characteristic words of the context appeared later in the conversation.

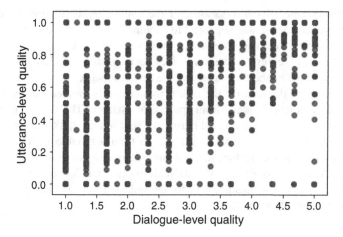

Fig. 3.7 Relationship between dialogue-level and utterance-level quality scores

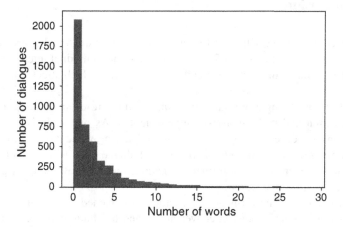

Fig. 3.8 Number of occurrences of top-15 representative words from the context in the dialogue

We defined the most characteristic words as words with the highest tf-idf score. This score is computed for a collection of documents (in our case a collection of paragraphs used as contexts) and is high for words which occur often in the current document and rarely in other documents—this means that these words are representative for this document. We computed tf-idf score for each word in all contexts. Then we took 15 words with the highest tf-idf score from each context and computed the number of times any of these words occurred in the corresponding dialogue. This gave an indication of whether the participants discussed the topic of the context.

It turned out that almost half of dialogues do not contain any of representative words (see Fig. 3.8). This means that in half of cases neither users nor bots tried to discuss the suggested paragraph. Another observation is that there is no correlation between the breadth of conversation and the use of representative words. The *breadth* evaluation metric was supposed to capture how good the conversation was in terms of coverage of a suggested topic. However, this weak correlation suggests that either the use of representative words does not mean that topic has been covered, or users did not understand the purpose of the *breadth* metric.

Finally, we used the data for the task it was primarily created for—we trained a metric that predicts dialogue-level quality of chatbot. The experiments were conducted only on the data collected during the first round (2,700 dialogues). This subset of data was shown to be insufficient to train a reliable metric. The best methods produced a metric that reached only moderate correlation with human judgments (Pearson score of 0.7). It is difficult to say if this low result is explained by small size of data or its unsuitability for the task. We leave the experiments with the full dataset for future work.

3.7   Conclusion

We presented the dataset of human-to-bot and human-to-human dialogues manually labelled for quality at the level of entire dialogues and individual utterances. Data collection experiment unravelled some flaws in our setup, which affected the quality of data.

First of all, providing a pre-dialogue *context* did not result in defining a goal of the conversation and making it more topic-oriented. As our analysis has shown, conversations were very rarely centered around the provided text. Moreover, as volunteers reported, *contexts* often harmed the dialogue: they were often too long, they contained much factual information (names, numbers) and did not give any interesting topics for discussion.

Secondly, the poor performance of chatbots was named as one of the reasons why users were losing interest in conversations and finishing dialogues very soon. Only around a half of dialogues contained at least three utterances from each user. Therefore, when aiming at collecting a particular number of *long* dialogues we should collect twice as many dialogues overall. Even when users managed to have relatively long conversations with chatbots, they were often rated low. This skews the distribution of quality labels in the dataset.

Small size and skewed distribution of labels in the dataset leads to poor quality of evaluation metrics trained on it. So far we were not able to develop a reliable metric.

Finally, the evaluation itself is not reliable enough. The use of multiple dialogue-level metrics proved useless, because volunteers often cannot distinguish between the different metrics. This resulted in strong correlation of these metrics. For the next rounds of data collection we plan to use only one metric (overall quality). Another problem is low reliability of scores. Since every dialogue is rated by one person, we cannot identify incorrect or random labels and cannot estimate the user agreement. We suggest that at least part of dialogues should be evaluated by multiple assessors.

On the other hand, this data was useful for developers of chatbots. The majority of participants of ConvAI challenge reported using the data collected during the first round to improve their models for the final round. Some of them were using only dialogues, because scores were too noisy. However, they still could use the dialogues and the utterance-level labels to train discriminators that decided if a candidate response is good enough or could choose between several candidate responses.

Acknowledgements The work was supported by National Technology Initiative and PAO Sberbank project ID 0000000007417F630002.

References

Burtsev, M., Logacheva, V., Malykh, V., Serban, I., Lowe, R., Prabhumoye, S., Black, A. W., Rudnicky, A., and Bengio, Y. (2018). The First Conversational Intelligence Challenge. *NIPS 2017 Competition track Springer Proceedings*.

Lowe, R., Noseworthy, M., Serban, I. V., Angelard-Gontier, N., Bengio, Y., and Pineau, J. (2017). Towards an Automatic Turing Test: Learning to Evaluate Dialogue Responses. *Acl*, pages 1–19.

Rajpurkar, P., Zhang, J., Lopyrev, K., and Liang, P. (2016). SQuAD: 100,000+ Questions for Machine Comprehension of Text. *Emnlp*, (ii):2383–2392.

Serban, I. V., Lowe, R., Charlin, L., and Pineau, J. (2015). A Survey of Available Corpora for Building Data-Driven Dialogue Systems. *CoRR*, page 46.

Serban, I. V., Sordoni, A., Lowe, R., Charlin, L., Pineau, J., Courville, A., and Bengio, Y. (2016). A Hierarchical Latent Variable Encoder-Decoder Model for Generating Dialogues. *Proceedings of the Advances in Neural Information Processing Systems 29 (NIPS 2016)*, pages 1–14.

Yu, Z., Xu, Z., Black, A. W., and Rudnicky, A. I. (2016). Chatbot Evaluation and Database Expansion via Crowdsourcing. *WOCHAT workshop*.

Chapter 4
A Talker Ensemble: The University of Wroclaw's Entry to the NIPS 2017 Conversational Intelligence Challenge

Jan Chorowski, Adrian Lancucki, Szymon Malik, Maciej Pawlikowski, Pawel Rychlikowski, and Pawel Zykowski

Abstract We present Poetwannabe, a chatbot submitted by the University of Wroclaw to the NIPS 2017 Conversational Intelligence Challenge, in which it shared the first place. It is able to conduct a conversation with a user in a natural language. The primary functionality of our dialogue system is context-aware question answering (QA), while its secondary function is maintaining user engagement. The chatbot is composed of a number of sub-modules, which independently prepare replies to user's prompts and assess their own confidence. To answer questions, our dialogue system relies heavily on factual data, sourced mostly from Wikipedia and DBpedia, data of real user interactions in public forums, as well as data concerning general literature. Where applicable, modules are trained on large datasets using GPUs. However, to comply with the competition's requirements, the final system is compact and runs on commodity hardware.

4.1 Introduction

The NIPS 2017 Conversational Intelligence Challenge promoted creation of conversational agents (chatbots), that could maintain a conversation with a human peer about a given news or encyclopedic article. Each conversation was opened with an article excerpt presented to both parties, after which they could communicate freely by asynchronously exchanging text messages. In this contribution we present the University of Wroclaw's chatbot called Poetwannabe.

The objective of the competition was to achieve high conversation quality which was evaluated by human judges. Such formulation gave chatbot designers much freedom in the system design. To simplify the problem, we have set a goal for our chatbot as enhancing the user's understanding of terms and concepts relevant

J. Chorowski · A. Lancucki (✉) · S. Malik · M. Pawlikowski · P. Rychlikowski · P. Zykowski
Institute of Computer Science, University of Wroclaw, Wroclaw, Poland
e-mail: adrian.lancucki@cs.uni.wroc.pl

© Springer International Publishing AG, part of Springer Nature 2018
S. Escalera, M. Weimer (eds.), *The NIPS '17 Competition: Building Intelligent Systems*, The Springer Series on Challenges in Machine Learning,
https://doi.org/10.1007/978-3-319-94042-7_4

to the discussed article. Therefore, the bot was primarily built to answer factual questions, propose follow-up topics, and serendipitously present interesting facts related to the article. What distinguishes Poetwannabe from a search engine is maintaining a constant dialogue interaction with the user. Thus, our secondary goal was responding to common utterances, regardless of the background article. To address this need, our system implements a general conversational module, supported by a large corpus of publicly available dialogues from on-line forums.

In general, we assumed asymmetry between the bot and the user: the bot is useful to its users and focuses on answering their needs. This assumption allows us to fully utilize the strength of computer programs, such as their super-human ability to index and memorize large bodies of data. It follows from this assumption, that the chatbot should not examine user's understanding on the contents of the article. Our interpretation of the rules means that, by design, the bot is easy to tell apart from a human, and would be a poor contestant in the Turing test.

4.2 Background and Related Work

Conversational systems spur the imagination since the inception of Alan Turing's famous paper on the "Imitation Game", now known as the Turing test (Turing 1950). To pass the test, the agent has to deceive a human judge into thinking they talk to another person. Throughout the years, the test evolved into various competitions, the oldest and one of the most notable of them being the Loebner Prize,[1] introduced in 1991. Thus far, no bot managed to win the one-time-only prize, awarded to a program able to truly fool the judges.

Early successful dialogue systems follow a *pattern-response* paradigm. We can point to ELIZA (Weizenbaum 1966) as a prime example of this approach. The idea for ELIZA was to simulate a psychoanalyst, who reflects interlocutor's statements in their responses. ELIZA incorporates linguistic rules, keyword matching and ranking as well as "memory". Another famous chatbot, A.L.I.C.E. (Wallace 2009), or Alicebot, can be thought of as an updated and more developed version of ELIZA. In Alicebot those rules are written in an XML dialect called Artificial Intelligence Markup Language (AIML).

Participants of the recent conversational intelligence competitions, including the NIPS 2017 Conversational Intelligence Challenge and the Alexa Prize,[2] have established the *ensemble* paradigm, in which independent responses collected from different modules are combined by a response selection policy. Poetwannabe follows this broad paradigm, and shares many traits with other submissions to the above competitions. Two examples of similar chatbots are MILABOT (Serban et al. 2017), an Alexa Prize contestant, and Bot#1337 (Yusupov and Kuratov 2017) the

---

[1] http://www.aisb.org.uk/events/loebner-prize

[2] https://developer.amazon.com/alexaprize

second winner of NIPS 2017 Conversational Challenge. MILABOT, created by a team from Montreal Institute for Learning Algorithms is an ensemble of multiple agents, including deep learning ones, as well as variants of ELIZA and Alicebot. It chooses its responses using a dialogue manager trained with reinforcement learning on rewards received from users. Bot#1337, created by the Moscow Institute of Physics and Technology, implements a set of skills (chit-chat, QA, topic detection, text summarization, etc.) and employs a dialogue manager trained in a supervised setting to select appropriate responses.

Poetwannabe utilizes a similar ensemble-based architecture, although instead of training a dialogue manager, we have employed confidence scores calibrated on selected dialogues.

4.3   System Description

The design of our chatbot is modular. Several subsystems, called *talkers*, independently monitor the conversation state and propose responses. This modularity made for easy development and parallelization of talkers, with minimum coordination between talker developers. Moreover, it enhanced the reliability of our chatbot: failures or timeouts of individual talkers can degrade particular responses, but the chatbot is guaranteed to always reply within the allocated time budget. The modular approach also introduces some downsides: it is difficult to endow the bot with a consistent persona, and to fine-tune the policy, which selects the best response among those proposed by the talkers.

The talkers can be broadly grouped into three categories by their responsibility: question answering, fact generation and general conversation handling. The QA talkers achieve the main objective of question answering. The fact generation talker displays to the user facts that are relevant, but missing from the initial article. The general conversation talkers respond to prompts in a way that creates the illusion of having a real conversation with an intelligent peer. They also respond to users' quirks, that we have observed during the preliminary stage of the competition. For instance, curious users investigate if the chatbot speaks in languages other than English, or if it can evaluate mathematical expressions. Finally, we include an open-source implementation of the Alicebot as a fall-back mechanism. We list all talkers in Table 4.1 and their exemplary response proposals in Table 4.2.

4.3.1   Detailed Response Generation Algorithm

In addition to being able to choose the best reply from the candidate list calculated by independent subsystems, we wanted to enable aggregation of responses coming from several talkers. For example, it makes sense to combine the answer to the user's query from the Wikipedia QA Talker with a related Simple Wikipedia fact.

Table 4.1 Talkers grouped by role

Question answering	
Wikipedia QA	Paragraph indexing, neural QA trained on large dataset
DBpedia fact indexer	Fuzzy triple matching using word embeddings
Simple Wikipedia definitions	Uses extracted definitions
Article topic finder	Article summarization and noun phrase extraction, finding similar Wikipedia titles
Fact generation	
Simple Wikipedia facts	Extracts interesting sentences and scores their similarity to the given article
General conversation handling	
Matching utterance embeddings	NN search over single utterances and pairs (Wikiquote, Reddit comments, handcrafted)
Trivia questions	Matched using word embeddings
Alice chatbot	Avoid boring answer by rewarding new terms
Misc behaviors	Handling non-english prompts and math

Table 4.2 Example of talkers' responses

Article: Cyclone Monica degraded

Cyclone Monica was expected to hit Darwin as a category five storm, with winds of up to 350 km/h (220 mph). But the national weather bureau downgraded it to category two on the morning of April 25, 2006, when it lost power after making landfall. Monica was a category five cyclone when it touched down in the remote Aboriginal community of Maningrida, in the Northern Territory, late on 24th night.

A spokeswoman for the Northern Territory Police, Fire and Emergency Services said some parts of the area had been damaged by the storm. Maningrida "certainly suffered extensive damage to some buildings and structures," she told the Sydney Morning Herald, although no serious injuries have been reported.

User: What continent did cyclone Monica impact?

Wikipedia QA	1.12	I'd say Australia.
DBpedia	0.46	A continent is one of several very large landmasses on Earth.
Wikiquote	0.41	A life is not important except in the impact it has on other lives.
Alice	0.40	That's not something I get asked all the time.
Simple Wikipedia	0.23	A continent is a large area of the land on Earth that is joined together.
Simple facts	0.22	Interesting fact: Monica is a female given name.
Trivia	0.20	I know the answer, do you: What theme is central to the movies The Lost Weekend, The Morning After and My Name Is Bill W.??
Forum comments	0.08	Like this guy surrounded by ignorance overcame it all.
Topic guess	0.01	It's about the remote Aboriginal community of Maningrida.
Popular dialogues	0.01	What is it that you want to know?
Abacus	0.00	I have no idea.
Gimmick	0.00	Well…

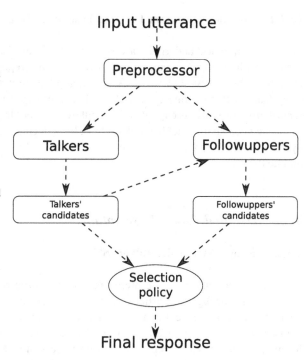

Fig. 4.1 Response generation algorithm. The user utterance first goes through a common preprocessing pipeline, which involves spell checking and coreference resolution. Then, the talkers can propose their responses. Afterward, the talkers' replies are modified during the follow-up stage. Finally, the set of candidate responses and follow-ups is ordered by the confidence and a response is selected to be shown to the user

Those considerations led us to a two-round response selection algorithm (Fig. 4.1). During the proposal round, all talkers independently propose candidate responses and state their confidence scores. Next, during the follow-up round, each talker can inspect the ranked list of candidate responses, and freely modify its reply. The new proposal can, for example, be an extension of the old one. Again, all talkers execute their follow-up methods independently and update their confidence scores. Versatility of the follow-up mechanism allowed us to easily aggregate responses of multiple talkers (e.g., responding to a user question and adding a related factoid statement), as well as to implement complex response selection rules for certain user prompts.

We note that since the follow-up mechanism can combine responses of several talkers, we do not keep track of which talker was active in which turn of the conversation. Instead, the talkers are assumed to record the state of the conversation themselves, and respond whenever the past dialogue matches their triggering patterns. If a talker wants to be active during several consecutive dialogue turns, it can indicate it to the dialogue system by responding with a high confidence. For instance, QA talkers propose answers with high confidence if they classify user's utterance as a question, and with low confidence otherwise. Conversely, general dialogue talkers typically reply with a medium confidence.

4.3.1.1   Common Utterance Pre- and Post-processing

Each user utterance undergoes a common set of transformations: we first spell-check it with Hunspell,[3] making sure that we do not replace words that are in the vocabulary lists of the QA modules. We then tokenize it and resolve coreferences using CoreNLP (Manning et al. 2014). This form is passed to the talkers. Finally, each chatbot response is capitalized and filtered for foul language. We have used an extensive vocabulary blacklist, although we have decided to whitelist words entered by the user. This way the chatbot is able to respond to sensitive topics, but cannot initiate them by itself.

4.3.2   Detailed Talker Descriptions

4.3.2.1   Simple Wikipedia Talker (SWT)

Analysis of the data from the preliminary competition round revealed that users, when given a background article, tend to ask about definitions. We identify such queries with a heuristic function, which considers presence of common asking phrases (*tell me about, what is*, etc.) accompanied by pronouns, as well as the location of single-word prepositions. Two talkers independently recognize query questions and assess their confidence score with this heuristic: Simple Wikipedia Talker and DBpedia Talker. This section describes the former.

Simple Wikipedia Talker responds with either: the opening sentences of a Simple Wikipedia (SW) article, or a definition from Wiktionary. It assigns the highest confidence score when the question contains SW article title, or a Wiktionary term. Otherwise, it uses a built-in off-line search engine to search for the definitions of related entities, and retrieves the opening sentence of the best matching SW article. When SWT is highly confident about its response, it also suggest other related topics. If the user happens to ask about them later on, SWT gives a big boost to its confidence score to maintain a coherent conversation. Example suggestions are shown in Table 4.3.

Calculating SW Match Quality

Given an article, we find the best follow-ups using cosine similarity between embeddings of Wikipedia article titles. Those embeddings are pre-computed using Word2vec (Mikolov et al. 2013). For a Wikipedia page, we try to predict what entries it links to, and what entries link to it. We used an artificially created corpora of tuples (title, linked_title). Every tuple consisted of an article title, and a title of another article it links to. Word2vec algorithm was used to embed links and titles, like if they were ordinary words.

---

[3]https://hunspell.github.io/

Table 4.3 Examples of SWT suggestions

Wikipedia title	Suggested topics
Hamburger	Kfc, barbecue, hot dog, french fries, maple syrup
Mathematics	Number theory, logic, set theory, number, geometry
England	Wales, bristol, yorkshire, uk, sheffield
Mozart	Sonata, counterpoint, accompaniment (music), symphony, virtuoso
Marie Curie	Pierre curie, irène joliot-curie, dmitri mendeleev, ivan pavlov, george gamow
Software	Personal computer, computer game, computer program, computer hardware, apple macintosh
European union	Euro, social democracy, european commission, european union budget, euroscepticism
Sandstone	Limestone, shore, sediment, silt, sand
Hamlet	Othello, twelfth night, english literature, the importance of being earnest, falstaff
The lord of the rings	The hobbit, middle-earth characters, luke skywalker, jedi, middle-earth

Wikipedia Indexer

Our Wikipedia indexer can either return a list of paragraphs rated by their similarity to the query, or an entire Wikipedia article containing the most relevant paragraph. The first option is usually used when dealing with a user's question. The second one comes in handy when we just want to know more about the subject, in which case we feed the entire main article into the search engine.

We gather all unigrams and bigrams from the query. Wikipedia paragraphs are then rated based on the number of occurrences of those phrases in them. We use inverse document frequency (idf) scores of n-grams to accentuate the presence of the most important words. Idf of a phrase is the percentage of documents in the corpus, that phrase occurs in. The scores were computed on Wikipedia texts. Due to RAM limitations, indexes are stored in cached databases on the hard drive.

4.3.2.2   Wikipedia QA

Our primary question answering module combines our implementation of FastQA (Weissenborn et al. 2017) with a Wikipedia indexer described above. A similar idea is proposed in Chen et al. (2017). The indexer finds a set of Wikipedia paragraphs most related to a user's question, and scores their relevancy to the topic. FastQA then proceeds to find an answer in each of them. The best response is chosen using the quality of a given paragraph according to the indexer and the confidence returned by FastQA. The module usually processes between 20 and 40 passages per question, within the competition time limit.

Answers to many questions can also be found in the article that started the conversation. To make use of that, we form a set of on-topic excerpts at the beginning of the conversation. It contains the article as well as fragments of a Wikipedia page which most resembles the article. Those paragraphs help answer questions regarding the main subject. However, we do not use them if the question is not similar enough with the article.

Wikipedia QA rephrases the question before performing a Wikipedia search. The first verb occurring after a question word (*what, when, who,* etc.) is placed just after the first noun phrase, which follows that verb. The form of a verb is changed to be grammatically correct. For example, *when did the war start* is transformed into *when the war started*. This heuristic slightly improved the quality of retrieved paragraphs.

The talker usually has problems answering simple definition questions like *Who was Niels Bohr?* We adjust confidence scores of our talkers so that SWT and DBpedia talker would take over on this kind of queries. If the highest idf word in the query still has low idf, we lower the confidence score of Wikipedia QA to refrain it from participating in chit-chat conversations.

We trained the model on SQuAD training set (Rajpurkar et al. 2016), using 300d GloVe word embeddings (Pennington et al. 2014). Our training process was similar to that of Weissenborn et al. (2017). Best model was achieved after 9 epochs. We used early stopping to stop the training after epoch 21. Unfortunately we were not able to replicate the result from Weissenborn et al. (2017). Our best model got only 72.34 F1 on SQuAD development set. For comparison, (Weissenborn et al. 2017) report 77.07 F1, which was slightly below 80.6 F1 presented by the top model from that time (Wang et al. 2017).

Negative Answers Experiment

In SQuAD, each question comes with a background document that contains the correct answer. Thus, a FastQA model trained on SQuAD often responds nonsensically when presented an off-topic text. We have performed an experiment to check if FastQA can be trained to not only point out the correct span in a fitting article (answer positively), but also decide if the span is missing from the text (answer negatively). Although it did not yield fully satisfying results, we briefly describe our approach.

We have prepared additional datasets for training to answer negatively. Questions from SQuAD training set have been coupled with paragraphs from Wikipedia found by the indexer. Most of them did not contain the correct answers. Analogous pairs were created for the SQuAD validation set, and used to test the models. A special neg token has been added at the end of every paragraph. The model could point to it, in order to answer negatively. The embedding of neg was learned. A perfect model would discard all off-topic contexts, while still finding correct answers in paragraphs that contain them. By training on additional examples from Wikipedia, we were able to reach 87% accuracy in discarding negative paragraphs. Unfortunately, this came with a severe drop in performance on the primary task: the model could only achieve 58 F1 on SQuAD validation set. Ultimately we found the trade-off too costly, and our final system does not use this feature.

4.3.2.3   DBpedia Talker

This talker answers questions, based on the knowledge in the form of RDF triples extracted from English Wikipedia infoboxes. Due to memory limits, we only utilize the top 100,000 resources according to the unofficial DBpedia PageRank.[4]

Each triple consists of a resource identifier, an attribute identifier, and a value of that resource's attribute. The same attributes are common for many resources, and one resource attribute can have many values. At the time of writing, the newest dataset contains information extracted from Wikipedia in October 2016.

DBpedia Talker tries to identify the topic of user's question among the known resources. In case of success, it looks for connections between parts of a question and facts about the topic. The best matching facts are formed into declarative sentences, e.g., *Albert Einstein birth date is 1879-03-14*, or *Christopher Columbus was an Italian explorer, navigator, colonizer, and citizen of the Republic of Genoa*.

Resource names are stored in a trie. Given a tokenized question, we try to match subsequences of tokens with known identifiers. Only one resource is returned. We prefer the ones with longer prefix match or higher PageRank. To optimize this step, we omit fragments which do not look like resource identifier (*who is, how old*, etc.), or would produce too many results, like *the*.

The crucial step is to find relations between the question and attributes. For this task we use word embeddings together with the English language thesaurus. In addition to checking words appearing in the query, we also look at their neighborhoods (in a sense of cosine distance) and synonyms. For example, when answering a question *Who was Albert Einstein's wife?* it turns out the word *wife* is closely related to the word *spouse*, and *spouse* is an attribute name of a formal relationship with a woman.

The connections are scored and the best one is chosen. We answer by combining the resource name, attribute name, and values of the attribute. The response to the question about Einstein's wife would be *Albert Einstein spouses are Mileva Maric, Elsa Löwenthal*. We have a dedicated submodule for handling age questions (*How old...*, *How many years...*, etc.). The talker returns the value of an *abstract* attribute when no interesting connections were found.

DBpedia Talker assigns partial confidence scores throughout the entire process. The final value is a combination of scores obtained during resource finding, connections finding and response building. Resource finding confidence comes from the matching quality and the PageRank of a given resource. The other partial scores

---

[4]http://people.aifb.kit.edu/ath/#DBpedia_PageRank

depend mostly upon the numbers of connections retrieved and sentences generated, as well as the Levenshtein distance between synonyms and matched attributes.

4.3.2.4 Topic Guess Talker

During the first stage of the competition we noticed that users often expected Poetwannabe to provide a short summary of the article. This talker is supposed to fill that role. Using phrases picked from the competition preliminary stage dataset, we handcrafted a small database of questions regarding general topic of the text. An example of such query would be *What is the article about?* User prompt is softly matched with those phrases using word vectors, and if the match is good enough, Topic Guess Talker answers with a high confidence.

We utilize a simple frequency-based extractive text summarizer to give a one-sentence overview of the article. We also gather the most interesting noun phrases from the passage, and use them to provide short answers like *The text is about <noun phrase>*. In addition, we try to find a Wikipedia title most closely related to the topic. If the indexer manages to get a close match, this title forms another short reply. From all these proposition we choose one and return it as a final response.

4.3.2.5 K-NN Talker

Large datasets of on-line dialogue records are scarce, especially those regarding a particular topic. In contrast, there is an abundance of publicly available conversations on forums concerning various entities like news, articles, blog posts, videos, pictures, etc. We focus on forum comment sections.

The character of comments differs from that of a conversation between two individuals. With many participants, comments typically form a tree in which an utterance is a node, and an edge signifies a response. Those trees tend to be rather shallow and wide. Even though a given path in the tree might not be a coherent dialogue, pairs and triplets of consecutive turns can form a short but logical chat.

We propose a talker that exploits local coherence of comment sections and treats each pair of subsequent comments (A, B) as a single training sample. All pairs from the corpus are embedded as pairs of 300d vectors (E_A, E_B), and stored in a database. For user utterance U, we retrieve a pair (A, B) with the highest cosine similarity $\cos(E_A, E_U)$, and respond with B. The data for this module comes from a publicly available dump of Reddit forums[5] and a `chatterbot-corpus` Python package.[6] We also experimented with the Hacker News corpus,[7] but found the

---

[5]https://bigquery.cloud.google.com/dataset/fh-bigquery:reddit_comments

[6]https://github.com/gunthercox/chatterbot-corpus

[7]https://cloud.google.com/bigquery/public-data/hacker-news

responses to be too technical to be used in a chatbot. We use two independent K-NN Talkers for Reddit and `chatterbot-corpus`.

Let $S = (w_1, w_2, \ldots, w_n)$ be a sentence of length n, and E_{w_i} a pre-trained embedding of word w_i (Mikolov et al. 2013). We embed sentence S as a Bag-of-Words Embedding (BoWE)

$$E_S = \frac{\sum_i \log tf(w_i) E_{w_i}}{\|\sum_i \log tf(w_i) E_{w_i}\|_2},$$

where $tf(w)$ denotes term frequency of word w in the corpus. In addition, when computing a BoWE we drop out-of-vocabulary words and greedily couple together neighboring words to form long phrases (e.g., consecutive words *Michael* and *Jordan* are embedded as *Michael_Jordan*).

Censorship

Reliance on comments scraped from Internet forums poses the obvious risk of unconsciously using foul language, hate speech, or touching on controversial and delicate topics. Filtering out such toxic utterances is a challenging task itself, and requires some level of comprehension of the utterance and its context.

We quickly found that using a list of forbidden words, which are mainly curse words, is not sufficient. We trained a binary discriminator neural network, tasked with rating the "toxicity" of an utterance.

A pair (Q, A) was converted to a 600d vectorial representation, where both utterances were embedded as 300d bags-of-words. Due to lack of data, we trained the toxicity predicting network in a semi-supervised fashion. We used a small corpus of curse words and banned terms and phrases. If at least one utterance in a (Q, A) pair contained a forbidden entity, the pair was labeled as positive (i.e., toxic) example. A version of such utterance pair with prohibited terms removed was added to the training set as yet another positive example. Our conjecture is that sentences with toxic words are, with high probability, present in toxic contexts.

To facilitate the censorship task, we trade precision over recall and select utterance pairs, which are rated as being toxic with probability < 0.4.

4.3.2.6   Wikiquote Talker

The idea behind using Wikiquote was to create a module that would provide general responses with rare words, that could be blindly put into the conversation and still fit in. Quotes meet this condition and fit into a lot of scenarios, giving Poetwannabe a witty character. For instance, when the user says *I feel lucky*, Wikiquote talker could respond with a quote *Luck, that's when preparation and opportunity meet* (by Pierre Elliott Trudeau). We heuristically chose about 50,000 quotes from Wikiquote to form a database of possible responses.

The talker embeds each utterance as a tuple of dense and sparse vectors (v_d, v_s). Each dense vector $v_d \in \mathbb{R}^{300}$ is a bag of GloVe embeddings of words from the utterance. A sparse vector $v_s \in \mathbb{R}^{|V|}$ has a field for each word w in vocabulary V, set to $tf \times idf$ for words present in the utterance, and 0 for absent. Similarity between pairs of dense and sparse vectors (u_d, u_s) and (v_d, v_s), is calculated as a linear combination of their cosine similarities $\alpha \cos(u_d, v_d) + (1 - \alpha) \cos(u_s, v_s)$. The talker has an internal state, which stores dense and sparse representations of both the context of a dialogue and the article.

Context vectors are initialized to zero and updated each turn, using the current user sentence and the last bot response. We focus on the latest utterances, but we do not completely forget earlier parts of the conversation. The article is summarized as a bag of interesting words, which are chosen heuristically. Context vectors are combined with article vectors to produce dense and sparse summary of the dialogue.

We keep track of rare words occurring in both the dialogue and the article. When matching the best response, we prioritize those words, and the influence of the article naturally decays as the conversation progresses. To diversify the answers we randomly sample the reply among top scoring candidates. To avoid random topic changes, we lower the influence of utterances containing too many unknown words. The final response is also penalized if it is too similar to the user query, or if the query has only common words.

4.3.2.7 Alice Talker

This talker fulfills two objectives: maintains the conversation flow with reasonable generic responses to user's questions, and sustains a coherent personality of the chatbot. At the beginning of the conversation, we choose values for bot predicates describing its personality (gender, name, birthplace, age, hobbies, favorite color, and many others) – these values will be occasionally used in bot responses. Alice talker uses off-the-shelf AIML rules from A.L.I.C.E. (Wallace 2009). From the perspective of our code, AIML chatbot is treated as a black box talker. Generally speaking, every chatbot can be used in this way, provided it has a confidence assessment mechanism.

Since AIML rules do not provide a clear notion of the rule's fitness to a given utterance, Alice talker scores its confidence with the following principles:

- Shorter Alice responses are generally more natural (and preferable).
- Alice talker should not repeat itself during the conversation.
- Accurate responses are preferred (e.g., *It is Paris, of course* is better than generic reply like *Please, go on*, since the former is clearly related to the user's question).

This "originality score" is computed in the following way: we created a corpora of Alice conversations in which the user utterances were taken randomly from Wikiquote or from NIPS Conversation Challenge data. For every word generated by Alice, we computed its counts. The final score depended on the logarithmic count of the least common term introduced by the chatbot (i.e., contained in chatbot's answer, and not present in the user's utterance). Note that we had to use only terms introduced by a bot. Some general rules repeat fragments of user's prompts, which can contain very specific words.

4.3.2.8 Simple Fact Generator

Given the article, this talker tries to present some facts related to it. All facts are self contained Simple Wikipedia (SW) sentences. To obtain them, we perform a number of SW searches, and gather interesting sentences among the results.

We try to find definitions of phrases occurring in the article. In addition, we search for a SW entry most closely resembling the article. Then, we use a simple heuristic: interesting sentences on a SW page contain part of the title of that page, and do not have any pronouns occurring before it. Result of this filtering can be observed in the example below.

```
GOOD: Alan Turing was born in Maida Vale, London.
GOOD: Turing went to St. Michael's, a school at 20 Charles Road,
      St Leonards-on-sea, when he was six years old.
BAD: His father was part of a family of merchants from Scotland.
BAD: His mother, Ethel Sara, was the daughter of an engineer.
```

During the conversation, Simple Fact Generator presents these facts, starting from the most interesting ones. When rating a response, we consider the following questions:

- Do any key words suggest the user wants to learn about the main topic?
- Does a fact come from a highly scored article? Is it the first sentence of it?
- Does it contain words used previously by the user?
- Does it have proper length?

In order to prevent this talker from dominating the discussion, the confidence score is penalized if Simple Fact Generator already spoke.

4.3.2.9 Trivia Questions

The Trivia Questions talker was designed to ask potentially interesting questions to the user. Instead of building a general question asking model we have opted to use higher quality trivia question lists that can be found on the Internet. This way the chatbot would not leave the impression of drilling the user with a reading comprehension test. Instead, it has a possibility to entertain the user.

We have gathered a set of trivia questions found on Internet portals: Moxquizz,[8] Tat's Trivia[9] and an archive of the Irc-wiki.[10] The talker matches questions to the dialogue by computing a tf-idf weighting of terms in all candidates. Next, it expresses each Q-A pair as a single real-valued vector by computing a tf-idf weighted average of GloVe vectors for all words in that pair. It then computes similar vectors for the past user utterances and uses the cosine distance to select the best matching question. Finally, the talker samples its confidence score based on the quality of the best matching answer, to make sure that the questions will not be triggered each time a certain set of keywords was entered by the user.

4.3.2.10   Miscellaneous Talkers (Abacus, Gimmick)

These talkers were inspired by the analysis of dialogues from preliminary phase of the competition, as well as tests conducted during public events at our faculty. In order to add a nice touch to our system and correctly handle some non-standard situations, we designed a couple of small specialized rule-based mechanisms. They can detect and evaluate mathematical expressions, respond to greetings in different languages, and react to urls, e-mail addresses and emoji characters sent by the user.

Mathematical expressions can be embedded within an utterance, and possibly be written partly in English, e.g., *What is 2 plus 2*. These are parsed and evaluated heuristically with regular expressions. For urls and email addresses we randomly sample one of several handcrafted responses.

In order to handle non-English greetings we took advantage of multilingual sentences from Tatoeba[11] and trained a language classification model.[12] An utterance is classified as a foreign salutation if it is not in English, and has common words with any greeting from Tatoeba. If this rule is satisfied for more than one language, we check whether the language returned by the classifier is among them.

4.3.3   Balancing and Prioritizing Talker Confidences

Poetwannabe selects the final response based on talkers' self-assessments of confidence. More complicated selection rules and special cases were facilitated by the mechanism of follow-ups (described in Sect. 4.3.1). Each talker computed its confidence score based on linguistic features of the user's prompt, the context of the conversation, and its internal state. To balance the confidences and to ensure that

---

[8]http://moxquizz.de/download.html

[9]http://tatarize.nfshost.com/

[10]https://web.archive.org/web/20150323142257/http://irc-wiki.org

[11]www.tatoeba.org

[12]https://github.com/saffsd/langid.py

the talkers respond to utterances they were designed to handle, we have prepared a dialogue corpora containing users' prompts of several types (chit-chat, questions about definitions, general questions, offensive dialogues). We have then linearly scaled the confidence scores such that the talkers most relevant to each corpus are also the ones with the highest confidence scores on it. Additionally, the follow-up mechanism was used to jointly promote QA talkers for user prompts that were identified as questions.

4.4   Conclusions and Future Work

We are pleased with the outcome of our work, although the problem is far from solved. We see limitations of this system and possible improvements. Chatbots in general, including our system, struggle with maintaining rich context of the conversation. We suspect a solution to this problem would cause a noticeable boost in performance.

Dividing the chatbot into independent talkers proved convenient from the architectural point of view, but this decision has clear downsides. Selecting the best response (i.e., adjusting the confidence scores) turned out to be challenging. There definitely is a great potential in developing a more robust supervisor of talkers. Independence of individual subsystems resulted in our bot having a multitude of different, sometimes even contradictory, personalities. Advanced interactions with the user, like asking them to provide some details, also were more difficult to accomplish.

Our question answering module would benefit greatly from a large QA dataset where the context is not strictly necessary to find an answer. Queries from SQuAD are often very context-dependent. Questions like *Who was the medical report written for?* or *How many did this epidemic in China kill?* simply cannot be answered without an access to a specific paragraph. If not for this characteristic, we might be able to train a better Wikipedia indexer, which would increase the likelihood of finding the right passage.

It is worth mentioning that during the last few months the top performing models on SQuAD dataset almost matched human performance.[13] Having access to a better QA architecture would also bring an improvement to the system. On top of that, presenting the content of the article to the user could be made easier with more intelligent summarizer.

We found that data-driven modules, such as K-NN Talker, can carry a more engaging casual conversation than classic, rule-based mechanisms like Alicebot. However, in our opinion, conversational bots work best when combining both options.

---

[13] https://rajpurkar.github.io/SQuAD-explorer/

Using large amounts of raw text from the Internet turned out to be quite problematic. Sanitizing the data and ensuring our bot would not say anything inappropriate was a small challenge in and of itself. Similarly, making the system run on low resources with all the knowledge we wanted it to process, called for compromises.

Lastly, chatbots and conversational user interfaces still need to find their optimal use cases. The Conversational Intelligence Challenge stimulated answering this question by defining the necessary boundary conditions: a dialogue format and relevant quality measures. Beyond these, contestants were granted free choice in defining the main purpose of their chatbots. We decided on a rather narrow purpose for our chatbot, defined as the user's utility. Thus our bot was designed to be help the user understand the article by providing an elaborate contextual question answering mechanism and only basic general conversational abilities. Thus the bot was tasked not to impersonate a human, but to provide a conversational interface to bot's knowledge. However, there exist other viable chatbot goals, such as trying to act like a human and pass the Turing test. We believe that the jury is still out on the question of the purpose of conversational agents.

Acknowledgements The authors want to thank the NIPS 2017 Conversational Intelligence Challenge for organizing the competition, and especially Valentin Malykh for help with resolving technical issues with chatbot deployment. We thank our labmates Adam Kaczmarek and Michal Zapotoczny for not complaining about our loud brainstorming sessions. We also thank the University of Wroclaw for providing a travel grant. Work on neural generators and QA systems was partially supported by Poland National Science Center under grant NCN Sonata 276459 2014/15/D/ST6/04402. Finally, we would like to thank everyone who was patient enough to talk to our chatbot during its development, for providing useful feedback and ideas.

Appendix: Sample Dialogues

We present a set of curated dialogues that best showcase all talkers.

Article: During the Second World War, Turing worked for the Government Code and Cypher School (GC&CS) at Bletchley Park, Britain's codebreaking centre that produced Ultra intelligence. For a time he led Hut 8, the section which was responsible for German naval cryptanalysis. Here he devised a number of techniques for speeding the breaking of German ciphers, including improvements to the pre-war Polish bombe method, an electromechanical machine that could find settings for the Enigma machine. Turing played a pivotal role in cracking intercepted coded messages that enabled the Allies to defeat the Nazis in many crucial engagements, including the Battle of the Atlantic, and in so doing helped win the war.

User: hello, let us chat!
Bot: Hi there!. I already started. [Alice]

User: what role did Alan Turing play in cracking german coded messages?

Bot: Wait a second... that enabled the Allies to defeat the Nazis in many crucial engagements? [Wikipedia QA]

User: why did Allies defeat Nazis?

Bot: Based on what I know to attack their lines of communications. [Wikipedia QA]

User: who won the Battle of the Atlantic?

Bot: I would say Turing. [Wikipedia QA]

User: Maybe in a metaphorical sense...

Bot: Sometimes it is an illustration of what is happening. [K-NN]

User: when was the Battle of the Atlantic?

Bot: Maybe the answer is 1866. Well... A cypher (or cipher) is an algorithm for performing encryption (coding) or decryption (decoding). [Wikipedia QA + Simple Fact Generator]

User: what happened in 1866

Bot: It has to be the police caught the murderers. [Wikipedia QA]

User: is it a historical event, are you sure?

Bot: There is only one thing in your life YOU can be sure of. [Wikiquote]

User: which one? death or taxes?

Bot: Nothing is more important in the face of a war than cutting taxes. [Wikiquote]

User: Let us come back to the article, ok?

Bot: Well, this is an interesting subject: the Second World War. [Topic Guess]

User: how many submarines were in German Navy during the Second World War.

Bot: It has to be 8. [Wikipedia QA]

User: Not more? Are you sure?

Bot: Indeed I am. [K-NN]]

Article: "I Like Chopin" is a song by Italian singer Gazebo. It was produced in Italy in 1983 by Pierluigi Giombini. It is generally regarded as one of the most significant Italo disco tracks of the mid-1980s. It peaked at number one in several European national charts. The music was composed by Giombini (contrary to popular belief without themes from Chopin), the lyrics were written by Gazebo.

User: buongiorno!

Bot: Ciao! Parlate inglese? It's so much I know in Italian :(Let's speak in English from now on, shall we? [Miscellaneous]

User: who was the author of the song "I like Chopin"?

Bot: An author is narrowly defined as the originator of any written work and can thus also be described as a writer. [DBPedia]

User: who composed the song "I like Chopin"?

Bot: I guess Pierluigi Giombini. [Wikipedia QA]

User: who was Chopin?

Bot: Fryderyk Franciszek Chopin (1 March 1810 – 17 October 1849) was a Polish-French composer and virtuoso pianist. [Simple Wikipedia]

User: what Chopin composition do you like best?

Bot: I don't have a favorite Chopin composition. My favorite band is Pink Floyd. [Alice]

User: can you play piano?

Bot: I know what you mean. It's always nice to just -get- the music. [K-NN]

User: i can play guitar

Bot: Do you mostly play Electric or Acoustic? [K-NN]

User: acoustic

Bot: There are many interesting things related to it. Say "piano rock", or "gibson sg". [Simple Wikipedia]

User: what is gibson sg?

Bot: Gibson SG is a solid body electric guitar model that was introduced in 1961 (as Gibson Les Paul) by Gibson Guitar Corporation. Maybe we can talk about "slide guitar" or "rock (music)"? [Simple Wikipedia]

User: No thanks. But may I have the last question?

Bot: You have my thanks... [Wikiquote]

User: who composed Eine Kleine Nachtmusik?

Bot: I believe it's Mozart. [Wikipedia QA]

Article: A child prodigy is a child who is very smart at an early age. They can do things that average people can only do when they are adults. Child prodigies are often musicians or mathematicians. A child prodigy does not always grow up to be a world-famous genius. Some of them lose their exceptional gifts in adulthood.

User: what is a child prodigy?

Bot: In psychology research literature, the term child prodigy is defined as a person under the age of ten who produces meaningful output in some domain to the level of an adult expert performer. [DBpedia]

User: what can do child prodigies?

Bot: I am quite sure it's calculating skills. [Wikipedia QA]

User: could you name some musicians who were child prodigies?

Bot: Biologically, a child is a human being between the stages of birth and puberty. [DBpedia]

User: I know. But are there any child prodigies playing music?

Bot: How, specifically, do you know? No I don't think there are any. [Alice]

User: You are wrong. Consider Mozart for example.

Bot: No, I am right. Can you think of another example? [Alice]

User: Franz Liszt for example.

Bot: Can you think of another example? World is strange... A child prodigy is a child who is very smart at an early age. [Alice + Simple Fact Generator]

Article: Python is an interpreted high-level programming language for general-purpose programming. Created by Guido van Rossum and first released in 1991, Python has a design philosophy that emphasizes code readability, and a syntax that allows programmers to express concepts in fewer lines of code, notably using significant whitespace. It provides constructs that enable clear programming on both small and large scales.

User: what is this article about?

Bot: The topic of this text is Guido van Rossum. [Topic Guess]

User: what else is this article about?

Bot: Created by Guido van Rossum and first released in 1991, Python has a design philosophy that emphasizes code readability, and a syntax that allows programmers to express concepts in fewer lines of code, notably using significant whitespace. [Topic Guess]

User: It is rather boring. Can we talk about something else?

Bot: This text is about high-level programming language for general-purpose programming. [Topic Guess]

User: I said: something else!

Bot: It depends. [K-NN]

User: Depends on what?

Bot: Good point, I should put what I like in the description. [K-NN]

User: Which programming language uses significant whitespace?

Bot: I am convinced that it's Python. Ever seen that one: R. Kelly sings: 'If I can see it then I can do it, if I just believe it, there's nothing to it'. What's the song title?? [Wikipedia QA + Trivia Questions]

References

Chen, D., Fisch, A., Weston, J., Bordes, A.: Reading wikipedia to answer open-domain questions. In: ACL (2017)

Manning, C.D., Surdeanu, M., Bauer, J., Finkel, J., Bethard, S.J., McClosky, D.: The Stanford CoreNLP natural language processing toolkit. In: Association for Computational Linguistics (ACL) System Demonstrations, pp. 55–60 (2014)

Mikolov, T., Sutskever, I., Chen, K., Corrado, G.S., Dean, J.: Distributed representations of words and phrases and their compositionality. In: Advances in neural information processing systems, pp. 3111–3119 (2013)

Pennington, J., Socher, R., Manning, C.D.: Glove: Global vectors for word representation. In: Empirical Methods in Natural Language Processing (EMNLP), pp. 1532–1543 (2014)

Rajpurkar, P., Zhang, J., Lopyrev, K., Liang, P.: Squad: 100, 000+ questions for machine comprehension of text. In: EMNLP (2016)

Serban, I.V., Sankar, C., Germain, M., Zhang, S., Lin, Z., Subramanian, S., Kim, T., Pieper, M., Chandar, S., Ke, N.R., Mudumba, S., de Brébisson, A., Sotelo, J., Suhubdy, D., Michalski, V., Nguyen, A., Pineau, J., Bengio, Y.: A deep reinforcement learning chatbot. CoRR **abs/1709.02349** (2017)

Turing, A.M.: Computing machinery and intelligence. Mind **LIX**(236), 433–460 (1950). DOI 10.1093/mind/LIX.236.433

Wallace, R.S.: The anatomy of alice. In: Parsing the Turing Test, pp. 181–210. Springer (2009)

Wang, W., Yang, N., Wei, F., Chang, B., Zhou, M.: Gated self-matching networks for reading comprehension and question answering. In: Proceedings of the 55th Annual Meeting of the Association for Computational Linguistics (Volume 1: Long Papers), pp. 189–198. Association for Computational Linguistics (2017). DOI 10.18653/v1/P17-1018

Weissenborn, D., Wiese, G., Seiffe, L.: Fastqa: A simple and efficient neural architecture for question answering. CoRR **abs/1703.04816** (2017)

Weizenbaum, J.: Eliza – a computer program for the study of natural language communication between man and machine. Commun. ACM **9**(1), 36–45 (1966). DOI 10.1145/365153.365168

Yusupov, I., Kuratov, Y.: Skill-based conversational agent. In: Presentation at Nips 2017 Conversational Intelligence Challenge (2017)

Chapter 5
Multi-view Ensemble Classification for Clinically Actionable Genetic Mutations

Xi Zhang, Dandi Chen, Yongjun Zhu, Chao Che, Chang Su, Sendong Zhao, Xu Min, and Fei Wang

Abstract This paper presents details of our solutions to the task IV of NIPS 2017 Competition Track that is called Classifying Clinically Actionable Genetic Mutations. It aims at classifying genetic mutations based on text evidence from clinical literature. A novel multi-view machine learning framework with ensemble classification models is proposed to solve this problem. During this Challenge, feature combinations deriving from three views including document view, entity text view, and entity name view to complement each other are comprehensively explored. Finally, an ensemble of 9 basic gradient boosting models win in the comparisons. Our approach scored 0.5506 and 0.6694 in Logarithmic Loss on a fixed split of stage-1 testing phase and 5-fold cross validation respectively, which is ranked as a top-3 team in NIPS 2017 Competition Track IV.

X. Zhang · D. Chen · Y. Zhu · F. Wang (✉)
Department of Healthcare Policy and Research, Weill Cornell Medicine, Cornell University, Ithaca, NY, USA
e-mail: few2001@med.cornell.edu

C. Che
Department of Healthcare Policy and Research, Weill Cornell Medicine, Cornell University, Ithaca, NY, USA

Key Laboratory of Advanced Design and Intelligent Computing, Ministry of Education, Dalian University, Dalian, China

C. Su
School of Electronic and Information Engineering, Xian Jiaotong University, Xi'an, China

S. Zhao
Research Center for Social Computing and Information Retrieval, Harbin Institute of Technology, Harbin, China

X. Min
Department of Healthcare Policy and Research, Weill Cornell Medicine, Cornell University, Ithaca, NY, USA

Department of Computer Science and Engineering, Tsinghua University, Beijing, China

© Springer International Publishing AG, part of Springer Nature 2018
S. Escalera, M. Weimer (eds.), *The NIPS '17 Competition: Building Intelligent Systems*, The Springer Series on Challenges in Machine Learning,
https://doi.org/10.1007/978-3-319-94042-7_5

5.1 Introduction

The NIPS 2017 Competition Track IV arises from gene mutation classification[1] using Natural Language Processing (NLP). Gene mutation classification aims at distinguishing the mutations that contribute to tumor growth (drivers) from the neutral mutations (passengers), is a significant problem in Precision Medicine. For instance, identifying the type of gene mutations are helpful in determining whether a molecular tumor emerges or what kind of drugs are available to treat it. For the purpose of classifying clinically actionable genetic mutations, the related research biomedical articles can be regarded as a wealth of knowledge (Peng et al. 2017). Currently, this interpretation of genetic mutations is being done manually. This is a quite time-consuming task where a clinical pathologist has to manually review and classify every single genetic mutation based on evidence from articles.[2]

The Competition Track releases a dataset of oncogenes (He et al. 2005), their corresponding mutations and related articles obtained from PubMed, an online biomedical literature repository. The goal is to ask participants to design machine learning approaches which can predict class labels for gene mutation samples very well. The target classes are predefined by the Challenge organizer Memorial Sloan Kettering Cancer Center (MSKCC). Specifically, they are Gain-of-function, Likely Gain-of-function, Loss-of-function, Likely Loss-of-function, Neutral, Likely Neutral, Switch-of-function, Likely Switch-of-function, Inconclusive. Therefore, it is a multi-class classification task.

Basically, this competition can be viewed as a text classification task based on clinical descriptions of gene mutations. However, the problem we faced with is more challenging than traditional document classification problem that is handled by natural language processing benchmarks. After analyzing the dataset carefully, we make the following three useful observations about the difficulties of the task.

- Different samples may share the same text entry, while their class labels are entirely different. From the statistics shown in Fig. 5.1, there are a bunch of similar cases that various samples share the same text. Instead of mining knowledge from original documents, more evidence from other perspective is necessary.
- Each sample was associated with an extremely long document with a large amount of noisy information that makes the problem cannot be easily addressed. As the word count distribution that is shown in Fig. 5.2, documents generally contain much more sentences than normal text classification dataset (Zhang et al. 2015).
- While a gene and its corresponding label distribution over classes could be a great hint in the prediction, the fact that there are only a few overlapped samples

---

[1] https://nips.cc/Conferences/2017/Schedule?showEvent=8748

[2] https://www.kaggle.com/c/msk-redefining-cancer-treatment

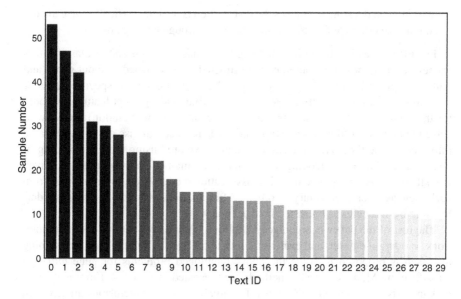

Fig. 5.1 Distribution of the counts of common text. The head of the distribution is shown here. When we give all the observed text a unique id, the most common text is used more than 50 times by gene mutation samples

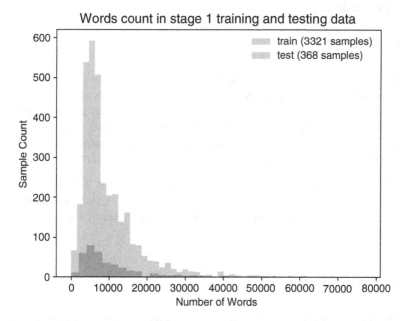

Fig. 5.2 Distribution of the text entry lengths. The median value of word count per text is 6,743 while the maximum word count in a text is 77,202

in training and testing set makes the distribution is useless. Basically, we can only summarize effective features from characters through entity names.

In order to deal with above challenges, a multi-view ensemble classification framework is proposed. Concretely, we extracted prior knowledge about genes and mutations globally from the sentences that have mentioned the specific genes or mutations in the text collection. Hence, we are able to design text features not only for the original document view but also for the entity (gene/mutation) text view to solve the first two difficulties above-mentioned. To make full use of the entity name information, the third view for names are also explored using word embedding or character-level n-gram encoding. Furthermore, we mainly combine features derived from three views to implement basic classification models and exploit features from each view as a complementary of others. After that, we ensemble the basic models together by strategies to boost the final accuracy.

The rest of the paper is organized as follows. Section 5.2 introduces main notations, validation dataset, and evaluation metric. In Sect. 5.3, multi-view text mining approach is proposed to solve the above-mentioned problems for gene mutation classification. Model ensemble methods are presented in Sect. 5.4. Empirical study and analysis are provided in Sect. 5.4. Eventually, several conclusions are given in Sect. 5.6.

5.2 Preliminary

5.2.1 Notations

Table 5.1 lists some main notations all through the paper. In the paper, genes, mutations, and their corresponding documents are respectively denoted by g, m, and d. Each sample is constructed by a triplet $< gene, mutation, document >$. The feature vector generated for each sample is denoted as the vector $\mathbf{x}$. Feature vectors in the three views can be represented as $\mathbf{x}^D$, $\mathbf{x}^{ET}$, and $\mathbf{x}^{EN}$ respectively. With notations presented in Table 5.1, our problem can be explicitly defined as:

Definition   Given sample sets $\{< g_i, m_i, d_i >\}_{i=1}^N$, our aim is to generate feature vectors $\{\mathbf{x}_i^D, \mathbf{x}_i^{ET}, \mathbf{x}_i^{EN}\}_{i=1}^N$ in multiple views, so that probabilities of label assignment over M possible class can be predicted.

5.2.2 Validation Set

The Challenge consists of 2 stages and releases a training set and validation set in stage-1. During stage-1, the labels of validation set are unknown and participants can verify their performances via online submitting the classification results of the

Table 5.1 Main notations used in this paper

Symbols	Definition
$\mathbf{x}$	Feature vector
$\mathbf{x}^D$	Feature vector in original document view
$\mathbf{x}^{ET}$	Feature vector in entity text view
$\mathbf{x}_g^{ET}$	Gene feature vector in entity text view
$\mathbf{x}_m^{ET}$	Mutation feature vector in entity text view
$\mathbf{x}^{EN}$	Feature vector in entity name view
$\mathbf{x}_g^{EN}$	Gene feature vector in entity name view
$\mathbf{x}_m^{EN}$	Mutation feature vector in entity name view
N	The number of samples
M	The number of classes
y_{ij}	Binary indicator whether label j is true for sample i
p_{ij}	Predicted probability of assigning label j to sample i
$\mathcal{T}^r$	Training set
$\mathcal{T}^v$	Validation set
$\mathcal{T}^s$	Testing set
$\hat{p}_{ij}^v$	Predicted probability for validation set data
$\hat{p}_{ij}^s$	Predicted probability for testing set data
α	Linear combination parameter for basic models

Table 5.2 Statistics of the datasets

	Training	Validation
# of samples	3,321	368
# of unique genes	264	140
# of unique mutations	2,996	328

validation set. The stage-1 of this Challenge is conducted for a couple of weeks, while the ongoing stage-2 conducted in the final week. For stage-2, the stage-1 training data, validation data, and new online test data without labels are given. The stage-1 training set contains 3,321 gene mutation samples with 264 unique genes and 2,996 unique mutations. The validation set contains 368 gene mutation samples with 140 unique genes and 328 unique mutations. In total, we have 3,689 training samples including 269 unique genes and 3,309 unique mutations. The detailed data statistics for the training set and validation set can be found in Table 5.2.

The stage 1 validation data is used to generate the rankings on the Leaderboard of the first stage. On the one hand, it can be used to extend the size of training set during the second stage of this competition. On the other hand, we conduct offline validation without submitting classification results using the validation set. In this work, we denote the stage-1 training set (3,321 samples) by $\mathcal{T}^r$, and denote the stage-1 validation set (368 samples) by $\mathcal{T}^v$. The online testing set for submission is denoted by $\mathcal{T}^s$.

5.2.3 Evaluation Metric

The Challenge utilizes Logarithmic Loss (Log Loss) as the evaluation metric. It can measure the performance of a multi-class classification model where the prediction is a probability distribution over classes between 0 and 1. Mathematically Log Loss is defined as:

$$-\frac{1}{N}\Sigma_{i=1}^{N}\Sigma_{j=1}^{M}y_{ij}log(p_{ij}) \tag{5.1}$$

where N is the number of samples, M is the number of the possible class label. y_{ij} is a binary indicator of whether or not label j is the correct classification for sample i, and p_{ij} is the output probability of assigning label j to instance i. By minimizing Log Loss, the accuracy of the classifier is maximized. In other words, a smaller value of the metric indicates a more accurate classifier.

5.3 The Proposed Approach

Given the gene mutations and their associated articles, one straightforward approach is to extract features directly from the documents and entity names. As we introduced, this approach might suffer the limitation that two samples share same text but have different class labels. Considering a gene *BRCA1*, it owns two possible mutations: *T1773I* and *M1663L* in two different samples. And their gene mutation types are Likely Loss-of-function and Likely Neutral, respectively. The article descriptions, however, are exactly same for the two samples. The straightforward document classification approach cannot work well in this case, since it is fairly difficult for the classifier to categorize the samples into correct classes only via the name of mutations (normally a few characters construct the names).

Figure 5.3 presents an overview of our multi-view framework for solving this problem. The original input data includes training and testing variants (the name information of gene mutations), training and testing texts (the associated articles[3]). In our solution, we perform feature extraction and engineering from the following three views:

- Document View: original documents associated with gene mutation samples (denoted by blue arrows in Fig. 5.3);
- Entity text View: sentences globally extracted from the document collection associated with genes and mutations (denoted by green arrows in Fig. 5.3);
- Entity name View: characters of the gene names and mutation names (denoted by purple arrows in Fig. 5.3).

---

[3] We use articles and documents interchangeably in this paper

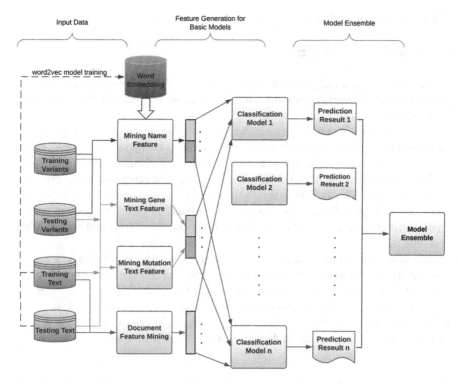

Fig. 5.3 The classification framework (best viewed in color). For data files are released by the Challenge: training/testing variants and training/testing text. The three color arrows from data to feature mining module indicate three aspects of feature engineering. Entity name features derive from gene/mutation names provided in training/testing variants as well as text provided in training/testing text that can train word embedding model; document features are only derived from text of samples given in training/testing text; entity text features need both training/testing variants and training/testing text

After feature engineering, we first concatenate the gene text feature with mutation text feature to represent each sample. In particular, $\mathbf{x}_g^{ET}$ and $\mathbf{x}_m^{ET}$ are concatenated to form the feature vector of entity text $\mathbf{x}^{ET} = \mathbf{x}_g^{ET} \| \mathbf{x}_m^{ET}$, where $\|$ denotes concatenation operation. Similarly, the feature vector of entity name is formed by concatenation $\mathbf{x}^{EN} = \mathbf{x}_g^{EN} \| \mathbf{x}_m^{EN}$. Then features from three views are combined to train multiple classification models and generate multiple prediction results. Various combination schema are explored to decide the feature sets with the best accuracy (see Sect. 5.4). The feature generation and combination will be introduced in following sections.

5.3.1 Document View

5.3.1.1 Domain Knowledge

Domain knowledge usually provides extra priors for the classification task. To incorporate biomedical domain knowledge, feature dimensions indicating bioentities and keywords are extracted.

Genes and mutations may have another alias in PubMed articles. Also, there are more bioentities are not included in the name of samples but appears in the text. How to use this bioentity information is critical. Thanks to a Name Entity Recognition (NER) tool PubTator (Wei et al. 2013), we can extract the entity dictionary existing in the text data. The PubTator is used to enrich the dictionaries of genes and mutations with the abstracts of the related PubMed articles. The tool includes GeneTUKit (Huang et al. 2011), GenNorm (Wei and Kao 2011) and tmVar (Wei et al. 2013).

Additionally, apart from the document corpus provided by the challenge, we also built a dictionary by *Keywords* extracted from related PubMed articles obtained from OncoKB.[4] The underlying assumption is that the keywords detected from titles of the related articles are the essential terms in the research domain. In particular, the keywords are extracted from the titles of those articles by removing the stop words and punctuations. The keywords dictionary has 3,379 unique words.

5.3.1.2 Document-Level Feature

Although traditional feature engineering will always be staples of machine learning pipelines, representation learning has emerged as an alternative approach to feature extraction. In order to represent a document by natural language modeling, paragraph vectors or Doc2Vec (Le and Mikolov 2014) is exploited. Doc2Vec can be viewed as a generalization of Word2Vec (Mikolov et al. 2013) approach. In addition to considering context words, it considers the specific document when predicting a target word, and thus it can exploit the word ordering along with their semantic relationships. With a trained Doc2Vec model, we can get a vector representation with a fixed length for any given document with arbitrary lengths.

Doc2Vec provides two training strategies to model the context in documents, which are distributed memory model (PV-DM) and distributed bag-of-word model (PV-DBOW). PV stands for paragraph vector here. Given sequences of training words in paragraphs, the PV-DM model is trained to get paragraph vectors, word vectors, softmax weights and bias to maximize the probability of seen texts. The difference between the two versions are: PV-DM simultaneously uses the context words and a paragraph matrix to predict the next word while PV-DBOW ignores the context words in the input but use the parameter matrix to predict words randomly

---

[4]http://oncokb.org/

sampled from the paragraphs, which leads to less storage. As recommended in Le and Mikolov (2014), we combine the outputs of PV-DM with PV-DBOW together to achieve the best performance (concatenation of 150 dimension PV-DM vector and 250 dimension PV-DBOW).

5.3.1.3   Sentence-Level Feature

When it comes to extracting features from very noisy long documents, filtering sentences might be a choice to obtain effective knowledge. Regarding sentences mentioned the genes or mutations as key sentences, the context of key sentences is also used to capture the useful information. The basic assumption behind is that words in the same context tend to have similar meanings. For the reason that the articles have sufficient sentences to satisfy the distributional hypothesis theory (Harris 1954), we extend the concept "word" to "sentence" for form contexts.

Considering a key sentence s_t and its Term Frequency-Inverse Document Frequency (TF-IDF) feature vector $\mathbf{x}_{s,t}$, the context can be represented as concatenation: $\mathbf{x}_{s,t-1} \| \mathbf{x}_{s,t} \| \mathbf{x}_{s,t+1}$ when the window size is set as 3. Then the representation for documents in samples can be calculated by the average the key contexts. Here we adopt average values and call the defined feature as sentence-level TF-IDF.

5.3.1.4   Word-Level Feature

Because of the importance, Nouns, verbs, adjectives, and adverbs are four major word types we considered in Part-of-Speech(PoS) Tagging (Jurafsky and Martin 2014; Fellbaum 1998). In the scenario of genetic mutation classification, nouns could be the name of proteins, diseases, drugs, etc. which serve as important cues for deciding mutation class. The verb type includes most of the words referring to actions and processes such as *interact*, *affect*, *detect*, and so on. In addition, adjectives are considered since they reflect properties of nouns while adverbs might semantically reflect some discoveries or conclusions like *interestingly*, *consequently*, or *therefore*. Our method takes all of the word tokens as input with preprocessing steps including filtering out stop words and punctuations, stemming and lemmatization, and PoS tagging. Then a dictionary with 9,868 words of all the four types is constructed.

Term Frequency-Inverse Document Frequency (TF-IDF) is one of the common used measure that computes the importances of each word in a document (Manning and Decleer 1995). Traditionally, we are given a collection of N documents. TF-IDF scheme assigns to term t a weight in document d given by $\mathrm{tfidf}_{td} = \mathrm{tf}_{td} \times \mathrm{idf}_t$, where inverse document frequency can be defined as $\mathrm{idf}_t = log \frac{N}{\mathrm{df}_t}$. Document frequency df_t means the number of documents in the collection that contain term t. Our new strategy is to embed the discriminative power of each term. Intuitively the idf_t should be calculated by class frequency, that is, $\mathrm{idf}_t = log \frac{M}{\mathrm{cf}_t}$, where M is the number of class and cf_t the number of classes that contain a term t.

Table 5.3 Dimensions of sentence-level and word-level features before and after using dimension reduction.(the statistics is computed in document view)

Features	Dimension
n/v./adj./adv. counts	9,868
ngram	9,473,363
Sentence-level TFIDF	28,368
Term frequency	9,456
n/v./adj./adv. counts+NMF	60
ngram+NMF	120
Sentence-level TFIDF+SVD	100
Term frequency+LDA	50

Except for the designed novel TF-IDF, we compare several different value computation methods such as word counts, TF, and TF-IDF based on bag-of-words to determine their values.

5.3.1.5 Dimension Reduction

In general, original features based on bag-of-words or bag-of-n-grams may have thousands of dimensions. For example, the dimension can reach more than 9 million when we adapt unigram/bigram/trigram simultaneously. The designed features and their corresponding dimensions are shown in the Table 5.3. To solve the problem for high-dimensional input, dimension reduction for feature vectors is taken into account. Dimension reduction is the process of reducing the number of features (Roweis and Saul 2000). On the one hand, it can help the classification models improving their computational efficiency. On the other hand, it can reduce the noise and sparsity of the raw features. Popular dimension reduction techniques including Singular-Value Decomposition(SVD) (Golub and Van Loan 2012), Non-negative Matrix Factorization(NMF) (Lee and Seung 1999), and Latent Dirichlet Allocation(LDA) (Blei et al. 2003) have been demonstrated promising results on multiple text analysis tasks. Hence, SVD, NMF, and LDA are implemented in our solution.

We combine the bag-of-words or bag-of-n-grams with SVD, NMF, or LDA, and choose the feature combinations according to their achieved performance. Finally, we obtain feature vectors with dimensionality 50, 60, 100, and 120. Table 5.6 reports the detailed settings for dimension reduction. The feature vector from document view is represented as $\mathbf{x}^D$.

5.3.2 Entity Text View

As we mentioned before, documents are too long and it would be helpful to analyze the view of texts containing individual genes or mutations. Correspondingly, we developed a two-step method including view construction and feature generation in the procedure of entity text view.

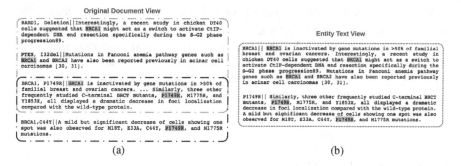

Fig. 5.4 A toy example of constructing the entity text view. (**a**) Original document view is the data provided by the Challenge. (**b**) Entity text view is the extracted sentences from the overall documents globally that mentioned the specific gene or mutation. The entity texts for gene mutations are collected separately. The given example illustrates the view construction of a gene *BRCA1* and its mutation *P1749R*. Then we can understand the knowledge not only from the document view but also from the entity text view

5.3.2.1 View Construction

Figure 5.4 shows an illustrative example of entity text extraction. Basically, we firstly match strings contains genes and mutations name in the documents and then extract the sentences containing those strings. A trie tree-like fast string search algorithm named Aho-Corasick (AC) automaton (Aho and Corasick 1975) is adopted. The complexity of the AC algorithm is linear $\mathcal{O}(n + m + z)$, where n is the length of the strings, m is the length of the texts that need to be searched, and z is the number of output matches. Without AC automaton, the time complexity of exact string matching is $\mathcal{O}(n + km)$ where k is the number of patterns (genes or mutations in our scenario) that need to be found, and hence it could take days to extract sentences with thousands of genes or mutations from original text to entity text, which is computationally prohibitive. As the computation complexity shown, AC automation is capable to solve the efficiency problem to a large extent.

5.3.2.2 Feature Generation

Once the sentences containing gene or mutation names are extracted, we collect all sentences mentioning a specific gene or a specific mutation as a separate entity text. Then the document feature engineering approaches introduced in the last subsection can be applied to these entity texts to generate feature vectors. Fortunately, both sentence-level features and word-level features show impressive performance on the top of entity texts. Note that the sentence-level TF-IDF is changed use the key sentences instead of context. Nevertheless, the assumption of document-level features mining technique paragraph vector is not consistent with the entity view, since it lacks rationale to optimize the paragraph vector (Le and Mikolov 2014).

We concatenate the gene feature vector $\mathbf{x}_g^{ET}$ and mutation feature vector $\mathbf{x}_m^{ET}$ to get the combined feature vector $\mathbf{x}^{ET} = \mathbf{x}_g^{ET}||\mathbf{x}_m^{ET}$ for a specific gene mutation sample, as shown in Fig. 5.3. For instance, suppose a gene and a mutation are given, the n-gram feature for the given sample with a gene and a mutation is generated separately, on the basis of their corresponding extracted text. Then the concatenated n-gram vector can be used to represent the sample. The feature vector generated from entity text view is represented as $\mathbf{x}^{ET}$.

5.3.3 Entity Name View

Although most of the gene names and mutation names are short and are only consist of few characters and numbers, the name itself contains useful information for classification. Two encoding approaches are designed to capture patterns from names, which are character-level n-gram and word embedding.

5.3.3.1 Character-Level Feature

Different with word-level n-gram, we can set a large n ($n = 8$) as names are typically short strings. As a consequence, the feature dimension is extremely high. We apply SVD to reduce the dimensionality to 20. The other encoding approach uses label encoder is to transform the letters and numbers in gene or mutation name into digital labels (112 in total) that can be used as feature directly.

5.3.3.2 Word Embedding Feature

Word embedding is a technique aiming at representing (embedding) words in a continuous vector space where semantically similar words are mapped to nearby points. Representative word embedding techniques include Word2Vec (Mikolov et al. 2013) and GloVe (Pennington et al. 2014). The trained word embedding models can offer us feature vector representations for each specific gene or mutation according to their names. In this task, we choose Word2Vec (Skip-Gram) (Mikolov et al. 2013) because both Word2Vec and GloVe have similar classification performance during evaluation. The feature dimension for gene or mutation name vectors is set to 200 according to cross-validation.

Similar to entity text view, the feature vector extracted from entity name view is concatenated by gene feature vector $\mathbf{x}_g^{EN}$ and mutation feature vector $\mathbf{x}_m^{EN}$, that is $\mathbf{x}^{EN} = \mathbf{x}_g^{EN}||\mathbf{x}_m^{EN}$. The feature vector generated from entity name view is represented as $\mathbf{x}^{EN}$.

5.3.4 Classifiers

Gradient Boosting Decision Tree (GBDT) (Friedman 2001) is a famous machine learning technique for regression and classification problems. Based on boosting, it aims to find an optimal model $f(\mathbf{x})$ that satisfies the following equation:

$$\hat{f}(\mathbf{x}) = \arg\min_{f(\mathbf{x})} E[L(y, f(\mathbf{x}))|\mathbf{x}] \tag{5.2}$$

for a given dataset, $\mathbf{x} \in \mathbb{R}^d$ is an instance or sample. Using an additive strategy similar to other "boosting" paradigm, the functions $f(\mathbf{x})$ can be learned by the model:

$$\hat{f}(\mathbf{x}) = \hat{f}_K(\mathbf{x}) = \Sigma_{k=0}^M f_k(\mathbf{x}) \tag{5.3}$$

where $f_0(\mathbf{x})$ is an initial guess and $f_k(\mathbf{x})_1^K$ are incremental functions. $\hat{f}(\mathbf{x}) = \hat{f}_K(\mathbf{x}) : \mathbb{R}^d \to \mathbb{R}$ is the objective function of the model. K is the number of training iterations, which also equals to the number of boosted trees. Then the function $f_k(\mathbf{x})$ contains the structure of the tree and leaf scores, which is a sort of weak classification model obtained at the k-th training iteration. In general, the tree boosting can be defined as the objective function $\mathscr{L}$ with a training loss term and regularization term:

$$\mathscr{L} = \Sigma_{i=1}^N l(y_i, \Sigma_{k=0}^M f_k(\mathbf{x}_i)) + \Sigma_{k=0}^M \Omega(f_k) \tag{5.4}$$

where N is the number of samples and l is the Logarithmic Loss for multi-class classification in our scenario. To take advantages of feature vectors: $\mathbf{x}^D$, $\mathbf{x}^{ET}$, and $\mathbf{x}^{EN}$, we concatenate vectors from different views into a new vector $\mathbf{x} = \mathbf{x}^D \| \mathbf{x}^{ET} \| \mathbf{x}^{EN}$ Then the single-view classification models can be applied straightforwardly on the concatenated vector. The symbol $\|$ denotes concatenation operation on vectors from views.

In practice, we exploit two effective versions of gradient boosting algorithms: XGBoost[5] and LightGBM[6]. XGBoost proposes to use a second-order approximation by Taylor expansion of the loss function for the problem optimization (Chen and Guestrin 2016). LightGBM can obtain a quite accurate estimation with a smaller data size and a fewer feature number so that it speeds up the conventional GBDT. Particularly, the specific gradient boosting algorithm in LightGBM we used is also GBDT. Through feature combinations across the given three views, multiple GBDT classifiers are trained independently.

---

[5]https://xgboost.readthedocs.io/en/latest/
[6]https://github.com/Microsoft/LightGBM

5.4 Model Ensembles

Many existing successful stories on data challenges demonstrated that combining multiple models together can gain better performance than a single model (Bell and Koren 2007; Wu et al. 2013). The rationale behind our framework is to combine features mined from original documents, entity texts, and entity names by different level features to form inputs of prediction models, and thus we can get numerous prediction results from these models (See Fig. 5.3). By setting a threshold of the Logarithmic Loss score (Mesnil et al. 2014), 9 qualified models finally win in the comparisons. Tables 5.4 and 5.5 show the feature combinations used in training these models by XGBoost and LightGBM respectively. Based on the results of basic models, ensemble strategies of 2 models, 3 models, and 9 models are applied. Through model ensemble, the system can eventually output a probability distribution over classes for each sample.

Formally, let $\hat{p}_{ij}^v$ be the final prediction result of validation data for sample i of label j and $\hat{p}_{ij}^s$ be the final prediction result of testing data for sample i on label j. They are computed by the linear combination of results of single models as:

$$\hat{p}_{ij}^v = \Sigma_c \alpha_c \hat{p}_{ijc}^v, \qquad \alpha_c > 0$$
$$\hat{p}_{ij}^s = \Sigma_c \alpha_c \hat{p}_{ijc}^s, \qquad \alpha_c > 0$$

(5.5)

Table 5.4 The details of feature combination for XGBoost models

| Model ID | Feature combination | | |
	Document view	Entity text view	Entity name view
GBDT_1	n/v/adj./adv. counts	n-gram+NMF	Word embedding
	n/v/adj./adv. counts+NMF		Character-level encoding
	n-gram+NMF		
	Bioentity counts		
GBDT_2	Paragraph vector	Sentence-level TFIDF+SVD	Word embedding
	Sentence-level TFIDF+SVD		Character-level encoding
	Term frequency+LDA		
	Bioentity/keywords counts		
GBDT_3	n/v/adj./adv. counts	Sentence-level TFIDF+SVD	Word embedding
	n/v/adj./adv.+NMF		
	Sentence-level TFIDF+SVD		
	Keywords counts		
GBDT_4	n/v/adj./adv. TFIDF	n/v/adj./adv. TFIDF	Word embedding
	Sentence-level TFIDF+SVD		Character-level encoding
	Bioentity counts		

Table 5.5 The details of feature combination for LightGBM models

Model ID	Feature combination		
	Document view	Entity text view	Entity name view
GBDT_5	n/v/adj./adv. counts	n/v/adj./adv. TFIDF	Word embedding
	n/v/adj./adv. counts+NMF		
	n/v/adj./adv. TFIDF		
GBDT_6	n-gram+NMF	n-gram+NMF	Word embedding
	n/v/adj./adv. counts		Character-level encoding
	n/v/adj./adv. counts+NMF		
	Bioentity counts		
GBDT_7	n/v/adj./adv. TFIDF	n/v/adj./adv. TFIDF+SVD	Word embedding
	n/v/adj./adv. counts+NMF		
	Sentence-level TFIDF+SVD		
	n-gram+NMF		
GBDT_8	Sentence-level TFIDF+SVD	Sentence-level TFIDF+SVD	Word embedding
	n/v/adj./adv. counts		Character-level encoding
	n/v/adj./adv. counts+NMF		
	keywords counts		
GBDT_9	n/v/adj./adv. TFIDF	n/v/adj./adv. TFIDF	Word embedding
	Sentence-level TFIDF+SVD		Character-level encoding
	Bioentity counts		

where $\hat{p}_{ijc}^{v}$ and $\hat{p}_{ijc}^{s}$ is the predicted probability of validation data and testing data by c-th single model. i is the index of triplet $< g_i, m_i, d_i >$, j is the index of class. α_c is the linear combination parameter for the c-th model, which is a positive weight.

Ensemble parameters α_c are computed by different manners: brute force grid searching and logarithmic loss minimization. The force grid searching quantizes the coefficient values in the interval $[0, 1]$ at increments of 0.01. It is an efficient way to find α when we need to ensemble 2 or 3 models. On the other hand, the logarithmic loss minimization problem on validation data can be mathematically defined as:

$$\alpha = \arg \min_{\alpha} \text{Logloss}(\Sigma_c \alpha_c \hat{p}_c^v) \qquad (5.6)$$

In above minimization problem, the Logloss is defined by:

$$\text{Logloss} = -\frac{1}{N} \Sigma_{i=1}^{N} \Sigma_{j=1}^{M} y_{ij} log(p_{ij}) \qquad (5.7)$$

where N is the number of triplet $< g, m, d >$ observations, M is the number of class label. It is consistent with the evaluation metric provided by the Challenge. One limitation of the ensemble method is that it treats the classes equally important. However, after statistical analysis, we find that the 9 classes are severely imbalanced.

In order to overcome the problem, we propose to use the loss computation on each class to optimize its own weight α_{cj}. Based on the Eqs. 5.6 and 5.7, the Logloss is updated by:

$$\text{Logloss} = -\Sigma_{j=1}^{M} \frac{1}{N_j} \Sigma_{i=1}^{N_j} y_{ij} log(p_{ij}) \qquad (5.8)$$

The new Logloss can help us to learn weight α_{cj} for different classes and different models. Also, we conduct a 9 model ensemble based on the improved ensemble method.

5.5 Experimental Results

5.5.1 Experimental Settings

In the empirical study, we apply two offline test strategies. The first strategy is stage-1 splitting which divides the entire samples into 3,321 training samples and 368 validation samples as shown in Table 5.2; the second strategy is 5-fold cross validation on the overall 3,689 samples. To show the effectiveness, the evaluation metric logarithmic loss is used, which have been introduced in Sect. 5.2.

5.5.2 Effects of Multi-view Features

In our method, features mainly come from three different views. To test the effectiveness of single feature, XGBoost implementation is utilized. In Table 5.6, the features are inputted into the 9 basic gradient boosting models, their dimensions, and performance on 5-fold cross-validation are shown. We test various bag-of-word and bag-of-n-gram features with or without dimension reduction methods, and there are 16 winner features in total built on three views. In each view, the most effective single feature can be easily observed.

To compare two feature combinations of two views, we concatenate the features obtained by the same extraction methods, i.e., two feature vectors of term frequency+LDA are computed based on original documents and entity texts, respectively. And then we train GBDT models to test the effects of multi-view features by XGBoost implementation. Experimental results are presented in Table 5.7. Same feature derived from both document view and entity text view consistently outperforms the one only generated from a single view. The empirical study can demonstrate the effectiveness of using a complementary view.

Table 5.6 The dimensions and logarithmic loss scores obtained by the single feature in 3 views on 5-fold cross-validation. (The classifier is implemented based on XGBoost)

Views	Feature	Dimension	5-fold cv
Document view	Bioentity counts	10,022	0.9914
	Keyword counts	3,379	**0.9583**
	Doc2Vec	400	1.0037
	Sentence-level TFIDF+SVD	100	0.9939
	n/v/adj./adv. counts	9,868	1.0018
	n/v/adj./adv. TFIDF	9,868	0.9825
	n/v/adj./adv. counts+NMF	60	1.0417
	n-gram+NMF	6 0	1.0370
	Term frequency+LDA	50	1.0348
Entity text view	Sentence-level TFIDF+SVD	200	0.9815
	n/v/adj./adv. TFIDF	9,868	**0.9788**
	n/v/adj./adv. TFIDF+SVD	200	1.0055
	n-gram+NMF	120	1.0029
Entity name view	Word embedding	200	**0.9811**
	Character-level encoding	40	1.1031

Table 5.7 Result comparisons of feature generated from single view and double views on 5-fold cross-validation. The double view contains document view and entity text view. (The classifier is implemented based on XGBoost)

Feature	Single view	Double views
n/v/adj./adv. TFIDF	**0.9825**	**0.8558**
Sentence-level TFIDF+SVD	0.9939	0.8845
n/v/adj./adv. counts+NMF	1.0417	0.9029
n/v/adj./adv. TFIDF+SVD	1.0055[a]	0.8775
Term frequency+LDA	1.0348	0.9098

[a]The score is based on feature in entity text view while others are computed in document view

5.5.3   Results of Basic Models

In the competition, 9 different models are used in the model ensemble. Corresponding to the feature settings presented in Tables 5.4, 5.5, Tables 5.8, and 5.9 shows the results of basic gradient boosting models. For a fair comparison, all the models share the same hyper-parameter setting. From the results, we can observe that GBDT models implemented by XGBoost overall perform slightly better than those implemented by LightGBM. Among the trained basic models using XGBoost, GBDT_3 has the best performance as a single model on 5-fold cross-validation, while GBDT_2 has the best performance on stage-1 testing set. The situation for LightGBM is that GBDT_7 wins other models on 5-fold cross-validation while GBDT_9 outperforms other models on stage-1 testing set.

Table 5.8 Results of GBDT model in terms of logarithmic loss on 5-fold cross-validation and stage-1 testing set

Model Id	5-fold cv	Stage-1 test
GBDT_1	0.7068	0.5997
GBDT_2	0.6930	**0.5638**
GBDT_3	**0.6870**	0.5743
GBDT_4	0.6901	0.5657

Table 5.9 Results of GBM model in terms of logarithmic loss on 5-fold cross-validation and stage-1 testing set

Model Id	5-fold cv	Stage-1 test
GBDT_5	0.7005	0.6090
GBDT_6	0.7121	0.6152
GBDT_7	**0.6967**	0.6139
GBDT_8	0.7028	0.6178
GBDT_9	0.7001	**0.6006**

Table 5.10 Results of 2 models ensemble by brute forcing grid search

Model_1 Id	Model_2 Id	Weight_1	Weight_2	5-fold cv
GBDT_1	GBDT_4	0.4	0.6	0.6786
GBDT_6	GBDT_7	0.4	0.6	0.6846
GBDT_1	GBDT_7	0.4	0.6	**0.6762**

Table 5.11 Results of 3 models ensemble by brute forcing grid search

Model_1 Id	Model_2 Id	Model_3 Id	Weight_1	Weight_2	Weight_3	5-fold cv
GBDT_1	GBDT_2	GBDT_4	0.32	0.30	0.38	0.6738
GBDT_5	GBDT_6	GBDT_7	0.40	0.32	0.28	0.6818
GBDT_1	GBDT_4	GBDT_5	0.30	0.38	0.32	**0.6695**

5.5.4 Results of Model Ensemble

Similarly, 5-fold cross-validation to the model ensemble is utilized here. In practice, brute force gird search strategy and logarithmic loss minimization strategy are used in the model ensemble. The combinations of basic models are shown in tables, if the evaluation of Logloss scores less than a threshold. Tables 5.10 and 5.11 respectively show ensemble results as well as weights by brute force grid search strategy to ensemble 2 models and 3 models.

Tables 5.12 and 5.13 respectively show 2 and 3 ensemble results under the target of logarithmic loss minimization. The best model ensemble can be found in the results. The improved logarithmic loss minimization considering the imbalanced labels are also tested by 5-fold cross-validation. The results in Table 5.14 show that the improved ensemble strategy can increase prediction accuracy on ensemble results of 9 models. To compare the ensemble effects of 9 models to 2 models and 3 models, the Fig. 5.5 plots the Log loss scores of main model ensemble methods concerned in this paper. Among different strategies, 9 model ensemble is the final winner, which slightly outperform the 3 model ensemble based on brute forcing grid search.

Table 5.12 Results of 2 models ensemble by logarithmic loss minimization

Model_1 Id	Model_2 Id	Weight_1	Weight_2	5-fold cv
GBDT_1	GBDT_4	0.49	0.51	0.6796
GBDT_6	GBDT_7	0.49	0.51	0.6860
GBDT_1	GBDT_7	0.49	0.51	**0.6771**

Table 5.13 Results of 3 models ensemble by logarithmic loss minimization

Model_1 Id	Model_2 Id	Model_3 Id	Weight_1	Weight_2	Weight_3	5-fold cv
GBDT_1	GBDT_3	GBDT_4	0.33	0.33	0.33	0.6745
GBDT_6	GBDT_8	GBDT_9	0.33	0.33	0.33	0.6832
GBDT_1	GBDT_4	GBDT_7	0.32	0.30	0.38	**0.6718**

Table 5.14 Results of the ensemble 9 models by logarithmic loss minimization

Ensemble method	Stage-1 test	5-fold cv
LogLoss_Min	0.5547	0.6711
LogLoss_Min_cl	**0.5506**	**0.6694**

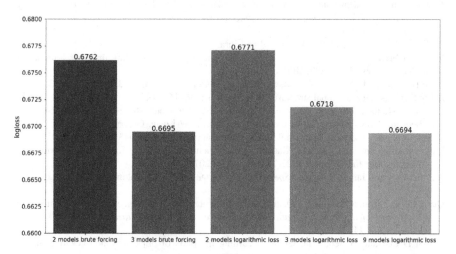

Fig. 5.5 Experimental results of different model ensemble strategies on 5-fold cross validation

5.6   Conclusion

The main contribution of our work is developing a comprehensive pipeline to perform gene mutation classification based on clinical articles. Our solution mines text features from tree views including original document view, entity text view, and entity name view. Various machine learning algorithms are exploited to generate text features from perspectives of domain knowledge, document-level, sentence-level, and word-level. In addition, word embedding and character-level encoding based on entity names are adopted. Multiple GBDT classifiers with different feature combinations are utilized in ensemble learning to achieve a satisfying genetic mutation classification accuracy. The reported results demonstrate that our multi-view ensemble classification framework yields promising performances in this competition.

Acknowledgements The work is partially supported by NSF IIS-1650723, IIS-1716432 and IIS-1750326.

References

Alfred V Aho and Margaret J Corasick. Efficient string matching: an aid to bibliographic search. *Communications of the ACM*, 18(6):333–340, 1975.

Robert M. Bell and Yehuda Koren. Lessons from the netflix prize challenge. *SIGKDD Explor. Newsl.*, 9(2):75–79, 2007.

David M Blei, Andrew Y Ng, and Michael I Jordan. Latent dirichlet allocation. *Journal of machine Learning research*, 3(Jan):993–1022, 2003.

Tianqi Chen and Carlos Guestrin. Xgboost: A scalable tree boosting system. In *Proceedings of the 22nd acm sigkdd international conference on knowledge discovery and data mining*, pages 785–794. ACM, 2016.

Christiane Fellbaum. *WordNet*. Wiley Online Library, 1998.

Jerome H Friedman. Greedy function approximation: a gradient boosting machine. *Annals of statistics*, pages 1189–1232, 2001.

Gene H Golub and Charles F Van Loan. *Matrix computations*, volume 3. JHU Press, 2012.

Zellig S Harris. Distributional structure. *Word*, 10(2-3):146–162, 1954.

Lin He, J Michael Thomson, Michael T Hemann, Eva Hernando-Monge, David Mu, Summer Goodson, Scott Powers, Carlos Cordon-Cardo, Scott W Lowe, Gregory J Hannon, et al. A microrna polycistron as a potential human oncogene. *nature*, 435(7043):828–833, 2005.

Minlie Huang, Jingchen Liu, and Xiaoyan Zhu. Genetukit: a software for document-level gene normalization. *Bioinformatics*, 27(7):1032–1033, 2011.

Dan Jurafsky and James H Martin. *Speech and language processing*, volume 3. Pearson London:, 2014.

Quoc Le and Tomas Mikolov. Distributed representations of sentences and documents. In *Proceedings of the 31st International Conference on Machine Learning (ICML-14)*, pages 1188–1196, 2014.

Daniel D Lee and H Sebastian Seung. Learning the parts of objects by non-negative matrix factorization. *Nature*, 401(6755):788–791, 1999.

David AC Manning and JGM Decleer. Introduction to industrial minerals. 1995.

Grégoire Mesnil, Tomas Mikolov, Marc'Aurelio Ranzato, and Yoshua Bengio. Ensemble of generative and discriminative techniques for sentiment analysis of movie reviews. *arXiv preprint arXiv:1412.5335*, 2014.

Tomas Mikolov, Kai Chen, Greg Corrado, and Jeffrey Dean. Efficient estimation of word representations in vector space. *arXiv preprint arXiv:1301.3781*, 2013.

Tomas Mikolov, Ilya Sutskever, Kai Chen, Greg S Corrado, and Jeff Dean. Distributed representations of words and phrases and their compositionality. In *Advances in neural information processing systems*, pages 3111–3119, 2013.

Nanyun Peng, Hoifung Poon, Chris Quirk, Kristina Toutanova, and Wen-tau Yih. Cross-sentence n-ary relation extraction with graph lstms. *arXiv preprint arXiv:1708.03743*, 2017.

Jeffrey Pennington, Richard Socher, and Christopher Manning. Glove: Global vectors for word representation. In *Proceedings of the 2014 conference on empirical methods in natural language processing (EMNLP)*, pages 1532–1543, 2014.

Sam T Roweis and Lawrence K Saul. Nonlinear dimensionality reduction by locally linear embedding. *science*, 290(5500):2323–2326, 2000.

Chih-Hsuan Wei, Bethany R Harris, Hung-Yu Kao, and Zhiyong Lu. tmvar: a text mining approach for extracting sequence variants in biomedical literature. *Bioinformatics*, 29(11):1433–1439, 2013.

Chih-Hsuan Wei and Hung-Yu Kao. Cross-species gene normalization by species inference. *BMC bioinformatics*, 12(8):S5, 2011.

Chih-Hsuan Wei, Hung-Yu Kao, and Zhiyong Lu. Pubtator: a web-based text mining tool for assisting biocuration. *Nucleic acids research*, 41(W1):W518–W522, 2013.

Jiaxiang Wu, Jian Cheng, Chaoyang Zhao, and Hanqing Lu. Fusing multi-modal features for gesture recognition. In *Proceedings of the 15th ACM on International Conference on Multimodal Interaction*, pages 453–460, 2013.

Xiang Zhang, Junbo Zhao, and Yann LeCun. Character-level convolutional networks for text classification. In *Advances in neural information processing systems*, pages 649–657, 2015.

Chapter 6
Learning to Run Challenge: Synthesizing Physiologically Accurate Motion Using Deep Reinforcement Learning

Łukasz Kidziński, Sharada P. Mohanty, Carmichael F. Ong, Jennifer L. Hicks, Sean F. Carroll, Sergey Levine, Marcel Salathé, and Scott L. Delp

Abstract Synthesizing physiologically-accurate human movement in a variety of conditions can help practitioners plan surgeries, design experiments, or prototype assistive devices in simulated environments, reducing time and costs and improving treatment outcomes. Because of the large and complex solution spaces of biomechanical models, current methods are constrained to specific movements and models, requiring careful design of a controller and hindering many possible applications. We sought to discover if modern optimization methods efficiently explore these complex spaces. To do this, we posed the problem as a competition in which participants were tasked with developing a controller to enable a physiologically-based human model to navigate a complex obstacle course as quickly as possible, without using any experimental data. They were provided with a human musculoskeletal model and a physics-based simulation environment. In this paper, we discuss the design of the competition, technical difficulties, results, and analysis of the top controllers. The challenge proved that deep reinforcement learning techniques, despite their high computational cost, can be successfully

Sharada P. Mohanty and Carmichael F. Ong contributed equally to this work.

Ł. Kidziński (✉) · C. F. Ong · J. L. Hicks · S. L. Delp
Stanford University, Stanford, CA, USA
e-mail: lukasz.kidzinski@stanford.edu; ongcf@stanford.edu; jenhicks@stanford.edu; delp@stanford.edu

S. P. Mohanty · S. F. Carroll · M. Salathé
Ecole Polytechnique Federale de Lausanne, Lausanne, Switzerland
e-mail: sharada.mohanty@epfl.ch; sean.carroll@epfl.ch; marcel.salathe@epfl.ch

S. Levine
Department of Electrical Engineering and Computer Sciences, University of California, Berkeley, CA, USA
e-mail: svlevine@eecs.berkeley.edu

© Springer International Publishing AG, part of Springer Nature 2018
S. Escalera, M. Weimer (eds.), *The NIPS '17 Competition: Building Intelligent Systems*, The Springer Series on Challenges in Machine Learning,
https://doi.org/10.1007/978-3-319-94042-7_6

employed as an optimization method for synthesizing physiologically feasible motion in high-dimensional biomechanical systems.

6.1 Overview of the Competition

Human movement results from the intricate coordination of muscles, tendons, joints, and other physiological elements. While children learn to walk, run, climb, and jump in their first years of life and most of us can navigate complex environments— like a crowded street or moving subway—without considerable active attention, developing controllers that can efficiently and robustly synthesize realistic human motions in a variety of environments remains a grand challenge for biomechanists, neuroscientists, and computer scientists. Current controllers are confined to a small set of pre-specified movements or driven by torques, rather than the complex muscle actuators found in humans (see Sect. 6.3.1).

In this competition, participants were tasked with developing a controller to enable a physiologically-based human model to navigate a complex obstacle course as quickly as possible. Participants were provided with a human musculoskeletal model and a physics-based simulation environment where they could synthesize physically and physiologically accurate motion (Fig. 6.1). Obstacles were divided into two groups: external and internal. External obstacles consisted of soft balls fixed to the ground to create uneven terrain, and internal obstacles included introducing weakness in the psoas muscle, a key muscle for swinging the leg forward during running. Controllers submitted by the participants were scored based on the distance

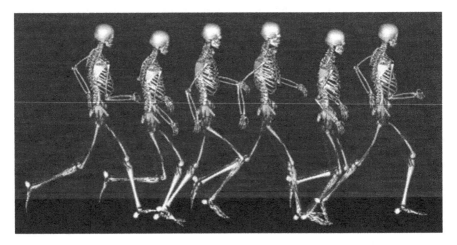

Fig. 6.1 Musculoskeletal simulation of human running in Stanford's OpenSim software. OpenSim was used to simulate the muscoloskeletal lower-body system used in the competition, and the competitors were tasked with learning controllers that could actuate the muscles in the presence of realistic delays to achieve rapid running gaits. Image courtesy of Samuel Hamner

the agents equipped with these controllers traveled through the obstacle course in a set amount of time. To simulate the fact that humans typically move in a manner that minimizes the risk of joint injury, controllers were penalized for excessive use of ligament forces. We provided competitors with a set of training environments to help build robust controllers; competitors' scores were based on a final, unknown environment that used more external obstacles (10 balls instead of 3) in an unexpected configuration (see Sect. 6.3.2).

The competition was designed for participants to use reinforcement learning methods to create their controllers; however, participants were allowed to use other optimization frameworks. As the benchmark, we used state-of-the art reinforcement learning techniques: Trust Region Policy Optimization (TRPO) (Schulman et al. 2015) and Deep Deterministic Policy Gradients (DDPG) (Lillicrap et al. 2015). We included implementations of these reinforcement learning models in the "Getting Started" tutorial provided to competitors.

This competition fused biomechanics, computer science, and neuroscience to explore a grand challenge in human movement and motor control. The entire competition was built on free and open source software. Participants were required to tackle three major challenges in reinforcement learning: large dimensionality of the action space, delayed actuation, and robustness to variability of the environments. Controllers that can synthesize the movement of realistic human models can help optimize human performance (e.g., fine-tune technique for high jump or design a prosthetic to break paralympic records) and plan surgery and treatment for individuals with movement disorders (see Sect. 6.3.1). In Sect. 6.5, we analyze accuracy of the top results from a biomechanical standpoint and discuss implications of the results and propose future directions. For a description of solutions from top participants please refer to Jaśkowski et al. (2018) and Kidziński et al. (2018).

To the best of our knowledge, this was the largest reinforcement learning competition in terms of the number of participants and the most complex in terms of environment, to date. In Sect. 6.4 we share our insights from the process of designing the challenge and our solutions to problems encountered while administering the challenge.

6.2 Prior Work

We identify two groups of prior challenges related to this proposal. The first set includes challenges held within the biomechanics community, including the Dynamic Walking Challenge[1] (exploring mechanics of a very simple 2D walker) and the Grand Challenge Competition to Predict In Vivo Knee Loads[2] (validation of musculoskeletal model estimates of muscle and joint contact forces in the knee). In

---

[1]http://simtk-confluence.stanford.edu:8080/pages/viewpage.action?pageId=5113821
[2]https://simtk.org/projects/kneeloads

the Dynamic Walking Challenge, the model used was highly simplified to represent the minimimum viable model to achieve bipedal gait without muscles. In the Grand Challenge, the focus was to predict knee loads given a prescribed motion rather than to generate novel motions.

The second class of prior challenges has been held in the reinforcement learning community. In the field of reinforcement learning, competitions have periodically been organized around standardized benchmark tasks.[3] These tasks are typically designed to drive advancements in algorithm efficiency, exploration, and scalability. Many of the formal competitions, however, have focused on relatively smaller tasks, such as simulated helicopter control (Dimitrakakis et al. 2014), where the state and action dimensionality are low. More recently, vision-based reinforcement learning tasks, such as the Arcade Learning Environment (ALE) (Bellemare et al. 2013) have gained popularity. Although ALE was never organized as a formal contest, the Atari games in ALE have frequently been used as benchmark tasks in evaluating reinforcement algorithms with high-dimensional observations. However, these tasks do not test an algorithm's ability to learn to coordinate complex and realistic movements, as would be required for realistic running. The OpenAI gym benchmark tasks (Brockman et al. 2016) include a set of continuous control benchmarks based on the MuJoCo physics engine (Todorov et al. 2012), and while these tasks do include bipedal running, the corresponding physical models use simple torque-driven frictionless joints, and successful policies for these benchmarks typically exhibit substantial visual artifacts and non-naturalistic gaits.[4] Furthermore, these tasks do not include many of the important phenomena involved in controlling musculoskeletal systems, such as delays.

There were three key features differentiating the "Learning to Run" challenge from other reinforcement learning competitions. First, in our competition, participants were tasked with building a robust controller for an unknown environment with external obstacles (balls fixed in the ground) and internal obstacles (reduced muscle strength), rather than a predefined course. Models experienced all available types of obstacles in the training environments, but competitors did not know how these obstacles would be positioned in the final test obstacle course. This novel aspect of our challenge forced participants to build more robust and generalizable solutions than for static environments such as those provided by OpenAI. Second, the dimensionality and complexity of the action space were much larger than in most popular reinforcement learning problems. It is comparable to the most complex MuJoCo physics OpenAI gym task Humanoid-V1 (Brockman et al. 2016) which had 17 torque actuators, compared to 18 actuators in this challenge. In contrast to many robotics competitions, the task in this challenge was to actuate muscles, which included delayed actuation and other physiological complexities, instead of controlling torques. This increased the complexity of the relationship between the control signal and torque generated. Furthermore, compared to torque actuators,

---

[3] see, e.g., http://www.rl-competition.org/
[4] see, e.g., https://youtu.be/hx_bgoTF7bs

more muscles are needed to fully actuate a model. Third, the cost of one iteration is larger, since precise simulations of muscles are computationally expensive. This constraint forces participants to build algorithms using fewer evaluations of the environment.

6.3 Competition Description

6.3.1 Background

Understanding motor control is a grand challenge in biomechanics and neuro-science. One of the greatest hurdles is the complexity of the neuromuscular control system. Muscles are complex actuators whose forces are dependent on their length, velocity, and activation level, and these forces are then transmitted to the bones through a compliant tendon. Coordinating these musculotendon actuators to generate a robust motion is further complicated by delays in the biological system, including sensor delays, control signal delays, and muscle-tendon dynamics. Existing techniques allow us to estimate muscle activity from experimental data (Thelen et al. 2003), but solutions from these methods are insufficient to generate and predict new motions in a novel environment.

Recent advances in reinforcement learning, biomechanics, and neuroscience can help us solve this grand challenge. The biomechanics community has used single shooting methods to synthesize simulations of human movement driven by biologically inspired actuators. Early work directly solved for individual muscle excitations for a gait cycle of walking (Anderson and Pandy 2001) and for a maximum height jump (Anderson and Pandy 1999). Recent work has focused on using controllers based on human reflexes to generate simulations of walking on level ground (Geyer and Herr 2010). This framework has been extended to synthesize simulations of other gait patterns such as running (Wang et al. 2012), loaded and inclined walking (Dorn et al. 2015), and turning and obstacle avoidance (Song and Geyer 2015). Although these controllers were based on physiological reflexes, they needed substantial input from domain experts. Furthermore, use of these controllers has been limited to cyclic motions, such as walking and running, over static terrain.

Modern reinforcement learning techniques have been used recently to train more general controllers for locomotion. These techniques have the advantage that, compared to the gait controllers previously described, less user input is needed to hand tune the controllers, and they are more flexible to learning additional, novel tasks. For example, reinforcement learning has been used to train controllers for locomotion of complicated humanoid models (Lillicrap et al. 2015; Schulman et al. 2015). Although these methods found solutions without domain specific knowledge, the resulting motions were not realistic. One possible reason for the lack of human-like motion is that these models did not use biologically accurate actuators.

Thus while designing the "Learning to Run" challenge, we conjectured that reinforcement learning methods would yield more realistic results with biologically accurate models and actuators. OpenSim is an open-source software environment which implements computational biomechanical models and allows muscle-driven simulations of these models (Delp et al. 2007). It is a flexible platform that can be easily incorporated into an optimization routine using reinforcement learning.

6.3.2 OpenSim Simulator

OpenSim is an open-source project that provides tools to model complex musculoskeletal systems in order to gain a better understanding of how movement is coordinated. OpenSim uses another open-source project, Simbody, as a dependency to perform the physics simulation. Users can employ either inverse methods, which estimate the forces needed to produce a given motion from data, or forward methods, which synthesize a motion from a set of controls. In this competition, we used OpenSim to (1) model the human musculoskeletal system and generate the corresponding equations of motion and (2) synthesize motions by integrating the equations of motion over time.

The human musculoskeletal model was based on a previous model (Delp et al. 1990) and was simplified to decrease complexity, similarly to previous work (Ong et al. 2017). The model was composed of 7 bodies. The pelvis, torso, and head were represented by a single body. Each leg had 3 bodies: an upper leg, a lower leg, and a foot. The model contained 9 degrees of freedom (dof): 3-dof between the pelvis and ground (i.e., two translation and one rotation), 1-dof hip joints, 1-dof knee joints, and 1-dof ankle joints.

The model included 18 musculotendon actuators (Thelen 2003), with 9 on each leg, to represent the major lower limb muscle groups that drive walking (Fig. 6.2). For each leg, these included the biarticular hamstrings, short head of the biceps femoris, gluteus maximus, iliopsoas, rectus femoris, vasti, gastrocnemius, soleus, and tibialis anterior. The force in these actuators mimicked biological muscle as the force depends on the length (l), velocity (v), and activation (a) level (i.e., the control signal to a muscle that is actively generating force, which can range between 0% and 100% activated) of the muscle. Biological muscle can produce force either actively, via a neural signal to the muscle to produce force, or passively, by being stretched past a certain length. The following equation shows how the total force was calculated, due to both active and passive force, in the each muscle (F_{muscle}),

$$F_{muscle} = F_{max-iso}(a f_{active}(l) f_{velocity}(v) + f_{passive}(l)),$$

where $F_{max-iso}$ is the maximum isometric force of a muscle (i.e., a stronger muscle will have a larger value), f_{active} and $f_{passive}$ are functions relating the active and passive force in a muscle to its current length, and $f_{velocity}$ is a function that scales the force a muscle produces as a function of its current velocity (e.g., a

Fig. 6.2 Musculoskeletal
model in OpenSim used in
this competition. Red/purple
curves indicate muscles,
while blue balls attached to
feet model contact

muscle can generate more force when lengthening than shortening). For a sense
of scale, in this model, values of $F_{max-iso}$ ranged between 557 and 9594 N. Force
is transferred between the muscle and bone by tendons. Tendons are compliant
structures that generate force when stretched beyond a certain length. Given the
physical constraints between the tendon and muscle, a force equilibrium must be
satisfied between them, governed by the relationship,

$$F_{tendon} = F_{muscle} \cos(\alpha),$$

where α is the pennation angle (i.e., the angle between the direction of the tendon
and the muscle fibers).

Additionally, arbitrary amounts of force cannot be generated instantaneously
due to various electrical, chemical, and mechanical delays in the biological system
between an incoming electrical control signal and force generation. This was
modeled using a first-order dynamic model between excitation (i.e., the neural signal
as it reaches the muscle) and activation (Thelen 2003).

The model also had components that represent ligaments and ground contact.
Ligaments are biological structures that produce force when they are stretched past
a certain length, protecting against excessively large joint angles. Ligaments were
modeled at the hip, knee, and ankle joints as rotational springs with increasing
stiffness as joint angle increases. These springs only engaged at larger flexion and

extension angles. Ground contact was modeled using the Hunt-Crossley model (1975), a compliant contact model. Two contact spheres were located at the heel and toes of each foot and generate forces depending on the depth and velocity of these spheres penetrating other contact geometry, including the ground, represented as a half-plane, and other obstacles, represented as other contact spheres.

6.3.3 Tasks and Application Scenarios

In this competition, OpenSim and the model described in Sect. 6.3.2 served as a black-box simulator of human movement. Competitors passed in excitations to each muscle, and OpenSim calculated and returned the state, which contained information about joint angles, joint velocities, body positions, body velocities, and distance to and size of the next obstacle. This occurred every 10 milliseconds during the simulation for 10 s (i.e., a total of 1000 decision time points).

At every iteration the agent receives the current observed state vector $s \in \mathbb{R}^{41}$ consisting of the following:

- Rotations and angular velocities of the pelvis, hip, knee and ankle joints,
- Positions and velocities of the pelvis, center of mass, head, torso, toes, and talus,
- Distance to the next obstacle (or 100 if it doesn't exist),
- Radius and vertical location of the next obstacle.

Obstacles were small soft balls fixed to the ground. While it was possible to partly penetrate the ball, after stepping into the ball the repelling force was proportional to the volume of intersection of penetrating body and the ball. The first three balls were each positioned at a distance that was uniformly distributed between 1 and 5. Then, each subsequent obstacle was positioned at u meters after the last one, where u was uniformly distributed between 2 and 4. Each ball was fixed at v meters vertically from the ground level, where v was uniformly distributed between -0.25 and 0.25. Finally, the radius of each ball was $0.05 + v$, where v was drawn from an exponential distribution with a mean of 0.05.

Based on the observation vector or internal states, current strength and distance to obstacles, participants' controllers were required to output a vector of current muscle excitations. These excitations were integrated over time to generate muscle activations (via a model of muscle's activation dynamics), which in turn generated movement (as a function of muscle moment arms and other muscle properties like strength and current length and lengthening velocity). Participants were evaluated by the distance they covered in a fixed amount of time. At every iteration the agent was expected to return a vector $v \in [0, 1]^{18}$ of muscle excitations for the 18 muscles in the model.

Simulation environments were parametrized by: difficulty, seed and max_obstacles. Difficulty corresponded to the number and density of obstacles. The seed was a number which uniquely identifies pseudo-random generation of the obstacle positions in the environment and participants could use it in training to obtain a robust controller. The seed ranges between 0 and $2^{63} - 1$. Both seed and difficulty of the final test environment were unknown to participants. Such a setup allowed us to give access to infinitely many training environments, as well as choose the final difficulty reactively, depending on users' performance leading up to the final competition round.

The controller modeled by participants was approximating functions of the human motor control system. It collected signals from physiological sensors and generated signals to excite muscles. Our objective was to construct the environment in such a way that its solutions could potentially help biomechanics and neuroscience researchers to better understand the mechanisms underlying human locomotion.

6.3.4 Baselines and Code Available

Before running the NIPS competition, we organized a preliminary contest, with similar rules, to better understand feasibility of the deep reinforcement learning methods for the given task. We identified that existing deep learning techniques can be efficiently applied to the locomotion tasks with neuromusculoskeletal systems. Based on this experience, for the NIPS challenge, we used TRPO and DDPG as a baseline and we included implementation of a simple agent in the materials provided to the participants.

One of the objectives of the challenge was to bring together researchers from biomechanics, neuroscience and machine learning. We believe that this can only be achieved when entering the competition and building the most basic controller is seamless and takes seconds. To this end, we wrapped the sophisticated and complex OpenSim into a basic python environment with only two commands: `reset(difficulty=0, seed=None)` and `step(activations)`. The environment is freely available on GitHub[5] and can be installed with 3 command lines on Windows, MacOS and Linux, using the Anaconda platform.[6] For more details regarding installation, refer to the Appendix.

6.3.5 Metrics

Submissions were evaluated automatically. Participants, after building the controller locally on their computers, were asked to interact with a remote environment. The objective of the challenge was to **navigate through the scene with obstacles to cover as much distance as possible in fixed time**. This objective was measured in

---

[5]https://github.com/stanfordnmbl/osim-rl

[6]https://anaconda.org/

meters from the origin on the X-axis the pelvis traveled during the simulation. To promote realistic solutions that avoid joint injury, we also introduced a penalty to the reward function for overusing ligaments.

We defined the objective function as

$$reward(T) = X(T) - \lambda \int_0^T \sqrt{L(t)}dt,$$

where $X(T)$ is the position of the pelvis at time T, $L(t)$ is the sum of squared forces generated by ligaments at time t and $\lambda = 10^{-7}$ is a scaling factor. The value of λ was set very low due to an initial mistake in the system and it turns the impact of ligament forces smaller than we initially designed. The simulation was terminated either when the time reached $T = 10s$ (equivalent to 1000 simulation steps), or when the agent fell, which was defined as when the pelvis fell below 0.65m.

In order to fairly compare the participants' controllers, the random seeds, determining muscle weakness and parameters of obstacles, were fixed for all the participants during grading.

6.4 Organizational Aspects

6.4.1 Protocol

Participants were asked to register on the crowdAI.org[7] platform and download the "Getting Started" tutorial. The guide led participants through installation and examples of training baseline models (TRPO and DDPG). After training the model, participants connected to the grader and interacted with the remote environment, using a submission script that we provided (Fig. 6.4). The remote environment iteratively sent the current observation and awaited response—the action of the participant in a given state. After that, the result was sent to the crowdAI.org platform and was listed on the leaderboard (as illustrated in Fig. 6.3). Moreover, an animation corresponding to the best submission of a given user was displayed beside the score.

By interacting with the remote environment, participants could potentially explore it and tune their algorithms for the test environment. In order to prevent this exploration and overfitting, participants were allowed to send only five solutions per day. Moreover, the final score was calculated on a separate test environment to which users can submit only 3 solutions in total.

At the beginning of the challenge we did not know, how many participants to expect, or if the difficulty would be too low or too high. This motivated us to introduce two rounds:

---

[7]http://crowdai.org/

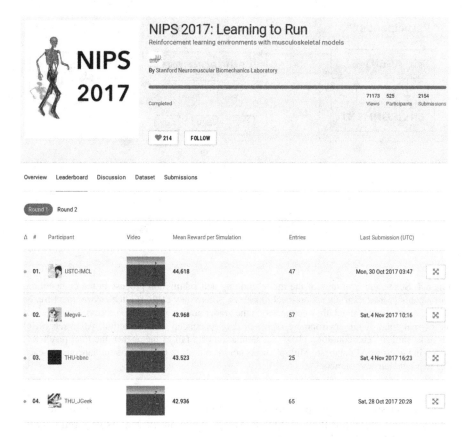

Fig. 6.3 The leaderboard from the first round (Open Stage) of the "Learning to Run" challenge on the crowdAI.org platform. We conjecture that animated simulations contributed to engagement of participants

1. The Open Stage was open for everyone and players were ranked by their result on the test environment. Every participant was allowed to submit 1 solution per day.
2. The Play-off Stage was open only for the competitors who earned at least 15 points in the Open Stage. Participants were allowed to submit only 3 solutions. Solutions were evaluated on a test environment different than the one in Open Stage.

The Play-off Stage was open for one week after the Open Stage was finished. This setting allowed us to adjust the rules of the Play-off before it starts, while learning more about the problem and dynamics of the competition in the course of the Open Stage.

We anticipated that the main source of cheating for locomotion tasks could be tracking of real or engineered data. To avoid this problem, we designed the

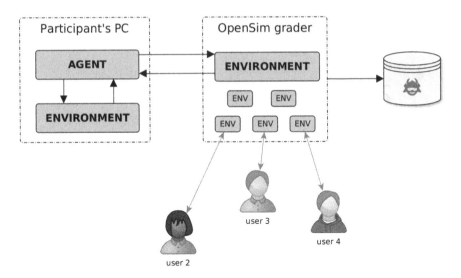

Fig. 6.4 Schematic overview of the model training and submission process in the competition. Participants trained their agents on local machines, where they could run the environment freely. Once the agent was trained, they connected to the grader and, in an iterative process, they received the current state of the environment to which they responded with an action. After successful iteration until the end condition (10 s of a simulation or a fall of the agent), the final result was stored in the crowdAI database. Multiple users could connect to the grader simultaneously—each one to a separate environment

competition such that competitors were scored on an unknown environment with obstacles, which means that a controller solely based on tracking is very unlikely to be successful.

To prevent overfitting as well as cheating, participants did not have access to the final test environment. Moreover, since participants were only interacting with a remote environment (as presented in Fig. 6.4), they were not allowed to change parameters of the environment, such as gravity or obstacles. In fact, they were constrained to send only action vectors in $v \in [0, 1]^{18}$ to the grader.

6.4.2 Execution

In the Open Stage, participants interacted with the environment through a lightweight HTTP API included in the osim-rl package. From a technical standpoint, in order to interact with a remote environment, they only needed to change the class from the local environment to HTTP API environment. The grader, on the remote host, was responsible for the life-cycle management of the environments. The cumulative rewards for each submission were added to the crowdAI leaderboard, along with visualization of the actual simulations. To judge submissions, 3 seeds for simulation environments were randomly chosen beforehand and were used to grade all submissions during this stage.

In the Play-off stage, participants packaged their agents into self-contained Docker containers. The containers would then interact with the grader using a lightweight redis API, simulating the process from the Open Stage. The grading infrastructure had a corresponding Docker image for the actual grading container. Grading a single submission involved instantiating the participant submitted Docker container, instantiating the internal grading container, mapping the relevant ports of the grading container and the submitted container, wrapping up both the containers in a separate isolated network, and then finally executing the pre-agreed grading script inside the participant submitted container.

6.4.3 Problems and Solutions

The major issues we encountered concerned the computational cost of simulations, over-fitting, and stochasticity of the results, i.e. high dependence of the random seed. Our solutions to each of these challenges are described below.

The Learning to Run environment was significantly slower than many visually similar environments such as the humanoid robot Mujoco-based simulations in OpenAI Gym.[8] This difference was due to the complex ground reaction model, muscle dynamics, and precision of simulation in OpenSim. Some of the participants modified the accuracy of OpenSim engine to trade off precision for execution speed[9]; even with these changes, the OpenSim-based Learning to Run environment continued to be expensive in terms of the actual simulation time. The computationally expensive nature of the problem required participants to find sample-efficient alternatives.

Another concern was the possibility of overfitting, since the random seed was fixed, and the number of simulations required for a fair evaluation of performance of submitted models. These issues were especially important in determining a clear winner during the Play-off stage. To address these issues, we based the design of the Play-off stage on Docker containers, as described in Sect. 6.4.2.

The design based on Docker containers has two main advantages for determining the top submissions. First, we could run an arbitrary number of simulations until we got performance scores for the top agents which were statistically significant. Given the observed variability of results in the Open Stage, we chose 10 simulations for the Play-off Stage and it proved to be sufficient for determining the winner. See Sect. 6.4.4 for details. Second, this setting prevents overfiting, since users do not have access to the test environment, while it allows us to use exactly the same environment (i.e., the same random seed) for every submission.

The main disadvantage of this design is the increased difficulty of submitting results, since it requires familiarity with the Docker ecosystem. For this reason, we

---

[8]https://github.com/stanfordnmbl/osim-rl/issues/78

[9]https://github.com/ctmakro/stanford-osrl#the-simulation-is-too-slow

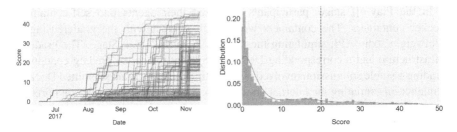

Fig. 6.5 Left: Progression of scores during the challenge. Each curve represents the maximum score of a single participant on the leaderboard at any point in time. The bold red line represents the baseline submission. Right: The final distribution of the scores for all the submitted solutions. The dotted gray line represents the score (20.083) of the baseline submission

decided to use this design only in the Play-off stage. This could potentially discourage participation. However, we conjectured that top participants who qualified to the Play-off stage will be willing to invest more time in preparing the submission, for the sake of fair and more deterministic evaluation. All top 10 participants from the Open Stage submitted their solutions to the Play-off stage.

6.4.4 Submissions

The competition was held between June 16th 2017 and November 13th 2017. It attracted 442 teams with 2154 submissions. The average number of submission was 4.37 per team, with scores ranging between -0.81 and 45.97 in both stages combined. In Fig. 6.5 we present the progression of submissions over time.

The design of the Play-off stage allowed us to vary the number of simulations used to determine the winner. However, our initial choice of 10 trials turned out to be sufficiently large to clearly determine the top places (Fig. 6.6).

From the reports of top participants (Kidziński et al. 2018; Jaśkowski et al. 2018), we observed that most of the teams (6 out of 9) used DDPG as the basis for their final algorithm while others used Proximal Policy Optimization (PPO) (Schulman et al. 2017). Similarly, in a survey we conducted after the challenge, from ten respondents (with mean scores 17.4 and standard deviation 14.1) five used DDPG, while two used PPO. This trend might be explained by the high computational cost of the environment, requiring the use of data efficient algorithms.

6.5 Results

We conducted a post-hoc analysis of the submitted controllers by running the solutions on flat ground with no muscle weakness (i.e., max_obstacles=0, difficulty=0). Only the last 5 s of each simulation were analyzed in order

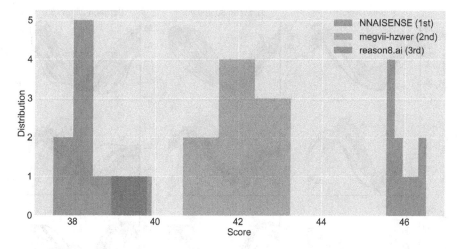

Fig. 6.6 Distribution of scores per simulation of the top 3 submitted entries in the Play-off Stage. In the final round of the challenge we ran 10 simulations in order to reduce the impact of randomness on the results. As it can be seen in the plot, the scores of top three participants were rather consistent between the simulations. This indicates that, despite stochasticity of simulations, our protocol allowed to determine the winner with high degree of confidence

to focus on the cyclic phase of running. To compare simulation results with experimental data, we segmented the simulation into individual gait cycles, which are periods of time between when a foot first strikes the ground until the same foot strikes the ground again. For each submission, all gait cycles were averaged to generate a single representative gait cycle. We compared the simulations to experimental data of individuals running at 4.00 m/s (Hamner and Delp 2013) as it is the closest speed to the highest scoring submissions.

Figure 6.7 compares the simulated hip, knee, and ankle joint angle trajectories with experimental data, separated by three bins of scores: (1) over 40, (2) between 30 and 40, and (3) between 25 and 40. These bins represent solutions with the following rankings: (1) 1st through 5th, (2) 6th through 24th, and (3) 25th through 47th. Solutions in all of the score bins show some promising trends. For example, solutions in all three score bins have joints that are extending, shown by decreasing angle values, through the first 40% of the gait cycle indicating that the models are pushing off the ground at this phase. Joint angles begin flexing, shown by increasing angle values during the last 60% of the gait cycle in order to lift the leg up and avoid tripping.

There were a few notable differences between the simulations and the running gait of humans. At the hip, simulations have a greater range of motion than experimental data as solutions both flex and extend more than is seen in human running. This could be due to the simple, planar model. At the knee, simulations had an excessively flexed knee at initial contact of the foot (i.e., 0% of the gait cycle) and had a delayed timing of peak knee flexion compared to experimental data (i.e., around 80% of the gait cycle compared to 65% of the gait cycle).

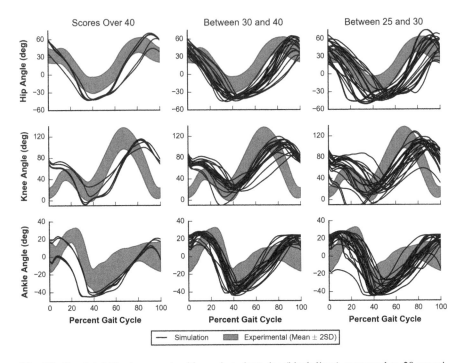

Fig. 6.7 Simulated hip, knee, and ankle angle trajectories (black lines) compared to 20 experimental subjects running at 4.00 m/s (gray regions) (Hamner and Delp 2013). Results are plotted from left to right with decreasing performance in three bins: scores over 40 (left), between 30 and 40 (middle), and between 25 and 30 (right). Positive values indicate flexion, and negative values indicate extension. 0% gait cycle indicates when the foot first strikes the ground

Future work can be done to improve the current results. Improving the fidelity of the model could yield better results. For example, allowing the hip to adduct and abduct (i.e., swing toward and away from the midline of the body) would allow the leg to clear the ground with less hip flexion and reduce the excessive hip range of motion. Testing different reward functions may also improve results, such as adding terms related to energy expenditure (Wang et al. 2012). Finally, it is likely that the best solution still has not been found, and further improvements in reinforcement learning methods would help to search the solution space more quickly, efficiently and robustly.

6.6 Discussion

The impact of the challenge ranged across multiple domains. First, we stimulated new techniques in reinforcement learning. We also advanced and popularized an important class of reinforcement learning problems with a large set of output parameters (human muscles) and comparatively small dimensionality of the input (state of a dynamic system). Algorithms developed in the complex biomechanical environment also generalize to other reinforcement learning settings with highly-dimensional decisions, such as robotics, multivariate decision making (corporate decisions, drug quantities), stock exchange, etc.

This challenge also directly impacted the biomechanics and neuroscience communities. The control models trained could be extended to and validated in, for example, a clinical setting to help predict how a patient will walk after surgery (Ackermann and Van den 2010). The controllers developed may also approximate human motor control and thus deepen our understanding of human movement. Moreover, by the analogy to Alpha Go, where reinforcement learning strategy outperforms humans (Silver et al. 2017) due to broader exploration of the solution space, in certain human movements we may potentially find strategies more efficient in terms of energy or accuracy. Reinforcement learning is also a powerful tool for identifying deficiencies and errant assumptions made when building models, and so the challenge can improve on the current state-of-the-art for computational musculoskeletal modeling.

Our environment was setup using an open-source physics engine—a potential alternative for commercial closed-source MuJoCo, which is widely used in the reinforcement learning research community. Similarly, crowdAI.org—the platform on which the challenge was hosted—is also an open-source alternative to Kaggle.[10] By leveraging the agile infrastructure of crowdAI.org and components from OpenAI reinforcement learning environments,[11] we were able to seamlessly integrate the reinforcement learning setting (which, to the date, is not available in Kaggle).

This challenge was particularly relevant to the NIPS community as it brought together experts from both neuroscience and computer science. It attracted 442 competitors with expertise in biomechanics, robotics, deep learning, reinforcement learning, computational neuroscience, or a combination. Several features of the competition ensured a large audience. Entries in the competition produced engaging (and sometimes comical) visuals of a humanoid moving through a complex environment. Further, we supplied participants with an environment that is easy to set-up and get started, without extensive knowledge of biomechanics.

Affiliations and Acknowledgments

Łukasz Kidziński, Carmichael Ong, Jennifer Hicks and Scott Delp are affiliated with Department of Bioengineering, Stanford University. Sharada Prasanna Mohanty, Sean Francis and Marcel Salath are affiliated with Ecole Polytechnique Federale de Lausanne. Sergey Levine is affiliated with University of California, Berkeley.

---

[10]https://kaggle.com/

[11]https://github.com/kidzik/osim-rl-grader

The challenge was co-organized by the Mobilize Center, a National Institutes of Health Big Data to Knowledge (BD2K) Center of Excellence supported through Grant U54EB020405. It was partially sponsored by NVIDIA, Amazon Web Services, and Toyota Research Institute.

Appendix

Installation

We believe that the simplicity of use of the simulator (independently of the skills in computer science and biomechanics) contributed significantly to the success of the challenge. The whole installation process took around 1–5 mins depending on the internet connection. To emphasize this simplicity let us illustrate the installation process. Users were asked to install Anaconda (https://www.continuum.io/downloads) and then to install our reinforcement learning environment by typing

```
conda create -n opensim-rl -c kidzik opensim git
source activate opensim-rl
pip install git+https://github.com/kidzik/osim-rl.git
```

Next, they were asked to start a python interpreter which allows interaction with the musculoskeletal model and visualization of the skeleton (Fig. 6.8) after running

```
from osim.env import GaitEnv
env = GaitEnv(visualize=True)
```

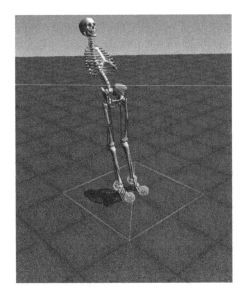

Fig. 6.8 Visualization of the environment with random muscles activations after. This simulation is immediately visible to the user after following simple installation steps as described in Appendix

```
observation = env.reset()
for i in range(500):
    observation, reward, done, info = env.step
    (env.action_space.sample())
```

References

Ackermann, M., Van den Bogert, A.J.: Optimality principles for model-based prediction of human gait. Journal of biomechanics **43**(6), 1055–1060 (2010)

Anderson, F.C., Pandy, M.G.: A dynamic optimization solution for vertical jumping in three dimensions. Computer methods in biomechanics and biomedical engineering **2**(3), 201–231 (1999)

Anderson, F.C., Pandy, M.G.: Dynamic optimization of human walking. Journal of biomechanical engineering **123**(5), 381–390 (2001)

Bellemare, M.G., Naddaf, Y., Veness, J., Bowling, M.: The arcade learning environment: An evaluation platform for general agents. Journal of Artificial Intelligence Research **47**, 253–279 (2013)

Brockman, G., Cheung, V., Pettersson, L., Schneider, J., Schulman, J., Tang, J., Zaremba, W.: Openai gym. arXiv preprint arXiv:1606.01540 (2016)

Delp, S., Loan, J., Hoy, M., Zajac, F., Topp, E., Rosen, J.: An interactive graphics-based model of the lower extremity to study orthopaedic surgical procedures. IEEE Transactions on Biomedical Engineering **37**(8), 757–767 (1990)

Delp, S.L., Anderson, F.C., Arnold, A.S., Loan, P., Habib, A., John, C.T., Guendelman, E., Thelen, D.G.: Opensim: open-source software to create and analyze dynamic simulations of movement. IEEE transactions on biomedical engineering **54**(11), 1940–1950 (2007)

Dimitrakakis, C., Li, G., Tziortziotis, N.: The reinforcement learning competition 2014. AI Magazine **35**(3), 61–65 (2014)

Dorn, T.W., Wang, J.M., Hicks, J.L., Delp, S.L.: Predictive simulation generates human adaptations during loaded and inclined walking. PloS one **10**(4), e0121,407 (2015)

Geyer, H., Herr, H.: A muscle-reflex model that encodes principles of legged mechanics produces human walking dynamics and muscle activities. IEEE Transactions on neural systems and rehabilitation engineering **18**(3), 263–273 (2010)

Hamner, S.R., Delp, S.L.: Muscle contributions to fore-aft and vertical body mass center accelerations over a range of running speeds. Journal of Biomechanics **46**(4), 780–787 (2013)

Hunt, K., Crossley, F.: Coefficient of restitution interpreted as damping in vibroimpact. Journal of Applied Mechanics **42**(2), 440–445 (1975)

Jaśkowski, W., Lykkebø, O.R., Toklu, N.E., Trifterer, F., Buk, Z., Koutník, J., Gomez, F.: Reinforcement Learning to Run. . . Fast. In: S. Escalera, M. Weimer (eds.) NIPS 2017 Competition Book. Springer, Springer (2018)

Kidziński, Ł., Mohanty, S.P., Ong, C., Huang, Z., Zhou, S., Pechenko, A., Stelmaszczyk, A., Jarosik, P., Pavlov, M., Kolesnikov, S., Plis, S., Chen, Z., Zhang, Z., Chen, J., Shi, J., Zheng, Z., Yuan, C., Lin, Z., Michalewski, H., Mio, P., Osiski, B., andrew, M., Schilling, M., Ritter, H., Carroll, S., Hicks, J., Levine, S., Salath, M., Delp, S.: Learning to run challenge solutions: Adapting reinforcement learning methods for neuromusculoskeletal environments. In: S. Escalera, M. Weimer (eds.) NIPS 2017 Competition Book. Springer, Springer (2018)

Lillicrap, T.P., Hunt, J.J., Pritzel, A., Heess, N., Erez, T., Tassa, Y., Silver, D., Wierstra, D.: Continuous control with deep reinforcement learning. arXiv preprint arXiv:1509.02971 (2015)

Ong, C.F., Geijtenbeek, T., Hicks, J.L., Delp, S.L.: Predictive simulations of human walking produce realistic cost of transport at a range of speeds. In: Proceedings of the 16th International Symposium on Computer Simulation in Biomechanics, pp. 19–20 (2017)

Schulman, J., Levine, S., Abbeel, P., Jordan, M.I., Moritz, P.: Trust region policy optimization. In: ICML, pp. 1889–1897 (2015)

Schulman, J., Wolski, F., Dhariwal, P., Radford, A., Klimov, O.: Proximal policy optimization algorithms. arXiv preprint arXiv:1707.06347 (2017)

Silver, D., Schrittwieser, J., Simonyan, K., Antonoglou, I., Huang, A., Guez, A., Hubert, T., Baker, L., Lai, M., Bolton, A., et al.: Mastering the game of go without human knowledge. Nature **550**(7676), 354 (2017)

Song, S., Geyer, H.: A neural circuitry that emphasizes spinal feedback generates diverse behaviours of human locomotion. The Journal of physiology **593**(16), 3493–3511 (2015)

Thelen, D.G.: Adjustment of muscle mechanics model parameters to simulate dynamic contractions in older adults. Journal of Biomechanical Engineering **125**(1), 70–77 (2003)

Thelen, D.G., Anderson, F.C., Delp, S.L.: Generating dynamic simulations of movement using computed muscle control. Journal of Biomechanics **36**(3), 321–328 (2003)

Todorov, E., Erez, T., Tassa, Y.: Mujoco: A physics engine for model-based control. In: Intelligent Robots and Systems (IROS), 2012 IEEE/RSJ International Conference on, pp. 5026–5033. IEEE (2012)

Wang, J.M., Hamner, S.R., Delp, S.L., Koltun, V.: Optimizing locomotion controllers using biologically-based actuators and objectives. ACM transactions on graphics **31**(4) (2012)

Chapter 7
Learning to Run Challenge Solutions: Adapting Reinforcement Learning Methods for Neuromusculoskeletal Environments

Łukasz Kidziński, Sharada Prasanna Mohanty, Carmichael F. Ong, Zhewei Huang, Shuchang Zhou, Anton Pechenko, Adam Stelmaszczyk, Piotr Jarosik, Mikhail Pavlov, Sergey Kolesnikov, Sergey Plis, Zhibo Chen, Zhizheng Zhang, Jiale Chen, Jun Shi, Zhuobin Zheng, Chun Yuan, Zhihui Lin, Henryk Michalewski, Piotr Milos, Blazej Osinski, Andrew Melnik, Malte Schilling, Helge Ritter, Sean F. Carroll, Jennifer Hicks, Sergey Levine, Marcel Salathé, and Scott Delp

Abstract In the NIPS 2017 *Learning to Run* challenge, participants were tasked with building a controller for a musculoskeletal model to make it run as fast as possible through an obstacle course. Top participants were invited to describe their algorithms. In this work, we present eight solutions that used deep reinforcement learning approaches, based on algorithms such as Deep Deterministic Policy Gradient, Proximal Policy Optimization, and Trust Region Policy Optimization.

Ł. Kidziński (✉) · C. F. Ong · J. L. Hicks · S. Delp
Department of Bioengineering, Stanford University, Stanford, CA, USA
e-mail: lukasz.kidzinski@stanford.edu; ongcf@stanford.edu; jenhicks@stanford.edu; delp@stanford.edu

S. Levine
Department of Electrical Engineering and Computer Sciences, University of California, Berkeley, CA, USA
e-mail: svlevine@eecs.berkeley.edu

S. P. Mohanty · S. F. Carroll · M. Salathé
Ecole Polytechnique Federale de Lausanne, Lausanne, Switzerland
e-mail: sharada.mohanty@epfl.ch; sean.carroll@epfl.ch; marcel.salathe@epfl.ch

Z. Huang · S. Zhou
Beijing University, Beijing, China
e-mail: huangzhewei@megvii.com; zsc@megvii.com

M. Pavlov · S. Kolesnikov · S. Plis
reason8.ai, San Francisco, CA, USA
e-mail: sergey@reason8.ai

© Springer International Publishing AG, part of Springer Nature 2018
S. Escalera, M. Weimer (eds.), *The NIPS '17 Competition: Building Intelligent Systems*, The Springer Series on Challenges in Machine Learning,
https://doi.org/10.1007/978-3-319-94042-7_7

Many solutions use similar relaxations and heuristics, such as reward shaping, frame skipping, discretization of the action space, symmetry, and policy blending. However, each of the eight teams implemented different modifications of the known algorithms.

7.1 Introduction

In the Learning to Run challenge participants were tasked to build a controller for a human musculoskeletal model, optimizing muscle activity such that the model travels as far as possible within 10 s (Kidziński et al. 2018). Participants were solving a control problem with a continuous space of 41 input and 18 output parameters with high order relations between actuations and actions, simulating human musculoskeletal system. Expensive computational cost of the musculoskeletal simulations encouraged participants to develop new techniques tailored for this control problem.

All participants whose models traveled at least 15 m in 10 s of the simulator time were invited to share their solutions in this manuscript. Nine teams agreed to contribute. The winning algorithm is published separately (Jaśkowski et al. 2018), while the remaining eight are collected in this manuscript. Each section in the reminder of this document describes an approach taken by one team. Sections are self-contained, they can be read independently, and each of them starts with

Z. Chen · Z. Zhang · J. Chen · J. Shi
Immersive Media Computing Lab, University of Science and Technology of China, Hefei, China
e-mail: chenzhibo@ustc.edu.cn; zhizheng@mail.ustc.edu.cn; chenjiale@ustc.edn.cn; cjuns@mail.ustc.edu.cn

A. Stelmaszczyk · H. Michalewski · P. Milos · B. Osinski
University of Warsaw, Warsaw, Poland
e-mail: a.stelmaszczyk@mimuw.edu.pl; H.Michalewski@mimuw.edu.pl; pmilos@mimuw.edu.pl; b.osinski@mimuw.edu.pl

Z. Zheng · C. Yuan · Z. Lin
Tunghai University, Taichung City, Taiwan
e-mail: zhengzb16@mails.tsinghua.edu.cn; yuanc@sz.tsinghua.edu.cn; lin-zh14@tsinghua.edu.cn

A. Pechenko
Yandex, Moscow, Russia

P. Jarosik
Institute of Fundamental Technological Research, Polish Academy of Sciences, Warsaw, Poland
e-mail: pjarosik@ippt.pan.pl

A. Melnik · M. Schilling · H. Ritter
CITEC, Bielefeld University, Bielefeld, Germany
e-mail: andmelnik@uni-osnabrueck.de; mschilli@techfak.uni-bielefeld.de; helge@techfak.uni-bielefeld.de

an introduction summarizing the approach. For information on compositions of teams, affiliations and acknowledgments please refer to section "Affiliations and Acknowledgments".

7.2   Learning to Run with Actor-Critic Ensemble

Zhewei Huang and Shuchang Zhou

We introduce an Actor-Critic Ensemble (ACE) method for improving the performance of Deep Deterministic Policy Gradient (DDPG) algorithm (Lillicrap et al. 2015; Silver et al. 2014). At inference time, our method uses a critic ensemble to select the best action from proposals of multiple actors running in parallel. By having a larger candidate set, our method can avoid actions that have fatal consequences, while staying deterministic. Using ACE, we have won the 2nd place in NIPS'17 Learning to Run competition.

7.2.1   Methods

7.2.1.1   Dooming Actions Problem of DDPG

We found that in the *Learning to Run* challenge environment legs of a fast running skeleton can easily be tripped up by obstacles. This caused the skeleton to enter an unstable state with limbs swinging and falling down after a few frames. We observed that it was almost impossible to recover from the unstable states. We call the action causing the skeleton to enter unstable state a "dooming action".

To investigate dooming actions, we let the critic network inspect the actions at inference time. We found that most of the time, the critic could recognize dooming actions by anticipating low scores. However, as there was only one action proposed by the actor network in DDPG at every step, the dooming actions could not be avoided. This observation led us to use an actor ensemble to allow the agent to avoid dooming actions by having a critic ensemble to pick the best action from the proposed ones, as shown in Fig. 7.1.

7.2.1.2   Inference-Time ACE

We first trained multiple actor-critic pairs separately, using the standard DDPG method. Then we built a new agent with many actor networks proposing actions at every step. Given multiple actions, a critic network was used to select the best action. The actor picked the action with the highest score in a greedy manner.

Empirically, we found that actors of heterogeneous nature, e.g. trained with different hyper-parameters, perform better than actors from different epochs of the

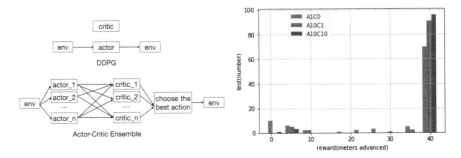

Fig. 7.1 Schema for DDPG and ACE (left), rewards for different combinations (right)

same training setting. This was in agreement with the observations in the original work on Ensemble Learning (Dietterich 2000).

To further improve critic's prediction quality, we built an ensemble of critics, by picking the pairing critics of actors. We combined the outputs of the critic networks by averaging them.

7.2.1.3 Training with ACE

If we put actor networks together to train, all the actor networks are updated at every step, even if a certain action was not used. The modified Bellman equation takes form

$$i_{t+1} = \arg \max_{j} Q(s_{t+1}, \mu_j(s_{t+1}))$$

$$Q(s_t, a_t) = r(s_t, a_t) + \gamma Q(s_{t+1}, \mu_{i_{t+1}}(s_{t+1})).$$

7.2.2 Experiments and Results

7.2.2.1 Baseline Implementation

We used the DDPG as our baseline. To describe the state of the agent, we collected three consecutive frames of observations from the environment. We performed feature engineering as proposed by Yongliang Qin,[1] enriching the observation before we feeding into the network.

As the agent was expected to run 1000 steps to finish a successful episode, we found the vanishing gradient problem (i.e. too small magnitude of the update step

---

[1] https://github.com/ctmakro/stanford-osrl

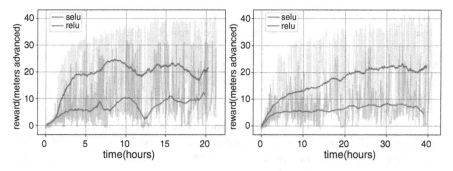

Fig. 7.2 Training with different activation functions and different number of processes for generating training data, by DDPG

Table 7.1 Hyper-parameters used in the experiments

Actor network architecture	$[FC800, FC400]$, Tanh for output layer and SELU for other layers
Critic network architecture	$[FC800, FC400]$, linear for output layer and SELU for other layers
Actor learning rate	3e−4
Critic learning rate	3e−4
Batch size	128
γ	0.96
replay buffer size	2e6

in the learning process) to be critical. We made several attempts to deal with this difficulty. First, we found that with the original simulation timestep, the DDPG converges slowly. In contrast, using four times larger simulation timestep, which was equivalent to changing the action only every four frames, was found to speedup convergence significantly.

We also tried unrolling DDPG as in $TD(\lambda)$ with $\lambda = 4$ (Anonymous 2018), but found it inferior to simply increasing simulation timestep. Second, we tried several activation functions and found that the activation function of Scaled Exponential Linear Units(SELU) (Klambauer et al. 2017) is superior to ReLU, as shown in Fig. 7.2. SELU also outperformed Leaky ReLU, Tanh and Sigmoid.

7.2.2.2 ACE Experiments

For all models we used an identical architecture of actor and critic networks, with hyper-parameters listed in Table 7.1. Our code used for competition can be found online.[2]

We built the ensemble by drawing models trained with settings of the last section. Figure 7.1b gives the distribution of rewards when using ACE, where AXCY stands

---

Table 7.2 Performance of ACE

Experiment	# Test	# Actor	# Critic	Average reward	Max reward	# Fall off
A1C0	100	1	0	32.0789	41.4203	25
A10C1	100	10	1	37.7578	41.4445	7
A10C10	100	10	10	39.2579	41.9507	4

for X number of actors and Y number of critics. It can be seen that A10C10 (having 10 critics and 10 actors) has a much smaller chance of falling (rewards below 30) compared to A1C0, which is equivalent to DDPG. The maximum rewards also get improved, as shown in Table 7.2.

Training with ACE was found to have similar performance as Inference-Time ACE.

7.2.3   Discussion

We propose Actor-Critic Ensemble, a deterministic method that avoids dooming actions at inference time by asking an ensemble of critics to pick actions proposed by an ensemble of actors. Our experiments found that ACE can significantly improve performance of DDPG, by reducing of the number of falls and increasing the speed of running skeletons.

7.3   Deep Deterministic Policy Gradient and Improvements

Mikhail Pavlov, Sergey Kolesnikov, and Sergey Plis

We benchmarked state of the art policy-gradient methods and found that Deep Deterministic Policy Gradient (DDPG) method is the most efficient method for this environment. We also applied several improvements to DDPG method, such as layer normalization, parameter noise, action and state reflecting. All this improvements helped to stabilize training and improve its sample-efficiency.

7.3.1   Methods

7.3.1.1   DDPG Improvements

We used standard reinforcement learning techniques: action repeat (the agent selects action every 5th state and selected action is repeated on skipped steps) and reward scaling. After several attempts, we choose a scale factor of 10 (i.e. multiply reward by ten) for remaining experiments. For exploration we used Ornstein-Uhlenbeck (OU) process (Uhlenbeck and Ornstein 1930) to generate temporally correlated noise, considered efficient in exploration of physical environments. Our DDPG implementation was parallelized as follows: n processes collected samples with fixed weights all of which were processed by the learning process at the end of an episode, which updated their weights. Since DDPG is an off-policy method, the stale weights of the samples only improved the performance providing each sampling process with its own weights and thus improving exploration.

7.3.1.2 Parameter Noise

Another improvement is the recently proposed parameters noise (Plappert et al. 2017) that perturbs network weights encouraging state dependent exploration. We used parameter noise only for the actor network. Standard deviation σ for the Gaussian noise was chosen according to the original work (Plappert et al. 2017) so that measure where $\tilde{\pi}$ is the policy with noise, equals to σ in OU. For each training episode we switched between the action noise and the parameter noise choosing them with 0.7 and 0.3 probability respectively.

7.3.1.3 Layer Norm

Henderson et al. showed that layer normalization (Ba et al. 2016) stabilizes the learning process in a wide range of reward scaling. We have investigated this claim in our settings. Additionally, layer normalization allowed us to use same perturbation scale across all layers despite the use of parameters noise (Plappert et al. 2017). We normalized the output of each layer except the last for critic and actor by standardizing the activations of each sample. We applied layer normalization before the nonlinearity.

7.3.1.4 Actions and States Reflection Symmetry

The musculoskeletal model to control in the challenge has bilateral body symmetry. State components and actions can be reflected to increase sample size by factor of 2. We sampled transitions from replay memory, reflected states and actions and used original states and actions as well as reflected as batch in training step. This procedure improves stability of learned policy. When we did not use this technique our model learned suboptimal policies, when for example muscles for only one leg are active and other leg just follows the first leg.

Table 7.3 Hyperparameters used in the experiments

Parameters	Value
Actor network architecture	[64, 64], elu activation
Critic network architecture	[64, 32], tanh activation
Actor learning rate	Linear decay from 1e−3 to 5e−5 in 10e6 steps with Adam optimizer
Critic learning rate	Linear decay from 2e−3 to 5e−5 in 10e6 steps with Adam optimizer
Batch size	200
γ	0.9
Replay buffer size	5e6
Rewards scaling	10
Parameter noise probability	0.3
OU exploration parameters	$\theta = 0.1$, $\mu = 0$, $\sigma = 0.2$, $\sigma_{min} = 0.05$, $dt = 1e-2$, n_{steps} annealing σ_{decay} 1e6 per thread

7.3.2 Experiments and Results

For all experiments we used environment with 3 obstacles and random strengths of the psoas muscles. We tested models on setups running 8 and 20 threads. For comparing different PPO, TRPO and DDPG settings we used 20 threads per model configuration. We have compared various combinations of improvements of DDPG in two identical settings that only differed in the number of threads used per configuration: 8 and 20. The goal was to determine whether the model rankings are consistent when the number of threads changes. For n threads (where n is either 8 or 20) we used $n - 2$ threads for sampling transitions, 1 thread for training, and 1 thread for testing. For all models we used identical architecture of actor and critic networks. All hyperparameters are listed in Table 7.3. Our code used for competition and described experiments can be found in a github repo.[3] Experimental evaluation is based on the non-discounted return.

7.3.2.1 Benchmarking Different Models

Comparison of our winning model with the baseline approaches is presented in Fig. 7.3. Among all methods the DDPG significantly outperformed PPO and TRPO. The environment is time expensive and method should utilized experience as effectively as possible. DDPG due to experience replay (re)uses each sample from environment many times making it the most effective method for this environment.

---

[3]Theano: https://github.com/fgvbrt/nips_rl and PyTorch: https://github.com/Scitator/Run-Skeleton-Run

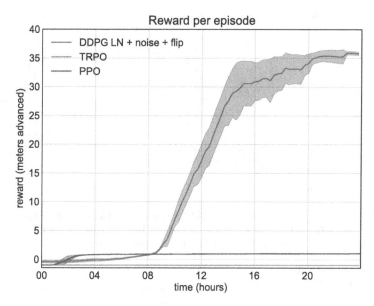

Fig. 7.3 Comparing test reward of the baseline models and the best performing model that we have used in the "Learning to run" competition

7.3.2.2 Testing Improvements of DDPG

To evaluate each component we used an ablation study as it was done in the rainbow article (Hessel et al. 2017). In each ablation, we removed one component from the full combination. Results of experiments are presented in Fig. 7.4a, b for 8 and 20 threads respectively. The figures demonstrate that each modification leads to a statistically significant performance increase. The model containing all modifications scores the highest reward. Note, the substantially lower reward in the case, when parameter noise was employed without the layer norm. One of the reasons is our use of the same perturbation scale across all layers, which does not work that well without normalization. Also note, the behavior is quite stable across number of threads, as well as the model ranking. As expected, increasing the number of threads improves the result.

Maximal rewards achieved in the given time for 8 and 20 threads cases for each of the combinations of the modifications is summarized in Table 7.4. The main things to observe is a substantial improvement effect of the number of threads, and stability in the best and worst model rankings, although the models in the middle are ready to trade places.

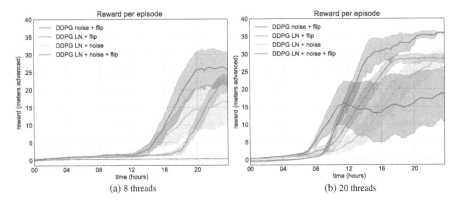

Fig. 7.4 Comparing test reward for various modifications of the DDPG algorithm with 8 threads per configuration (**a**) and 20 threads per configuration (**b**). Although the number of threads significantly affects performance, the model ranking approximately stays the same

Table 7.4 Best achieved reward for each DDPG modification

Agent		
Threads	8	20
DDPG + noise + flip	0.39	23.58
DDPG + LN + flip	25.29	31.91
DDPG + LN + noise	25.57	30.90
DDPG + LN + noise + flip	**31.25**	**38.46**

7.3.3 Discussion

Our results in OpenSim experiments indicate that in a computationally expensive stochastic environments that have high-dimensional continuous action space the best performing method is off-policy DDPG. We have tested 3 modifications to DDPG and each turned out to be important for learning. Action states reflection doubles the size of the training data and improves stability of learning and encourages the agent to learn to use left and right muscles equally well. With this approach the agent truly learns to run. Examples of the learned policies with and without the reflection are present at this URL https://tinyurl.com/ycvfq8cv. Parameter and Layer noise additionally improves stability of learning due to introduction of state dependent exploration.

7.4 Asynchronous DDPG with Deep Residual Network for Learning to Run

Zhibo Chen, Zhizheng Zhang, Jiale Chen, and Jun Shi

For improving the training effectiveness of DDPG on this physics-based simulation environment which has high computational complexity, we designed a parallel architecture with deep residual network for the asynchronous training of DDPG. In this work, we describe our approach and we introduce supporting implementation details.

7.4.1 Methods

7.4.1.1 Asynchronous DDPG

In our framework, the agent could collect interactive experiences and update its network parameters asynchronously. For the collection of experiences, the *Learning to Run* environments with different seeds and same difficulty-level settings were wrapped by multi-process programming. All step-by-step interactive experiences in every wrapped environment would be stored in a specific storage until this episode finished. Then we decided which step experiences to put into the experience replay memory according to their corresponding step rewards and episode rewards. In terms of the updating of networks' parameters, the updating process would sample a batch from the replay memory after each interaction with the RL environments no matter which specific environment process this interaction takes place in.

7.4.1.2 The Neural Network Structure

Whether for the human body in real-world or the musculoskeletal model used in this simulation, the accurate physical motions are determined by multiple joints and implemented by the excitations of multiple different muscles. Taking it naturally, we applied 1D convolution modules in the neural networks for both actor and critic networks with the expectation of capturing the correlation among 41 values of the observation. And our experimental results indicated that 1D convolution neural networks were better able to prevent converging to the local optimal solution than fully connected networks. In order to improve the efficiency and stability of training, we added the residual blocks (see Fig. 7.5) to make our model easier to train and converge.

We also tried to take advantage of 2D convolution to process the 1D observation information and learn the features from historical actions, inspired by the work on 3D convolution neural network for human action recognition (Ji et al. 2013). However, the performance of the RL agent with 2D convolution was less likely to converge steadily.

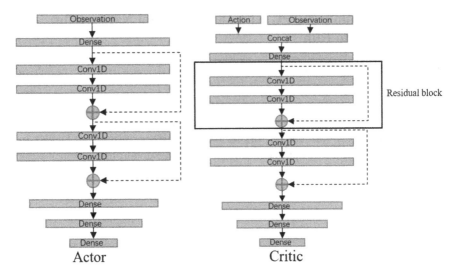

Fig. 7.5 The diagram of our network structure with residual blocks

7.4.1.3 Noise for Exploration

We tried both parameter space noise (Plappert et al. 2017) and action space noise for the exploration in this task. For parameter space noise, it was really hard to fine-tuning and get an optimal solution in *Learning to Run* environment, which might be caused by the structure of our neural network. In terms of action space noise, we found that Ornstein-Uhlenbeck noise would lead to inefficient exploration and convergence to local optimal solution. Instead, correlated Gaussian noise was more suitable in this task. Additionally, considering there should be the continuity among actions as the outputs of the actor, we designed a so-called random walk Gaussian noise for this continuous task, which brought us the highest grade but with a little large variance. Hence, we thought that normal correlated Gaussian noise and the random walk Gaussian noise were both effective for exploration in this environment, but each had its advantages and disadvantages.

7.4.1.4 Detailed Implementation

We would like to discuss the stability in this section, which included the stability of training and the stability of the policy for obstacles crossing. For the stability of training, we applied some common techniques in our model, such as layer normalization, reward scaling, prioritized experience replay (Schaul et al. 2015) and action repetition. Additionally, we applied a training trick with a small learning rate, named "trot". In detail, we sampled one batch and used it to implement back-propagation for multiple times with a small learning rate. For the stability of the policy for obstacles crossing, a ceil option for the radius of the obstacle turned out to be significant to improve the agent's performance. The obstacles for the agent would be slightly larger than their real sizes and the mathematic space to be fitted by neural network will be also reduced by this method. Hence, we could make it easier for the learning by neural network and improve the stability of obstacles crossing meanwhile.

7.4.2 Experiments and Results

7.4.2.1 The Number of Parallel Process

Based on the experimental verification, we found the number of environment process would have a large impact on the learning performance of the agent. We tested our model with setting 12, 24, and 64 processes. The experimental results indicated that the more processes we used, the more samples we could get but not inevitably the better for the learning performance. In our settings, the model with 24 environment process would get the highest grade. Excessive number of the parallel environment processes could cause that too much similar transitions were pushed into the experience replay memory, which adversely affected the training of agent.

7.4.2.2 The Neural Network Structure

The neural network structure seriously affects the learning ability of the agent. According to our training results (see Fig. 7.6), the 1D convolution neural network with residual blocks was the best fit for both actor and critic in DDPG whether for the maximum learning ability or the stability. Moreover, the 1D convolution neural network without residual blocks was also better than the fully connection network. Moreover, widening the network was more effective than deepening the network in this task, because it was easier to get the gradient in a suitable range for wide networks to implement policy updating.

7.4.3 Discussion

In this section, we discuss the difference between the first and the second round of the competition. Due to the setting of that the current episode will be finished if you fall down, the requirements on stability of obstacles crossing were significantly higher than it in the first round. More precisely, the obstacles only appeared in the beginning of the journey, it was easier for an agent to cross the obstacles in the set time, because the agent had not accelerated yet to a great speed. In the second round, the agent should cross the obstacles when it runs with a high speed, which made it easy to fall down. As our previous description, a ceiling constraint for the radius of obstacles could solve this problem effectively to some extent.

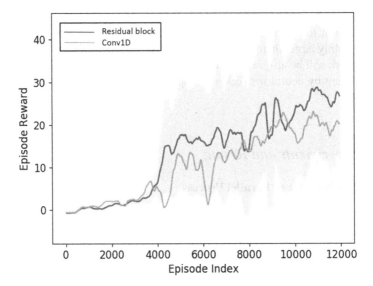

Fig. 7.6 The results of the comparison of network structure with and without residual module

Interestingly, our agent discovered a really smart trick by itself in the training process. Instead of avoiding the obstacles, it would try to deliberately step on a large obstacle and then used it as a stepping stone. Although it didn't master this trick due to the limitation of training time, we were really surprised by this exploitation of the environment.

7.5 Proximal Policy Optimization with Policy Blending

Henryk Michalewski, Piotr Miłoś, and Błażej Osiński

Our solution was based on the distributed Proximal Policy Optimization algorithm combined with a few efficiency-improving techniques. We used the *frameskip* to increase exploration. We changed rewards to encourage the agent to *bend its knees*, which significantly stabilized the gait and accelerated the training. In the final stage, we found it beneficial to transfer skills from small networks (easier to train) to bigger ones (with more expressive power). For this purpose we developed *policy blending*, a general cloning/transferring technique.

7.5.1   Methods

7.5.1.1   Combining Cautious and Aggressive Strategies

In the first stage of the competition our most successful submission was a combination of 2 agents. The first agent was cautious and rather slow. It was designed to steadily jump over the three obstacles (approx. first 200 steps of an episode). For the remaining 800 steps we switched to a 20%-faster agent, trained beforehand in an environment without obstacles.

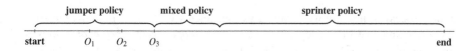

The switching of policies was a rather delicate task. Our attempts to immediately change from the first policy left the agent in a state unknown to the second one and caused the agent to fall. Eventually, we switched the policies gradually by applying the linear combination $(1 - \frac{k}{n})a_\eta + \frac{k}{n}a_v$, where k is the transition step, a_η, a_v are actions of the jumper and sprinter respectively; $n = 150$ was required to smooth the transition. A more refined version of this experiment should include learning of a macro policy which would decide on its own how the jumper and sprinter should be combined (see Sutton et al. 1999; Wiering and Schmidhuber 1997 for a broader introduction to hierarchical learning).

7.5.1.2 Frameskip

Our initial experiments led to suboptimal behaviors, such as kangaroo-like jumping (two legs moving together). We conjectured that the reason was a poor exploration and thus applied frameskip. In this way we obtained our first truly bipedal walkers. In particular, frameskip set to 4 led to a slow but steadily walking agent capable of scoring approximately 20 points.

7.5.1.3 Reward Shaping

In the process of training we obtained various agents walking or running, but still never bending one of the legs. We decided to *shape agent's behavior* (Dorigo and Colombetti 1997) through adding of an extra reward for bending of knees. More specifically, we added a reward for getting the angle α (Fig. 7.7) into a prescribed interval, see the figure on the left. This adjustment resulted in significant improvements in the walking style. Moreover, training with the knee reward caused our policy to train significantly faster, see Fig. 7.8. We experimented with various other rewards. Perhaps the most interesting was explicit penalization of falling over. As a consequence we created an ultra-cautious agent, who always concluded the whole episode but at the cost of a big drop of the average speed.

7.5.1.4 Final Tuning: Policy Blending

We found it easier to train a reasonable bipedal walking policy π when using small nets. However, small nets suffered from unsatisfactory final performance in environment with many obstacles. We used pretrained π and a method we called *policy blending* to softly guide the learning process. Namely, we kept π fixed and trained new η; the agent was issuing actions $\alpha a_\pi + (1 - \alpha)a_\eta$, $\alpha \in (0, 1)$. One can see blending as a simplified version of progressive networks considered in Rusu et al. (2016).

Even with $\alpha \approx 0.1$ the walking style of π was coarsely preserved, while the input from bigger net of η led to significant improvements in harder environments. In some cases blended policies could successfully deal with obstacles even though π was trained in an obstacle-free environment. In some experiments after an initial period of training with $\alpha > 0$, we continued with $\alpha = 0$, which can be seen as knowledge transfer from π to η. In our experience, such knowledge transfer worked better than direct behavioral cloning.

To test cloning we followed a procedure of Bratko et al. (1995), first copying the original policy to a new neural net through supervised learning followed by further training of the new policy on its own. However, in our experiments policies obtained through cloning showed at best the same performance as the original policies. Conversely, as can be seen in Fig. 7.9 transferring a policy from obstacle-free environment using policy blending performed better than simple retraining.

Fig. 7.7 Blending of π and η

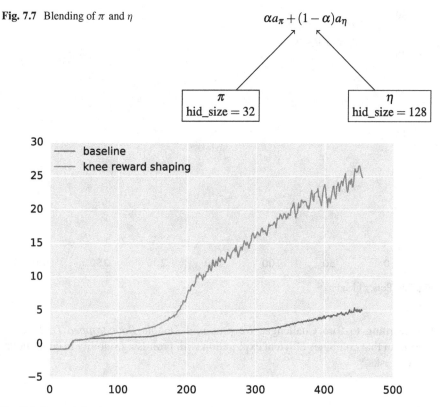

Fig. 7.8 Reward shaping

7.5.2 Experiments and Results

Overall, we performed approximately 5000 experiments of lengths up to 72 h. We used the PPO optimization algorithm (Schulman et al. 2017). In Fig. 7.8 we present how the knee reward helps in the training. Figure 7.9 we compare retraining with blending of policies.

7.6 Double Bootstrapped DDPG for Continuous Deep Reinforcement Learning

Zhuobin Zheng, Chun Yuan, and Zhihui Lin

Deep Deterministic Policy Gradient (DDPG) provides substantial gains in sample efficiency on off-policy experience data over on-policy methods. However, vanilla DDPG may explore inefficiently and be easily trapped into local optima in

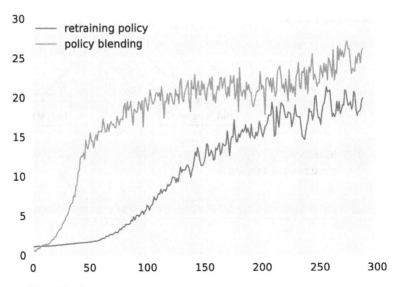

Fig. 7.9 Policy blending

the Learning to Run Challenge. We proposed *Double Bootstrapped DDPG*, an algorithm that combines efficient exploration with promising stability in continuous control tasks.

7.6.1 Methods

7.6.1.1 Double Bootstrapped DDPG

Inspired by Bootstrapped DQN (Osband et al. 2016), Double Bootstrapped DDPG, abbreviated with DB-DDPG, extends the actor-critic architecture to completely bootstrapped networks (see Fig. 7.10 for an overview of the approach). Both actor and critic networks have a shared body for feature extraction, followed by multiple heads with different random initialization.

A simple warm-up is applied before training: the actor heads are randomly selected to interact with the environment and pre-train during every episode, together with their paired critic heads as vanilla DDPGs.

During one single training episode, the k_{th} pair of actor and critic heads are randomly activated to learn. Given a state s_t, multiple actor heads output candidate actions $a_t = (a^1, a^2, \ldots, a^K)_t$, which are concatenated to the critic network. Multiple critic heads output an E-Q value matrix($\mathbb{R}^{K \times K}$) for the actions a_t according to the state s_t. The final ensemble action with highest Q-value sum which is determined by the E-Q value matrix as Eq. (7.1),

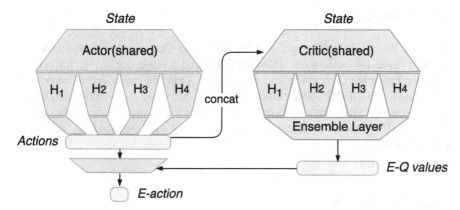

Fig. 7.10 Structure of Double Bootstrapped DDPG. When the actor(green) receives a state, each head outputs an action vector($\mathbb{R}^{18}$). Given the same state, the critic(blue) concatenates these actions($\mathbb{R}^{K \times 18}$) in the hidden layer and outputs an *Ensemble-Q* value matrix($\mathbb{R}^{K \times K}$) by K heads. The actor chooses the final *Ensemble*-action determined by the *Ensemble-Q* values

$$a_t = \arg\max_{a} \{ \sum_{i=1}^{K} Q_i(s_t, a)|_{a=\mu_k(s_t)} \}_{k=1}^{K}, \tag{7.1}$$

is chosen to execute for the state receiving a new state s_{t+1} and a reward r_t.

Moreover, a random mask $m_t = (m^1, m^2, \ldots, m^K)_t$ is generated with Bernoulli distribution simultaneously. A new transition $(s_t, a_t, r_t, s_{t+1}, m_t)$ is stored in experience memory. The selected k_{th} heads together with respective shared bodies and target networks are trained as a DDPG given a minibatch of samples. The i_{th} experience with mask $m_i^k = 0$ is ignored when training for bootstrapping (Osband et al. 2016). A more detailed procedure can be found in Algorithm 1.

Besides, we also used common reinforcement learning techniques, such as: frame skipping (Mnih et al. 2013) (the agent performs the same action every k consecutive observations. we set $k = 4$), prioritized experience replay (Schaul et al. 2015) and a reward trick (Heess et al. 2017) which utilizes velocity instead of distance as reward encouraging the agent to make more forward process along the track.

7.6.1.2 Observation Preprocessing

Since the original observation vector given by the environment does not satisfy the Markov property, we extended the observation by calculating more velocities and acceleration of the remaining body parts. During the experiments, we found that obstacles may be extremely close to each other. In this case, when an agent overstepped the first obstacle with one single leg, a new observation about the next obstacle was immediately updated. As a result, it probably fell down since another leg hit the previously invisible obstacle. To solve this problem, information about the previous obstacle was appended to the observation vector.

7.6.1.3 Noise Schedule

Ornstein-Uhlenbeck (OU) process (Uhlenbeck and Ornstein 1930) was used to generate noise for exploration. DB-DDPG utilized a noise decay rate for action noise for balancing exploration and exploitation. Once the noise decreased below a threshold, DB-DDPG acted without noise injection and focused on exploiting the environment. Exploration noise recovered when the uncertainty of the agent decreased. This process could be switched iteratively and fine-tuned manually for stability until convergence.

7.6.2 Experiments

7.6.2.1 Details

We used Adam (Kingma and Ba 2014) for learning the parameters with a learning rate of $1e^{-4}$ and $3e^{-4}$ for the actor and the critic network respectively. For the Q networks we set a discount factor of $\gamma = 0.99$ and $\tau = 1e^{-3}$ for soft target updates. All hidden layers utilized exponential linear units(ELU) (Clevert et al. 2015) while the output layer of the actor utilized a $tanh$ layer to bound the actions followed by scale and shift operations. The shared network of the actor had two hidden layers with 128 and 64 units respectively. This was followed by multiple heads with 64 and 32 units. The critic had similar architecture except actions which were concatenated in the second hidden layer.

7.6.2.2 Results

We evaluated the algorithm on a single machine. Results in Fig. 7.11 showed that multi-head architecture brought significant performance increase. These models with different multiple heads were pre-trained using previous experience memory in the warm-up phase before training. The single-head model could be regarded as vanilla DDPG. These agents were trained using the same techniques and hyperparameters mentioned above following Algorithm 1. The figure showed that DB-DDPGs outperformed vanilla DDPG on performance ensuring faster training and stability. The model with 10-head scored the highest cumulative reward by more efficient exploration and ensemble training.

7.6.3 Discussion

We proposed the *Double Bootstrapped DDPG* algorithm for high-dimensional continuous control tasks. It was demonstrated that DB-DDPG with multiple heads

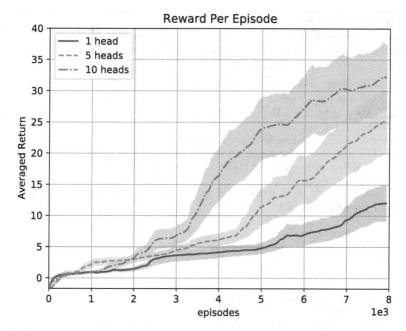

Fig. 7.11 Episode reward comparison among three modifications of DB-DDPG with different number of bootstrapped heads. Single-head model could be regarded as vanilla DDPG. Multi-head models scored higher rewards than single-head model

led to significantly faster learning than vanilla DDPG while retaining stability in the Learning to Run challenge.

Going forward, DB-DDPG can be not only efficient on a single machine, but parallelizable up to more machines boosting the learning. Furthermore, we believe this architecture is also available for dealing with multi-task reinforcement learning problems, which means each head only concentrates on its own sub-task when training then makes its own professional decision for ensemble collaboratively.

7.7 Plain DDPG with Soft Target Networks

Anton Pechenko

We used DDPG with soft target networks and Ornstein-Uhlenbeck process. Discount factor was 0.99, replay buffer was 1,000,000, batch size was 64. For training we used 7 simulators which was run in parallel.

Algorithm 1 Double Bootstrapped DDPG

Input: head number K, mini-batch size N, maximum training episode E

Initialize: Randomly initialize critic network $Q(s, a|\theta^Q)$ with K outputs $\{Q_k\}_{k=1}^K$, and actor network $\mu(s|\theta^\mu)$ with K outputs $\{\mu_k\}_{k=1}^K$.

Initialize critic target networks $\theta_1^{Q'}, \ldots, \theta_K^{Q'}$ with weights $\theta_k^{Q'} \leftarrow \theta_k^Q$ and actor target networks $\theta_1^{\mu'}, \ldots, \theta_K^{\mu'}$ with weights $\theta_k^{\mu'} \leftarrow \theta_k^\mu$

Initialize replay buffer R, masking distribution M

for episode $e = 1, E$ **do**

    Initialize a random process $\mathcal{N}$ for action exploration

    Receive initial observation state s_0

    Pick a pair of activated critic and actor networks using $k \sim Uniform\{1, \ldots, K\}$

    for step $t = 1, T$ **do**

        Select action a_t from actions $\{a|a^k = \mu(s_t|\theta_k^\mu)\}_{k=1}^K$ according to the policies and exploration noise as following,

$$a_t = \arg\max_a \{\sum_{i=1}^K Q_i(s_t, a)|_{a=\mu_k(s_t)}\}_{k=1}^K + \mathcal{N}_t$$

        Execute action a_t then observe reward r_t and new state s_{t+1}

        Sample bootstrapped mask $m_t \sim M$

        Store transition $(s_t, a_t, r_t, s_{t+1}, m_t)$ in R

        Sample a random minibatch of m transitions $(s_i, a_i, r_i, s_{i+1}, m_i)$

        Set $y_i = r_i + \gamma Q'(s_{i+1}, \mu'(s_{i+1}|\theta_k^{\mu'})|\theta_k^{Q'})$

        Update critic network by minimizing the loss: $L = \frac{1}{N}\sum_i m_i^k (y_i - Q(s_i, a_i|\theta_k^Q))^2$

        Update actor network using the sampled policy gradient:

$$\nabla_{\theta_k^\mu} \approx \frac{1}{N}\sum_i \nabla_a Q(s, a|\theta_k^Q)|_{s=s_i, a=\mu(s_i)} \nabla_{\theta_k^\mu} \mu(s|\theta_k^\mu)|_{s=s_i}$$

        Update the target networks:

$$\theta_k^{Q'} \leftarrow \tau \theta_k^Q + (1 - \tau)\theta_k^{Q'}$$

$$\theta_k^{\mu'} \leftarrow \tau \theta_k^\mu + (1 - \tau)\theta_k^{\mu'}$$

    end for

end for

7.7.1 Method

7.7.1.1 State Description

To remove redundancy from the state space and make training more efficient it is often reasonable to exploit state space symmetry. That is why we used *first person view* transformation of the observation vector. That means we subtracted coordinates and angle of pelvis from others bones coordinates and angles. Also we assigned zero to X coordinate of the pelvis to collapse observation space along X coordinate to make run performance independent of X coordinate. We had no information about ground reaction forces in observation vector. Since it seemed very important for running it was needed to estimate it. To that end, we constructed a state vector from a sequence of the three last observation vectors.

7.7.1.2 Training Process

We used two separated multilayer perceptrons (Rumelhart et al. 1986) for actor and critic with 5 hidden layers, 512 neurons each. In three out of seven agents we random 20–40 actions at start and then started collecting (S, A, R, S') experience items, i.e. a previous state state, an action, a reward and a result state. This increases variety of starting points and increases quality of replay buffer experience. For 30% of simulations we turned off obstacles in order to increase the variety of replay buffer. Training consisted of two steps. The first step was optimization with Adam (Kingma and Ba 2014) with $1e - 4$ learning rate till agents increase its score at maximum, which, in our case, turned out to be approximately 37 m. In the second step, we trained the network with the stochastic gradient descent (SGD) using the learning rate of $5e - 5$. During the SGD step agents decreased running velocity but increase robustness to falls and obstacles overcoming resulting in 26 m score.

7.7.2 Experiments and Results

The implementation of this solution can be found as a part of the RL-Server software available at github.[4] The RL-Server is a python application using Tensorflow (Abadi et al. 2015), with DQN (Mnih et al. 2013) and DDPG algorithms included. The entire training process, including replay buffer, training and inference steps is performed within the RL-Server application. A lightweight client code can be included in parallel running environments. It enables multiple languages thanks to an open communication protocol.

7.8 PPO with Reward Shaping

Adam Stelmaszczyk and Piotr Jarosik

We trained our final model with PPO on 80 cores in 5 days using reward shaping, extended and normalized observation vector. We recompiled OpenSim with lower accuracy to have about $3\times$ faster simulations.

---

[4] https://github.com/parilo/rl-server

7.8.1 Methods

Our general approach consisted of two phases: exploration of popular algorithms and exploitation of the most promising one. In the first phase we tried 3 algorithms (in the order we tried them): Deep Deterministic Policy Gradient (DDPG) (keras-rl implementation (Plappert 2016)), Proximal Policy Optimization (PPO) Schulman et al. (2017) (OpenAI baselines implementation (Dhariwal et al. 2017)), Evolution Strategies (ES) (Salimans et al. 2017) (OpenAI implementation (Salimans et al. 2017)). We also tried 3 improvements: changing the reward function during training (reward shaping), improving observations (feature engineering) and normalizing observations.

We started our experiments with DDPG (without improvements) and we could not achieve good results. That was probably because of the bad normalization or not enough episodes. We had problems parallelizing keras-rl and we were using only one process. Therefore, we switched to PPO and ES, for which learning plots and parallelization looked better. We were incrementally adding improvements to these two techniques. In the end we used the default hyperparameters for all the algorithms, their values can be found in the full source code (Stelmaszczyk and Jarosik 2017).

7.8.1.1 Reward Shaping

We guided learning to promising areas by shaping the reward function. We employed: a penalty for straight legs, a penalty for `pelvis.x` greater than `head.x` (causing a skeleton to lean forward), adding 0.01 reward for every time step (to help take the first step and get out of local maximum) and using velocity instead of distance passed, found in Heess et al. (2017). Using velocity rewards passing the same distance in less time steps.

7.8.1.2 Feature Engineering

We changed all `x` positions from absolute to relative to `pelvis.x`. Thanks to that similar poses were represented by similar observations. We also extended the observation vector from 41 values to 82 by adding: the remaining velocities and accelerations of the body parts, ground touch indicator for toes and talus, a queue of two obstacles: the next one (preserved from the original observation) and the previous one. Without this, when passing over an obstacle, agent would lose sight of the obstacle underneath it as it would immediately switch to the next one.

7.8.1.3   Normalizing Observations

We logged the mean and standard deviation of all the observations to see if the normalization was done correctly. By default, baselines PPO implementation used a filter which automatically normalized every observation. For every observation, it was keeping its running mean and standard deviation. It did normalization by subtracting the mean and dividing by std. This worked well for most of the observations, however for some it was problematic. For constants, e.g. the strength of psoas, the standard deviation would be 0. The code in that case was just passing this observation as it is. The magnitude of an observation was treated as an importance when passed to a network. Too big values would saturate all the other smaller inputs (which may be more important). Also, the first strength of psoas had a different value than the following ones (due to a bug in the challenge environment, later fixed). So, the filter would calculate some arbitrary mean with standard deviation and later use them. Another problem was that some observations were most of the time were close to 0, but were shooting up in some moments to greater values, e.g. velocity. This resulted in huge values (because initial standard deviation was close to 0), saturating the network.

Because all of these problems, we skipped the auto normalizing and manually normalized every observation. Iteratively, we were running our model and visualizing mean with standard deviation for all the observations. Then we were correcting the normalization of observations which mean was far from 0 or standard deviation far from 1.

7.8.2   Experiments and Results

We found that OpenSim simulator was the bottleneck, accounting for about 99% of the CPU time. To speed it up about 3×, we changed the simulator's accuracy from default 0.1% to 3%, following https://github.com/ctmakro/stanford-osrl#the-simulation-is-too-slow. Any change made in our environment could have introduced a bias when grading on the server, however we didn't notice any significant score changes.

We conducted our experiments on: *Chuck*, an instance with 80 CPU cores (Intel Xeon), provided by Faculty of Mathematics, Informatics, and Mechanics, University of Warsaw. *Devbox*, an instance with 16 CPU and 4 CUDA GPU cores, provided by Institute of Fundamental Technological Research, Polish Academy of Sciences. AWS c5.9×large and c4.8×large instances, in the last 4 days, sponsored by Amazon.

We checked OpenSim simulator performance on Nvidia GPU cores (with NVBLAS support), however it didn't reduce the computation time. Final training was done on *Chuck* due to its large number of CPU cores. Different training runs were often resulting in very different models, some of which were stuck in local maxima early. Because of that, we started 5–10 separate training runs. We monitored

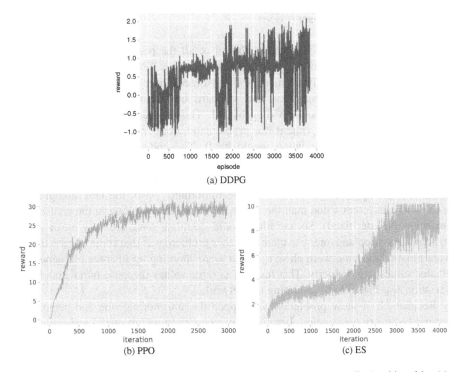

Fig. 7.12 Mean rewards (after reward shaping, so higher than during grading) achieved by (a) DDPG, (b) PPO, (c) ES in one training run. The x axis in the DDPG plot stands for episodes, in PPO and ES – for iterations (multiple episodes), because of the different implementations used (keras-rl for DDPG and OpenAI baselines for PPO & ES). The mean reward of DDPG was very variable. We experienced the most stable learning with PPO. ES gave us worse results, after 3000 iterations the skeleton stayed still for 1000 time steps, scoring around 10, because we rewarded 0.01 for every survived time step

their plots and visualized the current policy from time to time. If we judged that the model was not promising—e.g. it was stuck in local maxima or looked inferior to some other one—we stopped it and gave the resources to the more promising trainings.

In Fig. 7.12 we present mean episode reward obtained by DDPG, PPO and ES during one training run. We achieved the best result using PPO, our score in the final stage was 18.63 m. The final score was taken as the best score out of 5 submissions. The remaining scores were: 18.53, 16.14, 15.19, 14.5. The average of our 5 final submissions was 16.6.

7.8.3 Discussion

The average score during DDPG training was fluctuating a lot, sometimes it could also drop and never regain. We tried to tune the hyperparameters, without any gain though. Our problems were most probably due to bad data normalization or not enough episodes. The average score with PPO was not fluctuating as much and did not suddenly drop. That is why we switched to PPO and stayed with it until the end of the competition. ES usage in the Learning to Run environment should be more thoroughly examined.

There are a few things we would do differently now. We would try DDPG OpenAI baselines implementation. We would use simpler and well-known environment in the beginning, e.g. Walker2d and reproduce the results. We would make sure normalization is done correctly. We would try Layer Normalization instead of tedious manual normalization. We would tune hyperparameters in the end and in a rigorous way (Henderson et al. 2017). We would repeat an action n times (so-called *frame skip*). We would learn also on mirror flips of observations as shown in Pavlov et al. (2017). Finally, we would use TensorBoard or similar for visualizations.

7.9 Leveraging Emergent Muscles-Activation Patterns: From DDPG in a Continuous Action Space to DQN With a Set of Actions

Andrew Melnik, Malte Schilling, and Helge Ritter

A continuous action space with a large number of dimensions allows for complex manipulations. However, often, only a limited number of points in the action space is used. Furthermore, approaches like Deep Deterministic Policy Gradient (DDPG) may stick to a local optimum, where different optima have different sets of points in use. Therefore, to generalize over several local optima, we collected such points in the action space from different local optima and leveraged them in Deep Q-Network (DQN) (Mnih et al. 2015) learning.

7.9.1 Methods

Our approach consisted of two parts. In the first part, we applied the DDPG model to the Learning to Run environment. Our model consisted of actor and critic sub-networks with parameters used as recommended by the Getting Started guide.[5] For the initial exploration of the continuous 18-dimensional action space,

---

[5]https://github.com/stanfordnmbl/osim-rl

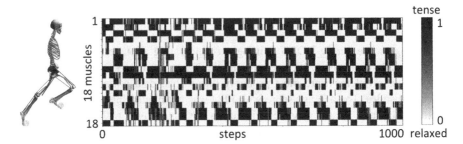

Fig. 7.13 Muscle activations in an episode. Columns are actor NN outputs after training

we used Ornstein-Uhlenbeck (OU) process (Uhlenbeck and Ornstein 1930) to generate temporally correlated noise which we added to the actor Neural Network (NN) output values. The model learned reliable muscles-activation patterns to perform successful locomotion (Fig. 7.13). After training, when the agent reached a performance plateau, the outputs of the actor NN became either equal to 0 or 1 (vectors of 18 binary values). We let the agents run further and collected a set of actor NN outputs (Table 7.5, Fig. 7.14). To generalize over many successful locomotion strategies, we collected patterns from different independently trained agents.

In the second part, we used the set of collected patterns in two different scenarios. In the first scenario, we continued with training of DDPG models and used Q-values of the set of collected patterns for exploration, as, according to the critic NN, actor's outputs were close, but not equal to the highest Q-values of the set of collected patterns (Fig. 7.15). The collected set allowed us to vastly reduce the action-search-space to a moderate set of useful muscles-activation patterns. Exploration by selection of patterns with highest Q-values allowed, in many cases, to increase the score further by 10–20%, after the DDPG agent reached a plateau of performance. In the second scenario, following the DQN approach, we used solely the critic NN (Fig. 7.16) to train new agents. To get Q-values for the set of collected muscles-activation patterns we concatenated them with state values and fed the batch to the critic NN (Fig. 7.16).

While a binary vector of 18 values would have $2^{18} = 262,144$ potential combinations, we found only a set of 214 muscles-activation patterns for trained models. That reduced exploration space to a moderate set of meaningful patterns. Certain patterns occurred more frequently than other (Table 7.5) with the 8 most frequent patterns representing already more than 30% of all executed actions. About a half of the collected patterns (108 patterns) occurred only once (per episode of 1000 steps). Occurrence frequencies of the collected patterns (Table 7.5) demonstrated a Pareto distribution (Fig. 7.14).

Table 7.5 Patterns of muscles activation and occurrence frequencies

Patt. ID	Muscles-activation pattern	Occur. freq.(%)	Sum (%)
1	110100001101001110	8.1	8.1
2	110100001100000110	4.5	12.6
3	000100001101001110	4.0	16.6
4	111001110110100001	3.5	20.1
5	101001110110100001	3.5	23.6
6	111001101100000110	2.7	26.3
7	110100001100011110	2.4	28.7
8	010100001101001110	2.3	31.0
...	...	...	...
214	000000001101001001	0.1	100.0

Fig. 7.14 Pareto distribution of occurrence frequencies of the muscles-activation patterns

7.9.2   Discussion

We presented alternative (DQN based) approaches to explore and select actions in the continues action space. However, the prerequisite is to have a set of meaningful actions for the task. Exploiting the set of collected muscles-activation patterns for further training has shown to lead to better performance and overall we want to consider in the future how to bootstrap the information further from emerging activation patterns and updating this collection. As a possible extension, we could take into account the reflection symmetry of muscles-activation patterns for the left and right legs. The set of 214 unique muscles-activation patterns for 18 muscles (two legs) contains only a set of 56 unique muscles-activation patterns for 9 muscles (per leg). In a way, this work is related to the ideas of hierarchical reinforcement learning (Heess et al. 2016) and the work on learning Dynamic Movement Primitives (Schaal 2006; Ijspeert et al. 2013) which are attractor systems of a lower dimensionality on the lower levels of such hierarchical systems.

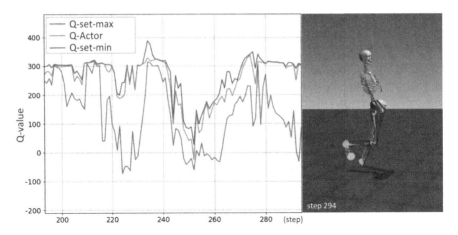

Fig. 7.15 Q-value range. Upper and lower curves represent maximum and minimum Q-values for the set of collected muscles-activation patterns in given states. The middle curve represents Q-values of the muscles-activation patterns proposed by the actor NN

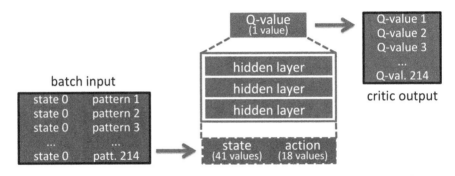

Fig. 7.16 Q-value estimation for a set of collected patterns

Affiliations and Acknowledgments

Organizers: Łukasz Kidziński, Carmichael Ong, Jennifer Hicks and Scott Delp are affiliated with Department of Bioengineering, Stanford University. Sharada Prasanna Mohanty, Sean Francis and Marcel Salathé are affiliated with Ecole Polytechnique Federale de Lausanne. Sergey Levine is affiliated with University of California, Berkeley.

    Team PKU (place 2nd, Section 7.2): Zhewei Huang and Shuchang Zhou are affiliated with Bejing University. **Team reason8.ai (place 3rd, Section 7.3):** Mikhail Pavlov, Sergey Kolesnikov and Sergey Plis are affiliated with reason8.ai. **Team IMCL (place 4th, Section 7.4):** Zhibo Chen, Zhizheng Zhang, Jiale Chen and Jun Shi are affiliated with Immersive Media Computing Lab, University of Science and Technology of China. **Team deepsense.ai (place 6th, Section 7.5):**

Henryk Michalewski is affiliated with Institute of Mathematics, Polish Academy of Sciences and deepsense.ai. Piotr Milos and Blazej Osinski are affiliated with Faculty of Mathematics, Informatics, and Mechanics, University of Warsaw and deepsense.ai. **Team THU-JGeek (place 8th, Section 7.6):** Zhuobin Zheng, Chun Yuan and Zhihui Lin are affiliated with Tunghai University. **Team Anton Pechenko (place 16th, Section 7.7):** Anton Pechenko is affiliated with Yandex. **Team Adam Stelmaszczyk (place 22nd, Section 7.8):** Adam Stelmaszczyk is affiliated with Faculty of Mathematics, Informatics, and Mechanics, University of Warsaw. Piotr Jarosik is affiliated with Institute of Fundamental Technological Research, Polish Academy of Sciences. **Team Andrew Melnik (place 28th, Section 7.9):** Andrew Melnik, Malte Schilling and Helge Ritter are affiliated with CITEC, Bielefeld University.

Team deepsense.ai was supported by the PL-Grid Infrastructure: Prometheus and Eagle supercomputers, located respectively in the Academic Computer Center Cyfronet at the AGH University of Science and Technology in Krakw and the Supercomputing and Networking Center in Poznan. The deepsense.ai team also expresses gratitude to NVIDIA and Goodeep for providing additional computational resources used during the experiment.

The challenge was co-organized by the Mobilize Center, a National Institutes of Health Big Data to Knowledge (BD2K) Center of Excellence supported through Grant U54EB020405. The challenge was partially sponsored by Nvidia who provided DGX Station for the first prize in the challenge, and GPUs Titan V for the second and the third prize, by Amazon Web Services who provided 30000 USD in cloud credits for participants, and by Toyota Research Institute who funded one travel grant.

References

Abadi, M., Agarwal, A., Barham, P., Brevdo, E., Chen, Z., Citro, C., Corrado, G.S., Davis, A., Dean, J., Devin, M., Ghemawat, S., Goodfellow, I., Harp, A., Irving, G., Isard, M., Jia, Y., Jozefowicz, R., Kaiser, L., Kudlur, M., Levenberg, J., Mané, D., Monga, R., Moore, S., Murray, D., Olah, C., Schuster, M., Shlens, J., Steiner, B., Sutskever, I., Talwar, K., Tucker, P., Vanhoucke, V., Vasudevan, V., Viégas, F., Vinyals, O., Warden, P., Wattenberg, M., Wicke, M., Yu, Y., Zheng, X.: TensorFlow: Large-scale machine learning on heterogeneous systems (2015). URL https://www.tensorflow.org/. Software available from tensorflow.org

Anonymous: Distributional policy gradients. International Conference on Learning Representations (2018). URL https://openreview.net/forum?id=SyZipzbCb

Ba, J.L., Kiros, J.R., Hinton, G.E.: Layer normalization. arXiv preprint arXiv:1607.06450 (2016)

Bratko, I., Urbancic, T., Sammut, C.: Behavioural cloning: Phenomena, results and problems. IFAC Proceedings Volumes **28**(21), 143–149 (1995). DOI https://doi.org/10.1016/S1474-6670(17)46716-4. URL http://www.sciencedirect.com/science/article/pii/S1474667017467164

Clevert, D.A., Unterthiner, T., Hochreiter, S.: Fast and accurate deep network learning by exponential linear units (elus). arXiv preprint arXiv:1511.07289 (2015)

Dhariwal, P., Hesse, C., Plappert, M., Radford, A., Schulman, J., Sidor, S., Wu, Y.: OpenAI Baselines. https://github.com/openai/baselines (2017)

Dietterich, T.G., et al.: Ensemble methods in machine learning. Multiple classifier systems **1857**, 1–15 (2000)

Dorigo, M., Colombetti, M.: Robot Shaping: An Experiment in Behavior Engineering. MIT Press, Cambridge, MA, USA (1997)

Heess, N., Sriram, S., Lemmon, J., Merel, J., Wayne, G., Tassa, Y., Erez, T., Wang, Z., Eslami, A., Riedmiller, M., et al.: Emergence of locomotion behaviours in rich environments. arXiv preprint arXiv:1707.02286 (2017)

Heess, N., Wayne, G., Tassa, Y., Lillicrap, T.P., Riedmiller, M.A., Silver, D.: Learning and transfer of modulated locomotor controllers. CoRR **abs/1610.05182** (2016). URL http://arxiv.org/abs/1610.05182

Henderson, P., Islam, R., Bachman, P., Pineau, J., Precup, D., Meger, D.: Deep Reinforcement Learning that Matters. ArXiv e-prints (2017)

Hessel, M., Modayil, J., Van Hasselt, H., Schaul, T., Ostrovski, G., Dabney, W., Horgan, D., Piot, B., Azar, M., Silver, D.: Rainbow: Combining improvements in deep reinforcement learning. arXiv preprint arXiv:1710.02298 (2017)

Ijspeert, A., Nakanishi, J., Pastor, P., Hoffmann, H., Schaal, S.: Dynamical movement primitives: Learning attractor models for motor behaviors. Neural Computation **25**, 328–373 (2013). URL http://www-clmc.usc.edu/publications/I/ijspeert-NC2013.pdf. Clmc

Jaśkowski, W., Lykkebø, O.R., Toklu, N.E., Trifterer, F., Buk, Z., Koutník, J., Gomez, F.: Reinforcement Learning to Run. . .Fast. In: S. Escalera, M. Weimer (eds.) NIPS 2017 Competition Book. Springer, Springer (2018)

Ji, S., Xu, W., Yang, M., Yu, K.: 3d convolutional neural networks for human action recognition. IEEE transactions on pattern analysis and machine intelligence **35**(1), 221–231 (2013)

Kidziński, Ł., Sharada, M.P., Ong, C., Hicks, J., Francis, S., Levine, S., Salathé, M., Delp, S.: Learning to run challenge: Synthesizing physiologically accurate motion using deep reinforcement learning. In: S. Escalera, M. Weimer (eds.) NIPS 2017 Competition Book. Springer, Springer (2018)

Kingma, D.P., Ba, J.: Adam: A method for stochastic optimization. CoRR **abs/1412.6980** (2014). URL http://arxiv.org/abs/1412.6980

Klambauer, G., Unterthiner, T., Mayr, A., Hochreiter, S.: Self-normalizing neural networks. arXiv preprint arXiv:1706.02515 (2017)

Lillicrap, T.P., Hunt, J.J., Pritzel, A., Heess, N., Erez, T., Tassa, Y., Silver, D., Wierstra, D.: Continuous control with deep reinforcement learning. arXiv preprint arXiv:1509.02971 (2015)

Mnih, V., Kavukcuoglu, K., Silver, D., Graves, A., Antonoglou, I., Wierstra, D., Riedmiller, M.A.: Playing atari with deep reinforcement learning. CoRR **abs/1312.5602** (2013). URL http://arxiv.org/abs/1312.5602

Mnih, V., Kavukcuoglu, K., Silver, D., Rusu, A.A., Veness, J., Bellemare, M.G., Graves, A., Riedmiller, M., Fidjeland, A.K., Ostrovski, G., et al.: Human-level control through deep reinforcement learning. Nature **518**(7540), 529–533 (2015)

Osband, I., Blundell, C., Pritzel, A., Van Roy, B.: Deep exploration via bootstrapped dqn. In: Advances in Neural Information Processing Systems, pp. 4026–4034 (2016)

Pavlov, M., Kolesnikov, S., Plis, S.M.: Run, skeleton, run: skeletal model in a physics-based simulation. ArXiv e-prints (2017)

Plappert, M.: keras-rl. https://github.com/matthiasplappert/keras-rl (2016)

Plappert, M., Houthooft, R., Dhariwal, P., Sidor, S., Chen, R.Y., Chen, X., Asfour, T., Abbeel, P., Andrychowicz, M.: Parameter space noise for exploration. arXiv preprint arXiv:1706.01905 (2) (2017)

Rumelhart, D.E., Hinton, G.E., Williams, R.J.: Parallel distributed processing: Explorations in the microstructure of cognition, vol. 1. chap. Learning Internal Representations by Error Propagation, pp. 318–362. MIT Press, Cambridge, MA, USA (1986). URL http://dl.acm.org/citation.cfm?id=104279.104293

Rusu, A.A., Rabinowitz, N.C., Desjardins, G., Soyer, H., Kirkpatrick, J., Kavukcuoglu, K., Pascanu, R., Hadsell, R.: Progressive neural networks. CoRR **abs/1606.04671** (2016). URL http://arxiv.org/abs/1606.04671

Salimans, T., Ho, J., Chen, X., Sidor, S., Sutskever, I.: Evolution Strategies as a Scalable Alternative to Reinforcement Learning. ArXiv e-prints (2017)

Salimans, T., Ho, J., Chen, X., Sidor, S., Sutskever, I.: Starter code for evolution strategies. https:// github.com/openai/evolution-strategies-starter (2017)

Schaal, S.: Dynamic movement primitives -a framework for motor control in humans and humanoid robotics. In: H. Kimura, K. Tsuchiya, A. Ishiguro, H. Witte (eds.) Adaptive Motion of Animals and Machines, pp. 261–280. Springer Tokyo, Tokyo (2006). DOI 10.1007/4-431-31381-8_23. URL https://doi.org/10.1007/4-431-31381-8_23

Schaul, T., Quan, J., Antonoglou, I., Silver, D.: Prioritized experience replay. arXiv preprint arXiv:1511.05952 (2015)

Schulman, J., Wolski, F., Dhariwal, P., Radford, A., Klimov, O.: Proximal policy optimization algorithms. CoRR **abs/1707.06347** (2017). URL http://arxiv.org/abs/1707.06347

Schulman, J., Wolski, F., Dhariwal, P., Radford, A., Klimov, O.: Proximal Policy Optimization Algorithms. ArXiv e-prints (2017)

Silver, D., Lever, G., Heess, N., Degris, T., Wierstra, D., Riedmiller, M.: Deterministic policy gradient algorithms. In: Proceedings of the 31st International Conference on Machine Learning (ICML-14), pp. 387–395 (2014)

Stelmaszczyk, A., Jarosik, P.: Our NIPS 2017: Learning to Run source code. https://github.com/AdamStelmaszczyk/learning2run (2017)

Sutton, R.S., Precup, D., Singh, S.: Between MDPs and semi-MDPs: A framework for temporal abstraction in reinforcement learning. Artificial Intelligence **112** (1999)

Uhlenbeck, G.E., Ornstein, L.S.: On the theory of the brownian motion. Physical review **36**(5), 823 (1930)

Wiering, M., Schmidhuber, J.: HQ-learning. Adaptive Behaviour **6** (1997)

Chapter 8
Reinforcement Learning to Run... Fast

Wojciech Jaśkowski, Odd Rune Lykkebø, Nihat Engin Toklu,
Florian Trifterer, Zdeněk Buk, Jan Koutník, and Faustino Gomez

Abstract This paper describes the approach taken by the NNAISENSE Intelligent
Automation team to win the NIPS '17 "Learning to Run" challenge involving a
biomechanically realistic model of the human lower musculoskeletal system.

8.1 Introduction

This paper describes the approach taken by the NNAISENSE Intelligent Automation team to win the NIPS '17 "Learning to Run" challenge. The learning environment is a simulation of a biomechanically realistic model of the human lower
musculoskeletal system (Kidziński et al. 2018), where the goal is to control the 18
muscles (9 per leg) such that it traverses the greatest distance possible in the forward
direction in 10 s of simulation time while avoiding obstacles placed in its path.

This task poses a number of interesting challenges from a reinforcement learning
perspective:

1. Control complexity: the task is arguably more challenging than those commonly
   found in continuous control benchmark suites (Duan et al. 2016), requiring the
   precise coordination of 18 actuators to control a highly unstable system.
2. Partial observability: the muscles have an internal state "activation" which
   accurately models hysteresis. Therefore, the state of the runner consists not only
   of the position of the joints, but also the hidden muscle activations.
3. Local minima: learning can easily get lured into and trapped in regions of
   policy space that yield reward but represent suboptimal behaviors which are
   qualitatively unrelated to the global optimum.

W. Jaśkowski (✉) · O. R. Lykkebø · N. E. Toklu · F. Trifterer · Z. Buk · J. Koutník · F. Gomez
NNAISENSE SA, Lugano, Switzerland
e-mail: wojciech@nnaisense.com; oddrune@nnaisense.com; engin@nnaisense.com;
florian@nnaisense.com; zdenek@nnaisense.com; jan@nnaisense.com; tino@nnaisense.com

© Springer International Publishing AG, part of Springer Nature 2018
S. Escalera, M. Weimer (eds.), *The NIPS '17 Competition: Building Intelligent
Systems*, The Springer Series on Challenges in Machine Learning,
https://doi.org/10.1007/978-3-319-94042-7_8

4. Computationally intensive: the task environment is a very detailed biomechanical simulation implemented in OpenSim (Delp et al. 2007). Consequently, interacting with the environment is three to four orders of magnitude more computationally expensive than with the most popular locomotion tasks found in the popular MuJoCo library (Todorov et al. 2012).

The next section provides an overview of the RL algorithm used to learn to run (Sect. 8.2), followed by an account of how we exploited domain knowledge to inform design decisions for both the policy representation (Sect. 8.3) and the training procedure (Sect. 8.4), in order to address the above challenges.

8.2 Proximal Policy Optimization

The RL algorithm used was Proximal Policy Optimization (PPO, Schulman et al. 2017), which belongs to the family of policy gradient methods. Given a stochastic policy, $\pi_\theta(s, a)$, parametrized by θ, where s is a state and a is an action, PPO optimizes the following objective function:

$$J(\theta) = \mathbb{E}_t \left[\min(r_t(\theta)\hat{A}_t, \text{clip}(r_t(\theta), 1 - \epsilon, 1 + \epsilon)\hat{A}_t) \right], \qquad (8.1)$$

where r_t is the ratio of the action probability under the new and old policies, respectively:

$$r_t(\theta) = \frac{\pi_\theta(a_t | s_t)}{\pi_{\theta_{old}}(a_t | s_t)},$$

ϵ is a clip hyperparameter, usually $\epsilon \in \{0.1, 0.2\}$, and $\hat{A}_t$ is the estimated advantage at time t. The expectation is taken over the timesteps and is approximated by samples from trajectories produced using the current (old) policy, $\pi_{\theta_{old}}$. The clipping mechanism imposes a constraint on the size of the policy change.

For $\hat{A}$, the Generalized Advantage Estimator (GAE, Schulman et al. 2015) was used:

$$\hat{A}_t = \sum_{\tau=0}^{\infty} (\gamma\lambda)^\tau \delta_{t+\tau},$$

where the error, $\delta_t = r_t + \gamma V(s_{t+1}) - V(s_t)$, is the TD-residual, $0 < \gamma \leq 1$ is the discount factor, and $0 \leq \lambda \leq 1$ plays a similar role as λ in TD(λ) (Sutton and Barto 1998).

The state value function, V, is approximated by V_ϕ, parametrized by ϕ, by minimizing the loss:

$$L(\phi) = \sum_{n=1}^{N} \left\| V_\phi(s_n) - \hat{V}_n \right\|,$$

where N is the number of samples and

$$\hat{V}_t = \sum_{\tau=0}^{\infty} (\gamma\lambda)^\tau \delta_{t+\tau} + V_\phi(s_t) = \hat{A}_t + V_\phi(s_t).$$

At each iteration, PPO first collects N samples using the current policy $\pi_{\theta_{old}}$. Then, for a number of epochs, it maximizes $J(\theta)$ and minimizes $L(\phi)$. Note that N is constant and does not depend on the trajectory length. Thus, for unfinished trajectories in the samples, to estimate $\hat{V}_t$ when $r_{t+\tau}$ is not yet known for a given τ, the algorithm needs to fallback to V_ϕ as an estimator of the future rewards according to the following rule:

$$\delta_t = r_t + \begin{cases} -V_\phi(s_t) & \text{if } s_{t+1} \text{ is terminal} \\ \gamma V_\phi(s_{t+1}) - V_\phi(s_t) & \text{otherwise.} \end{cases} \tag{8.2}$$

8.3 Policy Representation

Both the stochastic policy, π_θ, and the value function, V_ϕ, were implemented using feed-forward neural networks with two hidden layers, each layer with 256 tanh units. The inputs to each network were arranged in the following way.

The simulation provides 39 **unique** observations:

1–7 x-coordinate of the 7 joints
8 x-coordinate of the center of mass
9–15 y-coordinate of the 7 joints
16 y-coordinate of the center of mass
17–20 pelvis and center of the mass velocities
21–27 7 joint angles
28–34 7 joint angular velocities
35–37 distance to, vertical position of, and radius of the next obstacle
38–39 muscle strengths of the legs (constant throughout a given episode)

Of these, 31 of them (9–39) were used directly in the input vector, plus the following 24 aggregated features:

32–37 x joint coordinates relative to the pelvis x
38 x center of the mass coordinate relative the the pelvis x
39 a binary indicator whether any obstacles are still ahead
40–41 x,y distance between taluses

42–43 relative talus velocities
44–45 x, y distance between toes
46–47 relative toe velocities
48–51 x, y distance between the start of the next obstacle and toes
52–55 x, y distance between the end of the next obstacle and taluses

These 55 features from the current time-step, t, were complemented by 33 features representing the differences (hence velocities and accelerations) of observations 1–34 (excluding the pelvis x velocity) from the previous $h - 1$ time-steps, and the 18 muscle activations from the previous h time steps for a total of $55 + 33(h - 1) + 18h$ features.

Access to these muscle activations (which the simulator computes using a first-order dynamic muscle model based on Thelen et al. (2003)) provides additional state information but no guarantee that the state is fully observable since other state variables may still be hidden in the simulator. For this reason, the time-delay window of size h was used to try to capture sufficient task-relevant internal state.[1] Of course, it is not obvious how large the window should be to effectively disambiguate observations, and many of the variables are likely redundant. However, given the negligible affect on training time, it was decided to err on the side of overestimating this value with $h = 8$ for a total of 430 features in the network input.

Instead of using continuous actions, the value of each output unit, [0, 1], in the policy network was treated as the probability of the action corresponding to the unit being 1.0, i.e. the p parameter in a Bernoulli distribution. This "bang-bang" control strategy would be too coarse to work in many classical RL benchmarks such as the double pole balancer, but here, because of the muscle activation transients due to hysteresis, setting the actuator commands to their extremes still allows muscle activations to take intermediate values through a kind of pulse-width modulation (see Fig. 8.1). Restricting control in this way reduces the policy space dramatically from $\Re^{18}$ to 2^{18}, and allows for more efficient exploration than real-valued actions drawn from a Gaussian distribution (as is usually the case) because it biases the policy toward action sequences that are more likely activate the muscle enough to actually generate movement. Moreover, binary actions promote maximum muscle activation, which is ultimately required to run fast.

---

[1]The obvious alternative would have been to use recurrent networks, but this option was discarded due to time contraints.

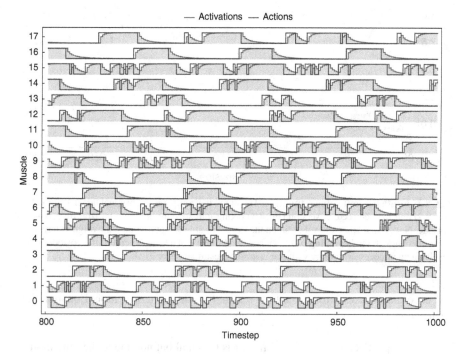

Fig. 8.1 Learned muscle activations. Each row shows the activation of one of the 18 muscles produced by the best policy over the course of roughly four strides at maximum speed. Some of the muscles (e.g. muscles 7, 8, 11, and 16) exhibit regular periodic behavior, while the control regime for other muscles is more complex (e.g. muscle 0 and 6)

8.4 Training Approach

8.4.1 Dealing with the Finite Horizon

Each training episode terminates either when the agent falls down or once the 1000-step time limit is reached. Given the purely proprioceptive nature of the state observation, in practice, the policy should not take time into account unless it wants to e.g., push out its chest at the finish line as human runners do (this would have only a tiny effect on the agent's score). However, notice that for RL methods that use value functions in finite horizon tasks, not knowing the current timestep means that $V_\phi(s_t)$ is not able to precisely approximate $\hat{V}_t$ because it does not know when the episode will terminate due to the timeout. Thus, $V_\phi(s_t)$ will be underestimated at the beginning of the episode and overestimated at the end. As a result, the variance of the Eq. 8.1 is unnecessarily high.

There are two possible solutions to this problem. The first is to treat the current timestep as part of the observation vector. This allows $V_\phi(s_t)$ to estimate $\hat{V}_t$ precisely. The second is to pretend there is no time limit by correcting the training

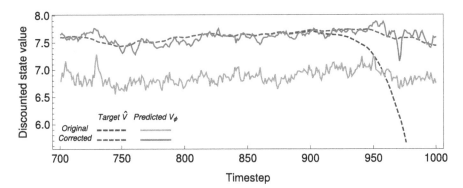

Fig. 8.2 Finite horizon value estimation. The graph the compares the original target $\hat{V}$ for GAE (Eq. 8.2) and the "corrected" version (Eq. 8.3) taking into account the finite horizon for a typical episode. Notice that since the value function, V_ϕ, is not able to approximate the original target, it underestimates in the beginning of the episode and overestimates at the end of the episode. This results in an unnecessarily large variance in gradient estimation for PPO

target so that it takes into account the reason for episode termination. Equation 8.2 then becomes:

$$\delta_t = r_t + \begin{cases} -V_\phi(s_t) & \text{if } s_{t+1} \text{ is terminal but not due to the time limit} \\ \gamma V_\phi(s_{t+1}) - V_\phi(s_t) & \text{otherwise.} \end{cases}$$

(8.3)

Note that the latter case now covers the situation in which s_T is a terminal state due to exceeding the time limit. Correcting the target in this way decreases the loss on the value function from 0.49 to 0.02 (Fig. 8.2).

8.4.2 Exploiting Task Symmetry

Intuitively, the runner should move symmetrically with the trajectory of one leg mirroring that of the other, out of phase. Notice, however, that the musculoskeletal model is not bilaterally symmetric because the legs have different muscle strengths. In order to achieve a symmetric gait, it is not enough to simply copy the actions of one leg to the other and apply them in the appropriate phase. Formally, we define a perfectly bilaterally symmetric policy as one that for each state s

$$\pi(s) = \text{flip}(\pi(\text{flip}(s))),$$

(8.4)

where flip($\cdot$) swaps features or actions of one side of the body with corresponding features or actions of the other side. This applies to such features as the y-coordinate of a talus or the distance of a talus to the next obstacle, but not to the position of the head or pelvis since they lie on the symmetry plane. To enforce this kind of symmetry the policy was trained on both the trajectory it would normally generate and its symmetric image. Without the symmetry constraint, we were unable

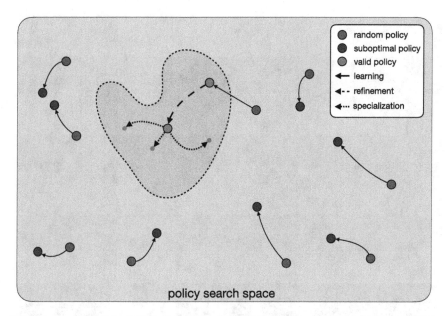

Fig. 8.3 Conceptual depiction of the staged training process. Training starts by sampling random points in policy space (black dots), and training them for a fixed number of iterations with PPO (red dots), after which the policy exhibiting the most convincing runner-like behavior (green dot, situated in the runner behavioral region shown in gray) is identified. This policy is then specialized into three sub-policies that form part of the final hybrid controller

to produce a believable controller. Most of the runs would converge quickly to behaviors where one leg was used to push forward, while the other served to stabilize the runner, and keep it from falling.

8.4.3 Staged Training Regime

Any single-agent RL algorithm that relies solely on scalar reward will be susceptible to local minima when using only local information (e.g. error gradient). In complex control tasks involving high-dimensional state/action spaces, there are often too many ways to accumulate some reward that bear little resemblance to the desired behavior. Therefore, some method is needed to guide the learning process toward favorable regions of the policy space. The approach take here, given the time constraints imposed by the competition, was to structure the training into three stages. Figure 8.3 shows a conceptual depiction of the training process in a hypothetical 2D search space.

Stage I: Global Policy Initialization

The purpose of the first stage is to identify a favorable region of the policy space where qualitatively correct behaviors reside. This involved generating 50

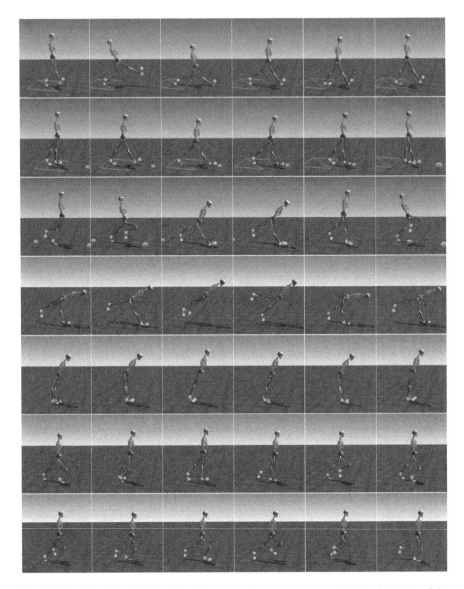

Fig. 8.4 Global policy initialization. Each row shows a sequence of frames from one of the behaviors discovered during the initial global exploration (stage I). Most gaits are suboptimal, often exhibiting pathological asymmetry, with stiff legs, one-leg dragging, or jumping. The "promising" candidate policy which formed the basis for the final hybrid controller is shown in the bottom row

policy networks with random weights and then using each as a starting point for 250 iterations of learning (4096 timesteps per iteration; for a detailed list of hyperparameter values see Table 8.2 in the Appendix). The best gaits, measured according to the final score, were visually inspected, and the policy network with the most promising behavior was selected for the second stage (Fig. 8.4).

Stage II: Policy Refinement

The policy identified in the first stage was trained further to fine-tune the running behavior. PPO was run for 1150 iterations with the number of samples per iteration being increased gradually from 24 K to 300 K. In total, this stage required 75 million timesteps.

For this stage and the policy specialization stage, a time limit of 5s was imposed on each time-step, which, if exceeded, caused the episode to terminate with a reward of -1. This limit made training significantly quicker by aborting in certain states that seemed to be causing some episodes to take as long as 100 mins on a single CPU.

Stage III: Policy Specialization

At this point the refined policy is already running with a high level of proficiency. In order to squeeze out the last bit of performance, the refined policy was specialized into three sub-policies, one for each distinct task mode: (i) *ready-set-go*, used for the first 75 timesteps; (ii) *through-obstacles* used when obstacles are present; and (iii) *max-speed* used when there are no obstacles ahead.

Starting from the "mother" policy from stage II, each sub-policy was trained using data only from its respective mode, i.e. *through-obstacles* was only trained on data from the period when obstacles are present. For *ready-set-go*, the symmetry constraint (see Sect. 8.4.2) was removed to promote asymmetrical behavior for maximum launch (Fig. 8.5). Once trained the sub-policies were assembled into a hybrid controller that switches between sub-policies depending on which mode it is in (Fig. 8.6). The three training stages together took 20 days of computation time.

Fig. 8.5 Optimized launch. The top row shows the relatively inefficient starting strategy that was learned in stage II. Both legs are simultaneously bent at the knee causing the torso to lean back before falling forward into a position from which the runner can push forward. The bottom row shows the specialized *ready-set-go* sub-policy learned in stage III where the runner first lifts its right leg, leaning the torso forward to shift its weight over the front foot before pushing forward in a natural motion seen in human standing starts

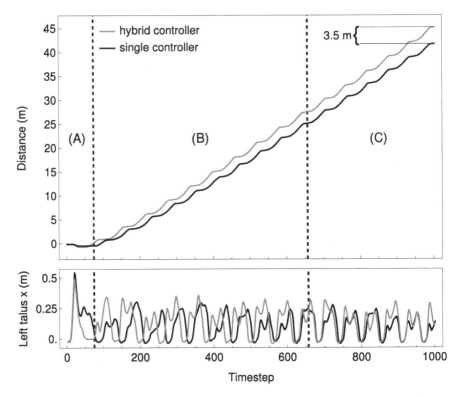

Fig. 8.6 Single policy vs hybrid controller. The upper graph shows the distance travelled by the left talus over time, for both the monolithic "mother" policy learned in stage II and the hybrid controller consisting of three specialized policies (A: *ready-set-go*, B: *through-obstacles*, C: *max-speed*) that was learned in stage III, which is able to run approximately 3.5 m further in 1000 time-steps. The vertical lines indicate the points at the which the controller switches sub-policies. The lower graph illustrates how the specialized controllers behave compared to the "mother" policy in terms of the vertical movement of the left talus over the course of the run

8.5   Results

The performance of three policies, *plain*, *noisy*, and *robust* are shown in Table 8.1. All three were produced using the method described in the above sections except that for the *robust* policy, negative rewards were generated for falling down and for leaning the upper body too far forward, and, for the *noisy* policy, Gaussian noise was added during stage II to the obstacle-related features (distances to the next obstacle and its size), and the leg strengths. The latter makes the runner more insensitive to

Table 8.1 Comparison of the three trained policies. The upper section shows the statistics for all episodes, including those where the runner fell down. The middle section measures performance based only on those episodes which completed the entire run (i.e. without falling down). Both the *noisy* and *plain* policies where statistically significantly better in both cases than the *robust* policy in terms of average performance, but the *robust* policy fell down much less often. The "best of 5 runs of 10 random episodes" were obtained with bootstrapping, and all averages were computed over 4000 episodes

Policy		Noisy	Plain	Robust
All episodes	Average	43.53	43.23	41.52
	SD	8.56	9.14	8.56
	max	47.24	47.13	45.81
Did not fall	Average	46.01	46.06	43.92
	SD	0.35	0.38	0.73
Best 5 out of 10 random episodes		45.91	45.89	43.91
% fall		8.75	9.98	**8.20**

obstacle locations so that it is less likely to fall, resulting in the competition winner, with a score of 45.96, as measured by the organizers. Notice that the scores provided by the competition organizers for our agents were (luckily) on par with the expected maximum of the average value over 5 submissions, estimated in Table 8.1.[2] Except of some interactions with the obstacles (the agent can sometimes put its legs inside the obstacles), the gait of the competition winner looks natural, as can be seen in the accompanying videos.

---

[2]Our statistics are significantly more precise since they were calculated on three orders of magnitude more episodes.

Appendix: Hyperparameters

Table 8.2 The hyperparameters used during the training depending on the training stage. Note that the training time is a rough estimation since we used different machines for different training stages

Hyperparameter	Training stage		
	Global initialization	Refinement	Specialization
Parallel runs	50	1	1
Timesteps per run [$\times 10^6$]	1	85	175
Timesteps per iteration	4'096	24'576 $\rightarrow$ 327'680	327'680
Iter. per run (approx.)	250	1'150	600
Learning rate [$\times 10^{-4}$]	3	3 $\rightarrow$ 0.6	0.6 $\rightarrow$ 0.3
Policy networks	1	1	3
Time limit per timestep [s]	∞	5	10
Training time [approx. days]	3	10	7
λ in GAE	0.9	0.9	0.95
γ in GAE	0.99	0.99	0.994
Obstacles	3	3	10
PPO clip parameter (ϵ)	0.2		
PPO batch size	256		
PPO optimizations per epoch	10		
PPO input normalization clip	5 SD		
PPO entropy coefficient	0		

Acknowledgements The authors would like to thank Jürgen Schmidhuber, Jonathan Masci, Rupesh Srivastava, Christian Osendorfer, and Marco Gallieri for fruitful and inspiring discussions during the work on this competition.

References

S. L. Delp, F. C. Anderson, A. S. Arnold, P. Loan, A. Habib, C. T. John, E. Guendelman, and D. G. Thelen. OpenSim: open-source software to create and analyze dynamic simulations of movement. *IEEE Transactions on Biomedical Engineering*, 54(11):1940–1950, 2007.

Y. Duan, X. Chen, R. Houthooft, J. Schulman, and P. Abbeel. Benchmarking deep reinforcement learning for continuous control. In *International Conference on Machine Learning*, pages 1329–1338, 2016.

Ł. Kidziński, S. P. Mohanty, C. Ong, J. Hicks, S. Francis, S. Levine, M. Salathé, and S. Delp. Learning to run challenge: Synthesizing physiologically accurate motion using deep reinforcement learning. In S. Escalera and M. Weimer, editors, *NIPS 2017 Competition Book*. Springer, Springer, 2018.

J. Schulman, P. Moritz, S. Levine, M. Jordan, and P. Abbeel. High-dimensional continuous control using generalized advantage estimation. *arXiv preprint arXiv:1506.02438*, 2015.

J. Schulman, F. Wolski, P. Dhariwal, A. Radford, and O. Klimov. Proximal policy optimization algorithms. *CoRR*, 2017.

R. S. Sutton and A. G. Barto. *Reinforcement learning: An introduction*, volume 1. MIT press Cambridge, 1998.

D. G. Thelen et al. Adjustment of muscle mechanics model parameters to simulate dynamic contractions in older adults. *Transactions-American Society Of Mechanical Engineers Journal Of Biomechanical Engineering*, 125(1):70–77, 2003.

E. Todorov, T. Erez, and Y. Tassa. MuJoCo: A physics engine for model-based control. In *Proceedings of IEEE/RSJ International Conference on Intelligent Robots and Systems (IROS)*, pages 5026–5033. IEEE, 2012.

.

Chapter 9
Human-Computer Question Answering: The Case for Quizbowl

Jordan Boyd-Graber, Shi Feng, and Pedro Rodriguez

Abstract This article describes the 2017 Human-Computer Question Answering competition at NIPS 2017. We first describe the setting: the game of quiz bowl, argue why it makes a suitable game for human-computer competition, and then describe the logistics and preparation for our competition. After reviewing the results of the 2017 competition, we examine how we can improve the competition for future years.

9.1 What Is Quizbowl?

Quizbowl is a competition played between middle schools, high schools, and colleges across the English-speaking world. It sometimes takes different names—in the UK, it's called "University Challenge"—but the central idea is the same: questions that test academic knowledge are read to teams. Those teams interrupt the question when they know the answer. These games are fun, engaging, and help the players prove and improve their knowledge of the liberal arts, science, and broader culture.

There are many games that test knowledge from game shows to pub quizzes, but there is a key component that makes quizbowl unique and special: **questions are specially written so that they can be interrupted**. Other question answering frameworks focus on single sentence questions. If both players or neither players can answer the question, then the question is useless in determining who knows more. Thus, you need many more questions of wildly varying difficulty to figure

J. Boyd-Graber (✉)
Computer Science, iSchool UMIACS, Language Science, University of Maryland, College Park, MD, USA
e-mail: jbg@umiacs.umd.edu

S. Feng · P. Rodriguez
Computer Science, University of Maryland, College Park, MD, USA
e-mail: shifeng@cs.umd.edu; pedro@snowgeek.org

© Springer International Publishing AG, part of Springer Nature 2018
S. Escalera, M. Weimer (eds.), *The NIPS '17 Competition: Building Intelligent Systems*, The Springer Series on Challenges in Machine Learning,
https://doi.org/10.1007/978-3-319-94042-7_9

At its premiere, the librettist of this opera portrayed [a character who asks for a glass of wine with his dying wish]$_1$. [That character]$_1$ in this opera is instructed to ring some bells to summon his love. At its beginning, [a man]$_2$ who claims to have killed a serpent has a padlock put on [his]$_2$ mouth because of [his]$_2$ lying. The plot of this opera concerns a series of tests that Tamino $_2$ must undergo to rescue Tamina from Sorastro. For 10 points, name this Wolfgang Mozart opera titled for an enchanted woodwind instrument.
ANSWER: The Magic Flute

Fig. 9.1 An example quizbowl question. The question starts with difficult clues and gets easier through the course of the question. Solving the answer to the question requires deep knowledge (e.g., that Emanuel Schikaneder portrayed Papageno in the premiere even though neither is mentioned by name). Two coreference groups corresponding to Papageno (1) and Tamino (2) are highlighted to show the difficulty of aligning these mentions

out who knows more. Quizbowl rewards different levels of knowledge in the *same question*, making it more efficient (and fun).

To see how this works, take the example question in Fig. 9.1; it begins with obscure information and then gets to trivial wordplay. Players with deep knowledge of music history and the libretto can answer early. Players who have memorized the names of characters can answer midway through, and players who just know titles of Mozart operas can get it at the end through wordplay. Because players can interrupt the question as its being read, it is a more effective way of distinguishing who knows more.

9.2 Why Should This Be a Computer Competition?

We haven't yet mentioned computers. We have only argued that quizbowl is a fun game and an efficient way to figure out who know more about a subject. Why should we have computers playing quizbowl?

In this section, we briefly describe our rationale for using quizbowl as a question answering task before describing our human-computer question answering competition at NIPS 2017.

9.2.1 Who's Smarter?

The deluge of computer question answering systems and datasets shows that there is keen interest in knowing which computer systems are smartest and can learn most effectively from reading the web. However, most of the computer science community has ignored the lessons learned from decades (centuries?) of asking questions of humans to figure out who is smarter or a better learner. For the same reasons that quizbowl is the "gold standard" of knowledge-based competitions in humans, we should adopt the same lessons for computer-based question answering.

9.2.2 Machine Learning

The question answering process that allows competitors to buzz after every word makes the problem more interesting from a machine learning perspective. This means that the system needs to decide after every word whether it has enough information or not to answer the question. If the system decides that it does have enough information, it can buzz.

This machine learning challenge is similar to simultaneous interpretation (Alvin et al. 2014; He et al. 2016a): for example, translating from German to English one word at a time. Thus, a full solution needs reinforcement learning (He et al. 2016b) to learn how to adjust to the strategies of your opponent. However, a solution can be much simpler (Sect. 9.3).

9.2.3 Natural Language Processing

Let's return to the question in Fig. 9.1. Answering the question correctly requires extensive coreference resolution: recognizing that characters aren't explicitly mentioned by name (Schikaneder) or that pronouns can appear before the reference (Tamino). Moreover, quizbowl represents a super-difficult version of coreference (Anupam et al. 2015): if a system can do well solving these coreference tasks, it can do well just about anywhere.

9.3 A Simple System to Scaffold Users

This section describes a very simple system we developed for users to use as a starting point in creating their submissions.[1] There are two primary components to the system: a *guesser* that generates candidates to answer and a *buzzer* that decides when to take that as the answer. Unlike other question answering scenarios where the only challenge is to generate answers, quizbowl also requires players to select how much information was needed to answer the question.

9.3.1 Guesser

Our simple guesser is based on ElasticSearch (Clinton and Zachary 2015), a search engine that uses TF-IDF keyword matching. Given a query (part of the question),

---

[1] https://github.com/pinafore/qb-api

the system compares it with previously asked quizbowl questions, and sorts the corresponding entities based on the similarity. Our simple guesser was trained on 31862 quizbowl questions, which covers 6991 distinct entities.

9.3.2 Buzzer

The ElasticSearch guesser returns with each entity a score of the similarity between the document and the query. The scores provide information about how confident the guesser is and can be used to determine when to buzz. Our simple reference system uses a simple threshold to decide when to buzz. We normalize the scores of the top ten guesses, and buzz if and only if the top score exceed a threshold (0.3) that is roughly tuned on a small held-out dataset.

9.4 Client-Server Architecture

Now that participants have the starting position of a system, we also need to provide a submission framework. Unlike other question answering tasks where entire questions are revealed at once, the nature of quizbowl requires an interactive server.

The server waits for users to submit their systems; when participants are ready, they interact with the server, which provides questions one word at a time (Fig. 9.2). The server records the answer and associates it with the last word the client saw.

1 Human-Computer Question Answering: The Case for Quizbowl

C: I'm User 1. I'd like to play!
S: Hi, User 1! Available questions are [1,2,3,4]
C: I'd like to hear Word 1 of Question 1
S: It's Extremism
C: I'd like to hear Word 3 of Question 1
S: It's in
C: I'd like to hear Word 2 of Question 1
S: It's the
C: I'd like to answer Question 1 Barry_Goldwater
S: Got it! You've answered Question 1 at Position 3 with Barry_Goldwater

Fig. 9.2 Example interaction of a participant client (C) with the server (S). The client repeats the process for all of the questions in the dataset

9.5   Results

Our competition ran in two phases: a computer only competition and a human-computer competition. After the top computer teams were selected in the computer competition, they were then placed against a top human team.

9.5.1   Computer Results

Other than calculating the accuracies of each computer system on the evaluation dataset, we also run simulated games between each pair of them. Of the seven submissions, we run this "tournament" between the three systems that performed better than the baseline system (we also include the baseline system for comparison). We use 160 test questions from the held-out dataset for both evaluations.

9.5.1.1   Accuracy

We evaluate the accuracy of each system by comparing the guesses they provided for each question, without using the buzzing information. The numbers are shown in Table 9.1. All selected submissions beat the baseline system in terms of end-of-question accuracy, and Ousia's system out-performed other systems by a large margin.

9.5.1.2   Simulated Games

For each pair of the system we run games simulated using the test questions. We use the regular scoring system: 10 points for a correct answer, -5 for a incorrect one if not at the end of the question. Systems are only allowed to answer after each word, and we break tie randomly. To reduce the randomness in the final score, we ran three games and take the average for each pair (Table 9.2).

Studio Ousia's system significantly (see contributed chapter in this collection) out-performed all other systems. The other systems appear relatively conservative when it comes to buzzing, and they often only answer the question at the end. Studio Ousia's system is superior in terms of both accuracy and buzzing capability, and is thus selected to compete with top human players.

While Lunit.io (Kim et al.) had a lower accuracy than Acelove (Chen et al.), they won in more head-to-head matches, showing that knowing *when* to buzz is just as important as determining the correct answer with buzz *with*.

Table 9.1 Accuracy of the systems

System	Accuracy
OUSIA	0.85
Acelove	0.675
Lunit.io	0.6
Baseline	0.55

Table 9.2 Final points from simulated games

System	Points	Points	System
Acelove	60	**1220**	OUSIA
Acelove	320	**615**	Lunit.io
Acelove	**470**	400	Baseline
OUSIA	**1145**	105	Lunit.io
OUSIA	**1235**	15	Baseline
Lunit.io	**605**	75	Baseline

Fig. 9.3 Trivia experts facing off against the winner of the computer phase of the competition

9.5.2 Human-Computer Games

Los Angeles is an epicenter for trivia competitions and game show contestants. In preparation for the NIPS competition, we recruited strong players (including some in the NIPS community) to take part in the competition (right to left in Fig. 9.3).

- Raj Dhuwalia is an educator living in the LA area who is a Jeopardy champion, a winner of 250 thousand dollars on "Who Wants to be a Millionaire", and a top-two scorer at three consecutive national quizbowl championships.
- David Farris is a mathematician who was a member of national championship teams at all three levels: high school, undergrad (Harvard), and graduate school (Berkeley). This year he won the Karnataka Quiz Association championship in Bangalore on the Rest House Crescent quizzers.
- Hidehiro Anto is an undergraduate at UCAL and was a member of 3rd place Team California at 2014 HSAPQ NASAT and top scorer at 2015 NAQT ICT junior varsity competition.

- Charles Meigs is the only player to win All-Star in Division II in two consecutive years while playing for UCLA, and led the University of Maryland to a 2008 national championship.
- Sharad Vikram is a PhD candidate at UCSD but a veteran of quizbowl teams at Torrey Pines and Berkeley, where he served as president. As author of the quizBowl Database, he is also the creator of much of the data used to train these algorithms.
- James Bradbury is a research scientist at Salesforce, where he works on question answering (among many other things). As a quizbowler, he played on top 15 teams at Thomas Jefferson High School and Stanford.

In addition, the second place computer team (Lunit.io, Kim et al.) played against the University of Maryland quizbowl team, a team with some of the same members had won the Academic Competition Federation tournament the previous year.

For both games, a moderator reads questions and an assistant advances the text one word at a time, simulating the client-server framework participants used to submit answers.

9.5.2.1   First-Place Game

The competition against the first place team was slow to start.[2] The computer won the first tossup on *Les Fleur du Mal* (a poetry collection by Baudelaire), and the humans got the next question on *Bimetalism* wrong (although the computer could not get the answer at the end of the question). After another human mistake on *Newton (Surname)* (which the computer could convert), the score stood at 50 for the computer against -10 for the humans.

However, the humans began a comeback with Question 6, correctly answering a question about the programming language *SQL*. However, the computer still maintained an impressive lead at the end of the first half, 260–80. The humans had a much better second half, answering four questions in a row on mythology, popular culture, and social science. The computer also had its only incorrect answer in the second half, incorrectly answering a question about Chinese art.

Nevertheless, the computer won handily (Table 9.3), although we speculate that the humans could have done better with a little more practice playing with each other and against the computer.

Table 9.3 Final scores of the first place system against a strong human team

	First half	Second half	Final
Human	80	120	**200**
Computer	245	230	**475**

---

[2]https://youtu.be/gNWU5TKaZ2Q

9.5.2.2 Second-Place Game

The second place team (Lunit.io, Kim et al.) also played against the University of Maryland Academic Quiz Team in College Park, Maryland (without an audience). The human team decisively won this game, almost doubling the computer's score.[3] The results aren't strictly comparable, as the Maryland team obviously had different strengths (being different people) and had more experience playing with each other.

9.5.3 Are Computers Better at Quizbowl?

In many ways, we have engineered this version of the task to be generous to computer players: answers are all Wikipedia answers, we use hard questions about easy topics, and we provide the text signal perfectly to the systems without speech recognition.

While the systems submitted to this competition are indeed impressive, there is substantial room for improvement in making the task more challenging for computers and would be a more realistic comparison of human vs. computer performance. We discuss how to further increase the difficulty (and scientific value) of this competition.

9.5.4 Improving Participation

We did not have as many entrants in our competition as we had hoped. Some of this was our own fault: we did not have as extensive and clear documentation as we had hoped, nor did we have our example system available as quickly as we would have liked. We should have clear documentation, simple example systems, and clear points to improve the example systems easily.

Future compeitions could move to more well-known platforms suce as CodaLab;[4] while our client-server system is relatively straightforward, a visible framework with slightly more complexity might be wortwhile for the additional debugging and documentation. Integrating into a more flexible web platform could also create better presentations of games that might make the submission process more fun.

Finally, having backing in the form of a monetary prize would encourage competitions and help build visibility for the competition.

---

[3]https://youtu.be/0kgnEUDMeug

[4]https://competitions.codalab.org/

9.6 Long-Term Viability of Increasingly Difficult Competitions

9.6.1 Changing the Difficulty

We have chosen nearly the optimal level of competition for our matches: difficult questions on easy topics. If the questions were easier, humans would have a speed advantage because they would be able to process information more quickly; computers often need multiple clues to triangulate information correctly. If the questions were more difficult, there would be less redundant information available from previous questions and Wikipedia, which would expose the fragility of systems: the same information can be worded in many different ways, and most systems are not robust to these paraphrases.

9.6.2 Speech Recognition

The most obvious step to make the competition more realistic for computers is to provide a speech signal rather than a text signal.[5] In particular, infrequent, highly specific named entities (e.g., "phosphonium ylide", "Temujin", or "Techumseh") are often key clues but are very hard for existing ASR systems to perfectly detect.

9.6.3 Adversarial Question Writing

We have been using questions written in the same way that they are for human players. However, computer players have different strengths and weaknesses than computer players. By highlighting clues / phrases that are easy for a computer and asking question writers to rephrase or avoid those clues, we can focus the questions on that are truly challenging for computers to answer.

9.6.4 Bonus Questions

Quizbowl games are not just tossups; typically the team that answers a tossup correctly is rewarded with the opportunity to answer a "bonus" question. These questions are typically multipart, related questions that probe the depths of teams' knowledge (Fig. 9.4). Successfully answering these questions would require both deeper knowledge and cross-sentence reasoning.

---

[5]In a sense, our computers are playing quizbowl in the same way deaf students play.

In this play, Tobias jokes about his wife's concern that she may someday go mad. For 10 points each:

10 Name this play in which Tobias and Agnes allow the distressed couple Harry and Edna to stay in the bedroom of their daughter Julia, who is disturbed to find it occupied when she comes home after a divorce.
ANSWER: A Delicate Balance
10 Other odd couples in plays by this author of *A Delicate Balance* include *Zoo Story*'s Peter and Jerry, as well as George and Martha from *Who's Afraid of Virginia Woolf?*
ANSWER: Edward Albee
10 In *Who's Afraid of Virginia Woolf?*, Nick realizes this fact about George and Martha's family after George says an unseen character died trying to drive around a porcupine and Martha shouts, "you cannot do that!"

ANSWER: their alleged son does not exist [or that George and Martha are childless; or that George and Martha never had a child; accept other answers indicating that their male child is any of the following: not real; fictional; imaginary; made up; never existed; etc.; do not accept or prompt on "their son is dead"]

Fig. 9.4 An example of a bonus question; teams work together to answer these more difficult questions, which often require reasoning across the three individual component questions

9.6.5 Open Domain Answers

Most (over 80%, sometimes higher depending on format) answers in quizbowl map to Wikipedia page titles. However, answers sometimes do not fit into this mold. For example:

- *Computational math questions*: uncommon at higher competition levels, computational math questions do not map to Wikipedia pages in the same way as other questions.
- *Common link questions*: sometimes a question will ask about several entities at once, and request players respond with how they fit together ("coats" in literature, the word "journey" appearing in titles of works, "ways that Sean Bean has died in films")
- Some answers do not have Wikipedia pages because they are rare or do not fit into Wikipedia's organization (e.g., "Gargantua", a character by Rabelais)

9.7 Comparison to Other Tasks

Quizbowl is a factoid question answering tasks, among which it is unique for being pyramidal — questions consist of multiple clues arranged in descending order of difficulty, with the hardest information first and the easiest at the end. Questions are revealed word by word, and players can buzz in when they are confident to answer. As a result, quizbowl challenges a system to both effectively incoporate information on-the-fly and accurately determine when the information is sufficient. Finally since quizbowl questions are revealed word by word, computers no longer have the advantage of reading speed against humans. This makes quizbowl uniquely suitable for human-computer competitions.

There are several other question answering datasets that use trivia questions. But as pyramidality is unique to quizbowl, we will compare them on some different aspects. We focus on three main attributes: answer definition, support set, and query type. Answer definition refers to both the answer space (e.g., open domain vs closed domain), and how the answer is defined (e.g., an entity vs a span in a document). Support set refers to the context that is provided for each example. Query type concerns in general how the queries are formed and is closely related to the support set.

The task most similar to quizbowl is TriviaQA (Mandar et al. 2017), and we compare them in detail:

- **Answer**: Similar to Quizbowl, most of TriviaQA's answers are titles in Wikipedia. TriviaQA has 40,478 unique answers, while Quizbowl has 8,091.
- **Support**: Each quizbowl answer has on average thirteen previously asked questions, each composed of four sentences on average. Each TriviaQA question has on average six supporting documents collected automatically from Wikipedia and web search. Because this evidence collection process is automated, there is no guarantee that the answer will appear in the documents (79.7% from Wikipedia and 75.4% from web search). The support set of TriviaQA makes it more suitable for reading comprehension methods compared to quizbowl.
- **Query**: TriviaQA has single sentence questions, and the clues are usually given in the form of a relationship of the entity in question with another entity, for example "who is the author of King Lear?". Quizbowl questions have four sentences on average, and start with more obscure clues. The clues, especially those from the first two sentences, almost always require high-order reasoning between entities, for example "The title character of this short story describes himself as driven off the face of the earth." Quizbowl requires more complicated reasoning, across multiple sentences, and requires broader knowledge.

Other similar tasks include: SearchQA (Matthew Dunn et al. 2017), a dataset of *Jeopardy!* questions paired with search engine snippets as evidence; WikiQA (Yi et al. 2015), a dataset automatically constructed from Bing queries that focuses on answer sentence selection. We note that these tasks don't share the pyramidality feature of Quizbowl and are less suitable for human-computer competitions.

Unlike other claims of human-level ability on question answering tasks,[6] quizbowl is a computerized setting of a task that humans already do. This makes it more straightforward to make realistic comparisons of relative performance. Its inherent fun makes it exciting to use it as a lens for researchers and lay audiences alike to measure the progress of NLP and ML algorithms.

---

[6]https://www.theverge.com/2018/1/17/16900292/ai-reading-comprehension-machines-humans

9.8 Conclusion

Quizbowl is a fun activity that is engaging to audiences and participants. It is easy to begin but difficult to master, and mastery of Quizbowl requires significant advances in natural language processing and machine learning. We hope that this initial NIPS competition provides the foundation for future competitions on a wider scale.

References

Matthew Dunn, Levent Sagun, Mike Higgins, Ugur Guney, Volkan Cirik, and Kyunghyun Cho. 2017. SearchQA: A new Q&A dataset augmented with context from a search engine. *arXiv preprint arXiv:1704.05179* (2017).

Clinton Gormley and Zachary Tong. 2015. *Elasticsearch: The Definitive Guide*. O'Reilly.

Alvin Grissom II, He He, Jordan Boyd-Graber, John Morgan, and Hal Daumé III. 2014. Don't Until the Final Verb Wait: Reinforcement Learning for Simultaneous Machine Translation. In *Empirical Methods in Natural Language Processing*. docs/2014_emnlp_simtrans.pdf

Anupam Guha, Mohit Iyyer, Danny Bouman, and Jordan Boyd-Graber. 2015. Removing the Training Wheels: A Coreference Dataset that Entertains Humans and Challenges Computers. In *North American Association for Computational Linguistics*. docs/2015_naacl_qb_coref.pdf

He He, Jordan Boyd-Graber, and Hal Daumé III. 2016a. Interpretese vs. Translationese: The Uniqueness of Human Strategies in Simultaneous Interpretation. In *North American Association for Computational Linguistics*. docs/2016_naacl_interpretese.pdf

He He, Kevin Kwok, Jordan Boyd-Graber, and Hal Daumé III. 2016b. Opponent Modeling in Deep Reinforcement Learning. docs/2016_icml_opponent.pdf

Mandar Joshi, Eunsol Choi, Dan Weld, and Luke Zettlemoyer. 2017. TriviaQA: A Large Scale Distantly Supervised Challenge Dataset for Reading Comprehension.

Yi Yang, Wen-tau Yih, and Christopher Meek. 2015. WikiQA: A Challenge Dataset for Open-Domain Question Answering. In *Proceedings of the 2015 Conference on Empirical Methods in Natural Language Processing*. 2013–2018.

Chapter 10
Studio Ousia's Quiz Bowl Question Answering System

Ikuya Yamada, Ryuji Tamaki, Hiroyuki Shindo, and Yoshiyasu Takefuji

Abstract In this chapter, we describe our question answering system, which was the winning system at the Human–Computer Question Answering (HCQA) Competition at the Thirty-first Annual Conference on Neural Information Processing Systems (NIPS). The competition requires participants to address a factoid question answering task referred to as *quiz bowl*. To address this task, we use two novel neural network models and combine these models with conventional information retrieval models using a supervised machine learning model. Our system achieved the best performance among the systems submitted in the competition and won a match against six top human quiz experts by a wide margin.

10.1 Introduction

We present our question answering system, which was the winning solution at the Human–Computer Question Answering (HCQA) Competition held at the Thirty-first Annual Conference on Neural Information Processing Systems (NIPS) 2017. This competition requires a system to address a unique factoid question answering (QA) task referred to as *quiz bowl*, which has been studied frequently (Boyd-Graber et al. 2012; Iyyer et al. 2014, 2015; Yamada 2017). Given a question, the system is required to guess the entity that is described in the question (see Table 10.1). One unique characteristic of this task is that the question is given one word at a time,

I. Yamada (✉) · R. Tamaki
Studio Ousia, Chiyoda, Tokyo, Japan
e-mail: ikuya@ousia.jp; ryuji.tamaki@ousia.jp

H. Shindo
Nara Institute of Science and Technology, Takayama, Japan
e-mail: shindo@is.naist.jp

Y. Takefuji
Keio University, Fujisawa, Japan
e-mail: takefuji@sfc.keio.ac.jp

© Springer International Publishing AG, part of Springer Nature 2018   181
S. Escalera, M. Weimer (eds.), *The NIPS '17 Competition: Building Intelligent Systems*, The Springer Series on Challenges in Machine Learning,
https://doi.org/10.1007/978-3-319-94042-7_10

Table 10.1 Example of a quiz bowl question

Question: The protagonist of a novel by this author is evicted from the Bridge Inn and is talked into becoming a school janitor by a character whose role is often translated as the Council Chairman. A character created by this writer is surprised to discover that he no longer likes the taste of milk, but enjoys eating rotten food. The quest for Klamm, who resides in the title structure, is taken up by K in his novel The Castle. For 10 points, name this author who wrote about Gregor Samsa being turned into an insect in "The Metamorphosis."
Answer: *Franz Kafka*

and the system can output an answer at any time. Moreover, the answer must be an entity that exists in Wikipedia.

To address this task, we use two neural network models and conventional information retrieval (IR) models, and we combine the outputs of these models using a supervised machine learning model. Similar to past work (Iyyer et al. 2014, 2015; Yamada 2017), our first neural network model directly solves the task by casting it as a text classification problem. As the entities mentioned in the question (e.g., *Gregor Samsa* and *The Metamorphosis* in the question shown in Table 10.1) play a significant role in guessing the answer, we use words and entities as inputs to the model. We train the neural network model to predict the answer from a set of words and entities that appear in the question.

Given a question, our second neural network model predicts the entity types of the answer. For example, the expected entity types of the question shown in Table 10.1 are *author* and *person*. We train the neural network model to predict the entity types of the answer to a question. We adopted a convolutional neural network (CNN) (Kim 2014) to perform this task.

The outputs of these neural network models are used as the features of a supervised machine learning model. We train the model with these neural-network-based features and other features including the outputs of conventional IR models. All of these machine learning models are trained using our quiz bowl QA dataset, which was developed from two existing datasets.

Our experimental results show that the proposed approach achieved high accuracy on this task. Furthermore, our system achieved the best performance among the systems submitted in the competition and also won a live match against six top human quiz experts by a wide margin.

10.2 Proposed System

In this section, we provide an overview of the proposed system. Figure 10.1 shows the architecture of our system. We combine the outputs of two neural network models (the *Neural Quiz Solver* and the *Neural Type Predictor*) and conventional information retrieval (IR) models using the *Answer Scorer*, which is also based on a supervised machine learning model. We first describe the data used to develop our system and then present the technical details of our system.

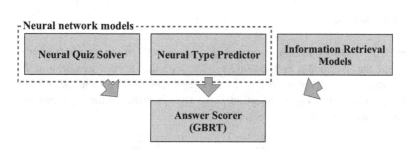

Fig. 10.1 Architecture of our proposed system

10.2.1 Data

We used several data sources to develop our system. First, we used the question–answer pairs available at the Protobowl website,[1] which contains over 100,000 quiz bowl questions and their answers and which was used as the official dataset of the competition. The dataset contained several questions whose answers did not exactly match their corresponding Wikipedia titles. We resolved the answers to the corresponding Wikipedia titles using simple string matching methods and a crowd-sourcing service and excluded the questions whose answers could not be matched to Wikipedia. In addition, we concatenated the Protobowl QA dataset with the public QA dataset provided by Iyyer et al. (2014), containing 20,407 quiz bowl questions and their answers.[2] Unlike the Protobowl dataset, the answers contained in this dataset were provided as Wikipedia titles. Finally, we removed the duplicate questions from the concatenated dataset. As a result, our final QA dataset contained 101,043 question–answer pairs.

We also used Wikipedia and Freebase as external data sources. We used a Wikipedia dump generated in June 2016 and the latest Freebase data dump as obtained from the website.[3]

10.2.2 Neural Quiz Solver

We developed two neural network models to solve the QA task. The first model is the Neural Quiz Solver, which addresses the task as a text classification problem over answers contained in the dataset.

---

[1] http://protobowl.com/

[2] The dataset was obtained from the authors' website: https://cs.umd.edu/~miyyer/qblearn/.

[3] https://developers.google.com/freebase/

10.2.2.1 Model

Figure 10.2 shows the architecture of this model. Given the words $(w_1, w_2, \ldots, w_N)$ and the Wikipedia entities $(e_1, e_2, \ldots, e_K)$ that appear in question D, our model first computes the word-based vector representation $\mathbf{v}_{D_w}$ and the entity-based vector representation $\mathbf{v}_{D_e}$ of question D by averaging the vector representations of the words and the entities, respectively.

$$\mathbf{v}_{D_w} = \frac{1}{N} \sum_{n=1}^{N} \mathbf{W}_w \mathbf{p}_{w_n}, \ \mathbf{v}_{D_e} = \frac{1}{K} \sum_{k=1}^{K} \mathbf{W}_e \mathbf{q}_{e_k}, \tag{10.1}$$

where $\mathbf{p}_w \in \mathbb{R}^d$ and $\mathbf{q}_e \in \mathbb{R}^d$ are the vector representations of word w and entity e, respectively, and $\mathbf{W}_w \in \mathbb{R}^{d \times d}$ and $\mathbf{W}_e \in \mathbb{R}^{d \times d}$ are projection matrices. Then, the vector representation of question $\mathbf{v}_D$ is computed as the element-wise sum of $\mathbf{v}_{D_w}$ and $\mathbf{v}_{D_e}$:

$$\mathbf{v}_D = \mathbf{v}_{D_w} + \mathbf{v}_{D_e} \tag{10.2}$$

Then, the probability that entity e_t is the answer to the question is defined using the following softmax function:

$$\hat{y}_{e_t} = \frac{\exp(\mathbf{a}_{e_t}{}^\top \mathbf{v}_D)}{\sum_{e' \in \Gamma} \exp(\mathbf{a}_{e'}{}^\top \mathbf{v}_D)}, \tag{10.3}$$

where Γ is a set containing all answers, and $\mathbf{a}_e \in \mathbb{R}^d$ denotes the vector representation of answer e. Further, we use categorical cross entropy as a loss function.

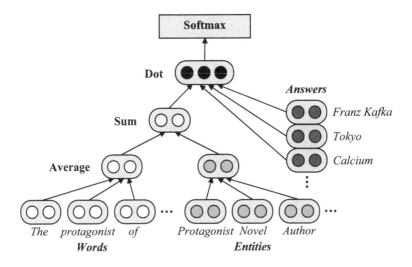

Fig. 10.2 Architecture of neural quiz solver

10.2.2.2   Entity Detection

Because the model requires a list of the entities appearing in a question, we automatically annotate entity names using a simple entity linking method. The method is based on *keyphraseness* (Mihalcea and Csomai 2007), which is the probability that an entity name is used as an anchor in Wikipedia. We detect an entity name if its keyphraseness is larger than 2%. Furthermore, as an entity name can be ambiguous (e.g., *Washington* can refer to the city and state in the U.S., a person's name, etc.), we use an entity name if it refers to a single entity with a probability of 95% or more in Wikipedia. The entities referred by the detected entity names are used as inputs to the model.

10.2.2.3   Pretrained Representations

To initialize the vector representations of words ($\mathbf{p}_w$), entities ($\mathbf{q}_e$), and answers ($\mathbf{a}_e$), we use Wikipedia2Vec[4] (Yamada et al. 2016), which is our method for learning vector representations of words and entities from Wikipedia. The model maps words and entities into the same continuous vector space; similar words and entities are placed close to one another in the vector space.

The representations of words and entities are trained by jointly optimizing the following three sub-models: (1) the conventional word-based skip-gram model, which learns to predict neighboring words given the target word in Wikipedia, (2) the *anchor context model*, which learns to predict neighboring words given the target entity based on each anchor link pointing to the target entity and its context words in Wikipedia, and (3) the *knowledge base graph model*, which learns to estimate neighboring entities given the target entity in the internal link graph between entities in Wikipedia.

We train the representations using the Wikipedia dump described in Sect. 10.2.1. Note that we use the same pretrained entity representations to initialize the representations of entities and answers.

10.2.2.4   Other Details

The model is trained by iterating over the QA dataset described in Sect. 10.2.1. Because a question is given one word at a time, the model must perform accurately for incomplete questions. To address this, we truncate a question at a random position before inputting it to the model during training.

The proposed model is implemented using PyTorch[5] and trained using minibatch stochastic gradient descent (SGD) on a GPU. The minibatch size is fixed as 32, the learning rate is automatically controlled by Adam (Kingma and Ba 2014), and the number of representation dimensions is set as $d = 300$. We keep the parameters in

---

[4]https://wikipedia2vec.github.io/
[5]http://pytorch.org

the answer representations static and update all the other parameters. To prevent overfitting, we randomly exclude the words and entities in the question with a probability of 0.5 (Iyyer et al. 2015; Srivastava et al. 2014).

Using this model, we compute two scores for each answer: (1) the predicted probability and (2) the unnormalized value inputted to the softmax function $(\mathbf{a}_{e_t}{}^{\top}\mathbf{v}_D)$.

10.2.3 Neural Type Predictor

The second neural network model is the Neural Type Predictor, which aims to predict the entity types for a question. For example, if the target question is the one shown in Table 10.1, the target entity types are *person* and *author*. We use the FIGER entity type set (Ling and Weld 2012), which consists of 112 fine-grained entity types, as the target entity types. We automatically assign entity types to each answer by resolving the answer's Wikipedia entity to its corresponding entity in Freebase and obtaining FIGER entity types based on the mapping[6] and Freebase data.

We use two separate models with the following different target entity types: all *fine-grained* entity types and only eight *coarse-grained* entity types (i.e., *person, organization, location, product, art, event, building,* and *other*). We address this task as a multiclass text classification task over entity types. In the former setting, we address the task as a *multilabel* text classification problem because many answers have multiple entity types (e.g., *person* and *author*).

We use a CNN (Kim 2014) to address this task. Given a question consisting of a sequence of N words $w_1, w_2, \ldots, w_N$, our task is to predict the probability for each entity type $t \in T$. Here, a one-dimensional convolution layer of width $h \in H$ in the CNN works by moving a sliding window of size h over the sequence of words. Let the vector representation of word w be $\mathbf{x}_w \in \mathbb{R}^{d_{word}}$, and let the vector corresponding to the i-th window be

$$\mathbf{s}_i = \mathbf{x}_{w_i} \oplus \mathbf{x}_{w_{i+1}} \oplus \ldots \oplus \mathbf{x}_{w_{i+h-1}}, \tag{10.4}$$

where $\oplus$ is the concatenation operator. The result of the convolution layer consists of m vectors $\mathbf{u}_1, \mathbf{u}_2, \ldots, \mathbf{u}_m$, each of which is computed by the following:

$$\mathbf{u}_i = \text{relu}(\mathbf{W}_{conv}\mathbf{s}_i + \mathbf{b}_{conv}), \tag{10.5}$$

where relu is a rectifier function, $\mathbf{W}_{conv} \in \mathbb{R}^{d_{conv} \times h \cdot d_{word}}$ is a weight matrix, and $\mathbf{b}_{conv} \in \mathbb{R}^{d_{conv}}$ is a bias vector. Note that because we use *wide convolution* (Kalchbrenner et al. 2014), m equals $N + h + 1$ in our model. Then, we use max pooling to combine the m vectors into a single d_{conv}-dimensional feature vector $\mathbf{c}$,

---

[6]The mapping was obtained from FIGER's GitHub repository: https://github.com/xiaoling/figer/.

each of whose components is computed as follows:

$$c_j = \max_{1 < i \leq m} \mathbf{u}_i[j],\tag{10.6}$$

where $\mathbf{u}[j]$ denotes the j-th component of $\mathbf{u}$. We apply multiple convolution operations with varying window sizes to obtain multiple vectors $\mathbf{c}_1, \mathbf{c}_2, \ldots, \mathbf{c}_{|H|}$, and obtain the concatenated feature vector $\mathbf{z} \in \mathbb{R}^{|H| \cdot d_{conv}}$ by

$$\mathbf{z} = \mathbf{c}_1 \oplus \mathbf{c}_2 \oplus \ldots \oplus \mathbf{c}_{|H|}.\tag{10.7}$$

Finally, we predict the probability corresponding to each entity type. In the coarse-grained model, the probability corresponding to the k-th entity type is computed by the following softmax function:

$$\hat{y}_k = \frac{\exp(\mathbf{w}_k^\top \mathbf{z} + b_k)}{\sum_{l=1}^{|T|} \exp(\mathbf{w}_l^\top \mathbf{z} + b_l)},\tag{10.8}$$

where $\mathbf{w}_k \in \mathbb{R}^{|H| \cdot d_{conv}}$ and $b_k \in \mathbb{R}$ are the weight vector and the bias, respectively, of the k-th entity type. The model is trained to minimize categorical cross entropy. Further, for the fine-grained model, we use the sigmoid function to create $|T|$ *binary* classifiers; the probability of the k-th entity type being correct is computed by

$$\hat{y}_k = \sigma(\mathbf{w}_k^\top \mathbf{z} + b_k),\tag{10.9}$$

where σ is the sigmoid function. The model is trained to minimize binary cross entropy averaged over all entity types.

These two models are trained by iterating over our QA dataset. We use the same configurations to train these models: they are trained using SGD on a GPU, the minibatch size is fixed as 32, and the learning rate is controlled by Adamax (Kingma and Ba 2014). For the hyper-parameters of the CNN, we use $H = \{2, 3, 4, 5\}$, $d_{word} = 300$, and $d_{conv} = 1,000$. We use filter window sizes of 2, 3, 4, and 5, and 1,000 feature maps for each filter. We use the GloVe word embeddings (Pennington et al. 2014) trained on the 840 billion Common Crawl corpus to initialize the word representations. As in the neural network model explained previously, a question is truncated at a random position before it is input to the models. The models are implemented using PyTorch.[7]

Given a question and an answer, each model outputs two scores: the sum and the maximum probability[8] based on the predicted probabilities of the entity types assigned to the answer.

---

[7]http://pytorch.org/

[8]We aggregate probabilities because an entity can have multiple entity types in both the coarse-grained and the fine-grained models.

10.2.4 Information Retrieval Models

As others have in past studies (Iyyer et al. 2014; Yih et al. 2013; Yu et al. 2014), we use conventional IR models to enhance the performance of our QA system. In particular, we compute multiple relevance scores against the documents associated with the target answer using the words in a question as a query.

Specifically, for each answer contained in the dataset, we create the target documents using the following two types of data sources: (1) *Wikipedia text*, which is the page text in the answer's Wikipedia entry, and (2) *dataset questions*, which are the questions contained in our QA dataset and associated with the answer. Regarding Wikipedia text, we use two methods to create documents for each answer: treating page text as a single document and treating each paragraph as a separate document. We also use two similar methods for dataset questions: creating a single document by concatenating all questions associated with the answer and treating each question as a separate document. Further, because the latter methods of both data sources create multiple documents for each answer, we first compute the relevance scores for all documents and reduce them by selecting their maximum score.

We preprocess the questions and documents by converting all words to lowercase, removing stop words,[9] and performing snowball stemming. We use two scoring methods: Okapi BM25 and the number of words in common between the question and the document. Further, we generate four types of queries for a question using (1) its words, (2) its words and bigrams, (3) its noun words, and (4) its proper noun words.[10] There are four target document sets, two scoring methods, and four query types; thus, given a question and an answer, we compute 32 relevance scores.

10.2.5 Answer Scorer

Given a question as an input, the Answer Scorer assigns a relevance score to each answer based on the outputs of the neural network models and IR models described above. Here, we use gradient boosted regression trees (GBRT) (Friedman 2001), a model that achieves state-of-the-art performance in many tasks (Chapelle and Chang 2011; Yin et al. 2016). In particular, we address the task as a binary classification problem to predict whether an answer to a given question is correct, and we use logistic loss as the loss function.

We use the probability predicted by the model as the relevance score for each answer. Furthermore, to reduce computational cost, we assign scores only for a small number of top answer candidates. We generate answer candidates using the

---

[9]We use the list of stop words contained in the scikit-learn library.

[10]We use Apache OpenNLP to detect noun words and proper noun words.

union of the top five answers with the highest scores among the scores generated by the Neural Quiz Solver and the IR models.

The features used in this model are primarily based on the scores assigned by the neural network models and IR models described above. For each score, we generate three features using (1) the score, (2) its ranking position in the answer candidates, and (3) the margin between the score and the highest score among the scores of the answer candidates. Further, we use the following four additional features: (1) the number of words in the question, (2) the number of sentences in the question, (3) the number of FIGER entity types associated with the answer, and (4) the binary value representing whether the question contains the answer.

The model is trained using our QA dataset. We use the GBRT implementation in LightGBM[11] with the learning rate being 0.02 and the maximum number of leaves being 400. To maintain accuracy for incomplete questions, we generate five questions truncated at random positions per question. One problem is that we use the same QA dataset for training both the neural network models and the target documents of the IR models; this likely causes overfitting. To address this, we use two methods during the training of the Answer Scorer. For the neural network models, we adopted stacked generalization (Wolpert 1992) based on 10-fold cross validation to compute scores used to train the Answer Scorer. For the IR models, we dynamically exclude the question used to create the input query from the documents.

10.3   Experiments

In this section, we describe the experiments we conducted to evaluate the system presented in the previous section. We first evaluated the performance of our Neural Type Predictor independently and then tested the performance of our question answering system.

10.3.1   Setup

To train and evaluate the models presented in the previous section, we used our QA dataset. We preprocessed the dataset by excluding questions whose answers appear fewer than five times in the dataset. Then, we randomly sampled 10% of the questions to use as a development set and 20% to use as a test set and used the remaining 70% of the questions as a training set. Thus, we obtained 49,423 training questions, 7,060 development questions, and 14,121 test questions with 5,484 unique answers. We denote this dataset as *Dataset QA*. From this dataset, we created another dataset to train and evaluate the performance of the Neural Type

---

[11] https://github.com/Microsoft/LightGBM

Predictor by excluding questions whose answers have no entity types. This dataset contained 39,318 training questions, 5,662 development questions, and 11,209 test questions and is denoted as *Dataset Type*.

We used the training set to train the machine learning models, the development set for early stopping (i.e., detecting the best epoch for testing), and the test set to evaluate the performance of the models. For the IR models, we simply concatenated the training set and the development set and used this as the target documents.

We used accuracy as the performance measure of our question answering system. To evaluate the Neural Type Predictor, we adopted different measures for the coarse-grained model and the fine-grained model. Because the coarse-grained model

Table 10.2 Results for neural type predictor

Model name	Metric	Sentence 1	Sentences 1–2	Sentences 1–3	Full
Coarse-grained CNN	Accuracy	0.95	0.96	0.97	0.98
Fine-grained CNN	Precision@1	0.93	0.95	0.96	0.97
	Accuracy	0.56	0.64	0.69	0.73
	F1	0.83	0.87	0.89	0.91

addresses the task as a single-label text classification, we used accuracy as the metric of its performance, and as the fine-grained model performs multi-label text classification, we used Precision@1, accuracy (prediction is correct if all the predicted types and no incorrect types are predicted), and F1 score (F1 score of all type predictions) as its performance metrics. Moreover, in order to evaluate the performance for incomplete questions, we tested the models using not only the full set of sentences in a question but also the first sentence only, the first and second sentences, and the first through the third sentences.

10.3.2 Results

Table 10.2 shows the performance of our Neural Type Predictor evaluated using *Dataset Type*. The coarse-grained model performed very accurately; the accuracies exceeded 95% for incomplete questions and 98% for full questions. The fine-grained model also achieved good results; its Precision@1 scores were comparable to the accuracies of the coarse-grained model. However, the model suffered when it came to predicting all the fine-grained entity types, resulting in the relatively degraded performance in its accuracy and its F1 score.

Table 10.3 shows the performance of our question answering system. Here, we tested the performance using *Dataset QA*, and used the output of the Answer Scorer to predict the answer. Our system performed very accurately; it achieved 56% accuracy when given only a single sentence and 97% accuracy given the full set of sentences. To further evaluate the effectiveness of each sub-model presented above, we added the sub-models incrementally to the Answer Scorer. Note that the features not based on sub-models (e.g., the number of words in a question) were included in all instances. As a result, all of the sub-models effectively contributed to the performance. We also observed that the neural network models (i.e., Neural Quiz Solver and Neural Type Predictor) achieved good performance only for longer questions. Further, the IR models substantially improved the performance, especially for shorter questions.

Table 10.3 Accuracies of our question answering system. NQS and NTP stand for neural quiz solver and neural type predictor, respectively

Name	Sentence 1	Sentences 1–2	Sentences 1–3	Full
Full model (NQS + NTP + IR)	0.56	0.78	0.88	0.97
NQS	0.31	0.54	0.70	0.88
NQS + coarse-grained NTP	0.33	0.56	0.72	0.89
NQS + fine-grained NTP	0.33	0.57	0.73	0.89
NQS + NTP	0.34	0.57	0.73	0.89
NQS + NTP + IR-Wikipedia	0.48	0.71	0.84	0.95
NQS + NTP + IR-Dataset	0.49	0.73	0.86	0.96

Table 10.4 Accuracies of the top three QA systems submitted in the competition

Name	Accuracy
Our system	**0.85**
Acelove	0.675
Lunit.io	0.6
Baseline	0.55

10.4   Competing with Other Systems and Human Experts

To train our final models submitted in the competition, we again used our QA dataset. We randomly sampled 10% of the questions as a development set and used them for early stopping. For the IR models, we simply created the target documents using the whole dataset.

Since questions are given one word at a time, our system needed to decide whether or not to provide an answer at every word. To achieve this, we adopted a simple strategy: we output an answer if the relevance score of the top answer exceeds a predefined threshold, which is set as 0.6. Furthermore, as predictions frequently become unstable when the question is short, we restrict the system not to output an answer if the number of words in the question is less than 15.

Table 10.4 shows the accuracies of the top three systems submitted in the competition. Our system achieved the best performance by a wide margin. To further evaluate the actual performance of the systems in the quiz bowl, the competition organizers performed simulated pairwise matches between the systems following the official quiz bowl rules. Our system outperformed the Acelove system (our system: 1220 points; the Acelove system: 60 points) and the Lunit.io system (our system: 1145 points; the Lunit.io system: 105 points) by considerably wide margins. The experimental results are reported in detail in Chap. 9.

Furthermore, a live match between our system and a human team consisting of six quiz experts was held at the competition's workshop (see Fig. 10.3). The human team included top quiz experts such as Raj Dhuwalia, a Jeopardy! champion and winner of 250,000 dollars on the TV show *Who Wants to be a Millionaire*, and David Farris, a mathematician and three-time national champion. Our system won the match by a significantly wide margin; it earned 425 points, whereas the human team earned only 200 points.

Fig. 10.3 A live match between six top human quiz experts and our question answering system was held at the HCQA workshop at NIPS 2017

10.5 Conclusions

In this chapter, we describe the question answering system that we submitted in the Human–Computer Question Answering Competition held at NIPS 2017. We proposed two novel neural network models and combined these two models with conventional IR models using a supervised machine learning model. Our system achieved the best performance among the systems submitted in the competition and won the match against six human quiz experts by a wide margin.

References

Jordan Boyd-Graber, Brianna Satinoff, He He, and Hal Daume III. Besting the Quiz Master: Crowdsourcing Incremental Classification Games. In *Proceedings of the 2012 Joint Conference on Empirical Methods in Natural Language Processing and Computational Natural Language Learning*, pages 1290–1301, 2012.

Mohit Iyyer, Jordan Boyd-Graber, Leonardo Claudino, Richard Socher, and Hal Daumé III. A Neural Network for Factoid Question Answering over Paragraphs. In *Proceedings of the 2014 Conference on Empirical Methods in Natural Language Processing*, pages 633–644, 2014.

Mohit Iyyer, Varun Manjunatha, Jordan Boyd-Graber, and Hal Daumé III. Deep Unordered Composition Rivals Syntactic Methods for Text Classification. In *Proceedings of the 53rd Annual Meeting of the Association for Computational Linguistics and the 7th International Joint Conference on Natural Language Processing (Volume 1: Long Papers)*, pages 1681–1691, 2015.

Ikuya Yamada, Hiroyuki Shindo, Hideaki Takeda, and Yoshiyasu Takefuji. Learning Distributed Representations of Texts and Entities from Knowledge Base. *Transactions of the Association for Computational Linguistics*, 5:397–411, 2017.

Yoon Kim. Convolutional Neural Networks for Sentence Classification. In *Proceedings of the 2014 Conference on Empirical Methods in Natural Language Processing*, pages 1746–1751, 2014.

Rada Mihalcea and Andras Csomai. Wikify!: Linking Documents to Encyclopedic Knowledge. In *Proceedings of the Sixteenth ACM Conference on Information and Knowledge Management*, pages 233–242, 2007.

Ikuya Yamada, Hiroyuki Shindo, Hideaki Takeda, and Yoshiyasu Takefuji. Joint Learning of the Embedding of Words and Entities for Named Entity Disambiguation. In *Proceedings of the 20th SIGNLL Conference on Computational Natural Language Learning*, pages 250–259, 2016.

Diederik Kingma and Jimmy Ba. Adam: A Method for Stochastic Optimization. *arXiv preprint arXiv:1412.6980v9*, 2014.

Nitish Srivastava, Geoffrey Hinton, Alex Krizhevsky, Ilya Sutskever, and Ruslan Salakhutdinov. Dropout: A Simple Way to Prevent Neural Networks from Overfitting. *Journal of Machine Learning Research*, 15:1929–1958, 2014.

Xiao Ling and Daniel S. Weld. Fine-Grained Entity Recognition. In *Proceedings of the Twenty-Sixth AAAI Conference on Artificial Intelligence*, pages 94–100, 2012.

Nal Kalchbrenner, Edward Grefenstette, and Phil Blunsom. A Convolutional Neural Network for Modelling Sentences. In *Proceedings of the 52nd Annual Meeting of the Association for Computational Linguistics (Volume 1: Long Papers)*, pages 655–665, Baltimore, Maryland, 2014. Association for Computational Linguistics.

Jeffrey Pennington, Richard Socher, and Christopher D Manning. GloVe: Global Vectors for Word Representation. In *Proceedings of the 2014 Conference on Empirical Methods in Natural Language Processing*, pages 1532–1543, 2014.

Wen-tau Yih, Ming-Wei Chang, Christopher Meek, and Andrzej Pastusiak. Question Answering Using Enhanced Lexical Semantic Models. In *Proceedings of the 51st Annual Meeting of the Association for Computational Linguistics (Volume 1: Long Papers)*, pages 1744–1753, 2013.

Lei Yu, Karl Moritz Hermann, Phil Blunsom, and Stephen Pulman. Deep Learning for Answer Sentence Selection. *arXiv preprint arXiv:1412.1632v1*, 2014.

Jerome H. Friedman. Greedy Function Approximation: A Gradient Boosting Machine. *The Annals of Statistics*, 29(5):1189–1232, 2001.

O Chapelle and Y Chang. Yahoo! Learning to Rank Challenge Overview. In *Proceedings of the Learning to Rank Challenge*, volume 14 of *Proceedings of Machine Learning Research*, pages 1–24, 2011.

Dawei Yin, Yuening Hu, Jiliang Tang, Tim Daly, Mianwei Zhou, Hua Ouyang, Jianhui Chen, Changsung Kang, Hongbo Deng, Chikashi Nobata, Jean-Marc Langlois, and Yi Chang. Ranking Relevance in Yahoo Search. In *Proceedings of the 22nd ACM SIGKDD International Conference on Knowledge Discovery and Data Mining*, pages 323–332, 2016.

David H Wolpert. Stacked generalization. *Neural networks*, 5(2):241–259, 1992.

Chapter 11
Adversarial Attacks and Defences Competition

Alexey Kurakin, Ian Goodfellow, Samy Bengio, Yinpeng Dong,
Fangzhou Liao, Ming Liang, Tianyu Pang, Jun Zhu, Xiaolin Hu, Cihang Xie,
Jianyu Wang, Zhishuai Zhang, Zhou Ren, Alan Yuille, Sangxia Huang,
Yao Zhao, Yuzhe Zhao, Zhonglin Han, Junjiajia Long,
Yerkebulan Berdibekov, Takuya Akiba, Seiya Tokui, and Motoki Abe

Abstract To accelerate research on adversarial examples and robustness of machine learning classifiers, Google Brain organized a NIPS 2017 competition that encouraged researchers to develop new methods to generate adversarial examples as well as to develop new ways to defend against them. In this chapter, we describe

A. Kurakin (✉) · I. Goodfellow · S. Bengio
Google Brain, Mountain View, CA, USA

Y. Dong · F. Liao · M. Liang · T. Pang · J. Zhu · X. Hu
Department of Computer Science and Technology, Tsinghua University, Beijing, China

C. Xie · Z. Zhang · A. Yuille
Department of Computer Science, The Johns Hopkins University, Baltimore, MD, USA

J. Wang
Baidu Research, Sunnyvale, CA, USA

Z. Ren
Snap Inc., Los Angeles, CA, USA

S. Huang
Sony Mobile Communications, Lund, Sweden

Y. Zhao
Microsoft Corporation, Redmond, WA, USA

Y. Zhao
Department of Computer Science, Yale Univerisity, New Haven, CT, USA

Z. Han
Smule Inc, San Francisco, CA, USA

J. Long
Department of Physics, Yale University, New Haven, CT, USA

Y. Berdibekov
Independent Scholar, Almaty, Kazakhstan

T. Akiba · S. Tokui · M. Abe
Preferred Networks, Inc., Tokyo, Japan

© Springer International Publishing AG, part of Springer Nature 2018
S. Escalera, M. Weimer (eds.), *The NIPS '17 Competition: Building Intelligent Systems*, The Springer Series on Challenges in Machine Learning,
https://doi.org/10.1007/978-3-319-94042-7_11

the structure and organization of the competition and the solutions developed by several of the top-placing teams.

11.1 Introduction

Recent advances in machine learning and deep neural networks enabled researchers to solve multiple important practical problems like image, video, text classification and others.

However most existing machine learning classifiers are highly vulnerable to adversarial examples (Biggio et al. 2013; Szegedy et al. 2014; Goodfellow et al. 2014; Papernot et al. 2016b). An adversarial example is a sample of input data which has been modified very slightly in a way that is intended to cause a machine learning classifier to misclassify it. In many cases, these modifications can be so subtle that a human observer does not even notice the modification at all, yet the classifier still makes a mistake.

Adversarial examples pose security concerns because they could be used to perform an attack on machine learning systems, even if the adversary has no access to the underlying model.

Moreover it was discovered (Kurakin et al. 2016; Sharif et al. 2016) that it is possible to perform adversarial attacks even on a machine learning system which operates in physical world and perceives input through inaccurate sensors, instead of reading precise digital data.

In the long run, machine learning and AI systems will become more powerful. Machine learning security vulnerabilities similar to adversarial examples could be used to compromise and control highly powerful AIs. Thus, robustness to adversarial examples is an important part of the AI safety problem.

Research on adversarial attacks and defenses is difficult for many reasons. One reason is that evaluation of proposed attacks or proposed defenses is not straightforward. Traditional machine learning, with an assumption of a training set and test set that have been drawn i.i.d., is straightforward to evaluate by measuring the loss on the test set. For adversarial machine learning, defenders must contend with an open-ended problem, in which an attacker will send inputs from an unknown distribution. It is not sufficient to benchmark a defense against a single attack or even a suite of attacks prepared ahead of time by the researcher proposing the defense. Even if the defense performs well in such an experiment, it may be defeated by a new attack that works in a way the defender did not anticipate. Ideally, a defense would be provably sound, but machine learning in general and deep neural networks in particular are difficult to analyze theoretically. A competition therefore gives a useful intermediate form of evaluation: a defense is pitted against attacks built by independent teams, with both the defense team and the attack team incentivized to win. While such an evaluation is not as conclusive as a theoretical proof, it is a much better simulation of a real-life security scenario than an evaluation of a defense carried out by the proposer of the defense.

In this report, we describe the NIPS 2017 competition on adversarial attack and defense, including an overview of the key research problems involving adversarial examples (Sect. 11.2), the structure and organization of the competition (Sect. 11.3), and several of the methods developed by the top-placing competitors (Sect. 11.4).

11.2 Adversarial Examples

Adversarial examples are inputs to machine learning models that have been intentionally optimized to cause the model to make a mistake. We call an input example a "clean example" if it is a naturally occurring example, such as a photograph from the ImageNet dataset. If an adversary has modified an example with the intention of causing it to be misclassified, we call it an "adversarial example." Of course, the adversary may not necessarily succeed; a model may still classify the adversarial example correctly. We can measure the accuracy or the error rate of different models on a particular set of adversarial examples.

11.2.1 Common Attack Scenarios

Scenarios of possible adversarial attacks can be categorized along different dimensions.

First of all, attacks can be classified by the type of outcome the adversary desires:

- **Non-targeted attack.** In this the case adversary's goal is to cause the classifier to predict any inccorect label. The specific incorrect label does not matter.
- **Targeted attack.** In this case the adversary aims to change the classifier's prediction to some specific target class.

Second, attack scenarios can be classified by the amount of knowledge the adversary has about the model:

- **White box.** In the white box scenario, the adversary has full knowledge of the model including model type, model architecture and values of all parameters and trainable weights.
- **Black box with probing.** In this scenario, the adversary does not know very much about the model, but can probe or query the model, i.e. feed some inputs and observe outputs. There are many variants of this scenario—the adversary may know the architecture but not the parameters or the adversary may not even know the architecture, the adversary may be able to observe output probabilities for each class or the adversary may only be to observe the choice of the most likely class.

- **Black box without probing** In the black box without probing scenario, the adversary has limited or no knowledge about the model under attack and is not allowed to probe or query the model while constructing adversarial examples. In this case, the attacker must construct adversarial examples that fool most machine learning models.

Third, attacks can be classifier by the way adversary can feed data into the model:

- **Digital attack.** In this case, the adversary has direct access to the actual data fed into the model. In other words, the adversary can choose specific `float32` values as input for the model. In a real world setting, this might occur when an attacker uploads a PNG file to a web service, and intentionally designs the file to be read incorrectly. For example, spam content might be posted on social media, using adversarial perturbations of the image file to evade the spam detector.
- **Physical attack.** In the case of an attack in the physical world, the adversary does not have direct access to the digital representation of provided to the model. Instead, the model is fed input obtained by sensors such as a camera or microphone. The adversary is able to place objects in the physical environment seen by the camera or produce sounds heard by the microphone. The exact digital representation obtained by the sensors will change based on factors like the camera angle, the distance to the microphone, ambient light or sound in the environment, etc. This means the attacker has less precise control over the input provided to the machine learning model.

11.2.2 Attack Methods

Most of the attacks discussed in the literature are geared toward the white-box digital case.

11.2.2.1 White Box Digital Attacks

L-BFGS One of the first methods to find adversarial examples for neural networks was proposed in Szegedy et al. (2014). The idea of this method is to solve the following optimization problem:

$$\left| x^{adv} - x \right|_2 \to \text{minimum}, \quad \text{s.t.} \quad f(x^{adv}) = y_{target}, \quad x^{adv} \in [0, 1]^m \quad (11.1)$$

The authors proposed to use the L-BFGS optimization method to solve this problem, thus the name of the attack.

One of the main drawbacks of this method is that it is quite slow. The method is not designed to counteract defenses such as reducing the number of bits used to store each pixel. Instead, the method is designed to find the smallest possible attack perturbation. This means the method can sometimes be defeated merely by degrading the image quality, for example, by rounding to an 8-bit representation of each pixel.

Fast gradient sign method (FGSM) To test the idea that adversarial examples can be found using only a linear approximation of the target model, the authors of Goodfellow et al. (2014) introduced the *fast gradient sign method* (FGSM).

FGSM works by linearizing loss function in L_∞ neighbourhood of a clean image and finds exact maximum of linearized function using following closed-form equation:

$$x^{adv} = x + \epsilon \, \text{sign}\big(\nabla_x J(x, y_{true})\big) \tag{11.2}$$

Iterative attacks The L-BFGS attack has a high success rate and high computational cost. The FGSM attack has a low success rate (especially when the defender anticipates it) and low computational cost. A nice tradeoff can be achieved by running iterative optimization algorithms that are specialized to reach a solution quickly, after a small number (e.g. 40) of iterations.

One strategy for designing optimization algorithms quickly is to take the FGSM (which can often reach an acceptable solution in one very large step) and run it for several steps but with a smaller step size. Because each FGSM step is designed to go all the way to the edge of a small norm ball surrounding the starting point for the step, the method makes rapid progress even when gradients are small. This leads to the **Basic Iterative Method (BIM)** method introduced in Kurakin (2016), also sometimes called **Iterative FGSM (I-FGSM)**:

$$x_0^{adv} = X, \quad x_{N+1}^{adv} = Clip_{X,\epsilon}\Big\{X_N^{adv} + \alpha \, \text{sign}\big(\nabla_X J(X_N^{adv}, y_{true})\big)\Big\} \tag{11.3}$$

The BIM can be easily made into a target attack, called the Iterative Target Class Method:

$$X_0^{adv} = X, \quad X_{N+1}^{adv} = Clip_{X,\epsilon}\Big\{X_N^{adv} - \alpha \, \text{sign}\Big(\nabla_X J(X_N^{adv}, y_{target})\Big)\Big\} \tag{11.4}$$

It was observed that with sufficient number of iterations this attack almost always succeeds in hitting target class (Kurakin 2016).

Madry et al.'s Attack Madry et al. (2017) showed that the BIM can be significantly improved by starting from a random point within the ϵ norm ball. This attack is often called **projected gradient descent**, but this name is somewhat confusing because (1) the term "projected gradient descent" already refers to an optimization method more general than the specific use for adversarial attack, (2) the other attacks use the gradient and perform project in the same way (the attack is the same as BIM except for the starting point) so the name doesn't differentiate this attack from the others.

Carlini and Wagner attack (C&W) N. Carlini and D. Wagner followed a path of L-BFGS attack. They designed a loss function which has smaller values on adversarial examples and higher on clean examples and searched for adversarial examples by minimizing it (Carlini and Wagner 2017b). But unlike (Szegedy et al. 2014) they used Adam (Kingma and Ba 2014) to solve the optimization problem and dealt with box constraints either by change of variables (i.e. $x = 0.5(\tanh(w) + 1)$) or by projecting results onto box constraints after each step.

They explored several possible loss functions and achieved the strongest L_2 attack with following:

$$\|x^{adv} - x\|_p + c \max\left(\max_{i \neq Y} f(x^{adv})_i - f(x^{adv})_Y, -\kappa\right) \rightarrow \text{minimum} \qquad (11.5)$$

where x^{adv} parametrized $0.5(\tanh(w) + 1)$; Y is a shorter notation for target class y_{target}; c and κ are method parameters.

Adversarial transformation networks (ATN) Another approach which was explored in Baluja and Fischer (2017) is to train a generative model to craft adversarial examples. This model takes a clean image as input and generates a corresponding adversarial image. One advantage of this approach is that, if the generative model itself is designed to be small, the ATN can generate adversarial examples faster than an explicit optimization algorithm. In theory, this approach can be faster than even the FGSM, if the ATN is designed to use less computation is needed for running back-propagation on the target model. (The ATN does of course require extra time to train, but once this cost has been paid an unlimited number of examples may be generated at low cost)

Attacks on non differentiable systems All attacks mentioned about need to compute gradients of the model under attack in order to craft adversarial examples. However this may not be always possible, for example if model contains non-differentiable operations. In such cases, the adversary can train a substitute model and utilize transferability of adversarial examples to perform an attack on non-differentiable system, similar to black box attacks, which are described below.

11.2.2.2 Black Box Attacks

It was observed that adversarial examples generalize between different models (Szegedy et al. 2014). In other words, a significant fraction of adversarial examples which fool one model are able to fool a different model. This property is called "transferability" and is used to craft adversarial examples in the black box scenario. The actual number of transferable adversarial examples could vary from a few percent to almost 100% depending on the source model, target model, dataset and other factors. Attackers in the black box scenario can train their own model on the same dataset as the target model, or even train their model on another dataset drawn from the same distribution. Adversarial examples for the adversary's model then have a good chance of fooling an unknown target model.

It is also possible to intentionally design models to systematically cause high transfer rates, rather than relying on luck to achieve transfer.

If the attacker is not in the complete black box scenario but is allowed to use probes, the probes may be used to train the attacker's own copy of the target model (Papernot et al. 2017, 2016b) called a "substitute." This approach is powerful because the input examples sent as probes do not need to be actual training examples; instead they can be input points chosen by the attacker to find out exactly where the target model's decision boundary lies. The attacker's model is thus trained not just to be a good classifier but to actually reverse engineer the details of the target model, so the two models are systematically driven to have a high amount of transfer.

In the complete black box scenario where the attacker cannot send probes, one strategy to increase the rate of transfer is to use an ensemble of several models as the source model for the adversarial examples (Liu et al. 2017). The basic idea is that if an adversarial example fools every model in the ensemble, it is more likely to generalize and fool additional models.

Finally, in the black box scenario with probes, it is possible to just run optimization algorithms that do not use the gradient to directly attack the target model (Brendel et al. 2017; Chen et al. 2017). The time required to generate a single adversarial example is generally much higher than when using a substitute, but if only a small number of adversarial examples are required, these methods may have an advantage because they do not have the high initial fixed cost of training the substitute.

11.2.3 Overview of Defenses

No method of defending against adversarial examples is yet completely satisfactory. This remains a rapidly evolving research area. We given an overview of the (not yet fully succesful defense methods) proposed so far.

Since adversarial perturbations generated by many methods look like high-frequency noise to a human observer[1] multiple authors have suggested to use image preprocessing and denoising as a potential defence against adversarial examples. There is a large variation in the proposed preprocessing techniques, like doing JPEG compression (Das et al. 2017) or applying median filtering and reducing precision of input data (Xu et al. 2017). While such defences may work well against certain attacks, defenses in this category have been shown to fail in the white box case, where the attacker is aware of the defense (He et al. 2017). In the black box case, this defense can be effective in practice, as demonstrated by the winning team of the

---

[1]This may be because the human perceptual system finds the high-frequency components to be more salient; when blurred with a low pass filter, adversarial perturbations are often found to have significant low-frequency components

defense competition. Their defense, described in Sect. 11.5.1, is an example of this family of denoising strategies.

Many defenses, intentionally or unintentionally, fall into a category called "gradient masking." Most white box attacks operate by computing gradients of the model and thus fail if it is impossible to compute useful gradients. Gradient masking consists of making the gradient useless, either by changing the model in some way that makes it non-differentiable or makes it have zero gradients in most places, or make the gradients point away from the decision boundary. Essentially, gradient masking means breaking the optimizer without actually moving the class decision boundaries substantially. Because the class decision boundaries are more or less the same, defenses based on gradient masking are highly vulnerable to black box transfer (Papernot et al. 2017). Some defense strategies (like replacing smooth sigmoid units with hard threshold units) are intentionally designed to perform gradient masking. Other defenses, like many forms of adversarial training, are not designed with gradient masking as a goal, but seem to often learn to do gradient masking when applied in practice.

Many defenses are based on detecting adversarial examples and refusing to classify the input if there are signs of tampering (Metzen et al. 2017). This approach works long as the attacker is unaware of the detector or the attack is not strong enough. Otherwise the attacker can construct an attack which simultaneously fools the detector into thinking an adversarial input is a legitimate input and fools the classifier into making the wrong classification (Carlini and Wagner 2017a).

Some defenses work but do so at the cost of seriously reducing accuracy on clean examples. For example, shallow RBF networks are highly robust to adversarial examples on small datasets like MNIST (Goodfellow 2014) but have much worse accuracy on clean MNIST than deep neural networks. Deep RBF networks might be both robust to adversarial examples and accurate on clean data, but to our knowledge no one has successfully trained one.

Capsule networks have shown robustness to white box attacks on the Small-NORB dataset, but have not yet been evaluated on other datasets more commonly used in the adversarial example literature (Geoffrey et al. 2018).

The most popular defense in current research papers is probably adversarial training (Szegedy et al. 2014; Goodfellow et al. 2014; Huang et al. 2015). The idea is to inject adversarial examples into training process and train the model either on adversarial examples or on mix of clean and adversarial examples. The approach was successfully applied to large datasets (Kurakin et al. 2016), and can be made more effective by using discrete vector code representations rather than real number representations of the input (Buckman et al. 2018). One key drawback of adversarial training is that it tends to overfit to the specific attack used at training time. This has been overcome, at least on small datasets, by adding noise prior to starting the optimizer for the attack (Madry et al. 2017). Another key drawback of adversarial training is that it tends to inadvertently learn to do gradient masking rather than to actually move the decision boundary. This can be largely overcome by training on adversarial examples drawn from an ensemble of several models (Tramr et al. 2017). A remaining key drawback of adversarial training is that it tends to overfit to specific constraint region used to generate the adversarial examples (models trained to resist adversarial examples in a max-norm ball may not resist adversarial examples based on large modifications to background pixels (Gilmer et al. 2018) even if the new adversarial examples do not appear particularly challenging to a human observer).

11.3 Adversarial Competition

The phenomenon of adversarial examples creates a new set of problems in machine learning. Studying these problems is often difficult, because when a researcher proposes a new attack, it is hard to tell whether their attack is strong, or whether they have not implemented their defense method used for benchmarking well enough. Similarly, it is hard to tell whether a new defense method works well or whether it has just not been tested against the right attack.

To accelerate research in adversarial machine learning and pit many proposed attacks and defenses against each other in order to obtain the most vigorous evaluation possible of these methods, we decided to organize a competition.

In this competition participants are invited to submit methods which craft adversarial examples (attacks) as well as classifiers which are robust to adversarial eaxmples (defenses). When evaluating competition, we run all attack methods on our dataset to produce adversarial examples and then run all defenses on all generated adversarial examples. Attacks are ranked by number of times there were able to fool defenses and defenses are scored by number of correctly classified examples.

11.3.1 Dataset

When making a dataset for these competition we had following requirements:

1. Large enough dataset and non-trivial problem, so the competition would be interesting.
2. Well known problem, so people potentially can reuse existing classifiers. (This ensures that competitors are able to focus on the adversarial nature of the challenge, rather than spending all their time coming up with a solution to the underlying task)
3. Data samples which were never used before, so participants unlikely to overfit to well known dataset.

These requirements were satisfied by choosing image classification problem and creating a dataset with ImageNet-compatible images (Deng et al. 2009). To do this we collected a set of images which were never used in publicly available datasets, labelled them using pretrained ImageNet classifier and then manually verified that these labels are correct.

The original (non-adversarial) ImageNet challenge (Russakovsky et al. 2015) is a complex and interesting problem, and thus satisfies requirement number 1. Additionally there are plenty of existing classifiers for ImageNet data, which satisfies requirement number 2. Because we collected new images and labelled them instead of using the already available dataset, our approach satisfies requirement number 3.

Overall we collected two datasets for this competitions:

- **DEV** dataset was released to participants in the beginning of the competition, so they can use it for development of their solutions. This dataset contained 1000 images.
- **FINAL** dataset was kept secret and was used to evaluate final submissions of participants. It contained 5000 images.

11.3.2 Tasks and Competition Rules

Our competition had three tracks. Each track had a different task:

- **Non-targeted adversarial attack.** In this track participants were invited to submit a method which performs a non-targeted black box attack, i.e. given an input image, generate an adversarial image which is likely be misclassified by unknown classifier.
- **Targeted adversarial attack.** In this track participants were invited to submit a method which performs a targeted black box attack, i.e. given an input image and a target class, generate an adversarial image which is likely be misclassified as a given target class by unknown classifier.
- **Defense against adversarial attacks.** In this track, participants were invited to submit a classifier which is robust to adversarial examples.

In all tracks participants submitted a program which performs the given task and we ran this code using our evaluation infrastructure.

The submitted program was given a set of images (and target classes in case of targeted attack) as an input, and had to produce either an adversarial image (for attack submission) or classification label (for defense submission) for each input image.

Input images were fed to each submission in batches of 100 images. To limit the budget required for computation, the rules of the competitions specified that each submission had to process a batch of 100 images in no more than 500 s. If a submission was not done after 500 seconds, then processing of the current batch was interrupted and the submission was fed the next batch. Only successfully processed images were included in the score of the submission (see details below in evaluation sub-section).

11.3.3 Evaluation Metrics

An attack got 1 point each time it was able to fool a defense on single image. If attack was unable to fool a defense or if it failed to generate an adversarial version of an image within the time limit then it got 0 points for that image. A defense got 1 point for each correctly classified image and 0 points for incorrect classification or failure to produce a classification label. A defense was used to score attacks only if it successfully processed all input images, so that attackers were neither rewarded nor penalized for making images that caused the defender to crash or time out—the competition is purely about classification accuracy. Likewise, an attack was used to score defenses only if it succesfully processed all inputs. Points for each submission were added together and then normalized (using the same normalization constant for all submissions), such that final scores of all submissions are in the range [0, 1], where 1 means success on all images and 0 means failure on all images.

Specifically, the score of each non-targeted attack $a(Image)$ was computed using the following formula:

$$\frac{1}{|D|N} \sum_{d \in D} \sum_{k=1}^{N} [d(a(I_k)) \neq TrueLabel_k] \tag{11.6}$$

The score of each targeted attack $a(Image, TargetLabel)$ was computed as:

$$\frac{1}{|D|N} \sum_{d \in D} \sum_{k=1}^{N} [d(a(I_k, TargetLabel_k)) = TargetLabel_k] \tag{11.7}$$

The score of each defense $d(Image)$ was computed in the following way:

$$\frac{1}{|A|N} \sum_{a \in A} \sum_{k=1}^{N} [d(a(I_k)) = TrueLabel_k] \tag{11.8}$$

Where:

- A is the set of all attacks (targeted and non-targeted) which were used for evaluation of defenses (attacks that crashed on some inputs or ran out of time for some inputs were not used to evaluate defense);
- D is the set of all defenses which were used for evaluation of attacks (defenses that crashed on some inputs or ran out of time for some inputs were not used to evaluate attacks);
- N is the number of images in the dataset;
- I_k is the k-th image from the dataset;
- $TrueLabelk$ is the true label of image I_k;
- $TargetLabel_k$ is the chosen target label for image k;

- [P] is an indicator function which equals to 1 when P is true, and 0 when P is false or undefined.
- $d(\bullet)$ is a defending classifier. If the binary fails to complete execution within the time limit, the output of $d(\bullet)$ is a null label that never equals the true label. If $d(\bullet)$ is called on an undefined image, it is defined to always return the true label, so an attacker that crashes receives zero points.

Additionally to metrics used for ranking, after the competition we computed worst case score for each submission in defense and non-targeted attack tracks. These scores were useful to understand how submissions act in the worst case. To compute worst score of defense we computed accuracy of the defense against each attack and chosen minimum:

$$\frac{1}{N} \min_{a \in A} \sum_{k=1}^{N} [d(a(I_k)) = TrueLabel_k] \tag{11.9}$$

To compute worst case score of non-targeted attack we computed how often attack caused misclassification when used against each defense and chosen minimum misclassification rate:

$$\frac{1}{N} \min_{d \in D} \sum_{k=1}^{N} [d(a(I_k)) \neq TrueLabel_k] \tag{11.10}$$

Worst case score of targeted attack could be computed in a similar way, but generally not useful because targeted attacks are much weaker than non-targeted and all worst scores of targeted attacks were 0.

11.3.4 Competition Schedule

The competition was announced in May 2017, launched in the beginning of July 2017 and finished on October 1st, 2017. The ompetition was run in multiple rounds. There were three development rounds followed by the final round:

- August 1, 2017 – first development round
- September 1, 2017 – second development round
- September 15, 2017 – third development round
- October 1, 2017 – deadline for final submission

Development rounds were optional and their main purpose was to help participants to test their solution. Only the final round was used to compute final scores of submissions and determine winners.

Algorithm 1 Algorithm of work of evaluation infrastructure

  ▷ PREPARE DATASET
1: Split dataset $D = \{I_1, \ldots, I_N\}$ into batches $\{B_1, \ldots, B_k\}$, such that each batch B_i contains
     100 image $\{I_{100(i-1)+1}, \ldots, I_{100i}\}$.
2: Assign size of maximum allowed perturbation ϵ_i to each batch B_i. Value of ϵ_i is randomly
     chosen from the set $\{\frac{4}{255}, \frac{8}{255}, \frac{12}{255}, \frac{16}{255}\}$
  ▷ RUN ALL ATTACKS
3: **for all** $b \in \{1, \ldots, k\}$ **do**   ▷ loop over all batches, b is batch index
4:     **for all** non-targeted attacks a **do**
5:         Run attack a on batch B_b and generate a batch of adversarial images $\hat{B}_b^a$. Size of
          maximum perturbation ϵ_b is provided to an attack.
6:         Project each adversarial image from $\hat{B}_b^a$ into L_∞ ϵ_b-neighborhood of corresponding
          clean image from B_b.
7:     **end for**
8:     **for all** targeted attacks t **do**
9:         Run attack t on batch B_b and generate a batch of adversarial images $\hat{B}_b^t$. Attack is
          provided with size of maximum perturbation ϵ_b as well as target classes for each
          image from the batch B_b.
10:        Project each adversarial image from $\hat{B}_b^t$ into L_∞ ϵ_b-neighborhood of corresponding
          clean image from B_b.
11:     **end for**
12: **end for**
  ▷ RUN ALL DEFENSES
13: **for all** $b \in \{1, \ldots, k\}$ **do**   ▷ loop over all batches, b is batch index
14:     **for all** defense d **do**
15:         **for all** non-targeted attacks a **do**
16:            Run defense d on all images from batch $\hat{B}_b^a$
17:         **end for**
18:         **for all** targeted attacks t **do**
19:            Run defense d on all images from batch $\hat{B}_b^t$
20:         **end for**
21:     **end for**
22: **end for**
  ▷ COMPUTE SCORES
23: Determine subset of targeted and non-targeted attacks A which produces all adversarial images
24: Determine subset of defenses D which output classification labels for all input images
25: Compute scores of all submissions using Equations 11.6, 11.7, 11.8

All rounds were evaluated in a similar way. For the evaluation of the round we gathered all submissions which were submitted before the round deadline, ran all of them and computed scores as described in Sect. 11.3.3.

We used DEV dataset to compute scores in development rounds and secret FINAL dataset to compute scores in the final round.

11.3.5   Technical Aspects of Evaluation

Competition participants were submitting pieces of code and we have run them ourselves. This approach posess several challanges. First of all we need to protect competition infrastructure from malicious code. Secondly, given the dataset size and number of submissions we had to run it in an efficient way.

We partnered with Kaggle[2] and used their platform as a frontend for the competition. Kaggle hosted competition web-site, leaderboard and participants were uploading submissions through Kaggle. For evaluation of each round we took all submissions from Kaggle and fed them into our evaluation infrastructure.

Evaluation infrastructure worked as described in Algorithm 1. As could be seen from the algorithm, attacks could be run independently of each other. Same for defenses. We took advantage of this fact and parallelized execution of all attacks and all defenses by spreading them across multiple machines.

For final evaluation we used 100 Google Cloud VMs. At any given moment one VM was running either one attack on one batch from the dataset or one defense on one batch of adversarial images. Submissions were run inside Docker containers to isolate submissions from our evaluation infrastructure and from the outside world.

11.4   Competition Results

For the final round we had 91 non-targeted attack submissions, 65 targeted attack submission and 107 defense submissions. During the course of competitions submissions kept improving their results compared to baselines which could be seen from Fig. 11.1.

Final results of the top submissions in each track are provided in Tables 11.1, 11.2 and 11.3. Meaning of the columns is following. **Rank** is submission rank in final scoring, **score** is submission score as described in Sect. 11.3.3, **raw score** is un-normalized score which is number of times submission got a point on the image, **worst score** is submission score in the worst case and **medial eval time** is median time needed for evaluation of one batch of 100 images. To put things into prospective, plots of all submission scores in final round from best to worst and comparison with provided baselines are depicted in Fig. 11.2.

As could be seen from the tables, best defenses achieved more than 90% accuracy on all adversarial images from all attacks. At the same time worst case scores of defenses are much lower. The highest worst case score among all defenses is only 53.6%.

---

[2]www.kaggle.com

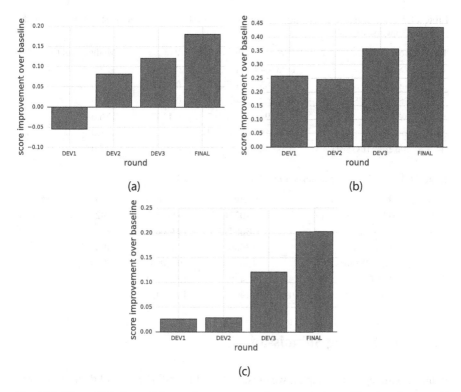

Fig. 11.1 Plots which shows difference between score of top submission and best baseline in each round in each track. As could be seen from the plot, submissions kept improving each round. (**a**) Defenses. (**b**) Non-targeted attacks. (**c**) Targeted attacks

Table 11.1 Top-5 defense submissions, best baseline and submission with maximum worst-case score

Rank	Team name or baseline	Score	Raw score	Worst score	Median eval time
1	TSAIL	0.953164	691044	0.1184	51.0
2	iyswim	0.923524	669555	0.2520	126.0
3	Anil Thomas	0.914840	663259	0.2666	97.0
4	erko	0.911961	661172	0.2920	87.0
5	Stanford & Suns	0.910593	660180	0.0682	129.0
24	Rafael Moraes	0.871739	632011	**0.5358**	17.0
56	Baseline (Ens. adv. ir_v2)	0.772908	560358	0.0186	17.0

This could be an indication that it's possible to achieve pretty high accuracy against adversarial examples in average case, however model will still be suspectible to adversarial examples and could be fooled if adversary will be able to find them.

Similar observation holds for attacks. Best attacks achieved up to 78% fooling rate against all defenses, at the same time worst case score of attacks was no more than 34%.

Table 11.2 Top-5 non-targeted attack submissions, best baseline and best submission with according to worst-case score

Rank	Team name or baseline	Score	Raw score	Worst score	Median eval time
1	TSAIL	0.781644	410363	0.1364	423.0
2	Sangxia	0.776855	407849	**0.3412**	421.0
3	Stanford & Sun	0.774025	406363	0.2722	497.0
4	iwiwi	0.768981	403715	0.1352	76.0
5	toshi_k	0.755598	396689	0.3322	448.0
44	Baseline (FGSM)	0.346400	181860	0.0174	17.0

Table 11.3 Top-5 targeted attack submissions and best baseline

Rank	Team	Score	Raw score	Median eval time
1	TSAIL	0.402211	211161.0	392.0
2	Sangxia	0.368773	193606.0	414.0
3	FatFingers	0.368029	193215.0	493.0
4	Anil Thomas	0.364552	191390.0	495.0
5	WNP	0.347935	182666.0	487.0
24	Baseline (Iter. T. C. 20)	0.199773	104881.0	127.0

11.5 Top Scoring Submissions

In the remainder of the chapter, we present the solutions of several of the top-scoring teams.

To describe the solutions, we use the following notation:

- x – input image with label y_{true}. Different images are distinguished by superscripts, for examples images x^1, x^2, ... with labels y^1_{true}, y^2_{true}, ...
- y_{target} is a target class for image x for targeted adversarial attack.
- Functions with names like $f(\bullet)$, $g(\bullet)$, $h(\bullet)$, ... are classifiers which map input images into logits. In other words $f(x)$ is logits vector of networks f on image x
- $J(f(x), y)$ – cross entropy loss between logits $f(x)$ and class y.
- ε – maximum L_∞ norm of adversarial perturbation.
- x_{adv} – adversarial images. For iterative methods x^i_{adv} is adversarial example generated on step i.
- $Clip_{[a,b]}(\bullet)$ is a function which performs element-wise clipping of input tensor to interval $[a, b]$.
- $\mathcal{X}$ is the set of all training examples.

All values of images are normalized to be in $[0, 1]$ interval. Values of ϵ are also normalized to $[0, 1]$ range, for examples $\epsilon = \frac{16}{255}$ correspond to uint8 value of epsilon equal to 16.

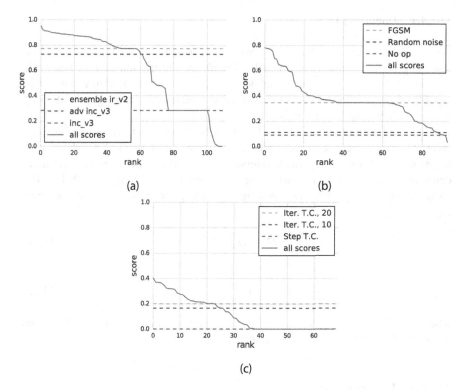

Fig. 11.2 Plots with scores of submissions in all three tracks. Solid line of each plot is scores of submissions depending on submission rank. Dashed lines are scores of baselines we provided. These plots demonstrate difference between best and worst submissions as well as how much top submissions were able to improve provided baselines. (**a**) Defenses. (**b**) Non-targeted attacks. (**c**) Targeted attacks

11.5.1   First Place in Defense Track: Team TsAIL

Team members Yinpeng Dong, Fangzhou Liao, Ming Liang, Tianyu Pang, Jun Zhu and Xiaolin Hu.

In this section, we introduce the high-level representation guided denoiser (HGD) method, which won the first place in the defense track. The idea is to train a neural network based denoiser to remove the adversarial perturbation.

11.5.1.1   Dataset

To prepare the training set for the denoiser, we first extracted 20 K images from the ImageNet training set (20 images per class). Then we used a bunch of adversarial attacks to distort these images and form a training set. Attacking methods included FGSM and I-FGSM and were applied to the many models and their ensembles to simulate weak and strong attacks.

11.5.1.2 Denoising U-net

Denoising autoencoder (DAE) (Vincent et al. 2008) is a potential choice of the denoising network. But DAE has a bottleneck for the transmission of fine-scale information between the encoder and decoder. This bottleneck structure may not be capable of carrying the multi-scale information contained in the images. That's why we used a denoising U-net (DUNET).

Compared with DAE, the DUNET adds some lateral connections from encoder layers to their corresponding decoder layers of the same resolution. In this way, the network is learning to predict adversarial noise only, which is more relevant to denoising and easier than reconstructing the whole image (Zhang et al. 2017). The clean image can be readily obtained by subtracting the noise from the corrupted input:

$$d\hat{x} = D_w(x^{adv}). \tag{11.11}$$

$$\hat{x} = x^{adv} - d\hat{x}. \tag{11.12}$$

where D_w is a denoiser network with parameters w, $d\hat{x}$ is predicted adversarial noise and $\hat{x}$ is reconstructured clean image.

11.5.1.3 Loss Function

The vanilla denoiser uses the reconstructing distance as the loss function, but we found a better method. Given a target neural network, we extract its representation at l-th layer for x and $\hat{x}$, and calculate the loss function as:

$$L = \| f_l(\hat{x}) - f_l(x) \|_1. \tag{11.13}$$

The corresponding models are called HGD, because the supervised signal comes from certain high-level layers of the classifier and carries guidance information related to image classification.

We propose two HGDs with different choices of l. For the first HGD, we define $l = -2$ as the index of the topmost convolutional layer. This denoiser is called feature guided denoiser (FGD). For the second HGD, we use the logits layer. So it is called logits guided denoiser (LGD).

Another kind of HGD uses the classification loss of the target model as the denoising loss function, which is supervised learning as ground truth labels are needed. This model is called class label guided denoiser (CGD). In this case the loss function is optimized with respect to the parameters of the denoiser w, while the parameters of the guiding model are fixed.

Please refer to our full-length paper (Liao et al. 2017) for more information.

11.5.2 First Place in Both Attack Tracks: Team TsAIL

Team members Yinpeng Dong, Fangzhou Liao, Ming Liang, Tianyu Pang, Jun Zhu and Xiaolin Hu.

In this section, we introduce the momentum iterative gradient-based attack method, which won the first places in both the non-targeted attack and targeted attack tracks. We first describe the algorithm in Sect. 11.5.2.1, and then illustrate our submissions for non-targeted and targeted attacks respectively in Sects. 11.5.2.2 and 11.5.2.3. A more detailed description can be found in Dong et al. (2017).

11.5.2.1 Method

The momentum iterative attack method is built upon the basic iterative method (Kurakin 2016), by adding a momentum term to greatly improve the transferability of the generated adversarial examples.

Existing attack methods exhibit low efficacy when attacking black-box models, due to the well-known trade-off between the attack strength and the transferability (Kurakin et al. 2016). In particular, one-step method (e.g., FGSM) calculates the gradient only once using the assumption of linearity of the decision boundary around the data point. However in practice, the linear assumption may not hold when the distortions are large (Liu et al. 2017), which makes the adversarial examples generated by one-step method "underfit" the model, limiting attack strength. In contrast, basic iterative method greedily moves the adversarial example in the direction of the gradient in each iteration. Therefore, the adversarial example can easily drop into poor local optima and "overfit" the model, which are not likely to transfer across models.

In order to break such a dilemma, we integrate momentum (Polyak 1964) into the basic iterative method for the purpose of stabilizing update directions and escaping from poor local optima, which are the common benefits of momentum in optimization literature (Duch and Korczak 1998; Sutskever et al. 2013). As a consequence, it alleviates the trade-off between the attack strength and the transferability, demonstrating strong black-box attacks.

The momentum iterative method for non-targeted attack is summarized as:

$$g^{t+1} = \mu \cdot g^t + \frac{\nabla_x J(f(x_{adv}^t), y_{true})}{\|\nabla_x J(f(x_{adv}^t), y_{true})\|_1}, \quad x_{adv}^{t+1} = \text{Clip}_{[0,1]}(x_{adv}^t + \alpha \cdot \text{sign}(g^{t+1}))$$

$$(11.14)$$

where $g^0 = 0$, $x_{adv}^0 = x$, $\alpha = \frac{\epsilon}{T}$ with T being the number of iterations. g^t gathers the gradients of the first t iterations with a decay factor μ and adversarial example x_{adv}^t is perturbed in the direction of the sign of g^t with the step size α. In each iteration, the current gradient $\nabla_x J(f(x_{adv}^t), y_{true})$ is normalized to have unit L_1 norm (however other norms will work too), because we noticed that the scale of the gradients varies in magnitude between iterations.

To obtain more transferable adversarial examples, we apply the momentum iterative method to attack an ensemble of models. If an example remains adversarial for multiple models, it may capture an intrinsic direction that always fools these models and is more likely to transfer to other models at the same time (Liu et al. 2017), thus enabling powerful black-box attacks.

We propose to attack multiple models whose *logit* activations are fused together, because the logits capture the logarithm relationships between the probability predictions, an ensemble of models fused by logits aggregates the fine detailed outputs of all models, whose vulnerability can be easily discovered. Specifically, to attack an ensemble of K models, we fuse the logits as

$$f(x) = \sum_{k=1}^{K} w_k f_k(x) \tag{11.15}$$

where $f_k(x)$ are the k-th model, w_k is the ensemble weight with $w_k \geq 0$ and $\sum_{k=1}^{K} w_k = 1$. Therefore we get a big ensemble model $f(x)$ and we can use the momentum iterative method to attack f.

11.5.2.2 Submission for Non-targeted Attack

In non-targeted attack, we implemented the momentum iterative method for attacking an ensemble of following models:

- Normally trained (i.e. without adversarial training) Inception v3 (Szegedy et al. 2016), Inception v4 (Szegedy et al. 2017), Inception Resnet v2 (Szegedy et al. 2017) and Resnet v2-101 (He 2016) models.
- Adversarially trained Inception v3$_{adv}$ (Kurakin et al. 2016) model.
- Ensemble adversarially trained Inc-v3$_{ens3}$, Inc-v3$_{ens4}$ and IncRes-v2$_{ens}$ models from (Tramr et al. 2017).

Ensemble weights (from Eq. 11.15) were $\frac{0.25}{7.25}$ for Inception-v3$_{adv}$ and $\frac{1}{7.25}$ for all other models. The number of iterations was 10 and the decay factor μ was 1.0.

11.5.2.3 Submission for Targeted Attack

For targeted attacks, we used a different formula of momentum iterative method:

$$g^{t+1} = \mu \cdot g^t + \frac{\nabla_x J(f(x_{adv}^t), y_{target})}{\text{std}(\nabla_x J(f(x_{adv}^t), y_{target})} \tag{11.16}$$

$$x_{adv}^{t+1} = \text{Clip}_{[0,1]}\left(x_{adv}^t - \alpha \cdot \text{Clip}_{[-2,2]}(\text{round}(g^{t+1}))\right) \tag{11.17}$$

Fig. 11.3 The pipeline of the proposed defense method. The input image x first goes through the random resizing layer with a random scale applied. Then the random padding layer pads the resized image x' in a random manner. The resulting padded image x'' is used for classification

where std($\bullet$) is the standard deviation and round($\bullet$) is rounding to nearest integer. Values of $\text{Clip}_{[-2,2]}(\text{round}(\bullet))$ are in set $\{-2, -1, 0, 1, 2\}$ which enables larger search space compared to sign function.

No transferability of the generated adversarial examples was observed in the targeted attacks, so we implement our method for attacking several commonly used white-box models.

We built two versions of the attacks. If the size of perturbation ϵ was smaller than $\frac{8}{255}$, we attacked ensemble of Inception v3 and IncRes-v2$_{ens}$ with weights $\frac{1}{3}$ and $\frac{2}{3}$; otherwise we attacked an ensemble of Inception v3, Inception-v3$_{adv}$, Inc-v3$_{ens3}$, Inc-v3$_{ens4}$ and IncRes-v2$_{ens}$ with ensemble weights $\frac{4}{11}$, $\frac{1}{11}$, $\frac{1}{11}$, $\frac{1}{11}$ and $\frac{4}{11}$. The number of iterations were 40 and 20 respectively, and the decay factor μ was 1.0.

11.5.3 Second Place in Defense Track: Team iyswim

Team members Cihang Xie, Jianyu Wang, Zhishuai Zhang, Zhou Ren and Alan Yuille

In this submission, we propose to utilize randomization as a defense against adversarial examples. Specifically, we propose a randomization-based method, as shown in Fig. 11.3, which adds a random resizing layer and a random padding layer to the beginning of the classification networks. Our method enjoys the following advantages: (1) no additional training or fine-tuning; (2) very few additional computations; (3) compatible with other adversarial defense methods. By combining the proposed randomization method with an adversarially trained model, it ranked **No.2** in the NIPS adversarial defense challenge.

11.5.3.1 Randomization as Defense

Intuitively, the adversarial perturbation generated by iterative attacks may easily get over-fitted to the specific network parameters, and thus be less transferable. Due to this weak generalization ability, we hypothesis that low-level image transformations, e.g., resizing, padding, compression, etc, may probably destroy the specific structure of adversarial perturbations, thus making it a good defense. It can even defend against white-box iterative attacks if random transformations are applied. This is because each test image goes through a transformation randomly and the attacker does not know this specific transformation when generating adversarial noise.

11.5.3.2   Randomization Layers

The first randomization layer is a random resizing layer, which resizes the original input image x with the size $W \times H \times 3$ to a new image x' with random size $W' \times H' \times 3$. Note that, $|W' - W|$ and $|H' - H|$ should be within a reasonably small range, otherwise the network performance on clean images would significantly drop. Taking Inception-ResNet network (Szegedy et al. 2017) as an example, the original data input size is $299 \times 299 \times 3$. Empirically we found that the network accuracy hardly drops if we control the height and width of the resized image x' to be within the range $[299, 331)$.

The second randomization layer is the random padding layer, which pads zeros around the resized image in a random manner. Specifically, by padding the resized image x' into a new image x'' with the size $W'' \times H'' \times 3$, we can choose to pad w zero pixels on the left, $W'' - W' - w$ zero pixels on the right, h zero pixels on the top and $H'' - H' - h$ zero pixels on the bottom. This results in a total number of $(W'' - W' + 1) \times (H'' - H' + 1)$ different possible padding patterns.

During implementation, the original image first goes through two randomization layers, and then we pass the transformed image to the original CNN for classification. The pipeline is illustrated in Fig. 11.3.

11.5.3.3   Randomization Layers + Adversarial Training

Recently, adversarial training (Kurakin et al. 2016; Tramr et al. 2017) was developed as an effective defense for single-step attacks. Thus by adding the proposed random transformations as additional layers to an adversarially trained model (Tramr et al. 2017), it is expected that this method is able to effectively defend against both single-step and iterative attacks, including both black-box and white-box settings.

11.5.3.4   Submission Details and Results

An adversarially trained model appended with randomization layers was submitted as our defense model to the challenge. Specifically, we (1) set the resizing range to be $[310, 331)$; (2) set the padding size to be $331 \times 331 \times 3$; (3) choose the adversarially trained model to be *ens-adv-Inception-Resnet-v2*[3]; (4) average the prediction results over 30 randomization patterns for each image; (5) flip the input image with probability 0.5 for each randomization pattern. The whole implementation is public available.[4]

By evaluating our model against 156 different attacks, it reaches a normalized score of 0.924 (ranked No.2 among 107 defense models), which is far better than using ensemble adversarial training (Tramr et al. 2017) alone with a normalized score of 0.773. This result further demonstrates that the proposed randomization method can effectively make deep networks much more robust to adversarial attacks.

11.5.3.5 Attackers with more Information

When submitting the proposed defense method to the NIPS competition, the randomization layers are remained as an unknown network module for the attackers. We thus test the robustness of this defense method further by assuming that the attackers are aware of the existence of randomization layers. Extensive experiments are performed in Xie et al. (2018), and it shows that the attackers still cannot break this defense completely in practice. Interested readers can refer to Xie et al. (2018) for more details.

11.5.4 Second Place in both Attack Tracks: Team Sangxia

Team members Sangxia Huang

In this section, we present the submission by Sangxia Huang for both non-targeted and targeted attacks. The approach is an iterated FGSM attack against an ensemble of classifiers with random perturbations and augmentations for increased robustness and transferability of the generated attacks. The source code is available online.[5] We also optimize the iteration steps for improved efficiency as we describe in more details below.

Basic idea An intriguing property of adversarial examples observed in many works (Papernot et al. 2017; Szegedy et al. 2014; Goodfellow 2014; Papernot et al. 2016b) is that adversarial examples generated for one classifier transfer to other classifiers. Therefore, a natural approach for effective attacks against unknown classifiers is to generate strong adversarial examples against a large collection of classifiers.

---

[3]https://download.tensorflow.org/models/ens_adv_inception_resnet_v2_2017_08_18.tar.gz

[4]https://github.com/cihangxie/NIPS2017_adv_challenge_defense

[5]https://github.com/sangxia/nips-2017-adversarial

Let $f^1, \ldots, f^k$ be an ensemble of image classifiers that we choose to target. In our solution we give equal weights to each of them. For notation simplicity, we assume that the inputs to all f^i have the same size. Otherwise, we first insert a bi-linear scaling layer, which is differentiable. The differentiability ensures that the correct gradient signal is propagated through the scaling layer to the individual pixels of the images.

Another idea we use to increase robustness and transferrability of the attacks is image augmentation. Denote by T_θ an image augmentation function with parameter θ. For instance, we can have $\theta \in [0, 2\pi)$ as an angle and T_θ as the function that rotates the input image clock-wise by θ. The parameter θ can also be a vector. For instance, we can have $\theta \in (0, \infty)^2$ as scaling factors in the width and height dimension, and T_θ as the function that scales the input image in the width direction by θ_1 and in the height direction by θ_2. In our final algorithm, T_θ takes the general form of a projective transformation with $\theta \in \mathbb{R}^8$ as implemented in `tf.contrib.image.transform`.

Let x be an input image, and y_{true} be the label of x. Our attack algorithm works to find an x^{adv} that maximizes the expected average cross entropy loss of the predictions of $f^1, \ldots, f^k$ over a random input augmentation [6]

$$\max_{x^{adv}:\|x-x^{adv}\|_\infty \leq \epsilon} \mathbf{E}_\theta \left[\frac{1}{k} \sum_{i=1}^{k} J\left(f^i(T_\theta(x)), y_{true} \right) \right]. \tag{11.18}$$

However, in a typical attack scenario, the true label y_{true} is not available to the attacker, therefore we substitute it with a psuedo-label $\hat{y}$ generated by an image classifer g that is available to the attacker. The objective of our attack is thus the following

$$\max_{x^{adv}:\|x-x^{adv}\|_\infty \leq \epsilon} \frac{1}{k} \sum_{i=1}^{k} \mathbf{E}_{\theta^i} \left[J\left(f^i(T_{\theta^i}(x)), g(x) \right) \right].$$

Using linearity of gradients, we write the gradient of the objective as

$$\frac{1}{k} \sum_{i=1}^{k} \nabla_x \mathbf{E}_{\theta^i} \left[J\left(f^i(T_{\theta^i}(x)), g(x) \right) \right].$$

For typical distributions of θ, such as uniform or normal distribution, the gradient of the expected cross entropy loss over a random θ is hard to compute. In our solution, we replace it with an empirical estimate which is an average of the gradients for a few samples of θ. We also adopt the approach in Tramr et al. (2017) where x is first randomly perturbed. The use of random projective transformation seems to be a natural idea, but to the best of our knowledge, this has not been explicitly described in previous works on generating adversarial examples for image classifiers.

---

[6]The distribution we use for θ corresponds to a small random augmentation. See code for details.

In the rest of this section, we use $\widehat{\nabla^i}(x)$ to denote the empirical gradient estimate on input image x as described above.

Let $x_{adv}^0 := x$, $x^{min} = max(x - \epsilon, 0)$, $x^{max} = min(x + \epsilon, 1)$, and let $\alpha^1, \alpha^2, \ldots$ be a sequence of pre-defined step sizes. Then in the i-th step of the iteration, we update the image by

$$x_{adv}^i = clip\left(x_{adv}^{i-1} + \alpha^i sign\left(\frac{1}{k}\sum_{i=1}^{k}\widehat{\nabla^i}(x)\right), x^{min}, x^{max}\right).$$

Optimization We noticed from our experiments that non-targeted attacks against pre-trained networks without defense (white-box and black-box) typically succeed in 3–4 rounds, whereas attacks against adversarially trained networks take more iterations. We also observed that in later iterations, there is little benefit in including in the ensemble un-defended networks that have been successfully attacked. In the final solution, each iteration is defined by step size α^i as well as the set of classifiers to include in the ensemble for the respective iteration. These parameters were found through trial and error on the official development dataset of the competition.

Experiments: non-targeted attack We randomly selected 18,000 images from ImageNet (Russakovsky et al. 2015) for which Inception V3 (Szegedy et al. 2015) classified correctly.

The classifiers in the ensemble are: Inception V3 (Szegedy et al. 2015), ResNet 50 (He et al. 2015), ResNet 101 (He et al. 2015), Inception ResNet V2 (Szegedy et al. 2017), Xception (Chollet 2016), ensemble adversarially trained Inception ResNet V2 (EnsAdv Inception ResNet V2) (Tramr et al. 2017), and adversarially trained Inception V3 (Adv Inception V3) (Kurakin et al. 2016).

We held out a few models to evaluate the transferrability of our attacks. The holdout models listed in Table 11.4 are: Inception V4 (Szegedy et al. 2017), ensemble adversarially trained Inception V3 with 2 (and 3) external models (Ens-3-Adv Inception V3, and Ens-4-Adv Inception V3, respectively) (Tramr et al. 2017).

Table 11.4 lists the success rate for non-targeted attacks with $\epsilon = 16/255$. The performance for $\epsilon = 12/255$ is similar, and somewhat worse for smaller ϵ. We see that a decent amount of the generated attacks transfer to the two holdout

Table 11.4 Success rate—non-targeted attack

Classifier	Success rate
Inception V3	96.74%
ResNet 50	92.78%
Inception ResNet V2	92.32%
EnsAdv Inception ResNet V2	87.36%
Adv Inception V3	83.73%
Inception V4	91.69%
Ens-3-Adv Inception V3	62.76%
Ens-4-Adv Inception V3	58.11%

adversarially trained network Ens-3-Adv Inception V3 and Ens-4-Adv Inception V3. The transfer rate for many other publicly available pretrained networks without defense are all close to or above 90%. For brevity, we only list the performance on Inception V4 for comparison.

Targeted attack Our targeted attack follows a similar approach as non-targeted attack. The main differences are:

1. For the objective, we now *minimize* the loss between a target label y_{target}, instead of maximizing with respect to y_{true} as in Eq. (11.18).
2. Our experiments show that doing random image augmentation severely decreases the success rate for even *white-box* attacks, therefore no augmentation is performed for targeted-attacks. Note that here success is defined as successfully make the classifier output the target class. The attacks with image augmentation typically managed to cause the classifiers to output some wrong label other than the target class.

Our conclusion is that if the success criteria is to trick the classifier into outputting some specific target class, then our targeted attack does not transfer well and is not robust.

11.5.5 Third Place in Targeted Attack Track: Team FatFingers

Team members Yao Zhao, Yuzhe Zhao, Zhonglin Han and Junjiajia Long

We propose a dynamic iterative ensemble targeted attack method, which builds iterative attacks on a loss ensemble neural networks focusing on the classifiers that are harder to perturb. Our methods are tested among 65 attackers against 107 defenders in NIPS-Kaggle competition and achieved 3rd in the targeted attack ranking.

11.5.5.1 Targeted Attack Model Transfer

In our experiments, we compared variants of single step attack methods and iterative attack methods including two basic forms of those two attack methods: fast gradient sign (FGS)

$$\mathbf{x}^{adv} = \mathbf{x} + \epsilon \cdot sign(\nabla_x J(f(\mathbf{x}), y_{true})) \tag{11.19}$$

and iterative sign attacks:

$$\mathbf{x}_{t+1}^{adv} = clip_{\epsilon, \mathbf{x}} \left\{ \mathbf{x}_t^{adv} + \alpha \cdot sign(\nabla_x J(f(\mathbf{x}_t^{adv}), y_{true})) \right\} \tag{11.20}$$

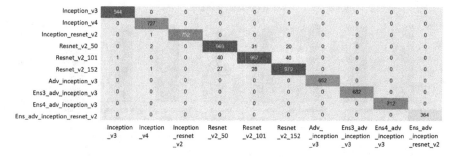

	Inception _v3	Inception _v4	Inception _resnet _v2	Resnet _v2_50	Resnet _v2_101	Resnet _v2_152	Adv_ inception _v3	Ens3_adv inception _v3	Ens4_adv inception _v3	Ens_adv inception _resnet_v2
Inception_v3	944	0	0	0	0	0	0	0	0	0
Inception_v4	0	727	0	0	0	1	0	0	0	0
Inception_resnet_v2	0	1	752	0	0	0	0	0	0	0
Resnet_v2_50	0	2	0	669	31	20	0	0	0	0
Resnet_v2_101	1	0	0	40	967	40	0	0	0	0
Resnet_v2_152	0	1	0	27	28	979	0	0	0	0
Adv_inception_v3	0	0	0	0	0	0	652	0	0	0
Ens3_adv_inception_v3	0	0	0	0	0	0	0	682	0	0
Ens4_adv_inception_v3	0	0	0	0	0	0	0	0	712	0
Ens_adv_inception_resnet_v2	0	0	0	0	0	0	0	0	0	364

Fig. 11.4 Target hitting matrix

	Inception _v3	Inception _v4	Inception _resnet _v2	Resnet _v2_50	Resnet _v2_101	Resnet _v2_152	Adv_ inception _v3	Ens3_adv _inception _v3	Ens4_adv _inception _v3	Ens_adv _inception _resnet_v2
Inception_v3	3	823	866	833	840	857	877	907	905	947
Inception_v4	738	30	864	800	822	845	868	906	907	940
Inception_resnet_v2	715	811	28	793	828	846	878	907	912	946
Resnet_v2_50	755	793	851	2	599	619	875	900	912	938
Resnet_v2_101	721	773	847	532	2	585	874	905	896	941
Resnet_v2_152	737	790	849	561	588	1	861	895	898	941
Adv_inception_v3	923	946	990	914	937	940	75	884	864	932
Ens3_adv_inception_v3	915	952	989	911	928	938	830	59	874	931
Ens4_adv_inception_v3	922	948	992	913	940	940	903	876	37	941
Ens_adv_inception_resnet_v2	932	949	993	922	943	930	824	895	879	153

Fig. 11.5 Defender accuracy matrix

To evaluate the ability of black-box targeted attacks, we built iterative attack methods (10 iterations) using single models against many single model defenders individually on 1000 images. Figure 11.4 demonstrates the matrix of target hitting for 10 attacking models, while Fig. 11.5 shows their capabilitis of defending.

White-box targeted adversarial attacks are generally successful, even against adversarial trained models. Though targeted adversarial attacks built on single models lower the accuracy of defenders based on a different model, the hit rate are close to zero.

11.5.5.2 Ensemble Attack Methods

Since targeted attacks against unknown models has very low hit rate, it is important to combine known models in a larger number and more efficiently to attack a pool of unknown models or their ensembles.

Probability ensemble is a common way to combine a number of classifiers (sometimes called majority vote). However, the loss function is usually hard to optimize because the parameters of different classifiers are coupled inside the logarithm.

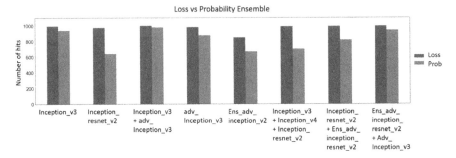

Fig. 11.6 Loss ensemble v.s. probability ensemble. Targeted attacks using the loss ensemble method outperforms probability ensemble at given number of iterations

$$J_{prob}(\mathbf{x}, y) = -\sum_{j}^{N} y_j \log\left(\frac{1}{M}\sum_{i}^{M} p_{ij}(\mathbf{x})\right) \tag{11.21}$$

By Jensen's inequality, an upper bound is obtained for the loss function. Instead of minimizing $J_{prob}(\mathbf{x}, y)$, we propose to optimize the upper bound. This way of combining classifiers is called loss ensemble. By using the following new loss function Eq. 11.4, the parameters of different neural networks are decoupled, which helps the optimization.

$$J_{prob}(\mathbf{x}, y) \leq -\frac{1}{M}\sum_{j}^{N}\sum_{i}^{M} y_{ij} \log\left(p_{ij}(\mathbf{x})\right) = J_{loss}(\mathbf{x}, y) \tag{11.22}$$

Comparisons between results of targeted attacks using loss ensemble and probability ensemble at given iterations were shown in Fig. 11.6. In general, it demonstrates that capability of targeted attacking using loss ensemble is superior to that using probability ensemble.

11.5.5.3 Dynamic Iterative Ensemble Attack

The difficulty of attacking each individual neural network model within an ensemble can be quite different. We compared iterative attack methods with different parameters and found that number of iterations is most crucial, as shown in Fig. 11.7. For example, attacking an adversarial trained model at high success rate takes significantly more iterations than normal models.

$$\mathbf{x}_{t+1}^{adv} = clip_{\epsilon,\mathbf{x}}\left\{\mathbf{x}_t^{adv} + \alpha \cdot sign\left(\frac{1}{M}\sum_{k}^{M} \delta_{tk}\nabla_x J_k(f(\mathbf{x}_t^{adv}), y_{true})\right)\right\} \tag{11.23}$$

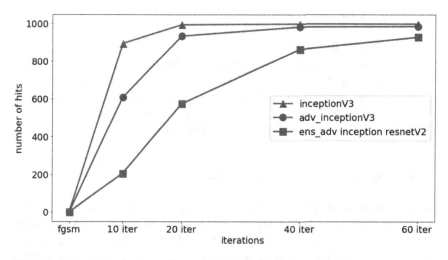

Fig. 11.7 Dynamic iterative ensemble attack results for three selected models

For tasks where computation is limited, we implemented a method that pre-assigns the number of iterations for each model or dynamically adjusts whether to include a model in each step of the attack by observing if the loss function for that model is small enough. As shown in Eq. 11.23, $\delta_{tk} \in \{0, 1\}$ determines if loss for model k is included in the total loss at time step t.

11.5.6 Fourth Place in Defense Track: Team erko

Team members Yerkebulan Berdibekov

In this section, I describe a very simple defense solution against adversarial attacks using spatial smoothing on the input of adversarially trained models. This solution took 4th place in the final round. Using spatially smoothing, in particularly median filtering with 2 by 2 windows on images and processing it by only adversarially trained models we can achieve simple and decent defense against black box attacks. Additionally this approach can work along with other defense solutions that use randomizations (data augmentations & other types of defenses).

Adversarially trained models are models trained on adversarial examples along with a given original dataset. In the usual procedure for adversarial training, during the training phase half of each mini-batch of images are replaced with adversarial examples generated on the model itself (white box attacks). This can provide robustness against future white-box attacks. However, like described in Tramr et al. (2017) *gradientmasking* makes the finding of adversarial examples a challenging task. Due to this, adversarially trained models cannot guarantee robustness against black-box attacks. Many other techniques have been developed to overcome these problems.

11.5.6.1 Architecture of Defense Model

Figure 11.8 below shows the architecture of my simple defense model: an input image is followed by median filtering, and then this filtered image is fed to ensemble of adversarially trained models. The resulting predictions are then averaged. However, like described in the sections below, many other variations of ensembles and single models were tested. The best results were achieved using an ensemble of all adversarially trained models with median filtering.

11.5.6.2 Spatial Smoothing: Median Filtering

Median filtering is often used in image/photo pre-processing to reduce noise while preserving edges and other features. It is robust against random high-magnitude perturbations resembling salt-and-pepper noise. Photographers also use median filtering to increase photo quality. ImageNet may contain many median filtered images. Other major advantages of image filtering include:

- Median filtering does not harm classification accuracy on clean examples, as shown below in experiments in Sect. 11.5.6.3
- Does not require additional expensive training procedures other than the adversarially trained model itself.

11.5.6.3 Experiments

I have experimentally observed that using median filtering only we cannot defend against strong adversarial attacks like described by Carlini and Wagner (2017b).

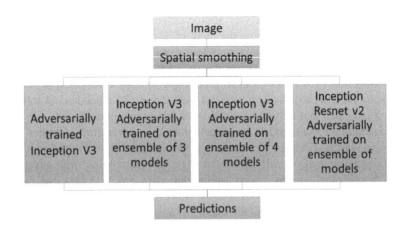

Fig. 11.8 Architecture of simple defense model, using median filtering with only adversarially trained models

However, I have also experimentally observed that using median filtering and only adversarially trained models we can obtain a robust defense against adversarial attacks.

In my experiments I used the dataset provided by competition organizers and used a modified C&W L2 attack to generate adversarial examples. These examples were later used to calculate the adversarial example misclassification ratio (number of wrong classifications divided by number of all examples) and to rank defenses. To generate adversarial examples I used either a single model or ensemble of models (a list of multiple models is indicated in each cell).

In all experiments I used a hold-out `inception_v4` model that was not used to generate adversarial examples (see Tables 11.5 and 11.6). This allowed us to test transferability of attacks and to test spatial smoothing effects.

11.5.6.4   Effects of Median Filtering

On our holdout `inception_v4` model, using median filtering performs nearly the same as without median filtering. Same results on other non-adversarially trained models. With median filtering or without, misclassification ratio differences are small.

Adversarially trained models with median filtering show good defense against attacks. An ensemble of these adversarially trained models with median filtered images is robust against black-box attacks and to attacks generated by an ensemble containing same models (see Tables 11.5 and 11.6). This is not exactly a white-box attack, because we generate adversarial examples on a model without a filtering layer. For example, we use a pre-trained `ens3_adv_inception_v3` model to generate adversarial examples. These images are median filtered and fed to model again to check the misclassification ratios.

All these attacks were generated using $\epsilon=16$ max pixel perturbations. In the case of the best ensemble defense against the best ensemble attacker, I tested other values of ϵ and plotted Fig. 11.9, showing that in case of lower ϵ values this defense approach is more robust against attacks(exact values in Table 11.7).

11.5.6.5   Submission Results

Following the competition results, we have seen that adversarially trained models with median filtering are indeed robust to most types of attacks. These results suggest more study on this effect of adversarially trained models in the future.

During the competition, new types of attacks were developed with smoothed adversarial examples that can fool spatially smoothed defenses with as high as 50–60% ratio and with high transferability. These are the best attackers developed in Non-Targeted/Targeted Adversarial Attack Competitions. Additional study is needed to defend against these new types of attacks.

Table 11.5 Misclassification ratio without filtering, percentage. Rows are defenders; columns are attackers. Even ensemble of adversarially trained models are not robust against good attackers

Defenders\Attackers	inception_v3	A	B	C
inception_v3	100.00	100.00	26.25	99.38
inception_v4	42.50	80.63	21.88	62.50
adv_inception_v3	20.62	41.25	100.00	100.00
ens3_adv_inception_v3	15.62	38.13	100.00	99.38
ens_adv_inception_resnet_v2	10.62	23.75	94.38	95.00
adv_inception_v3 ens3_adv_inception_v3	15.00	36.25	100.00	100.00
adv_inception_v3 ens3_adv_inception_v3 ens4_adv_inception_v3	16.25	33.13	100.00	99.38
adv_inception_v3 ens3_adv_inception_v3 ens_adv_inception_resnet_v2 ens4_adv_inception_v3	12.5	28.75	100.00	99.38

Where *A* is an ensemble of inception_v3, inception_resnet_v2, resnet_v1_101, resnet_v1_50, resnet_v2_101, resnet _v2_50, vgg_16

B is an ensemble of adv_inception_v3, ens3_adv_inception_v3, ens_adv_inception_resnet_v2, ens4_adv_inception_v3

C is an ensember of inception_v3, adv_inception_v3, ens3_adv_inception_v3, ens_adv_inception_resnet_v2, ens4_adv_inception_v3, inception_resnet_v2, resnet_v1_101, resnet_v1_50, resnet_v2_101

11.5.7 Fourth Place in Non-targeted Attack Track: Team iwiwi

Team members Takuya Akiba and Seiya Tokui and Motoki Abe

In this section, we explain the submission from team *iwiwi* to the non-targeted attack track. This team was Takuya Akiba, Seiya Tokui and Motoki Abe. The approach is quite different from other teams: training fully-convolutional networks (FCNs) that can convert clean examples to adversarial examples. The team received the 4th place.

11.5.7.1 Basic Framework

Given a clean input image x, we generate an adversarial example as follows:

$$x^{adv} = Clip_{[0,1]}(x + a(x; \theta_a)).$$

Here, a is a differentiable function represented by a FCN with parameter θ_a. We call a as an *attack FCN*. It outputs $c \times h \times w$ tensors, where c, h, w are the number of channels, height and width of x. The values of the output are in range $[-\varepsilon, +\varepsilon]$. During the training of the attack FCN, to confuse image classifiers, we maximize

Table 11.6 Misclassification ratio with filtering, percentage. Adversarially trained models with median filtering show better robustness against many kinds of attacks within these experiments. inception_v4 model with median filtering on all of attacks performs nearly same as without filtering. Same on other non-adversarial models. Therefore, I am speculating median filtering is not cleaning, or not mitigating adversarial examples

Defenders\Attackers	inception_v3	A	B	C
inception_v3	100.00	97.50	27.50	95.63
inception_v4	40.00	75.63	22.50	57.50
adv_inception_v3	21.88	43.13	33.13	40.00
ens3_adv_inception_v3	21.88	43.75	57.50	58.13
ens_adv_inception_resnet_v2	13.13	30.63	30.63	39.38
adv_inception_v3	17.50	40.00	43.75	47.50
ens3_adv_inception_v3 adv_inception_v3	17.50	38.75	43.75	48.75
ens3_adv_inception_v3 ens4_adv_inception_v3				
adv_inception_v3 ens3_adv_inception_v3 ens_adv_inception_resnet_v2 ens4_adv_inception_v3	14.38	35.00	39.38	43.13

Where *A* is an ensemble of inception_v3, inception_resnet_v2, resnet_v1_101, resnet_v1_50, resnet_v2_101, resnet_ v2_50, vgg_16;
B is an ensemble of adv_inception_v3, ens3_adv_inception_v3, ens_adv_inception_resnet_v2, ens4_adv_inception_v3;
C is an ensemble of inception_v3, adv_inception_v3, ens3_adv_inception_v3, ens_adv_inception _resnet_v2, ens4_adv_inception_v3, inception_resnet_v2, resnet_v1_101, resnet_v1_50, resnet_v2_101.

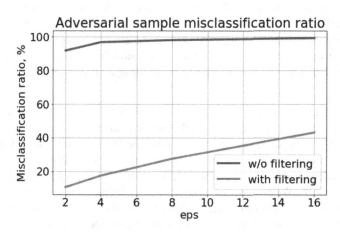

Fig. 11.9 Adversarial examples misclassification ratio, percentage

Table 11.7 Misclassification ratio on ϵ values, percentage. On smaller ϵ values, median filtering shows even better robustness to adversarial attacks

Defenders	$\epsilon=16$	$\epsilon=8$	$\epsilon=4$	$\epsilon=2$
Ensemble of adversarial models non-filtered input	99.375	98.125	96.875	91.875
Ensemble of adversarial models with filtered input	43.125	27.500	17.500	10.625

the loss $J(f(x^{adv}), y)$, where f is a pre-trained image classifier. We refer to f as a target model. Specifically, we optimize θ_a to maximize the following value:

$$\sum_{x \in \mathscr{X}} J\left(f\left(Clip_{[0,1]}\left(x + a\left(x; \theta_a\right)\right)\right), y\right).$$

This framework has some commonality with the work by Baluja and Fischer (2017). They also propose to train neural networks that produce adversarial examples. However, while we have the hard constraint on the distance between clean and adversarial examples, they considered the distance as one of optimization objective to minimize. In addition, we used a much larger FCN model and stronger computation power, together with several new ideas such as multi-target training, multi-task training, and gradient hints, which are explained in the next subsection.

11.5.7.2 Empirical Enhancement

Multi-Target Training To obtain adversarial examples that generalize to different image classifiers, we use multiple target models to train the attack FCN. We maximize the sum of losses of all models. In this competition, we used eight models: (1) ResNet50, (2) VGG16, (3) Inception v3, (4) Inception v3 with adversarial training, (5) Inception v3 with ensemble adversarial training (EAT) using three models, (6) Inception v3 with EAT using four models, (7) Inception ResNet v2, and (8) Inception ResNet v2 with EAT. All of these classifier models are available online.

Multi-Task Training A naive approach to construct a FCN so that it outputs values in the range $[-\epsilon, +\epsilon]$ is to apply the tanh function to the last output, and then multiply it by ϵ. However, in this way, the FCN cannot finely control the magnitude of perturbation, as ϵ is not given to the FCN. To cope with this issue, we take the advantage of discreteness. In this competition, ϵ can take 13 values: $\frac{4}{256}, \frac{5}{256}, \ldots, \frac{16}{256}$. We consider adversarial attack with different ϵ values as different tasks, and employ multi-task training. Specifically, the FCN outputs a tensor with shape $13 \times c \times h \times w$, where the first dimension corresponds to the ϵ value.

Gradient Hints Attack methods that use the gradients on image pixels work well. Therefore, these gradients are useful signals for generating adversarial examples. Thus, in addition to clean examples, we also use these gradients as input to the FCN. In this competition, we used gradients by Inception ResNet v2 with EAT, which was the strongest defense model publicly available.

Fig. 11.10 A clean example (left), adversarial example generated by our method (middle), and their difference (right),where $\epsilon = \frac{16}{255}$

11.5.7.3 Results and Discussion

The team ranked 4th among about one hundred teams. In addition, the team ranked 1st in 3rd-party PageRank-like analysis,[7] which shows that this attack method is especially effective for strong defense methods.

In addition to its effectiveness, the generated attack images have interesting appearance (Fig. 11.10, more examples are available online[8]). We observe two properties from the generated images: detailed textures are canceled out, and Jigsaw-puzzle-like patterns are added. These properties deceive image classifiers into answering the Jigsaw puzzle class.

11.6 Conclusion

Adversarial examples are interesting phenomenon and important problem in machine learning security. Main goals of this competition were to increase awareness of the problem and stimulate researchers to propose novel approaches.

Competition definitely helped to increase awareness of the problem. Article "AI Fight Club Could Help Save Us from a Future of Super-Smart Cyberattacks"[9] was published in MIT Technology review about the competition. And more than 100 teams were competing in the final round.

Competition also pushed people to explore new approaches and improve existing methods to the problem. In all three tracks, competitors showed significant improvements on top of provided baselines by the end of the competition. Additionally, top submission in the defense tracked showed 95% accuracy on all adversarial images

---

[7]https://www.kaggle.com/anlthms/pagerank-ish-scoring

[8]https://github.com/pfnet-research/nips17-adversarial-attack

[9]www.technologyreview.com/s/608288

produced by all attacks. While worst case accuracy was not as good as an average accuracy, the results are still suggesting that practical applications may be able to achieve reasonable level of robustness to adversarial examples in black box case.

References

S. Baluja and I. Fischer. Adversarial transformation networks: Learning to generate adversarial examples. 2017.

B. Biggio, I. Corona, D. Maiorca, B. Nelson, N. Šrndić, P. Laskov, G. Giacinto, and F. Roli. Evasion attacks against machine learning at test time. In *Joint European Conference on Machine Learning and Knowledge Discovery in Databases*, pages 387–402. Springer, 2013.

W. Brendel, J. Rauber, and M. Bethge. Decision-based adversarial attacks: Reliable attacks against black-box machine learning models. 2017.

J. Buckman, A. Roy, C. Raffel, and I. Goodfellow. Thermometer encoding: One hot way to resist adversarial examples. *Submissions to International Conference on Learning Representations*, 2018.

N. Carlini and D. Wagner. Adversarial examples are not easily detected: Bypassing ten detection methods. In *USENIX Workshop on Offensive Technologies*, 2017a.

N. Carlini and D. Wagner. Towards evaluating the robustness of neural networks. *IEEE Symposium on Security and Privacy*, 2017b.

P.-Y. Chen, H. Zhang, Y. Sharma, J. Yi, and C.-J. Hsieh. Zoo: Zeroth order optimization based black-box attacks to deep neural networks without training substitute models. 2017.

F. Chollet. Xception: Deep learning with depthwise separable convolutions, 2016.

N. Das, M. Shanbhogue, S.-T. Chen, F. Hohman, L. Chen, M. E. Kounavis, and D. H. Chau. Keeping the bad guys out: Protecting and vaccinating deep learning with jpeg compression. *arXiv preprint arXiv:1705.02900*, 2017.

J. Deng, W. Dong, R. Socher, L.-J. Li, K. Li, and L. Fei-Fei. Imagenet: A large-scale hierarchical image database. In *Computer Vision and Pattern Recognition, 2009. CVPR 2009. IEEE Conference on*, pages 248–255. IEEE, 2009.

Y. Dong, F. Liao, T. Pang, H. Su, X. Hu, J. Li, and J. Zhu. Boosting adversarial attacks with momentum. *arXiv preprint arXiv:1710.06081*, 2017.

W. Duch and J. Korczak. Optimization and global minimization methods suitable for neural networks. *Neural computing surveys*, 2:163–212, 1998.

N. F. Geoffrey E Hinton, Sara Sabour. Matrix capsules with em routing. In *International Conference on Learning Representations*, 2018.

J. Gilmer, L. Metz, F. Faghri, S. S. Schoenholz, M. Raghu, M. Wattenberg, and I. Goodfellow. Adversarial spheres. *Submissions to International Conference on Learning Representations*, 2018.

I. J. Goodfellow, J. Shlens, and C. Szegedy. Explaining and harnessing adversarial examples. *CoRR*, abs/1412.6572, 2014.

I. J. Goodfellow, J. Shlens, and C. Szegedy. Explaining and harnessing adversarial examples. *CoRR*, abs/1412.6572, 2014.

K. He, X. Zhang, S. Ren, and J. Sun. Deep residual learning for image recognition, 2015.

K. He, X. Zhang, S. Ren, and J. Sun. Identity mappings in deep residual networks. In *ECCV*, 2016.

W. He, J. Wei, X. Chen, N. Carlini, and D. Song. Adversarial example defense: Ensembles of weak defenses are not strong. In *11th USENIX Workshop on Offensive Technologies (WOOT 17)*, Vancouver, BC, 2017. USENIX Association.

R. Huang, B. Xu, D. Schuurmans, and C. Szepesvári. Learning with a strong adversary. *CoRR*, abs/1511.03034, 2015.

D. Kingma and J. Ba. Adam: A method for stochastic optimization. *arXiv preprint arXiv:1412.6980*, 2014.

A. Kurakin, I. Goodfellow, and S. Bengio. Adversarial examples in the physical world. In *ICLR'2017 Workshop*, 2016.

A. Kurakin, I. Goodfellow, and S. Bengio. Adversarial examples in the physical world. In *ICLR'2017 Workshop*, 2016.

A. Kurakin, I. J. Goodfellow, and S. Bengio. Adversarial machine learning at scale. In *ICLR'2017*, 2016.

F. Liao, M. Liang, Y. Dong, T. Pang, J. Zhu, and X. Hu. Defense against adversarial attacks using high-level representation guided denoiser. *arXiv preprint arXiv:1712.02976*, 2017.

Y. Liu, X. Chen, C. Liu, and D. Song. Delving into transferable adversarial examples and black-box attacks. In *Proceedings of 5th International Conference on Learning Representations*, 2017.

A. Madry, A. Makelov, L. Schmidt, D. Tsipras, and A. Vladu. Towards deep learning models resistant to adversarial attacks. 2017.

J. H. Metzen, T. Genewein, V. Fischer, and B. Bischoff. On detecting adversarial perturbations. In *ICLR*, 2017.

N. Papernot, P. McDaniel, and I. Goodfellow. Transferability in Machine Learning: from Phenomena to Black-Box Attacks using Adversarial Samples. *ArXiv e-prints*, May 2016b.

N. Papernot, P. McDaniel, I. Goodfellow, S. Jha, Z. B. Celik, and A. Swami. Practical black-box attacks against machine learning. In *Proceedings of the 2017 ACM on Asia Conference on Computer and Communications Security*, ASIA CCS '17, pages 506–519, New York, NY, USA, 2017. ACM.

B. T. Polyak. Some methods of speeding up the convergence of iteration methods. *USSR Computational Mathematics and Mathematical Physics*, 4(5):1–17, 1964.

O. Russakovsky, J. Deng, H. Su, J. Krause, S. Satheesh, S. Ma, Z. Huang, A. Karpathy, A. Khosla, M. Bernstein, A. C. Berg, and L. Fei-Fei. Imagenet large scale visual recognition challenge. *International Journal of Computer Vision*, 115(3):211–252, Dec 2015.

M. Sharif, S. Bhagavatula, L. Bauer, and M. K. Reiter. Accessorize to a crime: Real and stealthy attacks on state-of-the-art face recognition. In *Proceedings of the 23rd ACM SIGSAC Conference on Computer and Communications Security*, Oct. 2016. To appear.

I. Sutskever, J. Martens, G. Dahl, and G. Hinton. On the importance of initialization and momentum in deep learning. In *ICML*, 2013.

C. Szegedy, S. Ioffe, V. Vanhoucke, and A. A. Alemi. Inception-v4, inception-resnet and the impact of residual connections on learning. In *AAAI*, 2017.

C. Szegedy, V. Vanhoucke, S. Ioffe, J. Shlens, and Z. Wojna. Rethinking the inception architecture for computer vision, 2015.

C. Szegedy, V. Vanhoucke, S. Ioffe, J. Shlens, and Z. Wojna. Rethinking the inception architecture for computer vision. In *CVPR*, 2016.

C. Szegedy, W. Zaremba, I. Sutskever, J. Bruna, D. Erhan, I. Goodfellow, and R. Fergus. Intriguing properties of neural networks. In *International Conference on Learning Representations*, 2014.

C. Szegedy, W. Zaremba, I. Sutskever, J. Bruna, D. Erhan, I. J. Goodfellow, and R. Fergus. Intriguing properties of neural networks. *ICLR*, abs/1312.6199, 2014.

F. Tramr, A. Kurakin, N. Papernot, I. Goodfellow, D. Boneh, and P. McDaniel. Ensemble adversarial training: Attacks and defenses. In *arxiv*, 2017.

P. Vincent, H. Larochelle, Y. Bengio, and P.-A. Manzagol. Extracting and composing robust features with denoising autoencoders. In *International Conference on Machine learning*, pages 1096–1103, 2008.

C. Xie, J. Wang, Z. Zhang, Z. Ren, and A. Yuille. Mitigating adversarial effects through randomization. In *International Conference on Learning Representations*, 2018.

W. Xu, D. Evans, and Y. Qi. Feature squeezing: Detecting adversarial examples in deep neural networks. *CoRR*, abs/1704.01155, 2017.

K. Zhang, W. Zuo, Y. Chen, D. Meng, and L. Zhang. Beyond a gaussian denoiser: Residual learning of deep cnn for image denoising. *IEEE Transactions on Image Processing*, 2017.

Chapter 12
First Year Results from the IBM Watson AI XPRIZE: Lessons for the "AI for Good" Movement

Sean McGregor and Amir Banifatemi

Abstract The IBM Watson AI XPRIZE is a four-year competition awarding a $5 million prize purse to teams improving the world with artificial intelligence. The competition began in 2017 with 148 teams competing to solve problems in sustainability, robotics, artificial general intelligence, healthcare, education, and a variety of other grand challenge problem domains. The first round of judgment narrowed the field to 59 teams. The characteristics of the advancing and rejected problem domains highlight the opportunities and challenges of "AI for Good" as a social and technological movement. This work surveys the problem domains and technologies of teams, details the prize judging process executed to date, and explores several case studies from the first year of the competition. The results indicate where AI researchers may direct their efforts to address problems that are simultaneously important for humanity, technically challenging, and feasible to solve within the competition timeline.

12.1 Introduction

Investment in Artificial Intelligence (AI) has grown to more than $25 billion dollars annually (Bughin et al. 2017), but these investments place higher priority on financial returns than the general welfare of humanity. To focus AI development on direct societal benefits, the IBM Watson AI XPRIZE (AIXP) issued a $5 million prize purse to award AI startups and researchers producing the greatest

S. McGregor (✉)
Technical Lead, IBM Watson AI XPRIZE, XPRIZE Foundation, Culver City, CA, USA

Member of Technical Staff, Syntiant Corporation, Irvine, CA, USA
e-mail: NIPSCompetitionBook@seanbmcgregor.com

A. Banifatemi
Artificial Intelligence Lead and IBM Watson AI XPRIZE Lead, XPRIZE Foundation, Culver City, CA, USA
e-mail: amir.banifatemi@xprize.org

© Springer International Publishing AG, part of Springer Nature 2018
S. Escalera, M. Weimer (eds.), *The NIPS '17 Competition: Building Intelligent Systems*, The Springer Series on Challenges in Machine Learning,
https://doi.org/10.1007/978-3-319-94042-7_12

world-improving impact. The concept of grand challenge prizes exemplified by the AIXP has a long history. In 1919, the wealthy French hotelier Raymond Orteig pledged prize money for the first nonstop flight between New York and Paris. Within a decade, Charles Lindbergh won the Orteig prize to claim $25,000 over a field of nine teams spending a combined $400,000—16 times the value of the prize itself! A century later, these high multiples of investment to prize money are a consistent feature across the many prize competitions run by the XPRIZE Foundation (XPRIZE Foundation 2018).

The AIXP is unusual in the world of grand challenge science and technology. Rather than set a single shared objective for all teams, the AIXP invites teams to describe a grand challenge and demonstrate achievements over a four-year competition. This open prize structure allows teams to showcase a variety of approaches to the most significant problems faced by humanity.

Successfully executing an open competition structure poses many logistical challenges. We begin Sect. 12.2 by stepping through year one's team recruitment and judging process that began with nearly 700 teams and ended with 59 active teams. The lessons learned from running year one of the AIXP inform future flexible problem prize competitions.

Beyond the administration of prize execution, the advancement statistics produced by the first round indicate problem domains that are ready for additional private and public investment. The AIXP began with 148 teams gaining competitor status in 2017 for the problem domains listed in Table 12.1. In Sect. 12.3.1 we explore which problem domains had the strongest performing teams in the first

Table 12.1 High-level problem domain descriptions for teams competing for the IBM Watson AI XPRIZE. The rows are ordered from domains with the highest advancement rate (top) to the lowest advancement rate (bottom). Each of these groups will be explored in the case studies of Sects. 12.3.1, 12.3.2, and 12.3.3. If left unaddressed, these problems pose significant negative consequences for humanity, including loss of life, reduction in health, lack of access to basic human needs, lack of wellbeing, lack of education, environmental degradation, and increased inequality

Problem domain	Team count	Example problem area
Humanizing AI	7	Moral and ethical norming
Emergency management	5	Planning disaster response logistics
Health	13	Drug efficacy prediction
Life wellbeing	21	Augmenting the visually impaired
Environment	8	Automated recycling
Education/human learning	17	Intelligent tutoring system
Civil society	11	Popping online filter bubbles
Health diagnostics	12	Radiography image segmentation
Robotics	5	Robotic surgery
Knowledge modeling	7	Automated research assistant
Civil infrastructure	9	Earthquake resilience testing
Business	19	Optimizing social investment
Artificial general intelligence	8	* (all of them)
Brain modeling and neural networks	6	Cognition emulation

judged round of the competition. We then explore the problem domain areas where teams faced the lowest likelihood of advancement. Generally, these teams either failed to show sufficient advancement towards their goal (e.g., teams focused on artificial general intelligence), or failed to show how successful completion of their grand challenge would produce changes in the world that are overwhelmingly positive. We explore these cases in Sect. 12.3.2.

The XPRIZE Foundation recruited 33 judges for the first round of the AIXP. These judges distinguish themselves either through their technical capacities within the field of AI, or their knowledge for the deployment of these systems in the real world. Judges followed a similar review process to an academic AI conference. Team scorecards included fields for technical novelty, impact, etc., but they also included sections for real-world impact assessment. Some technologies were assessed to be blocked by factors outside the control of the proposed solution (e.g., systematic sociopolitical obstruction). We explore this case in Sect. 12.3.2.

For our final case study, we explore the ethical challenges inherent in developing AI aimed at improving the world. Our open-ended competition brings to the fore many issues of fairness, accountability, and transparency that require intensive review and effort to develop adequate safeguards. From our organizational perspective, we refer to this as the "AI IRB problem" and explore its solutions in Sect. 12.3.3.

12.2 Prize Process

The AIXP officially began in 2016 and closes after 3 annual judged rounds and a final competition at TED 2020. The judges award a $3,000,000 grand prize, a $1,000,000 second place prize, and a $500,000 third place prize. The judges award an additional $500,000 to teams with noteworthy successes achieved during the annual reporting periods. The process executed to date includes prize design, registration, project proposal submission, judge recruitment, First Annual Reports (FARs), and FAR milestone awards.

Prize Design The XPRIZE Foundation is an organization with more than 100 staff working on many prizes in parallel. Different staff members are responsible for generating prize ideas, designing prizes, and running the prizes that have been launched. Designing a prize for AI poses interesting difficulties. AI requires a prize plan that is simultaneously (1) technically feasible in a relatively short timeframe, (2) technically challenging, (3) not vulnerable to "bag of tricks" solutions, and most importantly (4) associated with real-world impact. Through collaboration with a distinguished board of advisors from academic and industrial AI, the prize developed into the open-prize concept, thereby ensuring that (1) teams will only be awarded if they successfully develop their technology during a fixed time period, (2) judges can assess the difficulty of solving the problem post-solution, (3) judges can assess whether the solution constitutes true advancement in AI and/or

Fig. 12.1 Example marketing collateral for the AIXP. XPRIZE Foundation marketing staff developed a campaign that included inspirational images and bold characters, such as innovation, collaboration, medication, exploration, and desalination

innovative application of existing AI technologies, and most importantly (4) judges can evaluate how the technology will be applied in the real world. After drafting the legal documents governing the prize process, the prize opened for registration.

Registration The first step to winning an XPRIZE is registering for the competition. To separate the teams that were potential contenders from the merely aspirational, the prize assessed a $1,500 registration fee. When assessing the fee, the nearly 900 pre-registered teams dropped to just over 150. The number of competing teams is so high in part due to two factors. First, the prize launched with a marketing strategy (e.g., Fig. 12.1) and contacted many media partners. Second, the Foundation established a network of regional partners to lead in the recruitment of companies and academics from local AI development ecosystems. Some of the regional partners that were particularly successful in their recruitment efforts include Ascender in Pittsburgh (22 fully registered teams, many in robotics), and District 3 in Montreal (18 fully registered teams, many in deep learning).

Project Proposal The fully registered teams were then invited to submit project proposals to the XPRIZE Foundation. The teams answered a series of questions about the problem they proposed to solve and the AI technologies they believed would be necessary in pursuit of the problem. The proposals were then read and categorized by XPRIZE Foundation staff. The resulting team count within the team taxonomy of Table 12.1 motivated the target list for judge recruitment.

Judge Recruitment Appropriately judging 148 teams working towards different grand challenges required a judging panel with diverse technical, philosophical, and personal experiences. Among the judges are leaders from the labs of multinational corporations, AI startups, academic research departments, non-governmental organizations, and public policy think tanks. These individuals collectively have expertise in natural language processing, deep learning, adversarial learning, computer security, social effects of technology, political campaigns, computational sustainability, ecology, robotics, and many other fields and applications of AI research. Judge biographies are available at ai.xprize.org/about/judges.

First Annual Report (FAR) In September of 2017, competing teams submitted their FARs as four-page extended abstracts detailing their problem areas, proposed solution, and the progress achieved to date. Of the 148 teams eligible to submit the FAR, only 118 teams opted to do so. This shows significant self-selection that we consider for the purposes of analysis to be similar to a judged rejection. The judges "bid" on the submissions via the EasyChair conference management site to select teams for which they did not have a conflict of interest and were eager to review. The resulting computer-assigned reviewers were then modified by XPRIZE staff to ensure every team received at least one judge whose professional background centered on the development of AI technologies. Each team received at least two full reviews.

The advancement criteria focused on world impact potential and technical progress indicators. Of the 118 teams submitting FARs, 40 teams were rated for acceptance in both judges' overall rating and were automatically accepted. Next, 44 teams joined the rejection list based on their overall ratings. Resolving the remaining 34 teams to accept/reject decisions required examination of more specific attributes of the scorecard. These included rejecting teams where at least one judge did not rate the problem as important for humanity, where neither judge rated the problem as previously unsolved, where neither judge rated the technology as having the capacity to solve the problem, or where neither judge indicated the team showed incremental progress. The remaining 19 teams were then accepted into the second year of the competition.

All FARs were reviewed by at least one judge who self-assessed at the medium level of technical proficiency or higher, and one judge who self-assessed at medium level of problem domain proficiency or higher. The box and whisker plots in Figs. 12.2 and 12.3 provide additional details on the spread of judge confidence levels. The charts and a post-hoc analysis of reviews for individual FARS show the panel of judges self-assessed the medium to high-level of confidence for most team problem domains, and the high-level of confidence for team technical areas.

Milestone Awards for First Annual Report Having established the list of teams accepted into year two of the competition, the next step was to award the first allocation of the \$500,000 milestone prize purse. The top ten performing teams were nominated for milestone prizes by taking the top ten average overall ratings assessed for the FARs. Producing a ranked list of the top ten teams required judges to review additional FARs, but doubling the review effort with ten additional reports, ranking

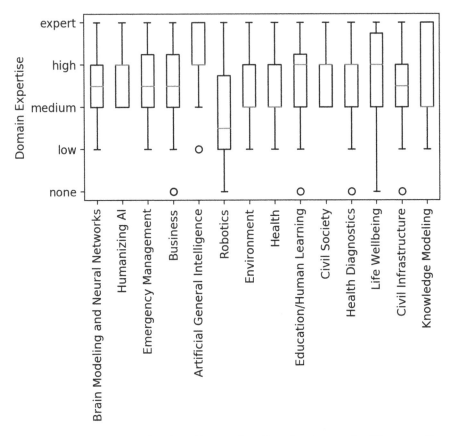

Fig. 12.2 Box and whisker plots for self-assessed problem domain expertise. The orange line indicates the median value and the box extends to the upper and lower quartiles. The whiskers show the extents. The circles are singleton outliers

them, and coming to a consensus before awarding first and second place at the NIPS conference was not feasible. To solve the ranking problem, XPRIZE staff employed collaborative ranking where each judge reviewed two additional reports they did not previously review. These review assignments were random, with the caveat that no judge reviewed the same pair of reports as another judge and no judge reviewed a team for which they have a conflict of interest. The judges then assessed one report as "better," and the resulting ordered pairs formed a scoring metric for milestone team ranking. The top two teams were selected from the ordered list with minimal weighted pairwise dissimilarity for all ordered judge pairs.

The Years Ahead In the coming year, additional teams have the opportunity to join the competition via a "wildcard round." The idea behind the wildcard is to solve a problem inherent in a multi-year, multi-round competition: the financial incentive only pushes teams starting at year one of the competition to develop their

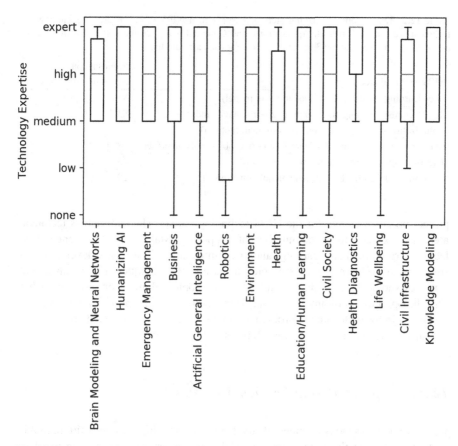

Fig. 12.3 Box and whisker plots for self-assessed technology expertise for team submissions. The orange line indicates the median value and the box extends to the upper and lower quartiles. The whiskers show the extents

solutions. By allowing for a limited number of wildcard entrants, the prize provides ongoing incentives for new breakthroughs in the most important problems faced by humanity. The competition has two wildcard rounds in which we expect a handful of teams to gain competition entry. Over the next two years, the field of regular and wildcard teams will be cut until three teams remain for a final round that takes place at TED 2020.

12.3   Case Studies in the AI for Good Movement

Real-world AI solution development often requires multiple AI components (e.g., solutions for perception, robotic control, and predictive state representation). Team application of multiple AI components is apparent in Table 12.2, which shows

Table 12.2 Team proposals having stemmed words in a NIPS technical areas, excluding the technical areas of Algorithms, Applications, and Competitions since the results for these areas are non-informative. The top 3 matching words for each area are listed

NIPS technical area	Proposal count containing reference
Deep learning (visual, predict model, gener model)	83
Reinforcement learning and planning (control, navig, mdp)	83
Optimization (optim, convex optim, combinatori optim)	78
Neuroscience and cognitive science (memori, problem solv, neurosci)	68
Theory (regular, comput complex, learn theori)	43
Probabilistic methods (bay, graphic model, topic model)	29

project proposal counts for the NIPS technology areas. The sum across technical areas far exceeds the total number of proposals. Many teams reference deep learning, reinforcement learning, and/or optimization. Since teams developing AI solutions to problem domains employ a variety of techniques, the advancement statistics should be regarded as indicators of problem domain opportunity rather than the opportunity of any individual AI technology for that problem domain.

We begin by exploring the problem domains where teams showed disproportionate success within the First Annual Reports.

12.3.1 Top Performing Problem Domains

Figure 12.4 shows the percentage of advancing teams within the competition. In this section we will explore the properties of the top performing seven team problem domains. When possible, we will center the exploration on the teams nominated for a milestone prize (Fig. 12.5).

Humanizing AI Teams involved in humanizing AI are concerned with solving the problems introduced by placing AI into the human context. For example, the milestone nominee from this group, Brown Human Centered Robotics Initiative (HCRI), aims to "create robots that obey social and moral norms." One example is mapping the attributes of a scene to behaviors, such as mapping "library" to a reduction in audio communication volume. While HCRI was primarily concerned with automatic inference of these norms, other teams took an end user programming approach whereby the system is more intentionally programmed by people in the environment. In both cases, these teams showed a greater success rate than the rest of the field because they are attempting to solve challenging problems faced by the deployment of all AI systems to the real world. Any solution to the humanizing problem would have the potential to greatly expand the domains AI systems can interface with.

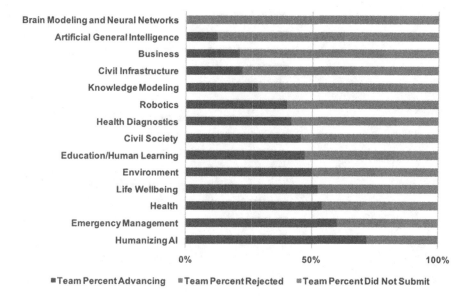

Fig. 12.4   Team advancement stacked bar chart showing percentages for advancement, rejection, and non-submitting within each of the problem domains. Figure 12.6 shows this stacked bar chart with team counts instead of percentages

Fig. 12.5   Group photo of the ten teams competing for the first milestone prize. The represented teams include **Aifred health** (Montreal, Canada), **Amiko AI** (Milan, Italy and London, UK), **BehAIvior** (Pittsburgh, PA), **Brown HCRI** (Providence, RI), **DataKind** (New York, NY), **Deep Drug** (Baton Rouge, LA), **emPrize** (Atlanta, GA), **EruditeAI** (Montreal, Canada), **Iris.ai** (Oslo, Norway), and **WikiNet** (Quebec, Canada)

Emergency Management Many teams involved in emergency management are data synthesis teams for performing operations research tasks in uncertain, fast-changing environments. Most of these teams gained entry into year two of the competition because they are (1) clearly working in an area that could have a

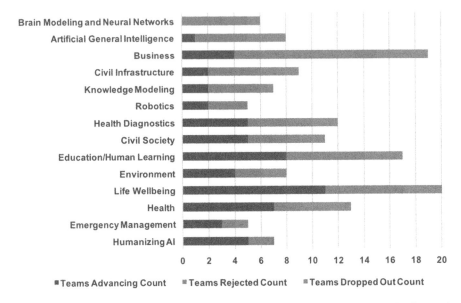

Fig. 12.6 Team advancement stacked bar chart showing counts for advancement, rejection, and non-submitting within each of the problem domains. 30 of 148 teams did not submit first annual reports. Judges then selected 59 of the 118 submitting teams to advance on to year two. Figure 12.4 shows this stacked bar chart with team percents instead of counts

real immediate impact for millions of people affected by natural and anthropogenic disasters, (2) working in a problem space that has fallen behind technological capacities, and (3) benefiting from a wealth of newly accessible datastreams (drones, daily satellite imagery, reliable emergency communications, etc.). The key attributes of these teams are either the development of specialized hardware for disaster management or models that can take immediate and ongoing surveys of the disaster area to prioritize rescues, resource deployment, and other disaster response activities.

Health Due to the high number of teams working on health-related problems, we split the health teams into "health" and "health diagnostics." The health diagnostics teams are largely concerned with diagnosing medical conditions through computer vision for radiography, biometric signal processing with always-on health sensors, and other applications of raw health data. After removing these health diagnostics teams, the remaining teams in the "health" category are working on problems of longevity (zero of three teams advancing), medical personalization (one of three teams advancing), mental health (five of six teams advancing), and drug discovery (one of one team advancing). The teams working on longevity may have fallen for the same trap as the teams working on artificial general intelligence (detailed in Sect. 12.3.2), whereby they attack the top-level problem without a concrete roadmap of deliverables. Only one of the three longevity teams submitted a FAR. Team Deep

Drug, a milestone nominee, was the one team working on drug discovery. This team distinguished itself by building on top of a history of successful academic research.

The most surprising aspect of the health advancement statistics is that so many of the mental health teams successfully advanced to year two. One team, BehAIvior Health, was nominated for a milestone award for predicting and preventing addiction relapses and overdoses using wearables. These teams have significant challenges in ensuring the safe and ethical deployment of their technologies, but the scale at which synthetic intellect can potentially serve mental health needs is ample justification for advancing these in-development solutions to year two. We will explore the ethical issues posed by these teams in more depth in Sect. 12.3.3.

The one medical personalization team admitted to year two placed second in the milestone competition. Aifred health submitted the following abstract,

Aifred health will be a deep-learning powered clinical decision aid for healthcare professionals in mental health care. Its primary outcomes will be to help clinicians select the most effective treatment plans (pharmacological, psychotherapeutic, etc.) and mitigate adverse side effects, allowing doctors to provide greater personalized care to a larger number of patients. We are addressing the field of mental health because there is currently an acute need for tailored treatments to improve efficacy and reduce recovery times. We begin our development with a focus on depression. Globally, depression affects 300 million people and is the leading cause of disability. Depression carries a socioeconomic burden of $210 billion per annum in the US alone. We have forged partnerships with various teams of experts and applied to major pharmaceutical company trial databases to gain access to critical datasets; prepared our deep learning model and created a backend pipeline to accept clinical data for training; validated our deep network on Fashion-MNIST; focused on preparing interpretability of treatment recommendations by implementing receptive field analysis and generating saliency maps; submitted an IRB ethics application to McGill University so that we will be able to accept the data for model training; innovated ethical concepts in order to guide model development; engaged in a systematic review of neuropsychiatric literature to better evaluate known predictors of treatment response in depression; and begun producing protocols for ease-of-use studies and clinical trials.

This is an excellent example of the sort of underserved use case in an otherwise heavily developed market sector. Drug companies have little incentive to develop methods for intelligently personalizing prescriptions since the intelligent agent may select the drugs of a competitor. Aifred health also excels in the systematic way they are pursuing interdisciplinary research. They are developing collaborations between people knowing the problem area and the technology, then executing a clear road map towards world impact.

Life Wellbeing Teams concerned with "life wellbeing" are attempting to solve quality of life issues, including AI designs for the hearing and vision impaired (three of four advancing), personal life management (six of eleven advancing), independent living assistance for the elderly or infirm (one in five advancing), and one team working to produce an online safety agent (advancing). Several successful teams from these groups are finding ways of promoting everyday wellness by extending the reach of clinical professionals beyond the doctor's office. The first prize milestone winner, AMIKO AI, submitted the following abstract,

Asthma affects over 300 million people worldwide. Each year, millions of hospitalizations and emergency department visits occur, driving costs over $50B in the US and €70B in Europe. And many, if not most, asthma-related exacerbations are preventable with proper treatment. In fact, despite the widespread availability of effective treatments, patients struggle to follow their treatment plans, to correctly administer their medications and to maintain habits that support their treatment, while physicians lack the tools and the information to understand how their patients are doing and to find the best therapy for each of them. Our solution is Respiro, a connected health platform that offers advanced medication sensors and digital health tools to assist healthcare professionals and empower asthma patients to achieve better outcomes. We are on track with the high-level timeline presented earlier this year, as we have successfully achieved our first milestone: the development of sensors to objectively monitor medication compliance, drug delivery technique and patients inhalation profiles.

AMIKO AI could easily be categorized a "Health" team, but their focus on continuously facilitating the doctor/patient relationship expands the boundaries of the medical profession into the capacity for promoting everyday wellness.

Environment Teams working on environmental problems are developing solutions within the subdomains of agriculture (one in four advancing), recycling (one of one advancing), species abundance (one of one advancing), water quality (zero of one advancing), and one team in pollution mitigation (advancing). WikiNet served as the pollution mitigation team and received a nomination for a milestone award for their work with the large unstructured corpus of environmental remediation documents to build a system that can recommend best practices on future remediation efforts. Their application of natural language processing to unforeseen datasets shows the promise of collaborative research.

Education and Human Learning The teams working on education are each developing different ways to make education more personalized, effective, scalable, or cost-efficient. Of the seventeen teams eligible to advance, eight teams were admitted into year two. Two of the education teams were nominated for milestone awards. emPrize is developing and deploying AI technologies to online classrooms, including components for cognitive tutoring, question answering, and formative assessment. Of particular interest to the judging panel was the early testing of system efficacy within real-world scenarios. This trait is shared by the other milestone nominee from the education domain, Erudite AI, who developed and began testing a system for connecting students that need help with a topic to students that are predicted to tutor the topic well. The complexities of educational systems are such that real-world demonstrations are crucial for establishing the efficacy of the system and gaining special recognition for the effort.

Civil Society Of the 11 teams in the competition in the subdomains of information consumption, equity, law, and safety, most of the five teams moving on to the next round were in safety. These teams work on problems of scaling up law enforcement for fighting sex trafficking advertised online, and making the roads safer with vehicle-mounted computer vision systems. We will return to the information consumption teams in the following section.

12.3.2 Underperforming Problem Domains

The underperforming problem domains generally did not advance for one of two reasons. They either failed to show that the problem they were working to solve would provide real-world benefit (e.g., they detailed a solution to a technical problem without an application), or failed to show a pathway to solving a grand challenge (i.e., they were overambitious).

Information Consumption (Civil Society Subdomain) Before covering the bottom seven problem domains, it is worth revisiting an underperforming subdomain from the higher-performing civil society domain. These three teams working on information consumption (the problems of filter bubbles, fake news, etc.) were all developing AI solutions to problems introduced by optimization algorithms applied to media consumption habits. In reading the judgment discussion surrounding information consumption, it appears that the failure was in presenting an AI technology to a complex sociopolitical problem without a clear solution. While an AI solution may exist in some form, there is no clear answer to how an AI can independently solve problems introduced by another AI. Still, in search of a solution these teams made commendable efforts in attempting to understand the problem. It is unfortunate that the competitive marketplace means third parties cannot experiment directly with the optimization algorithms performed by new media companies.

Health Diagnostics The health diagnostics teams were all working on worthy problems, but their apparent failure mode is that these solutions are generally under active development in many corporate and university research labs. Teams would be more successful in this domain if they were not implicitly competing with many researchers outside the competition.

Robotics The teams classified as "robotics" were so classified because their proposal involved the development of robotics without a clear problem solved by new robotic capacities. These teams were also at a significant disadvantage for showing progress since many planned to work with novel robotic architectures that can take years to develop. It is difficult to show progress compared to the more nimble machine learning problems. Further, the AIXP focus on real-world outcomes highlighted that many of the non-industrial applications of robotics have a backlog of fundamental advancements required before robotics can be a part of everyday life (e.g., the problems being solved by the "humanizing AI" teams).

Knowledge Modeling The heading of "knowledge modeling" spans practices within AI that could be described as applied data mining. One milestone nominee, Iris.ai, is working within this domain to produce a research assistant to greatly accelerate literature review and concept discovery. Iris.ai differentiates itself from the less successful teams in the domain by presenting a specific system that could be evaluated by judges for its fitness to purpose. Otherwise, building a knowledge base towards general purpose queries is too abstract to benchmark.

Civil Infrastructure The civil infrastructure teams suffered from one of two problems. First, the primary barrier to improvement within this domain is often not the absence of good ideas. There are many trivial optimizations of society that do not gain adoption due to budgetary or political reasons. The milestone nominee, DataKind, avoids these problems by building their solutions for countries that lack adequate measurement to perform basic civil services. Datakind processes satellite imagery to perform image segmentation of poverty and disease rates. The global automatic generation of these predictions have the capacity to selectively deploy scarce development interventions in the areas most needing them.

Business The business team category served as a catchall for teams not fitting into a category beyond building a business centered on AI. While a successful business proposition is often an indicator of a system's social utility, many business teams failed to articulate an advancement for society more generally. In some cases, the advancing business teams adjusted their project to more explicitly target social benefit, which may lead to their re-categorization in the future.

Artificial General Intelligence (AGI) Of the eight teams competing to develop the first AGI, only one of the teams advanced. The likely reason is that teams must show a plausible means of successfully completing their grand challenge, and establishing a plausible pathway to AGI within the timeframe of the competition is itself a grand challenge. The one team advancing from this category trimmed their ambitions to a sufficient degree so that they can plausibly produce their system within the competition timeframe.

Brain Modeling and Neural Networks Finally, many teams proposed to develop new approaches to neural networks. These teams often emphasized architectures that are inspired by the human brain. While some of the approaches may prove successful in the fullness of time, there is no shortage of proposals for new neural network architectures. Without a demonstrated capacity for solving a problem that was not solvable by previous neural network architectures, new proposed architectures don't represent a grand challenge. In the fullness of time we expect some of these teams will show empirical promise, but without preliminary evidence they are unlikely to advance.

12.3.3 Ethical Review for Artificial Intelligence Systems

The most challenging aspect of running an open-ended competition for artificial intelligence is the dual capacity for AI systems to solve global challenges, while introducing novel and unforeseen trade-offs. For instance, a hypothetical mental health dialog agent can serve the majority of the population, but a minority of users may suffer from conditions where the standard treatments developed for the system are inadequate or harmful. Mental health practitioners are trained to identify cases where their background is inadequate for effective treatment. In essence, they have solved the anomaly detection problem for the purpose of harm minimization. In

Table 12.3 Home countries, counts, and advancement rates for competing teams. We render the geographic extent of teams in Fig. 12.7

Country	Team count	Advancing count	Advancing percent
Barbados	1	1	100
Israel	1	1	100
Norway	1	1	100
Poland	1	1	100
Canada	20	11	55
UK	6	3	50
USA	71	30	42
China	6	2	33
Italy	6	2	33
Vietnam	3	1	33
France	7	2	29
Australia	8	2	25
Germany	4	1	25
India	5	1	20
Netherlands	2	0	0
Czech Republic	1	0	0
Ecuador	1	0	0
Japan	1	0	0
Romania	1	0	0
Spain	1	0	0
Switzerland	1	0	0

a global competitive marketplace, it is likely that these minority cases will not be protected without external forcing similar to an Institutional Review Board (IRB).

Many countries have rigorous systems of ethical review for research, but their standards have significant variation in process, requirements, ethical foundations, legal liability, and timelines. Further, current systems for ethical review do not adequately address the capacity for a deployed system to change through time. Assumptions valid for the initial version of a system may be violated as the system continues to explore the state space. The IBM Watson AI XPRIZE is a global competition (see Table 12.3 for a list of countries) with a potential for teams to deploy mental health dialog agents, medical recommender systems, and other technologies where the betterment of the many does not present an absence of harm to a few. The XPRIZE judges serve as arbiters of global beneficence and risk, but there is currently no expert body that has a global process for recommending the manner in which AI systems should be permitted to interface with the world. When an Australian XPRIZE team hypothetically proposes to deploy a system for HIV prevention to Africa based on training data gathered from Thailand, there is no established and systematic means of review. While the IBM Watson AI XPRIZE has developed responsive review processes for the teams competing to solve problems with AI, a near future where AI systems are commonplace requires a method that scales beyond a standing committee of the world's leading experts.

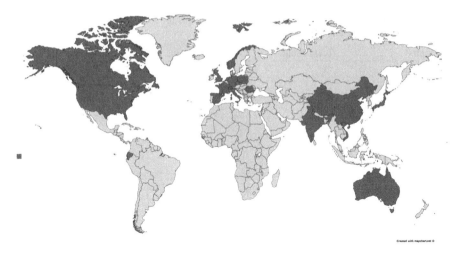

Fig. 12.7 Home countries for teams competing in the first year of the IBM Watson AI XPRIZE

12.4 Conclusions

The AI for Good movement borne of the efforts of governments, industry, academia, and AI competitions shows much progress towards producing beneficial AI. Notable efforts include the Partnership on AI (Partnership on AI 2018), the Asilomar principles (Asilomar Conference 2017), the IEEE recommendations on Ethics (IEEE Standards Association 2017), the UN AI for Good Summit (International Telecommunication Union 2017), and many university labs and research centers are beginning research programs for ethical, safe, and beneficial AI.

The teams competing for the IBM Watson AI XPRIZE support the movement with applications of AI that are beneficial for humanity, demonstrate human and machine collaboration, and identify the greatest opportunities for AI to make an impact on society. While AI techniques are developing quickly, we have an opportunity to better understand where research intersects with grand challenge applications to produce new opportunities. An open competition plan has allowed teams from many backgrounds to tackle hard problems with AI. The mixed teams bringing together AI and application domain experts is a validation of a multi-disciplinary approach to problem solving.

Areas of beneficence, fairness, explainable AI, and other aspects of AI governance will be a focus in round two of the competition. We look to feedback from our advisory board and judges to adapt the competition guidelines to ensure the ongoing execution of the competition process that is fair to competing teams and maximally impactful in the real world.

Great opportunities in the AI for Good space are being discovered, and as the competition proceeds to round two, the XPRIZE team along with the prize sponsor IBM and other supporting ecosystem partners look forward to seeing what an impassioned group of AI developers can solve.

Acknowledgements First and foremost, the teams competing to make the world a better place deserve special recognition for their efforts. Next, IBM has shown great vision in supporting such an open-ended endeavor.

The IBM Watson AI XPRIZE relies on an extraordinary advisory board to offer its insights and broad expertise to ensure maximum rigor in this competition.

- **Yoshua Bengio**, Full Professor of the Department of Computer Science and Operations Research, Head of the Montreal Institute for Learning Algorithms (MILA)
- **Francesca Rossi** Distinguished Research Scientist at the IBM T.J. Watson Research Centre and a professor of computer science at the University of Padova, Italy
- **Rob High** IBM Fellow, Vice President and Chief Technology Officer, IBM Watson
- **Babak Hodjat** Co-founder and CEO of Sentient
- **Neil Jacobstein** Chair of the Artificial Intelligence and Robotics Track at Singularity University
- **Subbarao (Rao) Kambhampati**, Professor of Computer Science at Arizona State University and President of AAAI
- **Peter Norvig** Director of Research at Google Inc.
- **Tim O'Reilly** Founder and CEO of O'Reilly Media Inc.
- **Jean Ponce** Professor at Ecole Normale Superieure in Paris, France.
- **Lav Varshney** Assistant professor of electrical and computer engineering at the University of Illinois at Urbana-Champaign.
- **Manuela M. Veloso** The Herbert A. Simon University Professor in the School of Computer Science at Carnegie Mellon University.

The judges perform the hard work of balancing imagination and critical review. They include Gabriel Skantze, Carla Gomes, Eric Van Gieson, Adam Cheyer, Robin Murphy, Danah Boyd, Ivan Laptev, Bistra Dilkina, Alex London, Al Kellner, Erin Walker, Madeleine Clare Elish, Franois Chollet, Sidney D'Mello, David Kale, Danielle Tarraf, Xiaoyang Wang, Evan Muse, Nicolas Papernot, Henry Kautz, Risto Miikkulainen, Pascal Van Hentenryck, Mark Crowley, Forent Perronnin, Bill Smart, Graham Taylor, Julien Mairal, Stefano Ermon, Antoine Bordes, Jonathan Zittrain, Michael Gillam, Peter Eckersley, Barry O'Sullivan, and Rayid Ghani.

Finally, the XPRIZE staff members Jennine Dwyer, Yvonne Cooper, Katherine Schelbert, Michael Martin, Sean Beougher, Daniel Miller, Stephanie Wander, and Ed McNierney have all been instrumental in organizing the IBM Watson AI XPRIZE.

References

Asilomar Conference. Asilomar AI Principles. *Future of Life Institute*, pages 1–25, 2017.

Jacques Bughin, Eric Hazan, Sree Ramaswamy, Michael Chui, Tera Allas, Peter Dahlstrom, Nicolaus Henke, and Monica Trench. Artificial intelligence the Next Digital Frontier? *McKinsey Global Institute*, 2017.

IEEE Standards Association. The IEEE Global Initiative on Ethics of Autonomous and Intelligent Systems Announces New Standards Projects, 2017.

International Telecommunication Union (ITU). AI for Good Global Summit, 2017.

Partnership on AI. Partnership on AI Home Page. partnershiponai.org, 2018.

XPRIZE Foundation. About XPRIZE. www.xprize.org/sites/default/files/xprize_backgrounder.pdf, 2018.

Chapter 13
Aifred Health, a Deep Learning Powered Clinical Decision Support System for Mental Health

David Benrimoh, Robert Fratila, Sonia Israel, Kelly Perlman, Nykan Mirchi, Sneha Desai, Ariel Rosenfeld, Sabrina Knappe, Jason Behrmann, Colleen Rollins, Raymond Penh You, and The *Aifred Health* Team

Abstract *Aifred Health*, one of the top two teams in the first round of the IBM Watson AI XPRIZE competition, is using deep learning to solve the problem of treatment selection and prognosis prediction in mental health, starting with depression. Globally, depression affects over 300 million people and is the leading cause of disability. While a range of effective treatments do exist, patients' responses to treatments vary to a large degree. Some patients spend years going through a frustrating 'trial-and-error' process in order to find an effective treatment. The

D. Benrimoh (✉)
Department of Psychiatry, McGill University, Montreal, QC, Canada

Wellcome Trust Center for Neuroimaging, University College London, London, UK

Aifred Health, Montreal, QC, Canada
e-mail: david.benrimoh@mail.mcgill.ca

R. Fratila
School of Computer Science, Montreal Neurological Institute, McGill University, Montreal, QC, Canada

Aifred Health, Montreal, QC, Canada
e-mail: robert.fratila@mail.mcgill.ca

S. Israel
Department of Psychiatry, McGill University, Montreal, QC, Canada

Douglas Mental Health University Institute, Montreal, QC, Canada

Aifred Health, Montreal, QC, Canada
e-mail: sonia.israel@mail.mcgill.ca

K. Perlman · N. Mirchi
Department of Neurology & Neurosurgery, McGill University, Montreal, QC, Canada

Montreal Neurological Institute, Montreal, QC, Canada

Aifred Health, Montreal, QC, Canada
e-mail: kelly.perlman@mail.mcgill.ca; nykan.mirchi@mail.mcgill.ca

© Springer International Publishing AG, part of Springer Nature 2018 251
S. Escalera, M. Weimer (eds.), *The NIPS '17 Competition: Building Intelligent Systems*, The Springer Series on Challenges in Machine Learning,
https://doi.org/10.1007/978-3-319-94042-7_13

Aifred Health solution is a deep learning-powered Clinical Decision Support System (CDSS) aimed at helping clinicians select the most effective treatment plans for depression in collaboration with their patients. In this chapter, we discuss problem of treatment selection in depression and explore the technical, clinical, and ethical dimensions of building a CDSS for mental health based on deep learning technology.

13.1   Introduction: What Is *Aifred Health*?

Artificial intelligence (AI) is one sector that has the potential to revolutionize healthcare, allowing for a better understanding, diagnosis and treatment of numerous diseases and an improved evaluation of prognosis. Specifically, recent advances in deep learning (Goodfellow et al. 2016) bring about new potential advantages over many classic prediction approaches in medicine (i.e., regression or naive Bayesian classifiers). Deep learning can leverage many clinical predictive features to find hidden patterns in data. Learning these patterns can bolster prediction accuracy. Deep learning is robust to missing attributes or data – this mitigates some of the

S. Desai
School of Computer Science, McGill University, Montreal, QC, Canada

Aifred Health, Montreal, QC, Canada
e-mail: sneha.desai@mail.mcgill.ca

A. Rosenfeld
Department of Computer Science and Applied Mathematics, Weizmann Institute of Science, Rehovot, Israel

S. Knappe
Department of Cognitive Science, McGill University, Montreal, QC, Canada

Aifred Health, Montreal, QC, Canada
e-mail: sabrina.knappe@mail.mcgill.ca

J. Behrmann
Aifred Health, Montreal, QC, Canada

C. Rollins
Department of Psychiatry, University of Cambridge, Cambridge, UK

Aifred Health, Montreal, QC, Canada
e-mail: colleen.rollins2@mail.mcgill.ca

R. P. You
School of Physical and Occupational Therapy, McGill University, Montreal, QC, Canada

Aifred Health, Montreal, QC, Canada
e-mail: raymond.you@mail.mcgill.ca

The *Aifred Health* Team
The *Aifred Health* Team, Montreal, QC, Canada
e-mail: info@aifredhealth.com

challenges associated with the diverse and incomplete datasets commonly existing in medical practice. Deep networks allow the learning of complex dependencies between variables that are useful for handling the often poorly understood relationships between variables in medicine. As an interdisciplinary team of computer scientists, psychiatrists and biomedical researchers, we tackle one of the biggest challenges of the twenty-first century: improving treatment in mental health.

Globally, depression affects over 300 million people and is the leading cause of disability (World Health Organization 2017). While a range of effective treatments do exist, patients' responses to treatments vary to a large degree; some patients spend years going through a frustrating trial-and-error process in order to find an effective treatment. We believe that AI and data science can expedite this process. The Aifred Health solution is a deep learning powered Clinical Decision Support System (CDSS) for general practitioners, psychiatrists, and nurse practitioners. Its primary aim is to help clinicians select the most effective treatment plans for depression. This will not only improve treatment quality but also enable clinicians to provide more personalized care to a larger number of patients. In addition to improvements in efficacy and reduction in recovery times, this system may significantly lower healthcare costs by reducing the amount of services required per patient to reach remission from depression. The following chapter will discuss our progress towards this CDSS from theoretical, technical, design, and ethical perspectives.

Team Aifred Health began development in 2016 as one of the 100+ teams competing for the IBM Watson AI XPRIZE. Teams winning the XPRIZE share a $5 million prize purse allocated to the projects most improving the world with artificial intelligence. During the first year of the competition, judges from the fields of AI, medicine, and other application areas nominated ten "Milestone Award" teams. The judges then selected two teams to win cash prizes during the Neural Information Processing Systems (NIPS) Competition Track. Aifred Health garnered the second place award for distinguishing itself in the importance of the problem being addressed and the progress achieved in addressing the problem.

13.2   Problem Description: What Is Depression and Why Is It Hard to Treat?

Major Depressive Disorder (MDD), known as 'depression', is a mood disorder that negatively affects feelings, thinking patterns, and behavior (American Psychiatric Association 2013). As the leading cause of disability burden in the world, over 322 million people currently struggle with depression (World Health Organization 2017). This debilitating health condition will affect globally more than one in ten people during the course of their lives, and up to one in six people in the United States (Bromet et al. 2011; Ferrari et al. 2013). In addition to significant suffering for individuals and their families, depression greatly increases the risk for self-harm and suicide (Turecki and Brent 2016).

The pathophysiology of major depression is complex and remains to be fully deciphered. Depressed patients typically experience changes in their neurophysiology, neuroanatomy, and neuroimmunology (Lener et al. 2015; Schmidt et al. 2016). Also of relevance are genetic factors, particular cognitive styles, and environmental conditions, such as childhood trauma or stressful life situations (Kemp et al. 2008). According to the current definition of depression in the Diagnostics and Statistical Manual of Mental Disorders (DSM-V), two patients with depression can have symptom profiles with little overlap; so while one patient could experience symptoms of insomnia and agitation, the other may experience periods of oversleeping and lethargy (American Psychiatric Association 2013). A cohesive description for the pathophysiology of depression is lacking, and when coupled with the varied phenomenology of depression, we understand why developing targeted treatments for this condition proves challenging: it is unlikely that there is simply *one kind* of depression.

Nevertheless, effective treatments do exist (Kennedy et al. 2016) and include various medications, psychotherapies, exercise, light therapy and several neuromodulation techniques (i.e., electroconvulsive therapy, transcranial magnetic stimulation, transcranial direct-current stimulation) (Cooney et al. 2013). What is striking is that many of these treatments are roughly equally effective (Khan et al. 2012). The heterogeneity of depression, the multitude of effective treatments, combined with the clinical observation that some patients do much better with some treatments than with others (even though they are all supposed to be equally effective), leads us to the following assessment: there is an opportunity to use an understanding of the differences between people all diagnosed with depression,to better target treatment.

Though best-evidence clinical guidelines such as those from Maudsley or the Canadian Network for Mood and Anxiety Treatments (CANMAT) provide valuable insights, current strategies for selecting effective treatments typically follow an educated guess and check approach (Kennedy et al. 2016; Taylor et al. 2015) and do not have extensive options for personalization. A patient and their physician will try one treatment, and then another, with the hope that some treatment or combination thereof will eventually be effective. Given the multitude of treatments available, the probability of selecting the ideal therapeutic option on the first try is low (Warden et al. 2008) and this trial-and-error process is demonstrably sub-optimal. Consider observations from the Sequenced Treatment Alternatives to Relieve Depression (STAR*D) trial (Warden et al. 2008), the largest pragmatic trial of depression treatment thus far. In this study, response rates to one initial medication were low, with only a third of patients achieving remission. This trial complements clinical observations, where a number of patients must try two or more treatments before identifying one that works for them. Such guess-and-check trial periods can span months or years because medications require several weeks to take effect. Moreover, long wait times are typical when trying to access psychotherapy or neuromodulation, which themselves require weeks to complete. Possible side effects to treatment are also of concern, and remain difficult to predict for individual patients (Simon and Perlis 2010).

Improving our ability to identify the most effective treatment for each patient would mark a significant advancement in the treatment of depression. Indeed, current efforts to personalize medical treatment for other heterogeneous diseases like cancer do improve diagnostics, monitoring, and the selection of effective treatments (Shin et al. 2017). Can we use personalized medicine to improve outcomes in psychiatry? We believe so.

We propose combining clinical and sociodemographic features – such as symptom profile, marital status, ethnicity and age – with a panel of biomarkers, such as genetic polymorphisms and EEG responses. This combination will provide a rich set of data points for each patient that we can assess using a predictive model that in turn will recommend personalized treatments for individual patients. But which predictors should be considered?

We conducted a systematic meta-review assessing roughly 200 reviews or meta-analyses of predictors of antidepressant treatment response in patients with MDD. All papers were screened for relevance by title and abstract; selected papers were then read in detail by two independent reviewers. Papers determined not to contain any information about predictors of response were then excluded. All reviewers used an online data-extraction form to collect information about predictors of response. These predictors could be biomarkers, patient symptoms, demographic data, or information about comorbidities (co-occurring pathologies), medical history, and environmental factors (i.e., ongoing abuse). Though our results are preliminary, we have identified several evidence-based predictors of treatment response. We now discuss the state of the field of predictor research and some key predictors identified in the review.

These predictors fall roughly into the following domains: genetics, neuroimaging, peripheral (e.g., blood, serum) markers, demographics, symptom profile and patient history, and medical and psychiatric comorbidities.

Demographics   Only a few demographic features, such as age, ethnicity, or socioeconomic status have been robustly associated with antidepressant (AD) treatment response (De Carlo et al. 2016). Though such factors lack predictive power in isolation, they have been shown to interact with genetic or other factors to predict differential response to treatment (Klengel et al. 2013). For example, while ethnicity alone may not be a predictor of response, it interacts with the serotonin receptor genetic polymorphism: Caucasians with the S/S genotype are less responsive to citalopram and fluvoxamine, while Asians are more responsive to these drugs (Duval et al. 2006).

Symptom profile   Patients' clinical characteristics have been commonly investigated as pragmatic predictors of treatment response. Of these features, higher baseline symptom severity and early improvement are strongly correlated with treatment response (McIntyre 2010; Papakostas and Fava 2009).

Clinical comorbidities   As a general rule, MDD patients with a clinical comorbidity have lower rates of improvement and higher rates of relapse. For instance, concurrent neurological disorders, vitamin deficiency, viral infections, obesity, heart disease, obsessive compulsive disorder, alcohol and substance abuse/dependence, and personality disorder adversely affect the outcome of antidepressant treatment (Berlim et al. 2007, 2008; Miller et al. 2016; Lopresti et al. 2013).

Genetics A multitude of genetic markers are associated with treatment response. Though replication remains a significant barrier to translating genetic markers to clinical practice, among the most consistently demonstrated candidates are polymorphisms in the SLC6A4 gene, particularly the 5-HTTLPR region which codes for the 5-HT transporter (Porcelli et al. 2012).

Peripheral markers Peripheral immune-inflammatory markers, many of which are clinically accessible through urine, blood, saliva or cerebrospinal fluid (CSF) tests, are implicated in the pathoetiology of MDD (Schmidt et al. 2016) and have been shown to be predictive of treatment outcome. Levels of pro-inflammatory cytokines, inflammatory marker C-Reactive Protein (CRP), for example, are particularly associated with treatment response (Young et al. 2016).

Neuroimaging Neuroimaging predictors include brain structural, functional, and temporal measures, as assessed by structural magnetic resonance imaging (MRI), functional MRI/SPECT/PET, and EEG/MEG, respectively. Such measures have identified hippocampal volume, anterior cingulate activity, fronto-limbic connectivity, and certain EEG measurements, among others, as predictors of treatment response (Breitenstein et al. 2014; Chi et al. 2015; Dichter et al. 2016; Lener and Iosifescu 2015).

Biomarkers are ultimately only as valuable as they are practical. For this reason, the most pragmatic biomarkers of antidepressant treatment response emerge as peripheral markers, such as TNF-α, CRP, BDNF, IL-1β, IL-6, accessible through saliva or blood samples, and EEG indices like frontal EEG theta band activity, measured by placing low cost and portable electrodes on the patients' scalp for a short period. Clinical and sociodemographic variables may act as important moderators or mediators of treatment response for a given patient, or as important predictors in their own right.

Recent research strongly suggests that no single predictor or biomarker is sufficient to predict treatment response. Instead, our strategy should be to use research findings to define a panel of investigations and clinical questions which, together, will provide appropriate data on which to base predictions of response (Brand et al. 2015). We note that panels may include temporal components (i.e., measurements taken at different timepoints). Most biomarker research to date identifies predictors at baseline (i.e., prior to the initiation of treatment); however, future assessments should identify if there are additional metrics of interest at various time points early on in the course of treatment (Leuchter et al. 2010).

Note that in the rest of this chapter, we will use the words *predictor* and *patient feature* interchangeably. This is because the predictors (or potential predictors) of response defined in the medical literature serve as the input features for our machine learning model.

13.3 Solution Description and Rationale

We expect to accrue several benefits from a deep-learning based CDSS as a means to select effective treatments for depression. These systems should shorten the time patients need to find an effective treatment, thereby reducing their suffering while saving physicians time and healthcare costs. Following standard assessment of patient features, a clinician can then input the most salient features and obtain as output a personalized list of treatment options. Each treatment option is paired with a simple to understand percentage value that predicts likely effectiveness at reducing or eliminating symptoms or improving social and occupational functioning. The CDSS should eventually be able to appropriately recommend all approved treatments for depression, including medications, psychotherapy, neurostimulation, and lifestyle interventions. Using a software as a service business model, clinicians will access our CDSS as an application available on their at-work computer or as a plugin to an existing interface for electronic medical records. In addition to providing predictions, the application will provide an easy means for clinicians and patients to track symptoms; other features of the software application will include visuals of patient symptoms over time and their response to treatment.

We aim to use existing resources and knowledge more effectively rather than develop new treatments. Given the recent abandonment of research into neuropsychiatric disorders by several large pharmaceutical firms (Cressey 2011; Pfizer 2018), using existing treatment resources to their fullest potential is a necessary strategy to improve outcomes in mental health. In addition, a deep learning approach can identify patient subtypes or profiles through an unsupervised learning stage, identifying groups of patients that respond well to specific treatments. This in turn could enable us to identify patients that do not respond well to any existing therapies, knowledge which could encourage new research into therapeutics by providing a more targeted research question and a better defined population of study (Hahn et al. 2017). Given this context, the Aifred Health approach – targeting treatments – is reasonable, but rests on a fundamental assumption. We assume that there are useful differences between groups of patients that can be demarcated by measurable features that can predict response to treatments. Recall in the previous section, we outlined specific patient attributes (such as EEG measures or the presence of certain symptoms) that can predict the efficacy of a treatment. Research and clinical experience supports observations of heterogeneous responses to treatments. As such, our assumption appears well-grounded and supports our chosen approach to improving personalized care.

The precise form for our proposed CDSS merits further discussion, as identifying how this tool could best be used will determine a great number of technical and CDSS/user experience specifications. The specific problem that needs to be solved is determining, given certain features, what treatments a patient is most likely to respond to.

Firstly, how can we measure response to treatment? Many different validated symptom rating scales exist in psychiatry, such as the Montgomery-Asberg

Depression Rating Scale (MADRS) (Montgomery and Asberg 1979), as well as scales that measure social and occupational functioning (Goldman et al. 1992). Note that we can normalize different scales across studies in order to make comparisons. This enables the use of findings from diverse studies. Once normalized, we can define response as a clinically meaningful change in scores from baseline to a study's endpoint, and define remission as dropping below a score necessary for the diagnosis of depression on a given questionnaire. We can also code additional outcomes categorically, such as whether a patient attempts or commits suicide, or whether they gained employment or are currently on welfare. As such, there exist meaningful quantifiable measures useful as training objectives for a machine learning system.

Next, how do we determine which treatments to include in our model? The most reasonable course of action is to include only treatments that clinical trials demonstrate to be effective. This standard may exclude emerging effective treatments that require further study to prove their efficacy. Regardless, given the paucity of clinical trials for emerging therapies, there will be insufficient data at this time to train our model while incorporating them in a meaningful way. Focusing on established treatments also mitigates ethical concerns that would arise from an AI system recommending an unproven treatment.

Another consideration is the precise features to include in training. This is complicated because candidate predictors previously shown to be irrelevant in lower-dimensional and shallower models (i.e., models with comparably fewer features and less complex internal representations than what is commonly used in a deep learning model) might be of use when combined with new features or combinations of features due to previously unknown interactions. For example, if a mutation of a given gene increases response to a treatment in half the population but decreases it in the other half, this gene would be a poor predictor of response unless we also know what – if anything – differentiates these two halves of the population. As such, there is good reason to try many predictors in the model. On the other hand, a model with too many predictors will be too arduous to collect from a new patient (and may lead to overfitting and poor generalization). Some patient information can be very expensive to collect (e.g., MRI results) and using these as routine model input features would impractical in clinical practice. Feature selection (Guyon and Elisseff 2003) – the process of determining which subset of patient features to use for model training given a set of patient features in the training data – is therefore a critical step in the development of our CDSS. Our approach to feature selection and merging domain expertise with algorithmic methods for feature selection will be described in Sect. 13.3.

Next we will address data sources. We have defined a precise objective- learning to predict the efficacy of treatments for depression on a patient-by-patient basis; this objective places certain constraints on which datasets will be most useful to our work. The data should have rigorous baseline and outcome measurements; it should have a range of features we can select from, but not only those known to be good predictors in isolation; and it should include a wide variety of patients treated with all of the currently supported treatments for depression. In addition, the dataset should be large enough to make best use of machine learning approaches and to ensure the system has a sufficient number of training entries for lesser used treatments. How large is large enough? There is no direct answer to this problem, however, we can derive this estimate from the $10\times$ rule, a common standard employed in classification tasks of deep learning (Beleites et al. 2012). Given the various number of parameters inherent to our algorithm, we must be sure each parameter is trained with enough examples from different classes (i.e., treatments) to be able to distinguish them from other classes. A general heuristic is that 10 examples per trainable parameter is sufficient to extract discriminative patterns between patients. For instance, with 200 parameters we would require a minimum of 2000 training data points. To further avoid bias and maximize generalizability, the dataset should include people with a large array of medical and psychiatric comorbidities from different ethnic, socioeconomic, and cultural backgrounds. This ideal dataset does not exist. There are certainly large banks of electronic medical record data, but these records often lack rigorous outcome measures necessary to predict treatment outcomes since psychiatrists rarely collect this information (Gilbody et al. 2002). Regardless, medical record data is useful for unsupervised learning. To account for these deficiencies, we focus on clinical trials and research studies as our primary source of data. Trials, such as STAR*D, provide rigorous outcome measures, and every approved treatment has clinical trials by definition.

Not all trials record a large range of predictors, however, and many trials have strict inclusion and exclusion criteria that lead to a biased population sample. This selection bias (Lambert 2011), can counter our abilities to generalize findings to actual clinical populations. Some trials conducted at research universities are more inclusive of study populations typically overlooked by large industry-sponsored or more general trials, or have less-restrictive exclusion criteria. Our decision to focus on clinical trials to source higher quality data therefore provides benefits of acquiring large data sets (as well as collections of smaller, but still significant trials) to acquire sufficient diversity in patient populations to ensure generalizability of the findings. Another concern is publication bias in industry-sponsored trials and their overall quality (Kirsch 2014). When funded by industry, results from successful trials get published while the results from unsuccessful studies typically remain unpublished. Some trials are designed to acquire results faster instead of conducting higher-quality, rigorous studies (Walkup 2017). Sourcing trial data from quality sources matters. Walkup (2017) demonstrated how trials conducted under the NIMH had lower placebo response rates and much greater differences in terms of response between placebo and treatment groups. Therefore it is important to include in the training of our model datasets from sources like the NIMH, which focus on conducting quality trials and reporting of funded studies regardless of their results (Walkup 2017).

Collating these datasets requires reconciling different ways of representing the same variables and accounting for missing data – we discuss this process further in the technical section. Another difficulty is that most of the available data is from North America and Western Europe, potentially limiting the applicability of our model to these regions of the world until it can be validated in other geographic regions, or until we can acquire data of similar quality from other territories to further train our model.

Who ought to use this CDSS, and how? One determining factor is the type of features used for the prediction. If the features are blood tests, genetic tests, or complex clinical assessments, contact with a clinician will be required. However, if the treatment prediction model could remain accurate without the need for complex biomarker inputs, we question whether the model should be available directly to patients. We suspect this would result in the suboptimal use of our treatment selection model for several reasons.

First, in most jurisdictions, clinicians must prescribe drug treatments and neuro-modulation, and often provide psychotherapy. While AI-based therapy (Fitzpatrick et al. 2017) will be a welcome addition to the continuum of care, they will likely mostly help those without severe pathology and will not displace the role of clinicians in diagnosis and in providing appropriate treatment in the foreseeable future.

Clinician expertise and experience are valuable sources of information when it comes to assessing diagnosis, prognosis, and response; indeed, relying only on patient-reported measures in isolation would overlook a great deal of data. Beyond trust-building between AI and clinicians and the desire not to infringe on the patient-doctor relationship, this is one key reason why we decided to insist on the inclusion of physician-derived data in the input space for our predictive model of response.

An ideal model is one that makes use of clinician expertise and helps inform and enrich shared clinician-patient decision making (Braddock 2010). Part of the clinician's role in shared decision making is to provide information and help the patient consider treatment options. By providing clinicians with a set of personalized treatment recommendations and their underlying justification based on up-to-date medical data, aifred can enrich the dialog between clinician and patient. Our keeping of physicians *in the loop* also supports making safer medical decisions because the clinician serves as a filter that monitors a potentially fallible AI system.

This is not to say that clinicians are infallible – in fact, clinicians often do not follow evidence-based practice (Kenefick et al. 2008). A series of 'unofficial' and preliminary conversations with physicians confirm this. For example, because there are so many treatment options that are thought to be equally effective, many clinicians said they will simply pick three or so treatments – usually medications – become acquainted with their side effect profiles and use them in near exclusivity for most patients. Having a tool that will recommend diverse treatments based on a patient's individual features will give clinicians a principled reason to leave their "comfort zone" and explore treatment options they may not have considered otherwise.

Our view is that augmenting clinicians with AI-enhanced tools and giving patients digital tools that help them understand and manage their own conditions will produce the best outcomes. The best way forward is to enrich and augment, not displace, the clinician-patient relationship. Enrichment will come through better information (i.e., the predictive model) and through empowering patients to effectively participate in the management of their own care (i.e., through our patient-facing features).

Beyond prediction of treatment response, other predictive models we plan to develop may prove useful. Clinicians, family members and patients could benefit from predictive models of suicide or relapse, and from tools that help tailor lifestyle interventions and guide self-management to suit individual patient needs and preferences.

Having discussed the rationale underlying our work to build an AI-powered clinical decision support system, we now explain the process of building such a system and conclude by describing how this predictive model can become a commercialized product.

Building this CDSS is a step-wise process. After deciding on the model objective and the data required to train the model, we need to acquire this data from public and private repositories. This entails establishing data-sharing partnerships with researchers and companies from around the world. Once acquired, much effort must be diverted towards combining datasets with different variables. This requires collaboration between statisticians, data scientists, clinicians and domain experts in mental health and clinical trials. The model must then be trained with objective functions suitable to the overall objective of response prediction. Next we need to select input features by leveraging both domain expertise and statistical approaches, which requires collaboration between machine learning engineers, clinicians and mental health researchers. At the same time, a user interface must be designed to suit clinician needs and to integrate well within their workflow. Clinical validation obtained by testing our CDSS through clinical trials will be the last step before we progress to marketing, sales, customer support, and the harnessing of data collected as the CDSS is used to iteratively improve it. The inherent interdisciplinary nature of this project demonstrates how interdisciplinary work is a necessary and fruitful *modus operandi* in this information age.

Finally, how does aifred work as a *product*? What incentives will motivate clinicians or healthcare systems to purchase our innovation? Primary care clinicians (family doctors, nurse practitioners) treat large numbers of patients within tight time constraints (Tai-Seale 2007). Treating depression is time consuming for the patient and the clinician. Such conflicting demands on time and resources encourages primary care clinicians to find means to treat their depressed patients efficiently so that they can, free up time to treat additional patients while decreasing their overall clinical workload. Differing from primary care clinicians, psychiatrists focus their clinical activities towards depressed patients referred from primary care with treatment resistance or complex comorbidities. For these patients aifred's decision support system could be of particular use because medicine lacks personalized treatment guidelines for this patient population. Healthcare networks such as the public National Health Service in the United Kingdom typically must meet standards that aim to maximize quality of care while minimizing costs. Public institutions and private healthcare networks would thus benefit from our tool that will reduce the need for multiple treatment trials and follow-up appointments.

13.4 Technical Description

Deep learning (Goodfellow et al. 2016) has become a vast area of research with rapid advances propagating throughout the field, many of which manifested in medical applications. Perhaps the most common application is in medical imaging due to the popularization of convolutional neural networks (Ronneberger et al. 2015; Roth et al. 2015). However, the use of computational tools in mental health care, an emerging field often termed computational psychiatry (see Hahn et al. 2017), introduces various technical and theoretical challenges and opportunities.

At Aifred Health, we set a goal to develop a model that can produce individualized treatment suggestions for patients with depression. Let us pose the problem more formally: Given a diverse and heterogeneous group of patients, each characterized by many different features, we seek to predict how a given patient will respond to an array of treatments. We aim to provide a list of treatment options sorted by efficacy, and pair each option with an individualized side-effect profile. Moreover, we will assess if subtypes of patients exist, and if a specific subtype predicts differential responses to different types of treatment. Finally, we need to ensure our model produces outputs that a clinician can understand with ease so that they can make treatment decisions alongside their patient.

To produce a model that will predict which patients will respond best to which treatments, we must use a complex and potentially highly-dimensional set of input features. Model training proceeds in two steps: unsupervised and supervised. In the unsupervised step, the model learns the underlying distributions of variables in the data and how they interact without being required to make any predictions. In the supervised step, we then train this "knowledgeable" model to use its general understanding of the dataset to make specific predictions, namely, treatment efficacy scores and side effect profiles.

An efficient network structure will automatically pick up on the subtle patterns hidden in the patient data and then make accurate predictions on new patients. However, such a model still requires fine tuning of the hyperparameters. Generally, modifying hyperparameters requires: adjusting the number of artificial neurons for each hidden layer; determining a sufficient number of hidden layers; determining the optimal learning rate for the network and modifying additional parameters depending on the precise choice of learning function and network architecture. Through the use of a gradient descent algorithm such as Adam ("adaptive estimates of lower-order moments") (Kingma 2014), we can modify the parameters of the network to optimize the loss function specified for the model by trying to predict the treatment outcomes. In this situation, the network gradually learns which patient characteristics and in what combinations – such as age, diagnosis, genetics, previous therapies – are of value in determining which drug or therapy is best to use, and how effective we expect it to be. Such capacities would be of great utility for frontline clinicians that often have lots of clinical information about an individual patient but little guidance on how best to use it to guide treatment decisions. Compared to Bayesian techniques, we avoid the theoretical constraint of needing to assume independence between features in the feature set. If there is a pattern, the network finds it without human intervention. However, the model requires vast amounts of labelled data for training and validation. Given the low number of patient records with good outcome measures in clinical trials and research studies when compared to popular databases used for machine learning like ImageNet (Krizhevsky et al. 2012), one limitation of the model is that it must have a limited number of input features. This serves to avoid over specification due to the limited number of training examples. Working with a limited number of input features is also beneficial in clinical practice; a large input space would require a clinician or patient to enter a long list of patient features, thus rendering our innovation impractical and overly time consuming.

The data required to train our model is complex and heterogeneous, containing subtle dependencies between a large number of features. These attributes signifies that model training requires many levels of abstraction needed to express complex dependencies in the data and a need to experiment with various models and training techniques. To aid in this process we developed a new open-source deep learning framework, termed *Vulcan* (source code can be found at https://github.com/Aifred-Health/*Vulcan*). We built *Vulcan* on top of Theano (Bergstra 2010) and Lasagne (Dieleman 2015) using added functionality from the Scikit-learn library (Pedregosa et al. 2011) including data shuffling, preprocessing and decomposition methods. Together, these computer resources provide the tools we need for visualizing high-dimensional data, rapid prototyping of neural networks and several methods for evaluating and interpreting models, which will be discussed later in this section. We designed this framework with both modularity and ease-of-use in mind, which simplified constructing several architectures and made them easier to use across many machines. *Vulcan* is preloaded with various example training scripts using the Fashion-MNIST dataset (Xiao et al. 2017) where even the simplest implementation yields over 90% accuracy. Future versions of this framework will have the most recent version of TensorFlow (Abadi et al. 2016) as the backend tensor computation library.

Due to a deficiency of labelled data, we needed to employ certain strategies to improve the performance of our model. To this end, we conducted unsupervised learning on the unlabelled data as a means to model the underlying distributions and provide better weight initializations for the supervised learning step. Our network architecture (Fig. 13.1) uses a feed-forward autoencoder with self-normalizing Scaled Exponential Linear Units (SELUs) coupled with alpha-dropout layers for regularization (Klambauer et al. 2017). This network architecture allows for greater depth than standard activation functions for feed-forward artificial neural networks (ANNs), resulting in higher-order representations.

Using Snapshot learning (Huang et al. 2017), we will train several models to learn various optimized solutions in the cost function (e.g. categorical cross-entropy for classification tasks) by exploring more of the non-convexity cost space (i.e., each "snapshot" of the model will learn variations of a representation while the objective remains the same). This ensemble of networks can cover more of the solution space than a single network. The various models are queried in parallel

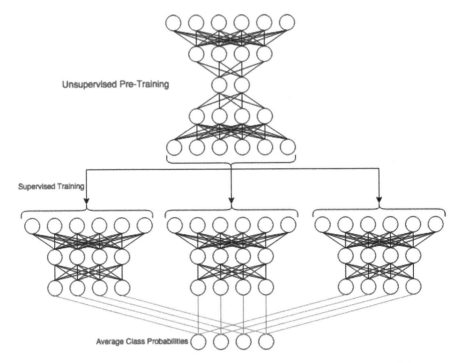

Fig. 13.1 A visual depiction of the general architecture. The unsupervised pre-training stage handles vast amounts of unstructured data followed by additional training of the assembled networks to optimize treatment predictions. At inference time, the models make their own predictions and the final results are averaged to get a global prediction

and all will have influence on the prediction, making for more robust classifications (Huang et al. 2017). Instead of having a majority vote, we have opted in for a soft-voting scheme where the class probabilities are averaged together so as to control extremes and have more stable performance. The autoencoder learns the distribution of the data by actively encoding and decoding the features. Doing so gives the network some implicit knowledge about the data by forcing it to be "summarized" – that is, reducing its dimensionality with respect to the input space. The self-normalizing units help to avoid extremes of gradients and orients the model progression towards a stable convergence point (lower error, increased accuracy) that together allow for deeper networks and therefore more faithful representations of the abstract relationships between input features (Klambauer et al. 2017).

Recall that the model will assess patient outcomes in terms of validated depression rating scales. We will use a separate autoencoder to model side effect profiles, producing a list of probable side effects for each recommended treatment course. Moreover, other validation methods such as calculating the confusion matrix, sensitivity & specificity (Lalkhen 2008), DICE score (Dice 1945), positive predictive value, negative predictive value, accuracy, F1 score, and the receptive operating curve (ROC) (Hajian-Tilaki 2013) along with the area under the ROC (AUC) for each class. To further examine all aspects of the classifier, we built into the test suite *Vulcan* a cumulative score for each metric. This will help identify the model's strengths and vulnerabilities so we can account for these vulnerabilities in the next training cycle (i.e., we will be able to determine if the model is sacrificing specificity for sensitivity, or the converse).

We plan to develop a neural network that allows for output of combined treatments (e.g., a specific medication plus a specific psychotherapy). However, the ability for the neural network to combine treatments within a single prediction may be limited because the medical literature labels outcomes for combination treatments as if that combination was a single treatment. This means that for model training purposes, a combination treatment is actually a separate class of treatment than its constituent treatments.

The network will always output a list of treatments, and will associate each treatment with a probability of effectiveness using the common *softmax* function. The need for clarity makes the ranking and presentation of results important. During supervised training, we will determine the accuracy of the model by comparing the efficacy of the treatment that the test patient actually received with the predicted efficacy for that treatment provided by the model. This does not, of course, validate all the other predicted efficacies on the list for that given patient, making clinical validation of the model critical (see below).

We will use k-fold cross validation where k is 5 (i.e. 20% split for each fold) on all of our metrics to ensure consistent model performance (Fushiki 2011). Dropout, with a probability of turning off an internal artificial neuron at each training cycle, will be used during training to prevent overfitting and improve generalizability (Srivastava et al. 2013). Clinical data collection is imperfect and often results in a great deal of missing data due to, for example, patients dropping out at different stages in the study for various reasons. We would need to remove a great deal of the data if we excluded patients that have incomplete records of all the measured features in the study. We can instead retain these records and include additional features to flag if a feature is valid (i.e., not missing) and train with additional dropout. We can initially train the network with large amounts of dropout on the input layer so as to embed several representations of an optimal solution to the neural network in the scenario where the input does not have a complete set of features for a patient. This would force the neural network to find alternative correlative patterns between available features and the outcome measure. This training procedure will act as a primer for the network to perform as well as it can in the validation stage when it must make a prediction on a patient whose medical record is missing data.

In order to maximize sample size and cover a wide range of treatments, we need to train our model on datasets collected by various research groups and institutions. This need presents a challenge: we will first need to homogenize the datasets in order to produce one dataset to train the model. We can combine the various datasets using normalization to allow for comparison of scores on depression questionnaires and by simplifying patient features in the data by converting them into categorical variables. However it is possible that in the worst case we have very little overlap in collected features between studies. To address this, and to address the much more common situation where rare features appear in only a few datasets, we can introduce an artificial complementary feature. This complementary feature tracks the validity of a patient feature. If the variable's value is in fact "true" for a patient, we can label it as "1". If that variable is missing, we can insert the label "0", signalling that feature was not collected. Given n features, in the worst case this method introduces an additional n artificial features to track variable validity. Doubling the dimensional space introduces a considerable amount of complexity to the neural network and causes it to suffer even more from the "curse of dimensionality" (Han et al. 2017) if we use these as features in the traditional sense. However, we can also use this complementary variable to void the weights connected to any missing feature so that it does not affect downstream decision-making and simplifies our cost function considerably by reducing the number of input features.

There are situations where one study will have multiple phases, with each phase acting as a trial of a new treatment modality. Such studies present an opportunity. We can separate phases to redefine them as different studies. This requires using identifying codes for each participant to append the results of the earlier phase to the participant record for the later phase of the study. With this strategy we can use multi-phase studies, like STAR*D, to train the model on the response of individuals to different kinds of treatments while using their response history from the first part of the trial as a new feature, to take the patient's medical history (i.e., treatment received in the first phase of the trial) into account.

To further reduce our feature set in order to simplify the optimization function of our network, we work with our human clinical advisors. They provide expert knowledge with respect to which features are redundant or unnecessary. The research literature provides additional insights as to how we may identify and eliminate redundant features. We will combine our expert-driven approach to feature reduction with traditional algorithm-based dimension reduction, such as the pruning of low-weighted input features or principal component analysis (Jolliffe 2002). These are designed to identify the most descriptive features of the dataset so as to prevent learning redundant representations in the predictive model. This will produce a highly performing model that is also practical in the clinical environment (i.e., which does not require large time and financial resources to collect a large number of patient features to make a treatment prediction).

Clinicians require interpretability in decision support tools, something that has been traditionally difficult with deep learning due to the increasingly abstract internal representations found in the hidden layers. However, we decided that this should not deter us from using powerful deep learning techniques, and as such we have committed to building tools for model interpretability. Such tools include: cross validating (Fushiki 2011) the final model input features and relating them to existing literature for domain validation, and using receptive field and saliency map analysis in order to get a sense of some of the low-level feature groupings and the magnitude of their contribution to the final prediction (Luo et al. 2016). Moreover, generating saliency maps has been shown to shine some light into which features of an input data sample have contributed to which class the network predicts (Simonyan 2013).

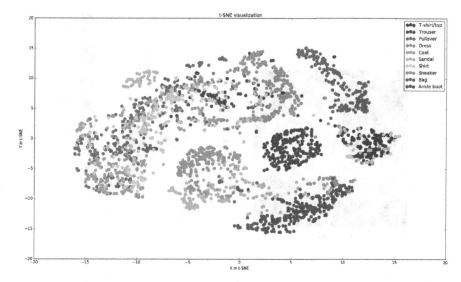

Fig. 13.2 Data visualization with t-SNE and network interpretability through saliency maps.
As a visual example of how we can cluster patients, we can identify several clusters in the Fashion-MNIST dataset (Xiao et al. 2017) with t-SNE (van der Maaten and Hinton 2008)

These analyses can also give us an insight into which features the network believes is generally most useful in predicting our outcome measure which can allow us to consult with some of our experts and potentially further reduce the feature set Some of the feature clusters we identify may also produce novel research questions. Such clusters correspond to similarities between certain patient types that we would be able to extract with t-SNE (van der Maaten and Hinton 2008) and displayed visually for ease of interpretability. Figures 13.2 and 13.3 depicts how these algorithms work on other datasets. This level of sophistication will allow for the identification of patient subgroups defined by input features, a type of result familiar and useful to clinicians. We will be presenting these results as reports that can be easily read by clinicians in order to provide them and their patients with more information.

We employed with success some of the techniques described above to predict lifetime suicidal ideations using the Canadian Community Health Survey (CCHS) – Mental Health component (Gravel 2005). We note that these results are preliminary; we have yet to complete our feature reduction and interpretability work on this model, though we were able to show the value of expert-driven dimension reduction and feature selection using machine learning techniques.

Predicting suicidal ideation is a good starting point because unlike the multiple classes of treatment we must assess for depression, having had suicidal thoughts can be assessed with a yes or no answer. We trained our model on 23,859 survey responses from the CCHS. Ninety percent of those surveyed answered no to having suicidal thoughts. How can we best use these findings to train our algorithm to predict suicidal ideation in future patients? Imagine if the algorithm learned to guess

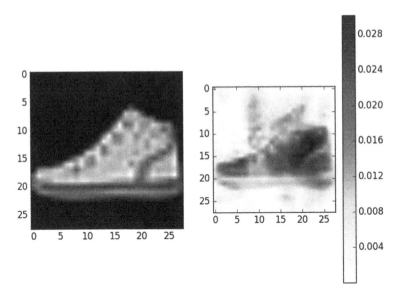

Fig. 13.3 Data visualization with t-SNE and network interpretability through saliency maps.
A visual depiction of how we can interpret which features contributed the most to the final
prediction through the saliency map (Simonyan et al. 2013). Calculating the gradients of the loss
with respect to the inputs show us which pixels led to the prediction of "shoe"

no for all future patients; it would be right 90% of the time, giving the illusion that
it is highly accurate in its predictions. To address the sparsity of the "no" class,
a subset of the dataset was created which consisted of all examples that had the
yes label (2262) and 2262 randomly sampled examples from the 'no' class. This
was passed to a cross validation function where the number of folds was equal to
5. Thus, the 4524 examples with equal amounts of 'yes' and 'no' was split into
5 chunks. For each fold, we trained on 4 chunks and validated on the last chunk
plus all of the extra 19,335 examples (all class no). Following training using the
training data set, we would be able to determine whether our algorithm is accurate
if it is capable of detecting the minority of yes respondents within the validation
data set.

An important part of this prediction was selecting which features to include in
the model. Features were answers to questions given by participants. There were
a total of 585 features, but with the consultation with a clinician, we were able
to reduce the feature set down to 177 features. This minimized redundancy and
confounding variables in the dataset, while maintaining clinically relevant features.
After expert feature reduction, features were further removed using a receptive field
technique. This technique allows us to determine which features have significant
and insignificant contributions to the prediction. Insignificant features were removed
5 at a time, for 15 iterations. This reduced the feature set size from 177 to 99.
Finally, a variance thresholding technique was used, where features that had 80% or

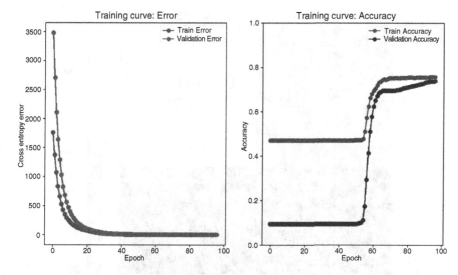

Fig. 13.4 Plot of the training and validation cross entropy errors of suicide ideation prediction over 100 epochs of training. Due to a larger class imbalance in the validation set (closer to the rate of suicidal ideation observed in the general population), the initial errors and accuracies are much higher and lower, respectively. However, the model was able to distinguish a difference between the two classes and performed more accurately on both the train and validation sets around 60 epochs

more examples with the same value were removed. This reduced the feature set size from 99 to 82. In Fig. 13.3 we have illustrated the training and validation errors and accuracy measurements across 100 training epochs for one of the folds within cross validation using 82 features.

We achieved an algorithm able to distinguish between yes and no responders for suicidal thoughts, with a sensitivity of 69.84% and specificity of 76.04%, a positive predictive value of 6.12% and a negative predictive value of 99.12%. As a reference point, the sensitivity and specificity prior to any feature removal was 71.42% and 73.44%, respectively. After expert feature reduction the values were 69.9% and 76.28%, respectively. Thus, the features removed on the basis of receptive fields and variance thresholding, changed the sensitivity and specificity by a negligible amount (Fig. 13.5).

Plotting results of a confusion matrix (Fig. 13.4) provides further proof of the accuracy of our predictive algorithm. If highly accurate, plotting the predicted classifications of the respondents versus their actual category should have virtually all data points have a value of (1,1), falling within the upper right quadrant. Cost sensitive learning could be used if the number of false positives (type 1 error) is unacceptable (Dmochowski et al. 2010); we will explore this in the future. We also note that in order to train our classifier we needed to use most of the subjects with suicidal ideations in the training set, leaving a validation set with only roughly 2% of respondents having suicidal ideations, as opposed to 10% in the general population.

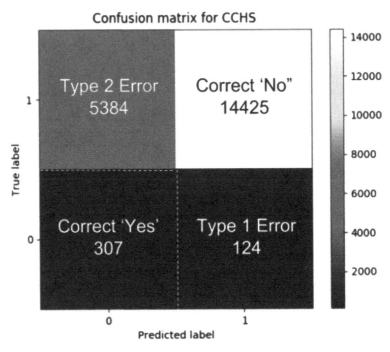

Fig. 13.5 Confusion matrix for suicidal prediction results. The X-axis represents how our algorithm classified respondents as either yes (0) or no (1) for suicidal thoughts (predicted label), while the Y-axis is the actual category for all respondents (true label)

Had we had more data and been able to avoid this class imbalance, we predict that our classifier would have performed even better.

We believe this result demonstrates several key concepts. The first is that deep learning can be used effectively to analyze psychiatric datasets. The second is that much smaller amounts of data (i.e., roughly 4000 examples in the training set) can be used for prediction in psychiatry than are needed in imaging-heavy fields such as oncology, given the lower number of features available for training the predictive model. The third is that domain expertise can be useful in feature selection in computational psychiatry applications (Hahn et al. 2017). In addition, we believe that with further refining this model may become clinically useful, potentially as an automated screening tool attached to a patients medical record that can alert physicians when a patient is predicted to be having suicidal thoughts, encouraging the clinician to discuss this with the patient.

13.5 Optimizing Physician-AI Interaction

Many researchers view healthcare as a promising domain to introduce AI technologies (Patel et al. 2009). AI technologies could improve health outcomes and quality of life for millions of people in the coming years – but only if they gain the trust of physicians and patients. In building our CDSS, we must consider three entities: the physician, the patient, and the CDSS. The three entities must work together as they are dependent on each other in determining the best choice of treatment. The physician provides input and diagnostic details; the patient provides self-assessments; the CDSS assists in ranking treatment solutions and providing information. The patient and physician then discuss these options together to make a medical decision. As noted in the *AI100* report in 2016, "the field of AI is shifting toward building intelligent systems that can collaborate effectively with people" (Stone et al. 2016). In order to support this goal, we are designing our CDSS to optimize physician-AI interaction.

Physicians must trust and use the treatment predictions from the predictive model in order for these prediction to have any impact. The literature discusses key factors in securing such trust, with a particular focus on the importance of natural interaction of AI with physicians, patients and families (Stone et al. 2016). We aim to accomplish this through three key elements: transparency, adaptability, and integration.

13.5.1 Transparency

To inspire trust, aifred must be easy to interpret The physician must view the CDSS as a tool whose internal processes can be understood rather than seen as inexplicable inputs and outputs. 'Interpretable' or 'explainable' AI is an important concept for policy makers and machine learning researchers, and deep learning systems are more difficult to interpret than other, sometimes less accurate, approaches such as K-nearest neighbour or Bayesian classifiers. However, we have decided that the often superior performance of deep learning over other approaches justified attempting to find ways to integrate them into clinical work. We focus on what we *can* tell clinicians about what the system is computing (such as the input features that were most important in generating a given prediction). Also, as some of the data used for each prediction comes from physicians, this might help improve physician trust and engagement with the system because they will know that the CDSS has taken their expertise into consideration.

13.5.2   Adaptability

A CDSS must be able to determine when and how to present information to the users. This requires striking a careful balance between ensuring clinical quality (e.g., reminding physicians whether to order blood tests and follow-up appointments as per best-practice guidelines) and usability (e.g., ensuring that reminders and notifications do not overwhelm clinicians). An important factor in this realm is to model and predict human (in this case, physician and patient) behavior and decision-making, whereby we use these models to guide the design of our artificially intelligent systems (Rosenfeld and Kraus 2018). Consider the recently developed CDSS by UCLA (Yoon et al. 2016) that monitors hospitalized patients' vital signs and sounds an alarm when the system identifies a patient's health deteriorating. The system, as with many other CDSS's, rely on explicit, and sometimes non-intuitive, physician-defined parameters (e.g., in the UCLA system, doctors are requested to define mathematical thresholds for when alarms should be triggered). According to the authors, this decision burden may significantly contribute to the barriers of adopting this potentially life-saving system in practice. From a technological research perspective, it is very easy for one to overlook physicians' doubt and resistance to implementing new technology. However, if the goal is to improve patient outcomes, then these systems must be implemented and widely used. Designing a CDSS to be adaptable will reduce barriers to clinician adoption of the CDSS in their practice.

In order to bring about a seamless and beneficial interaction with a physician, aifred should integrate into the physician's workflow (Fig. 13.4), as well as adapt to each physician's preferences while minimally resorting to explicitly soliciting physician feedback on its performance. This interaction setting is often referred to as *implicit interaction* (Schmidt 2000). The system should accommodate physician needs and preferences, learning how to do so based on use patterns. As an example, consider the task of scheduling a regular follow-up for a specific patient. A CDSS could rely on a standard model for "default" follow-up schedules, though this may not accord with an individual physician's usual practice or a given patient's preferences. Instead, it could provide personalized follow-up recommendations, relying on both the patient's characteristics and past follow-up schedules as well as the doctor's preferences, past decisions and best practices. These measures could save time for the physician, freeing them of the need to manually input follow-up appointments. Not only is the administrative load for the physician reduced, but a follow-up schedule that accords with patient preferences may lead to better attendance at follow-ups. On the other hand, certain follow-up schedules would fall outside the bounds of acceptable clinical practice (e.g., a patient should be seen within 2 weeks of starting an antidepressant, not 3 months later), and the CDSS must be programmed in such a way that its recommendations never contravene best-practices (a physician may choose to do so, but this should be an explicit act). As one would expect of a human medical assistant, a "one-size-fits-all(-physicians)" CDSS is likely to provide suboptimal assistance for a physician. Meeting the challenge of adaptability may require the development of both novel algorithmic approaches as well as the design of new interaction methods for improving aifred's integration into the clinical workflow.

The use of online learning (Shalev-Shwartz 2012) provides a promising approach for addressing the above challenges. Starting at a default configuration, (that could be learned in an offline fashion given physicians' past decisions), an online learning algorithm would first receive a prediction instance (e.g., a patient for which the next check-up must be scheduled). Then, the algorithm is required to predict the personalized desired outcome for both the specific patient and doctor (e.g., follow-up in 2 weeks) and presents the prediction to the physician. Following this prediction, the system obtains the correct output (e.g., the physician may modify the recommendation or accept it), and this information would be used to improve the model's future predictions. The online learning framework is popular in personalizing system configurations and decisions overtime (e.g., in automotive settings Rosenfeld et al. 2016). The possible predictions would be bounded by best-practice guidelines (to ensure, for example, that follow-ups are scheduled at safe intervals). This online learning framework, combined with our design philosophy should bring about a rapid personalization and adaptation of aifred to meet clinician, patient, and care quality needs.

13.5.3 Integration

Another question is *how* aifred should integrate into the clinician workflow. Clinicians commonly use medical calculators (such as the online FRAX score calculator for risk of hip fracture, https://www.sheffield.ac.uk/FRAX/) and online sources of information while they practice, but they are not used to structuring their time with a patient in order to make the best use of a CDSS. We propose the schematic in Fig. 13.6 to illustrate the integration of our CDSS with physician workflow. Working with the CDSS requires clinicians to ask certain questions and gather certain information that they may or may not be used to asking or gathering. It will require them to spend time inputting some of this information into the model and asking for a prediction, and then to spend more time reviewing the suggestions. They generally cannot do this outside of the interaction with the patient because the outcome of the use of the CDSS is the recommendation for the prescription or referral the patient needs to leave with. Since time is of the essence for many clinicians, the CDSS must integrate as closely as possible into the clinician's workflow and minimize the time it takes for a prediction to be made. For example, it should draw as much information as it can from patient self-report through a mobile application or waiting-room questionnaires filled out by tablet or from the electronic medical record. The data the clinician inputs must be simple and consist as much as possible of yes/no questions and simple scales in order to reduce input time. Reports generated by the predictive model should be easy to parse and translate into clinical action. Above all else, the model must be proven to work in order for clinicians to justify spending time using it (see Sect. 13.6).

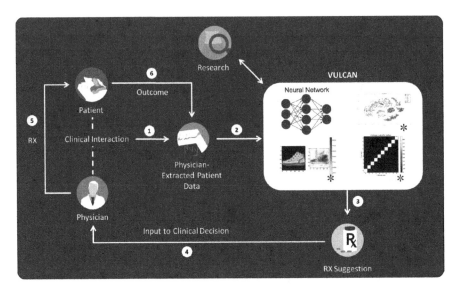

Fig. 13.6 **Integration of the aifred solution into the physician workflow.** Through clinical interactions between the physician and patient (1), relevant questionnaires and tests will be completed to extract patient data (2). This data will be fed into *Vulcan*, our machine-learning model which is continuously fed up-to-date research on treatment (and which will provide new questions for further research). Following analysis, the model will suggest (3) a list of treatments which will be proposed to the physician, as well as a report explaining these predictions, assisting in the clinical decision step (4). The physician will then select a treatment (Rx) (5). Patient outcome will continuously be recorded via patient-rated questionnaires on a mobile application and follow-up appointments with the physician and will be added to the patient database (6). This will then be fed into *Vulcan* again, allowing for the continuous evaluation and revisiting of the personalized treatment strategy

aifred is designed to incorporate our philosophy of integration, adaptability, and transparency. This will lead to the development of an experience that differentiates our product. According to research, "an iterative design process conducted by an interdisciplinary team improves the usability and favorability of a CDSS among providers" (Thum 2014). This means that collaboration between our different teams will be a key feature of our design process. Our small team size allows for open communication between physicians, designers, and researchers, as well as quick updates to the product. Our goal is to leverage these advantages to allow for quick and iterative updates that improve the experience of our end-users.

13.6 Clinical Validation

Physicians are not accustomed to using AI technologies. Building physician and patient trust will be critical to our solution's success. Clinical validation is key in order to ensure the safety and efficacy of our model under real clinical conditions, and to provide clinicians with confidence in our results. In our view, simply attaining high model accuracy and other measures in the validation set is not sufficient to demonstrate the utility of the model, and proof must be provided that the predictive model can generalize from the clinical trial to the real clinical population. We have set out a suite of premarket and clinical testing: an ease-of-use study in which clinicians will use the model and provide us with feedback on the experience and utility of the product; an open-label clinical trial in which we would be able to monitor safety and effectiveness; and a Randomized Controlled Trial (RCT) to evaluate efficacy by comparing our model to a 'dummy' model loaded with hard-coded suggestions based off of current clinical guidelines, such as the Canadian Network for Mood and Anxiety Treatments (CANMAT) guidelines (Kennedy et al. 2016). In this section we will expand on our planned clinical validation.

In medicine, the 'gold standard' proof that a given treatment or intervention is truly effective is a positive result from a well-designed Randomized Controlled Trial (Burns 2011). Moreover, a meta-analysis of multiple RCTs showing a positive overall effect would further increase physicians' confidence in a treatment's efficacy. RCTs randomize patients to two or more groups – at least one treatment group (which might be a new treatment or novel intervention), and a control group being treated either with a placebo or with the current best available treatment. A key component of randomized trials is blinding. Blinding means that the patients in the trial do not know whether they are in the treatment or control group. Among the best trials are the *double-blind* trials, where neither those being treated or those providing treatment know who is in which arm of the trial. Even more exacting is the *triple-blind* trial, where neither the patients, those administering treatment, or those evaluating outcomes are aware of who is in which arm. Blinding is important to reduce systemic bias and the chance that patients in the treatment arm show a significantly greater response because they *expect* to get better (or vice versa in the control group). Randomized controlled trials can often be expensive because of the need to hire staff and recruit a large number of physicians to ensure an adequate sample size. Due to the high expenses, we must ensure that our solution has been thoroughly tested and that we have a well thought-out methodology before investing in this final step.

Before proceeding with the description for planned clinical validation, let us answer a question several readers may have posed themselves: why bother? The clinical validation process is long and expensive, so why can we not just trust to standard machine learning estimates of accuracy and assume that this will generalize to the clinical environment? After all, the model is being trained on clinical trial data! There are several reasons. The first, as we have noted previously, is the concern about bias. Our data does not necessarily reflect the population at large. As such it is important to validate our model in a realistic clinical population. Secondly, just because a model can predict data collected as part of a research project, that does not mean that it will be able to perform well under clinical conditions where it must be integrated into the clinical workflow of a physician who is not participating in a clinical trial (and whose practice may therefore be less structured than that of a physician in a study). These concerns drive the third reason: even a model that performs well on a validation set has not been proven to work under clinical conditions. As previously mentioned, lack of clinical validation would drive distrust on the part of clinicians and patients. Distrust would result in severely limited adoption of our product, ensuring that it would never become accepted as part of evidence-based practice. As such, as arduous as they may be, clinical trials are a sine qua non for the translation of AI technology to the clinical setting.

13.6.1 Ease of Use Study

Our first trial, called an *ease-of-use* study, aims to determine if the system is easy to use and how best to integrate it into the clinical workflow. Each participant will be asked to engage in four simulation stations and one interview of 10–15 min each. The first station will be a technology familiarization station where participants will be asked to use different features of the aifred software and then answer questions about their experience and comfort with the model via a questionnaire.

The next three stations will feature written clinical scenarios which the participants will have a chance to read or an interaction with a simulated patient (this is similar to how medical students are trained). More clinical information (such as the fictional results of blood tests and neuroimaging) will be available in supplementary material present in the room. The participants will be asked to make a treatment recommendation with the help of the aifred model. They will be allowed to disagree with the model when writing their final recommendation. There will be three levels of difficulty – one station will be about a fairly standard case of first-episode depression; another will be about a treatment-resistant patient who has failed two treatments; and the third will be a patient with a complex history which includes medical or psychiatric comorbidity. The order of the three clinical simulation stations will be random for each participant in order to control for the bias towards or against the model that may occur in relation to the complexity of the case. For example, if all participants started with the simple case, they would be more likely to agree with the model's predictions, given the large number of first line therapies; this might positively bias them towards agreeing with the model in future stations. This process is called *counterbalancing*. After each clinical situation, participants will fill out a very short questionnaire asking them whether they agreed or disagreed with the model's recommendations and why. Information gained from this study will help us get a sense of how easy it is for different kinds of clinicians to start using our technology, and will give us a chance to evaluate how well the system can be incorporated into the clinical workflow. The results of this study will allow us to modify our software and UX in order to best meet the needs of clinicians and the clinician-patient relationship.

13.6.2 Open Label Trial

The next study is the open-label trial. An open-label trial is one in which participants, clinicians and study authors are aware of who is in which group, meaning that it is unblinded. These kinds of trials are less complicated to run than RCTs and allow for assessment of the safety of an intervention, as well as how effective it may be when compared to regular clinical practice under naturalistic conditions. Our two-arm, open-label, controlled, randomized, unblinded trial will test the effectiveness and safety of our clinical decision support system (CDSS) used by physicians to treat adults with major depressive disorder. Since the intervention is the use of the clinical decision support system itself, and not an actual treatment given to the patient, we need to randomize clinicians instead of patients. A trial in which clinicians switch back and forth between using the CDSS and not would be a very clunky design. We will be recruiting both psychiatrists and family doctors, because these are the physicians who treat the majority of depressed patients. Physicians will be randomized to the CDSS or control group. Randomization will control for clinician factors that could influence technology usage, patient populations and the severity of depression being treated. These clinician factors include gender, length of time in practice, whether the clinician is a family doctor or psychiatrist, location of practice, volume of depressed patients, current technology adoption, current rating scale use, and current practice of psychotherapy. Patients participating in the study will be recruited from these physicians' practices and will not be randomized.

We will follow patients selected for the study for 12 weeks from their initial visit. We will schedule minimum follow up appointments at 2 weeks, 4–6 weeks, and 12 weeks. The study will last a total of 6 months, with recruitment ending at three months so that all patients recruited by the end of the third month will have the required 12 weeks of follow up.

13.6.3 Outcomes

The primary outcome measure will be the severity of a patient's major depression and response to treatment, as measured by the MADRS, BDI, PHQ-9, CGI, and GAF (APA 2000; Beck 1996; Busner 2007; Kroenke 2001; Montgomery and Asberg 1979) and the safety of the model with respect to adverse events (e.g., suicide, side effects). We will use a pre-post treatment design with baseline measurements of outcome variables taken before commencement of treatment (i.e., first visit with physician) and repeated at each following visit. We will measure patient outcome variables between the pre- and post-treatment assessments (week 2, 4–6 and 12) to assess possible early therapeutic effects of treatment. Patients will be followed up to 6 months as part of this study. We will also measure how often physicians use our CDSS or follow CDSS recommendations.

Based on these outcomes, we will know if our model is effective and safe under clinical conditions. If it is, we would then be ready to move to a randomized control trial. In addition, because we are collecting both patient and clinician rated questionnaires we will be able to determine which questions have more predictive value if answered by the patient, and which are more useful when answered by the clinician. This would help us streamline our user experience by potentially allowing more patient-answered questions to be used, reducing clinician time burden for using our software.

13.6.4 Randomized Control Trial

How does one run a randomized control trial of an AI-powered software? Rather, how does one ensure proper blinding in the trial of a software?

The answer we have devised is the following: we will develop a version of the software that looks identical to the one employing the deep learning model, and takes in identical features, but which instead of producing recommendations based on the deep learning model, produces recommendations based on best practice guidelines in the field of psychiatry (e.g., CANMAT, Maudsley) (Kennedy et al. 2016; Taylor et al. 2015). There would also be a third, unblinded group of patients receiving treatment as usual, without the benefit of a software. This would allow us to directly compare having a software implementation of best practice guidelines with treatment as usual, which will then allow us to determine what value the AI adds to clinical decision support over and above a software that helps track patient symptoms and facilitates the use of validated questionnaires and guidelines. If we simply compared a software group to a non-software group, we would not know whether any improvement in patient outcomes was coming from the AI or simply access to a useful software that helps track patient outcomes.

Note that in both of our clinical trials our outcome measures are based on *patient outcomes*. We are not interested primarily in how often the system produces recommendations that agree with physician recommendations because the intention of this system is to supplement and improve upon the recommendations made by physicians. As such, simply approximating current physicians decisions would have little practical value. In addition, we take great care to ensure that clinicians and patients are always in control and are able to reject recommendations made by the AI. This information is crucial in order to simulate out-of-trial conditions and to gain insight into how often we can expect our system's recommendations to be used. Using these data, we can perform a subgroup analysis, looking at the differences between cases in which the highest-rank recommendations were accepted or rejected and see if this had any effect on outcome.

13.7 AI Ethics: Meticulous Transparency

The use of AI as a general problem-solving technology has immense promise in diverse sectors of society. However the application of this technology in multiple domains and for a myriad of purposes provides notable challenges for developing regulatory frameworks that can keep pace with rapid advances and evolving applications of this technology. A current challenge we face is that AI systems provide predictions and make decisions, but we often cannot explain how or why the software arrived at those conclusions (the "black box" problem) (Pasquale 2015). This lack of transparency impedes our ability to assess whether an algorithm is malfunctioning or misrepresenting people, which in turn can limit opportunities and reinforce inequalities (O'Neil 2016). Given its potential for both positive and negative uses, ensuring the ethical development and responsible use of AI systems is critical. However, a barrier to ensuring ethical development is that concepts and procedures used to regulate AI lags behind the rapid progress of AI technology. According to literature (Wallach and Allen 2010; Hughes 2017), there is a strong case to find a way to effectively regulate and guide the development of AI in a manner that maximizes its benefits and minimizes its harms (IEEE 2016). Various international (Asilomar AI Principles 2016; IEEE 2016) and industry-based groups (Intel 2017; ITIC 2017) have been developing principles of ethics for AI.

Beyond the aforementioned ethical principles, we are unaware of an existing framework that would allow for the rigorous ethical assessment of AI (i.e., how one should approach the task of determining whether or not a given AI system is ethical). Given the importance of ethical development when it comes to medical technology aimed at improving life for vulnerable people, we created a new ethics evaluation framework, *Meticulous Transparency* (MT), to help our team consider the ethical implications of our product. MT is an agile assessment framework that focuses on evaluating AI applications, namely its foreseen capabilities and the underlying intentions of the developers of the technology, rather than on evaluating its conformity to static regulations. MT shifts the focus of ethical evaluation from the technology itself to why it is being built and its potential consequences. We focus on the *why* of an AI system (the intentions of its developers) because AI systems are trained by developers, and so understanding the true objectives of this training is important for understanding the system's true capabilities and risks for bias. We note that the IEEE has similarly identified the importance of intentionality (IEEE 2016).

MT takes the form of a directed ethical analysis for a given AI product or system. An MT analysis must be completed for each system by its developers before it ever reaches consumers. MT is meticulous in the sense that it requires a high degree of detail and explanation, as well as documentation that would have to be made available to regulators and the public. The degree of explanation and rigor required in the reporting would be proportional to two variables: the autonomy of the technology (i.e., to what extent can an AI system make decisions without a human being part of the process?) and its potential impact (i.e., is the AI system making life-or-death recommendations? Will it have a significant impact on social dynamics?).

For a sense of the detail required, a good model would be to examine research ethics board applications commonly used in medical research. Low-risk projects (such as questionnaires) often require abridged applications; high-risk research (such as clinical trials) require more thorough documentation. We suggest applying similar standards to AI applications. In our experience, such documentation is not prohibitively time-consuming or difficult to complete.

13.7.1 Details of an MT Assessment

An MT assessment should contain the following sections:

A complete description of the system's purpose This description should be provided in fine detail and must reflect the intentions of those selling the product. Consider as example a company that is developing targeted advertisements. Such company would need to explain that their goal is to increase revenue for the marketed brands, and then explain in detail the markets being targeted, the products being prioritized, and some of the specific training parameters that are being used in model training. Intellectual Property (IP) protection would allow developers to keep obscured some of the input features and hyperparameters, as these form the basic IP of the system. However, other values, such as the possible output variables, most input variables, and a description of common input-cluster-output associations would be critical to provide. For instance, if a system's output is commonly targeting alcohol towards people with characteristic inputs suggestive of depressive features, then this should be noted and addressed. Some of this information may not be available prior to model training, and thus should be provided to regulators as soon as it is available via an addendum to the original MT assessment.

Scope of use The platforms and reach of the system should be carefully documented. For example, a product present in smartphones and aimed at children will have different ethical implications from a platform present in stores that uses internal camera footage to predict customer flow.

Data sources and bias control To reduce the occurrence of biased solutions, the provenance, quality, and characteristics of data used to train the model must be clearly discussed as a prerequisite to product approval. For example, the developers of an application using phone sensor and location data to provide information about risk of defaulting on a loan would need to be trained with a dataset that does not unfairly bias the AI against people living or working in poorer areas. A biased dataset could, for example, have an overrepresentation of loan defaulters who live in poor areas, leading the AI to overestimate the risk of defaulting based on where the person lives.

Human interpretability While the current state of technology does not allow access to a reliable narrative account of the decision processes of AI systems, standards based on best practice (and specific to the context) should be set and enforced when it comes to interpretability. A clear plan for introducing these features should be included in every MT assessment, and all products should be required to meet current best practice standards. Standards for interpretability ought to improve alongside technological development.

The projected risks and benefits of the product While this section is more speculative than the others, it serves two important functions. Firstly, it gives the developers a chance to explore at least some of the "known knowns" and perhaps identify some of the "known unknowns" when it comes to the impact of their product. Secondly, it gives regulators a chance to see how seriously a developer has considered the consequences of their product. Risks and benefits should be described in quantitative terms when possible, and, when available, up-to-date research should be used to justify assumptions or projections.

Monitoring and contingency plans for adverse events Before a developer is willing to put an AI system on the market, they must accept some responsibility for the downstream effects that it may have. For example, a targeted advertising company should have a system in place for monitoring, in aggregate, what kinds of products are being marketed to which kinds of consumers. Accordingly, they should also have a plan for how to intervene if unethical behavior occurs (e.g., alcohol being marketed to people who may be depressed). Though not all adverse events can be predicted, this exercise effectively assigns developers responsibility for their products' impacts, and allows them to plan their monitoring strategy and their possible responses to negative impacts.

MT assessments would need to be carried out early in the development cycle, with updates and resubmissions as development progresses. Application to new markets or to new populations would require a new proposal, and companies would need to stay up-to-date with respect to advances in interpretability and algorithmic bias control. Data curatorship would also need to become a stronger focus of companies and governments using AI systems.

Importantly, MT is not a value system; this framework does not contain guidance on moral judgements. This means that two different MT evaluations may produce the same data with respect to what an AI system is being used for, but those evaluating this data may arrive at different conclusions with respect to whether the system meets ethical norms. However, a common evaluation framework should facilitate the development of cross-national and cross-sectoral ethical norms.

Staffing of MT review boards should be handled in a similar fashion to current ethics review boards; in many cases, current REB/IRB's could, with the addition of relevantly trained members, become the MT review board. Companies would have internal boards; universities and governments would also employ their own boards. While the composition would vary by context, as a general rule review boards ought to include an ethicist or lawyer, experts with domain knowledge of the problem being addressed, someone with knowledge of AI technology, and a member of the public affected by the application (e.g., a consumer, a patient, an employee, etc.). The value of the MT assessment is that it provides a written, structured record for a review board, which means that members of that board will not necessarily need to be experts in the specific technologies used. The existence of such a record will also provide a legal document for use in auditing if an ethical violation occurs. We look forward to applying MT analysis to our own product, and collecting data from others using this technique in order to develop a more detailed handbook for its use.

13.8 Conclusion

The route from training our model to having it become integrated into routine clinical practice is challenging but ultimately navigable. In this chapter, we have laid out some of the theoretical, clinical, technical, design, and ethical challenges we are facing, along with our plans to meet them. Should aifred meet the goals set out herein, it could bring about a paradigm shift in the treatment of depression – and eventually in the treatment of other conditions as well.

It is important to emphasize that aifred would simply not be able to exist without interdisciplinary collaboration. Researchers, physicians, and computer scientists each bring unique skill sets, which are invaluable to the creation and design of our tool. Additionally, without data-sharing resources such clinical trial databases and the goodwill of individual researchers, we would not have sufficient data to train our model, nor would we be able to extend its utility to other conditions. Therefore, as Hahn et al. (2017) note, for computational psychiatry to succeed, the pivot towards open data must continue. We recognize that many researchers have qualms about sharing data with industry. As a team composed mostly of academics, we share these qualms and the concern about private industry profiting off of publicly-funded research. On the other hand, innovations led by startups like ours have the potential to translate research into products that have a real clinical impact. Governments could help in this regard, perhaps by having successful medical technology startups and corporations 'pay-it-forward' by creating compulsory funds that industry must contribute to if they have benefited in the past from publicly-funded data.

After implementing and refining our depression therapeutics model, we plan to train aifred to predict treatment efficacy for many other mental health conditions, including but not limited to psychotic disorders, anxiety disorders, and post-traumatic stress disorder. Though treatment efficacy is our current focus, improving adherence to treatment is another important objective. We believe that if we can use our model to minimize burdensome side effects and better match treatments to patients, patients will not abandon their regimens as frequently as they currently do. It has been estimated that approximately 50% of patients discontinue their antidepressant treatment plan, which likely contributes to the suboptimal efficacy of depression treatment today (Sansone and Sansone 2012).

With respect to ethics, we at Aifred Health plan to continually adhere to and improve upon our MT framework, and encourage ethical conduct in the use of artificial intelligence in medicine and more generally.

Using deep learning to increase treatment efficacy in psychiatry, we hope to improve the lives of those suffering from mental illness. Additionally, we expect that aifred will provide insights into specific disease subpopulations, the versatility of biomarkers, and treatment plan optimization. This will prompt novel research questions. By creating a clinically validated, reliably interpretable, evidence-based decision tool for physicians, we hope to encourage other researchers and innovators to invest increased effort in improving mental health care in general, using new computational approaches to usher in an era of computationally-powered precision psychiatry.

We began our effort to bring AI methods to depression treatment in late 2016 with the launch of the IBM Watson AI XPRIZE. Through the foundational work we conducted in our first year, we developed and validated methods for solving the technical, practical, and ethical challenges inherent in the practice of mental health. We look forward to continuing our pursuit of improving the world with AI and invite collaboration towards solving mental health via our open source *Vulcan* project: https://github.com/Aifred-Health/Vulcan.

References

Abadi M., et al. (2016). TensorFlow: Large–Scale Machine Learning on Heterogeneous Distributed Systems. arXiv preprint arXiv:1603.04467v2

American Psychiatric Association. (2000). Diagnostic and statistical manual of mental disorders: DSM–IV–TR. Washington, DC: American Psychiatric Association.

American Psychiatric Association. (2013). Diagnostic and statistical manual of mental disorders (5th ed.). Washington, DC. Author[1]

Asilomar AI Principles. 2016. Retrieved October 24 2017, from https://futureoflife.org/ai–principles/.

Beck A. T., Steer, R. A., & Brown, G. K. (1996). Manual for the Beck depression inventory–II. San Antonio, TX: Psychological Corporation.

Beleites, C., Neugebauer, U., Bocklitz, T., Krafft, C., Popp J. (2012). Sample Size Planning for Classification Models. arXiv:1211.1323 [stat.AP]

Bergstra J., et al. 2010. "Theano: A CPU and GPU Math Compiler in Python".

Berlim M.T., Fleck, M.P., Turecki, G., 2008. Current trends in the assessment and somatic treatment of resistant refractory major depression: An overview. Ann. Med. 40, 149–159.

Berlim M.T., Turecki, G., 2007. Definition, assessment, and staging of treatment–resistant refractory major depression: A review of current concepts and methods. Can. J. Psychiatry 52, 46–54.

Braddock C. H. (2010). The Emerging Importance and Relevance of Shared Decision Making to Clinical Practice. Medical Decision Making, 30(5_ suppl), 5–7. https://doi.org/10.1177/0272989X10381344

Busner J., & Targum, S. D. (2007). The Clinical Global Impressions Scale. Psychiatry (Edgmont), 4(7), 28–37.

Brand S. J., Möller, M., & Harvey, B. H. (2015). A Review of Biomarkers in Mood and Psychotic Disorders: A Dissection of Clinical vs. Preclinical Correlates. Current Neuropharmacology, 13(3), 324–368. http://doi.org/10.2174/1570159X13666150307004545

Breitenstein B., Scheuer, S., Holsboer, F., 2014. Are there meaningful biomarkers of treatment response for depression? Drug Discov. Today 19, 539–61.

Bromet E., Andrade, L. H., Hwang, I., Sampson, N. A., Alonso, J., de Girolamo, G., . . . Kessler, R. C. (2011). Cross–national epidemiology of DSM–IV major depressive episode. BMC Medicine, 9 – 90. https://doi.org/10.1186/1741-7015-9-90

Burns P. B., Rohrich, R. J., & Chung, K. C. (2011). The Levels of Evidence and their role in Evidence–Based Medicine. Plastic and Reconstructive Surgery, 128(1), 305–310. https://doi.org/10.1097/PRS.0b013e318219c171

Chi K.F., Korgaonkar, M., Grieve, S.M., 2015. Imaging predictors of remission to anti–depressant medications in major depressive disorder. J. Affect. Disord. 186, 134–144.

Cooney GM, Dwan K, Greig CA, Lawlor DA, Rimer J, Waugh FR, McMurdo M, Mead GE. Exercise for depression. Cochrane Database of Systematic Reviews 2013, Issue 9. Art. No.: CD004366. https://doi.org/10.1002/14651858.CD004366.pub6.

Cressey D. (2011). Psychopharmacology in crisis. Available at: https://www.nature.com/news/2011/110614/full/news.2011.367.html

De Carlo, V., Calati, R., Serretti, A., 2016. Socio–demographic and clinical predictors of non–response/non–remission in treatment resistant depressed patients: A systematic review. Psychiatry Res. 240, 421–430.

Dice L. R. 1945. Measures of the amount of ecologic association between species. Ecology.; 26(3):297–302. https://doi.org/10.2307/1932409.

Dichter G.S., Gibbs, D., Smoski, M.J., 2016. A systematic review of relations between resting–state functional–MRI and treatment response in major depressive disorder. J. Affect. Disord. 172.

Dieleman S., et al. 2015. "Lasagne: First release."

Dmochowski J. P., Sajda, P., Parra, L. C. (2010). Maximum Likelihood in Cost–Sensitive Learning: Model Specification, Approximations, and Upper Bounds. Journal of Machine Learning Research 11 3313–3332

Duval F., Lebowitz, B.D., Macher, J.P., 2006. Treatments in depression. Dialogues in. Clin. Neurosci. 8, 191–206.

Ferrari A. J., Charlson, F. J., Norman, R. E., Patten, S. B., Freedman, G., Murray, C. J. L., . . . Whiteford, H. A. (2013). Burden of Depressive Disorders by Country, Sex, Age, and Year: Findings from the Global Burden of Disease Study 2010. PLOS Medicine, 10 (11), e1001547. https://doi.org/10.1371/journal.pmed.1001547

Fitzpatrick K. K., Darcy, A., & Vierhile, M. (2017). Delivering Cognitive Behavior Therapy to Young Adults With Symptoms of Depression and Anxiety Using a Fully Automated Conversational Agent (Woebot): A Randomized Controlled Trial. JMIR Mental Health, 4(2), e19.

Fushiki T. (2011). Estimation of prediction error by using K–fold cross–validation. Statistics and Computing, Volume 21, Issue 2, pp 137–146

Gilbody S. M., House, A. O., & Sheldon, T. A. (2002). Psychiatrists in the UK do not use outcomes measures: National survey. The British Journal of Psychiatry, 180(2), 101–103. https://doi.org/10.1192/bjp.180.2.101

Goldman HH, Skodol AE, Lave TR: "Revising Axis V for DSM–IV: A Review of Measures of Social Functioning." American Journal of Psychiatry 149:1148–1156, 1992.

Goodfellow I., Bengio, Y., Courville, A., & Bengio, Y. (2016). Deep learning (Vol. 1). Cambridge: MIT press.

Gravel R., Beland, Y. The Canadian Community Health Survey: mental health and well–being. Can J Psychiatry. 2005 Sep;50(10):573–9.

Guyon I., Elisseff, A. (2003). An Introduction to Variable and Feature Selection. Journal of Machine Learning Research 3 1157–1182

Han J., Jentzen, A., Weinan, E. (2017). Overcoming the curse of dimensionality: Solving high–dimensional partial differential equations using deep learning. arXiv:1707.02568v1

Hahn T., Nierenberg, A. A., & Whitfield–Gabrieli, S. (2017). Predictive analytics in mental health: applications, guidelines, challenges and perspectives. Molecular psychiatry, 22(1), 37.

Hajian-Tilaki, K. 2013. "Receiver Operating Characteristic (ROC) Curve Analysis for Medical Diagnostic Test Evaluation".

Huang G., Li, Y., Pleiss, G., Liu, Z., Hopcroft, J.E., Weinberger, K.Q.(2017). Snapshot Ensembles: Train 1, get M for free. arXiv: 1704.00109v1 [Cs, Stat] . Retrieved from http://arxiv.org/abs/1704.00109

Hughes G. 2017. Montreal AI pioneer warns against unethical uses of new tech. CBC News.

IEEE. 2016. The IEEE Global Initiative for Ethical Consideration in Artificial Intelligence and Autonomous Systems. Institute of Electrical and Electronics Engineers.

Information Technology Industry Council. 2017. ITI AI Policy Principles. Retrieved from https://www.itic.org/resources/AI--Policy--Principles--FullReport2.pdf

Intel. 2017. Artificial Intelligence? The Public Policy Opportunity. Intel Corporation. Retrieved from http://blogs.intel.com/policy/files/2017/10/Intel--Artificial--Intelligence--Public--Policy--White--Paper--2017.pdf

Jolliffe IT. Principal Component Analysis. New York: Springer; 2002.

Kemp A., Gordon, E., Rush, A., & Williams, L. (2008). Improving the Prediction of Treatment Response in Depression: Integration of Clinical, Cognitive, Psychophysiological, Neuroimaging, and Genetic Measures. CNS Spectrums, 13(12), 1066–1086. https://doi.org/10.1017/S1092852900017120

Kenefick H., Lee J., Fleishman V. (2008). Improving Physician Adherence to Clinical Practice Guidelines, Barriers and strategies for change, New England Healthcare Institute, February 2008. http://www.nehi.net/writable/publication_files/file/cpg_report_final.pdf

Kennedy S. H., Lam, R. W., McIntyre, R. S., Tourjman, S. V., Bhat, V., Blier, P., et al. CANMAT Depression Work Group. (2016). Canadian Network for Mood and Anxiety Treatments (CANMAT) 2016 Clinical Guidelines for the Management of Adults with Major Depressive Disorder: Section 3. Pharmacological Treatments. Canadian Journal of Psychiatry. Revue Canadienne De Psychiatrie, 61(9), 540–560. https://doi.org/10.1177/0706743716659417

Khan A., Faucett, J., Lichtenberg, P., Kirsch, I., & Brown, W. A. (2012). A Systematic Review of Comparative Efficacy of Treatments and Controls for Depression. Plos One, 7(7), e41778. https://doi.org/10.1371/journal.pone.0041778

Kingma D. P., Ba, J. (2014). Adam: A Method for Stochastic Optimization. arXiv preprint arXiv:1412.6980v9

Kirsch I. (2014). Antidepressants and the Placebo Effect. Zeitschrift Fur Psychologie, 222(3), 128–134. https://doi.org/10.1027/2151--2604/a000176

Klambauer G., Unterthiner, T., Mayr, A., & Hochreiter, S. (2017). Self–Normalizing Neural Networks. arXiv:1706.02515 [Cs, Stat].

Klengel T., Binder, E.B., 2013. Gene x environment interactions in the prediction of response to antidepressant treatment. Int. J. Neuropsychopharmacol. 16, 701–711

Krizhevsky A., Sutskever, I., Hinton, G. 2012. ImageNet Classification with Deep Convolutional Neural Networks. Advances in Neural Information Processing Systems 25 (NIPS 2012)

Kroenke K., Spitzer, R. L., & Williams, J. B. W. (2001). The PHQ–9. Journal of General Internal Medicine, 16(9), 606–613. https://doi.org/10.1046/j.1525--1497.2001.016009606.x

Lalkhen A. G., & McCluskey, A. (2008). Clinical tests: sensitivity and specificity. Continuing Education in Anaesthesia Critical Care & Pain, 8(6), 221–223.

Lambert J. (2011). Statistics in Brief: How to Assess Bias in Clinical Studies? Clinical Orthopaedics and Related Research, 469(6), 1794–1796. https://doi.org/10.1007/s11999--010--1538--7

Lener M.S., Iosifescu, D. V, 2015. In pursuit of neuroimaging biomarkers to guide treatment selection in major depressive disorder: a review of the literature. https://doi.org/10.1111/nyas.12759

Leuchter A. F., Cook, I. A., Hamilton, S. P., Narr, K. L., Toga, A., Hunter, A. M., . . . Lebowitz, B. D. (2010). Biomarkers to predict antidepressant response. Curr. Psychiatry Rep. 12, 553–562. http://doi.org/10.1007/s11920--010--0160--4

Lopresti A.L., Maker, G.L., Hood, S.D., Drummond, P.D., 2013. A review of peripheral biomarkers in major depression: The potential of inflammatory and oxidative stress biomarkers, in: Progress in Neuro Psychopharmacology and Biological Psychiatry. 48.

Luo W., Li, Y., Urtason, R., Zemel, R. (2016). Understanding the Effective Receptive Field in Deep Convolutional Neural Networks. Advances in Neural Information Processing Systems, 29

McIntyre R.S., 2010. When should you move beyond first–line therapy for depression? J. Clin. Psychiatry 71, 16–20.

Miller A.H., Haroon, E., Felger, J.C., 2016. Therapeutic Implications of Brain–Immune Interactions: Treatment in Translation. Neuropsychopharmacology 42, 334–359.

Montgomery S.A., Asberg M. (1979) A new depression scale designed to be sensitive to change. British Journal of Psychiatry, 134, 382–389.

O'Neil, C. Weapons of Math Destruction: How Big Data Increases Inequality and Threatens Democracy. (2016); Penguin Books

Papakostas G.I., Fava, M., 2009. Predictors, moderators, and mediators (correlates) of treatment outcome in major depressive disorder. Dialogues Clin. Neurosci. 10, 439–451.

Pasquale F., The Black Box Society: The Secret Algorithms That Control Money and Information (2015); Harvard University Press

Patel V. L., Shortliffe, E. H., Stefanelli, M., Szolovits, P., Berthold, M. R., Bellazzi, R., & Abu–Hanna, A. (2009). The coming of age of artificial intelligence in medicine. Artificial intelligence in medicine, 46(1), 5–17.

Pedregosa F., Varoquaux, G., Gramfort, A., Michel, V., Thirion, B., Grisel, O., Blondel, M., Prettenhofer, P., Weiss, R., Dubourg, V., Vanderplas, J., Passos, A., Cournapeau, D., Brucher, M., Perrot, M., Duchesnay, E. 2011. Scikit–learn: Machine Learning in Python. The Journal of Machine Learning Research. Volume 12, pages 2825–2830.

Pfizer (2018). https://www.pfizer.com/news/featured_stories/featured_stories_detail/learn_more_about_our_neuroscience_r_d_decision

Porcelli S., Fabbri, C., Serretti, A., 2012. Meta–analysis of serotonin transporter gene promoter polymorphism (5–HTTLPR) association with antidepressant efficacy. Eur. Neuropsychopharmacol. 22, 239–258.

Ronneberger O., Fischer, P., Brox, T. (2015). U–Net: Convolutional Networks for Biomedical Image Segmentation. arXiv:1505.04597

Rosenfeld A., & Kraus S. (2018). Predicting Human Decision–Making: From Prediction to Action. Morgan and Claypool Publishing.

Rosenfeld A., Keshet, J., Goldman, C. V., & Kraus, S. (2016). Online Prediction of Exponential Decay Time Series with Human–Agent Application. In ECAI (pp. 595–603).

Roth H., Lu, L., Farag, A., Shin, A.C., Liu, J., Turkbey, E., Summers, R. (2015). DeepOrgan: Multi–level Deep Convolutional Networks for Automated Pancreas Segmentation. Arxiv:1506.06448v1

Sansone R. A., & Sansone, L. A. (2012). Antidepressant Adherence: Are Patients Taking Their Medications? Innovations in Clinical Neuroscience, 9(5–6), 41–46.

Schmidt A. (2000). Implicit human computer interaction through context. Personal technologies, 4(2), 191–199.

Schmidt F.M., Kirkby, K.C., Lichtblau, N., 2016. Inflammation and immune regulation as potential drug targets in antidepressant treatment. Curr. Neuropharmacol. 14, 674–687.

Shalev-Shwartz, S. (2012). Online learning and online convex optimization. Foundations and Trends in Machine Learning, 4(2), 107–194.

Shin S. H., Bode, A. M., & Dong, Z. (2017). Precision medicine: the foundation of future cancer therapeutics. Npj Precision Oncology, 1(1), 12. https://doi.org/10.1038/s41698–017–0016–z

Simon G.E., Perlis, R.H., 2010. Personalized medicine for depression: Can we match patients with treatments? Am. J. Psychiatry 167, 1445–1455.

Simonyan K., Vedaldi, A., Zisserman, A. (2013). Deep Inside Convolutional Networks: Visualising Image Classification Models and Saliency Maps. arXiv:1312.6034v2 [Cs, Stat].

Srivastava N., Hinton, G., Krizhevsky, A., Ilya Sutskever, I., Salakhutdinov, R. (2013). Dropout: A Simple Way to Prevent Neural Networks from Overfitting. Journal of Machine Learning Research, 15 (1929–1958)

Stone P., Brooks R., Brynjolfsson E., Calo R., Etzioni O., Hager G., Hirschberg J., Kalyanakrishnan S., Karmar E., Kraus S., Leyton–Brown K., Parkes D., Press W., Sanexian A., Shah J., Tambe M., Teller A. (2016). Artificial Intelligence and Life in 2030. One Hundred Year Study on Artificial Intelligence.

Tai-Seale, M., McGuire, T. G., & Zhang, W. (2007). Time Allocation in Primary Care Office Visits. Health Services Research, 42(5), 1871–1894. https://doi.org/10.1111/j.1475–6773. 2006.00689.x

Taylor D., Paton, C., & Kapur, S. (2015). The maudsley prescribing guidelines in psychiatry.

Thum F. et al. (2014) Usability Improvement of a Clinical Decision Support System. In: Marcus A. (eds) Design, User Experience, and Usability. User Experience Design for Everyday Life Applications and Services. DUXU 2014. Lecture Notes in Computer Science, vol 8519. Springer, Cham

Turecki G., & Brent, D. A. (2016). Suicide and suicidal behaviour. The Lancet, 387(10024), 1227–1239. https://doi.org/10.1016/S0140–6736(15)00234–2

van der Maaten L., Hinton G. (2008). Visualizing Data using t-SNE. Journal of Machine Learning Research, 9, 2579–2605. http://www.jmlr.org/papers/v9/vandermaaten08a.html

Walkup J. T. (2017). Antidepressant Efficacy for Depression in Children and Adolescents: Industry– and NIMH–Funded Studies. American Journal of Psychiatry, 174(5), 430–437. https://doi.org/10.1176/appi.ajp.2017.16091059

Wallach W., & Allen, C. 2010. Moral Machines: Teaching Robots Right from Wrong. New York, NY, USA: Oxford University Press.

Warden D., Rush, A.J., Trivedi, M.H., Fava, M., Wisniewski, S.R., 2008. The STAR*D Project results: a comprehensive review of findings. Curr Psychiatry Rep 9, 449–459.

World Health Organization. Depression and Other Common Mental Disorders: Global Health Estimates. Geneva: World Health Organization; 2017.

Xiao H., Rasul, K., Vollgraf, R. (2017) Fashion–MNIST: a Novel Image Dataset for Benchmarking Machine Learning Algorithms. arXiv:1708.07747

Yoon J., Alaa, A., Hu, S., & Schaar, M. (2016). ForecastICU: a prognostic decision support system for timely prediction of intensive care unit admission. In International Conference on Machine Learning (pp. 1680–1689).

Young J.J., Silber, T., Bruno, D., Galatzer–Levy, I.R., Pomara, N., Marmar, C.R., (2016). Is there progress? An overview of selecting biomarker candidates for major depressive disorder.

Printed in the United States
By Bookmasters